YITZHAK RABIN

YITZHAK RABIN

ISRAEL'S SOLDIER STATESMAN

MICHAEL G. KORT

The Millbrook Press
Brookfield, Connecticut

Library of Congress Cataloging-in-Publication Data
Kort, Michael, 1944–
Yitzhak Rabin: Israel's soldier statesman / by Michael G. Kort.
p. cm.
Includes bibliographical references and index.
ISBN 0-7613-0100-3 (lib. bdg.) ISBN 0-7613-0135-6 (tr. pbk.)
1. Rabin, Yitzhak, 1922–1995–Juvenile literature. 2. Prime ministers–
Israel–Biography–Juvenile literature. 3. Generals–Israel–Biography–
Juvenile literature. 4. Israel–History–Juvenile literature. I. Title.
DS126.6.R32K67 1996
956.9405'092–dc20 [B] 96–17595 CIP AC

Photographs courtesy and © Israel Government Press Office: pp. 24, 29,
50, 73; UPI/Corbis-Bettmann: pp. 37, 39, 45, 52, 76, 83, 86, 105, 111,
159; Wide World: pp. 69, 145, 161; Ruben Bittermann, Impact Visuals: pp.
137, 157; map by Frank Senyk.

Published by The Millbrook Press
2 Old New Milford Road, Brookfield, Connecticut 06804

For my uncles, Heini and Max
and their children, grandchildren,
and great-grandchildren,
in Israel.

I would like to thank Zvi Meth of Haifa, Israel, for his invaluable help in locating materials I needed for this book. I am very grateful to Norman H. Finkelstein and Lawrence Lowenthall, who read and critiqued the entire manuscript, and to Paula Fredriksen and Richard Landes, who read and discussed with me at length several sections of the manuscript that dealt with particularly difficult issues. My wife, Carol, deserves a special thanks, not just for editing the manuscript, as she always does so well, but for coming up with the idea for this book and then insisting that I write it.

Michael G. Kort

CONTENTS

YITZHAK RABIN

JERUSALEM

ISRAEL

WEST
BANK

0   5 Miles
0   5 Kilometers

Old City

West
Jerusalem
1949-67

Jewish
Quarter

1949 armistice line

No Man's Land 1949-67

SYRIA

LEBANON

GOLAN
HEIGHTS
(annexed by
Israel 1981)

Kiryat
Shemona

Sea of Galilee
(Israeli name:
Lake Kinneret)

Haifa

ISRAEL

Jordan River

Tel Aviv

Jerusalem

WEST BANK

Mediterranean Sea

GAZA STRIP

Dead Sea

Beersheba

NEGEV
DESERT

JORDAN

Suez
Canal

SINAI
PENINSULA

Elat

Gulf of Swez

Gulf of
Aqaba
(Israeli name:
Gulf of Elat)

SAUDI

0   50   100 Miles
0   50   100 Kilometers

EGYPT

Strait of Tiran

ARABIA

Red Sea

CHAPTER ONE

"The hopes of the Jewish people."

October 10, 1945, was a moonless night along the coast of the Mediterranean Sea in British-controlled Palestine. Eight miles (13 kilometers) south of the city of Haifa, 203 Jewish prisoners waited inside a makeshift detention camp called Atlit. The well-lit camp glowed against the surrounding darkness. The mood inside the camp's barbed-wire fences and barracks mirrored the stark contrast outside. There was despair as dark as the enveloping night as the prisoners awaited their fate at the hands of the British. Yet hope also glowed because the prisoners knew the Jewish community of Palestine had not abandoned them.

The Jews in the Atlit camp were not criminals. They were refugees, survivors of the Holocaust, whose murderous fires finally had been extinguished by the Allied victory over Nazi Germany only months before. The refugees in Atlit had left Europe and entered Palestine during 1945 by sneaking across the border from Syria on foot. This made them "illegal" immigrants according to the British, who controlled Palestine. British policy was to put strict limits on Jewish immigration into Palestine to avoid antagonizing the Arab population of the region. Jews who slipped into the country illegally and were caught were deported. Meanwhile, 250,000 Jewish survivors of the Holocaust in Europe wandered from place to place or waited in crowded and filthy detention camps with no place in the world to go.

The Jewish community of Palestine, which numbered about 650,000, was resisting British immigration policy. That is why on this night in October more than 200 Jewish soldiers waited in darkness about 100 yards (914 meters) outside the camp. These soldiers did not belong to a regular army. They were members of the Palmach, the elite military unit of the Hagana, the self-defense organization of Palestine's Jewish community. The Palmach's main job was to protect the Jewish population against increasingly serious attacks from local Arabs. At the same time it tried to help Jewish refugees from Europe avoid British authorities and get into Palestine.

The Palmach's task on October 10 was to free the refugees from the Atlit camp and hide them among the general population. Its troops outside the camp were divided into three groups. One group would wait outside to set up roadblocks and fight any British troops who tried to interfere with the planned operation. A second group prepared to take the refugees to nearby trucks after they were freed from the camp. They would then be driven to a Jewish agricultural settlement called Kibbutz Yagur. The third group had the job of breaking into the camp and getting the prisoners out beyond the fences. It was led by the second-in-command of the overall operation, a handsome twenty-three-year-old with a reputation for quick thinking and staying calm under fire. His name was Yitzhak Rabin.

Rabin was worried, less about his tough soldiers who were risking their lives than about the desperate people they were trying to liberate. He was thinking: "These people were survivors of the Holocaust, the few snatched from the conflagration. We would never forgive ourselves if any harm were to befall them."[1]

Inside Atlit the escape was carefully prepared. The Palmach had sent agents into the camp posing as teachers. They organized the refugees for the breakout. The "teachers" also secretly disabled the rifles of Arabs employed by the British to help guard the camp.

The job of getting the refugees out of the camp went quickly and smoothly. Rabin's men cut their way through the fence wires and entered the camp. They immediately met some "teachers" who told Rabin they had broken the firing pins on the rifles of the Arab guards. Thanks to their efforts, when Rabin and his men ran into the Arab guards, they "cocked their guns, pressed the triggers, and nothing happened." It also was very helpful, Rabin remembered later, that the British at the camp "were fast asleep."[2]

It took barely 30 minutes to get the refugees out of the camp. Then the trouble began. The men, women, and children freed from the camp refused to leave behind their few bundles and suitcases, as Rabin recalled, "the only possessions they had left."[3] Meanwhile, they could not help dropping bits and pieces of their possessions as they marched, leaving a perfect trail for British spotter planes that would soon be searching for them to follow. Making matters worse, infants, small children, and the weaker adults slowed up the group.

Rabin quickly conferred with the operation's overall commander, a veteran soldier named Nahum Sarig. Rabin and Sarig knew the entire group could never reach the waiting trucks before the British arrived. They decided to split the refugees. Sarig would take the stronger refugees, who could move fastest, to the waiting trucks and on to Kibbutz Yagur. Rabin with about 60 troops would look after the rest of the group. He would march them on foot to a nearer Jewish settlement, Kibbutz Bet Oren.

A difficult journey lay ahead of Rabin and the 100 Holocaust survivors "whose fate was now in my hands."[4] To reach Bet Oren, Rabin's group had to climb up a ridge about 1,800 feet (550 meters) high known as Mount Carmel, which extends about 15 miles (24 kilometers) along the Mediterranean shore. The Bible records that in ancient times the Israelite prophet Elijah performed miracles there. Rabin performed no miracles that October night, or the next day, but he must have seemed like a miracle worker to the terrified children and weakened adults under his care.

The climb up rugged Mount Carmel went far more slowly than planned. Rabin's soldiers had to carry the children on their shoulders. As Rabin carried one of them he thought of how "my shoulders bore the hopes of the Jewish people." Those shoulders also bore a child "paralyzed with fear." Rabin soon had evidence of how afraid the child was when he "suddenly felt a warm, damp sensation running down my back. Under the circumstances, I could hardly halt."[5]

During the march to Bet Oren a British patrol in a truck ran across Rabin's group. In the shooting that followed, a British sergeant was killed, the only casualty of the Atlit operation.

Sarig's group reached Kibbutz Yagur before dawn, and the refugees were scattered among the residents. Things went less smoothly for Rabin's weary troop. By the time it reached Bet Oren, it was daylight. British soldiers surrounded the settlement. Rabin hid his people in the woods outside the settlement and sent scouts to see if a way could be found through the encirclement. They found a gap in the British lines. Rabin quickly moved his people into the kibbutz. The refugees immediately were placed in different homes while Rabin and his men hid their weapons, which they carried illegally.

As these tasks were being completed, the British realized what had happened, and it seemed as if they would force their way into the settlement and carry off the refugees. Help arrived just in time from the nearby city of Haifa. The Hagana organized 15,000 people to get on buses and come to Bet Oren. As the British watched, unwilling to shoot unarmed Jewish civilians who were committing no crime, thousands of people poured into Bet Oren. Rabin remembered: "By afternoon the whole area was teeming with people, and the immigrants were swallowed up by a human sea. The British conceded defeat."[6]

Word quickly spread of the Atlit operation and Rabin's role in it. His girlfriend, Leah Schlossberg, who later became his wife, remembers how she was congratulated because of Yitzhak's success. As for Rabin, always a man of few words, he only said, "The planning and the execution weren't bad."[7]

CHAPTER TWO

"All right. You'll do."

In his memoirs, Yitzhak Rabin wondered about how his parents came to meet and set the stage for his own life:

> *Some marriages, I am told, are made in heaven. I cannot testify that some otherworldly force guided my parents toward their first meeting. But the crossing of their paths was such an unlikely event that it's almost a wonder that I am here to relate the subsequent story of my life.[1]*

Actually, what brought Rabin's parents together was Zionism. This movement was founded on the belief that Jews should return from the countries in which they lived all over the world and rebuild their ancient homeland in the land of Israel. The movement is as old as the disasters that befell the Jews almost 2,000 years ago, when the Romans crushed Jewish independence revolts in A.D. 70 and 135, destroyed the city of Jerusalem, and drove most Jews from the country where they had been living for more than 1,500 years. At the time of the rebellions against Rome, the country was called Judea. After the second Jewish revolt, the conquering Romans tried to cut the link between the Jews and their homeland by changing its name to Palestine.

That link, however, was never broken, regardless of whether the Romans, Byzantines, Persians, Arabs, Crusaders, Mamelukes, Turks, or British ruled in Palestine. Although Jews became a minority in Palestine, Jewish communities in Jerusalem and cities like Safed, Tiberias, and Hebron, as well as in other parts of the country, continued to exist and recover after periods of disaster and persecution. In their communities throughout the world outside Palestine, which the Jews called the Diaspora, they prayed to return to Jerusalem and the land of their ancestors. Zionism remained a belief rather than an organized movement until the late nineteenth century. Then, faced with growing anti-Semitism in Europe, Jews who believed in Zionism began to organize. By the 1880s the first large groups of Jews from Europe began returning to Palestine. They joined the old communities of Jews that throughout the centuries had lived in Jerusalem and other parts of the country. The new arrivals from Europe in turn were joined by several thousand Jews escaping Muslim persecution in Yemen, a country located on the Arabian Peninsula.

At that time Palestine was part of the Ottoman, or Turkish, Empire, which had conquered the territory in 1517. The Turks were Muslims, as were the Arabs who were the majority of Palestine's population.

Palestine was extremely poor and barren and thinly settled. In the 1880s the total Arab population in all of Palestine west of the Jordan River (which includes today's Israel *and* the West Bank and Gaza Strip) was about 250,000. Most Arabs were peasant farmers who lived in small isolated villages. Jews were the majority in Jerusalem, in those days a neglected and poverty-stricken city of less than 30,000 people, as well as in Tiberias and Safed. Wherever they lived in Palestine, Jews faced constant discrimination and periodic violence at the hands of the Muslim Arab majority.

The Jews who were returning to Palestine did not intend to displace the local Arabs. They were convinced that their efforts to rebuild the country would enable it to support all the people living there, both Arabs and Jews. In fact, as Jewish immigrants from Europe developed the local economy, many Arabs from surrounding territories immigrated into Palestine. After 1880 the population of Palestine, both Arab and Jewish, grew rapidly, both as a result of immigration and improved local health conditions. By 1914, Palestine west of the Jordan River had a population of about 650,000, about 85,000 of whom were Jews. However, the Arabs feared that Jews would eventually become a majority in Palestine and win control of the country. This they were unwilling to accept. The Arabs considered the Jews arriving from Europe to be intruders, and as early as the 1880s they began to oppose Jewish immigration.

Zionism took various forms. While some Zionists were deeply religious, most were not. Many Zionists were influenced by socialist ideas. They wanted to build a new Jewish society in Palestine based on the socialist principles of cooperation and equality. Both Nehemiah

Robichov, who was born in Russia in 1886 and who in 1917 changed his last name to Rabin, and Rosa Cohen, who was born in Russia in 1890, belonged to the socialist wing of the Zionist movement. Nehemiah and Rosa would become Yitzhak Rabin's father and mother.

Nehemiah Robichov was born in a poor village near Kiev, today the capital of Ukraine but in those days part of the huge Russian Empire. He started working when he was ten and left home at fourteen. At age eighteen, alone and without knowing a word of English, he left Russia and went to the United States. Nehemiah ended up in Chicago, working mainly as a tailor. He spent much of his free time with other poor Jewish workers who were interested in socialism and Zionism. They belonged to a group called Workers of Zion.

Although Nehemiah was very impressed with America, and especially with American democracy, he decided that his place was with the Jewish community in Palestine, which Jews called the *Yishuv*. In 1917, as World War I raged, he joined a newly formed group called the Jewish Legion and left America for Palestine. The Legion's goal was to help Allied forces free Palestine from Turkish control. Among its founders was David Ben-Gurion, who later became Israel's first prime minister. Years later Ben-Gurion told Yitzhak, "I recruited your father for the Jewish Legion, and that's why you were born in Palestine."[2]

By the time Nehemiah's unit arrived in Palestine most of the fighting against the Turks was over. In any event, the Allied victory in World War I removed Palestine from Turkish control. It was turned over to Great Britain by the League of Nations under what was called a mandate. According to the League's mandate system,

Britain was to govern Palestine until its people were ready for independence. One of its tasks was to make possible the "establishment of a Jewish National Home" in Palestine, an idea drawn from the Balfour Declaration issued by the British government in November 1917.[3] Exactly what that national home would look like, or what its borders would be, the Balfour Declaration did not say.

In 1920, when the British received their mandate, it included the entire region that today contains Israel, the West Bank and the Gaza Strip, the Golan Heights, and the Kingdom of Jordan. However, in 1921, the British separated what today is Jordan from Palestine and installed an Arab prince from the Arabian Peninsula as its ruler. They thereby closed about three-quarters of the original Palestine mandate to Jewish immigration. Two years later, in return for territory in Iraq, the British ceded the Golan Heights to the French-controlled mandate of Syria.

Four years after Nehemiah Robichov was born into poverty near Kiev, Rosa Cohen was born into a prosperous family in the town of Mogilev, in the part of the old Russian Empire that today is Belarus. Her father, a rabbi, opposed Zionism. He believed that Jews should await the Messiah promised in the Bible to lead them back to their ancient homeland. However, Rosa's uncle Mordechai was a convinced Zionist. During the 1870s and 1880s there were violent mob attacks on Jews in Russia known as pogroms. Severe government discrimination added to the hardship. As a result, several million Jews fled Russia between 1880 and 1914. Most went to the United States. A small minority decided to go to Palestine. In 1897, Rosa's uncle Mordechai and his family joined the migration eastward and settled in Jerusalem.

Rosa Cohen was an independent child. She convinced her father to let her attend a Christian secondary school for girls, then defied his wishes by attending classes on Saturday, the Jewish Sabbath. Rosa worked as a private tutor to pay her school fees. For years Rosa was attracted to socialism rather than to Zionism. She hoped that a socialist revolution in Russia would bring a better world for all people, whatever their religion. At the same time, Rosa stuck by her fellow Jews. After a pogrom in the town where she was going to school, Rosa became a medical assistant. She was not afraid to go out at night to help victims of mob violence.

In 1917 came the revolution that Rosa had hoped for. It turned out to be a bitter disappointment, however. The Bolshevik party that eventually seized power established a one-party dictatorship. In 1919, Rosa decided to leave Russia. She intended to go to America or Scandinavia, but the first ship she could find was headed for Palestine. On board were young Zionist pioneers who intended to build a new settlement in the northern part of the country near Lake Kinneret (the Sea of Galilee). Their idealism convinced her to join them. So, as with Nehemiah Rabin, Zionism brought Rosa Cohen to Palestine.

If Zionism brought Nehemiah and Rosa separately to Palestine, anti-Jewish violence brought them together in Jerusalem. By 1920, Jewish immigration into Palestine was encountering strong Arab opposition. The Arabs opposed Jewish immigration, even though many Arab residents of Palestine themselves were immigrants who had come to take advantage of job opportunities caused by Jewish economic activity. In April 1920, Arab mobs attacked Jews in the part of Jerusalem known as the Old City. Shouting "We shall drink Jewish blood," the mobs attacked the neighborhood known as the Jewish Quarter.

Nehemiah Rabin and other members of the Jewish Legion rushed from the town of Jericho to Jerusalem to defend their people. At that time Rosa Cohen was visiting her uncle Mordechai in his home in the new and main section of Jerusalem outside the Old City walls. Upon learning about the trouble in the Old City, she immediately put on a nurse's uniform and went to the Jewish Quarter to treat the wounded. It was there, in the middle of the rioting, that Rosa Cohen and Nehemiah Rabin met. A year later they were married in Haifa. Rosa kept her maiden name after her marriage. On March 1, 1922, she gave birth to a son, Yitzhak, in Jerusalem.

The Rabins settled in Tel Aviv, where their second child, Rachel, was born in 1925. Nehemiah went to work for the newly founded Palestine Electric Corporation, one of the most important Jewish-owned companies in the country. Rosa worked as an accountant for a large construction firm. Working near her as a cashier was Golda Meir, who later would become Israel's prime minister. Years later when Meir told Rabin she had been a cashier at the construction firm, he answered, "So was my mother." Golda, as Israelis called their grandmotherly prime minister, corrected him. "No. I was the cashier; your mother was the accountant."[4]

Earning a living was only a small part of Nehemiah's, and especially Rosa's, working day. Both parents were deeply involved in public affairs, "a duty owed to the community."[5] Nehemiah was active in trade-union activities at the Electric Company. Union meetings were held at the Rabin home, as were meetings related to Rosa's many activities. She was a virtual dynamo, involved in political and social work all over Tel Aviv. Rosa's main concern was the welfare of Tel Aviv's Jewish workers, but she had so many activities and obligations that she had to pin notes to her dress in order to remember them all.

No activity was more important than defending the Jewish community. Both Rabins belonged to the Hagana, which was founded in 1920. Military duties often took Nehemiah away from home for weeks at a time. Guns were stored and hidden in the Rabin apartment. Once, when a gun accidentally went off, a bullet almost hit Rachel.

Rosa was always on call, even when strolling with her children. "We would never get to our destination on time," Rabin remembered. "We were always being held up because on the way she would meet someone who took the opportunity to ask her something or to talk things over with her." Rachel, the younger child, at least took advantage of the delays. As she later recalled, "I used to pull on her dress, and she would buy me ice cream to keep me quiet."[6]

All these activities and commitments took a toll on the Rabin home life. Because the parents were so busy, the children often had to be cared for by neighbors, a situation that Yitzhak later admitted he did not like but understood. The only time reserved just for the family was Friday evenings, when the Jewish sabbath begins with a special meal. Still, the Rabin home was a happy place. Although Yitzhak's parents were not religious, they took great pride in being Jewish. They also stressed their socialist values by rejecting luxury and expecting their children to do chores. Waste was not tolerated. The chil-

*Six-year-old Yitzhak with his mother Rosa and sister Rachel.
Both children knew their mother had a heart condition and
were always careful not to upset her. Rosa died when
Yitzhak was in high school.*

dren helped make the beds, wash dishes, and sweep floors. They were taught that one "did not work merely to satisfy material needs; work was valuable in itself."[7]

Yitzhak's first school reflected his early training at home. It was a new school founded by workers' organizations in Tel Aviv called the Bet Hinuch (House of Education). The school was set up because working people in Tel Aviv who thought like Rosa were not satisfied with just teaching children basic academic subjects. They wanted to prepare children to be pioneers with the skills necessary to build new settlements and work the land. Bet Hinuch stressed practical training and socialist values. Along with their academic studies, students cooked their own meals, washed dishes, tended a vegetable garden, and worked in the school carpentry shop. To promote socialist egalitarianism, students called their teachers by their first names.

Students attended school six days a week. Many remained in school until 4 P.M. because of their parents' work schedules. Conditions were far from ideal, especially during the first years when the school was housed in a ramshackle wooden building. None of that bothered Yitzhak or the other students:

> *It was hot in the summer and wet in the winter, but we loved it, we loved the atmosphere that pervaded it. We loved to study in the hut—that is to say, on those days when it was possible to study—for if the flooding rose beyond a certain level, the students had to adjourn to the dining room.*[8]

When the school's facilities finally improved, it was, as usual, due in large part to Rosa's efforts. She convinced her uncle Mordechai to lend the school a large sum of money so it could move to better quarters. But a new building did not correct the academic weaknesses of Bet Hinuch. Nor were those weaknesses addressed after Yitzhak completed his studies and moved on to a regional intermediate school called Givat Hashalosha (Hill of the Three), which his mother had helped found. When he applied to enter high school Yitzhak found he was poorly prepared in mathematics and several other academic subjects. After failing his entrance examinations, he had to study hard for several months until he passed on his second try.

Yitzhak was a handsome boy with reddish-brown wavy hair, like his father. His intense eyes and facial expressions seem to have come from his mother. Yitzhak was strong and a good athlete who enjoyed sports, but also was very shy. He rarely spoke, whether in school or when he was with other children or adults. As he wrote in his memoirs, "Then, as now, I did not show my feelings or share them with others."[9] One feeling he hid was his concern for his mother. Rosa had a heart condition, and Nehemiah went into debt in a futile search for a doctor or treatment that could cure her.

In 1937 the family's dread became a reality. In October of that year Yitzhak became a student at the Kadoorie Agricultural High School. It was located in northern Palestine, far from Tel Aviv. In November he received an urgent message from his father to rush to Tel Aviv's Hadassah hospital. Rosa was dying. "I did not want to cry in front of her but I just couldn't help myself, and all my grief flooded out," Yitzhak remembered. More than 1,000 people attended Rosa's funeral in Tel Aviv. The principal of the Kadoorie school spoke for many when he wrote to the grieving Yitzhak:

*Your mother was one of the great women of Israel
whose names are associated with the idealism of
the nation....May you find comfort in studying
for the profession you have chosen, for your own
good and for the good of the public which your
mother loved so much and to which she gave so
much of her time in her short life.[10]*

Many years later, when Yitzhak entered politics, he found
many supporters who still remembered him as "Rosa
Cohen's son."

Yitzhak returned to school "with the feeling that I
had crossed over the threshold to manhood." He dedicated himself to his studies and became the best student
in his class. He fully intended to serve his country as a
farmer. But Yitzhak's studies and plans were about to be
interrupted by more pressing matters. In 1929, Yitzhak
had lived through Arab riots and attacks on Jews. In 1936
a far more serious outbreak of riots and attacks on Jews
began. It was organized by the Arab leadership in Palestine. The main issue behind what was called the "Arab
Revolt" once again was Jewish immigration, which had
surged upward after the Nazi rise to power in Germany.
The Arabs attacked Jewish settlements as well as Jews
living in cities. Several attacks were launched on the
Kadoorie school. The British authorities did little to stop
the attacks. The Jewish Yishuv would have to protect
itself. Yitzhak Rabin's military career was about to begin.

Yitzhak had been taught how to use a gun as a thir-
teen-year-old student in intermediate school. Now the
training became more serious. He and the other boys
were trained by a Hagana sergeant–and Kadoorie graduate–named Yigal Allon. More intensive training followed

at a nearby kibbutz when the British temporarily closed Kadoorie during 1938. Rabin's duties included guard duty and setting ambushes. Allon, who like Rabin became a leading Israeli general and politician, was impressed with Yitzhak's abilities:

He had a sort of analytical approach to problems. He would never say he understood something before he really did understand all that it involved. Once he said that he understood, you knew that he did.[11]

By the time Rabin and his fellow students returned to school in October 1939, World War II had broken out. Yitzhak found it difficult to concentrate on his studies, but did well enough to graduate at the top of his class in 1940.

By 1940 the Arab Revolt was over, but the Yishuv faced far greater problems. The start of World War II and the German victories that followed directly threatened millions of Jews in Europe. Already in 1938, Chaim Weizmann, the leader of the world Zionist movement, had warned that for European Jews the "world is divided into places where they cannot live and into which they cannot enter."[12] The situation became dramatically worse in May 1939 when the British announced their White Paper of that year. The White Paper was specifically designed to win over Arab public opinion, which was becoming increasingly pro-German. It ignored the desperate plight of millions of Jews by limiting Jewish immigration into Palestine to 75,000 over the next five years. After that, all Jewish immigration would be

In 1940 Yitzhak graduated from high school, intending to become a farmer. Events overtook him and turned him into a soldier. Within one year of graduation Yitzhak became one of the first members of the Palmach, a fighting force set up to protect the Jewish community of Palestine.

banned. The White Paper also forbade Jews to buy land in 95 percent of Palestine.

The Jews in Palestine were shocked and bitterly angry. Nonetheless, more than 32,000 Palestine Jews served in the British armed forces fighting the Nazis. (More than 130,000 actually volunteered.) As Chaim Weizmann put it, "Their war is our war." In terms of British immigration policy, however, the attitude was different. The Jews of Palestine simply could not accept the White Paper, which amounted to a death sentence for the Jews in Europe and the end of any hope for a Jewish national home. David Ben-Gurion, head of the Jewish Agency, the governing organization of the Jewish community in Palestine, summed up its attitude when he said, "We shall fight the war as if there were no White Paper, and the White Paper as if there were no war."[13]

One way of fighting was to set up a full-time military force to protect the Jewish community. This became essential by 1941 as German victories in North Africa meant that Germany might overrun Palestine. The new force, set up by the Hagana, was called the Palmach. The threat to Palestine was so grave that the British did not stop its formation and even trained some Palmach soldiers for commando and scouting missions. One of the first young people recruited into the Palmach was Yitzhak Rabin, who at the time was living on a kibbutz. Several weeks after he agreed to join, a Hagana officer came to see him. The officer was Moshe Dayan, who was destined to become one of Israel's legendary war heroes. Dayan was looking for men to undertake a dangerous mission. He had no time and did not waste it conducting a long interview:

Do you know how to fire a rifle?
Yes.

Have you ever thrown a hand grenade?
Yes.

Do you know how to operate a machine-gun?
No.

Can you drive?
No.

Can you ride a motorcycle?
No.

All right. You'll do.[14]

Only nineteen, Rabin had just been accepted for a sabotage mission into Lebanon. Lebanon and Syria were under control of the French puppet government that the Germans had set up after defeating and occupying France. The British planned to invade Lebanon and Syria to stop the Germans from using them as springboards to seize the Middle East and its invaluable oil resources. They sent in Palmach units first to destroy telephone communications lines, ambush enemy patrols, sabotage roads, and blow up installations. The young Jewish soldiers were warned that if they were caught they probably would be shot on the spot. Rabin's unit was ordered to cut key telephone wires:

> *The route to our objective was 30 miles (48 kilometers)—to be covered on foot, of course. As the youngest, I was given the job of climbing up the*

*telephone poles. We had received our climbing
irons only that day and hadn't had time to
practice. Unable to use the irons, I took off my
boots (which was the way I was used to climbing), shinnied up the pole, and cut the first wire,
only to find out that the pole was held upright by
the tension of the wires. The pole swayed, and I
found myself on the ground. But for a lack of
choice, up again I climbed, cut the wire, made my
way down, and repeated the operation on the
second pole. Mission completed, we...made our
way back...by a shortcut.*[15]

The successful Palmach operations in Lebanon boosted
its prestige, but its future remained uncertain. By 1943,
as the Nazi threat to Palestine faded, the British turned
against the Palmach and once again began arresting its
men if they carried weapons. Nor was the Yishuv leadership overly enthusiastic about the Palmach. Many
leaders believed that it cost too much to maintain and
should be disbanded.

The Palmach leadership believed that its force had
to stay together and remain prepared. Rabin was among
those who were convinced that as soon as the war ended
the Jews "would have to fight for our lives in Palestine"
and that only an independent Jewish military force could
give them a chance to survive.[16]

The organization was held together by a scheme in
which Palmach members lived in kibbutz settlements,
working half of the month for their keep and training or
taking on military tasks the other half. It often was a
monotonous routine and, as Rabin recalled, only "deep
faith and inner conviction held the Palmach together."[17]

Led by Yitzhak Sadeh, a veteran of the Soviet Union's Red Army, the Palmach stressed individual initiative, speed, and aggressiveness in battle. Building on Hagana tactics of "active defense" developed in the 1930s, Palmach troops were trained to move quickly on patrol and attack day or night, before the Arab gangs could strike. The Palmach even managed secretly to start a naval program and a tiny air force disguised as a flying club.

Rabin meanwhile advanced into a leadership position. He became a platoon leader in 1943. One of his assignments was helping illegal Jewish immigrants cross into Palestine from the north. He earned a reputation as a first-rate leader whose men were tough and well trained in hit-and-run tactics. Rabin also was known and highly respected as a thorough, careful, and innovative military strategist. Early in 1945, as World War II drew to a close, the Palmach reorganized its small force into several battalions. Rabin was made second-in-command of the First Battalion. He also was put in charge of training section leaders for the Palmach.

Rabin's personal life also advanced. In 1944 he met a pretty, dark-haired, blue-eyed fifteen-year-old schoolgirl in Tel Aviv named Leah Schlossberg. She had been born in Germany and immigrated to Palestine with her parents in 1933. Their first few encounters amounted to what Yitzhak remembered as "a glance, a word, a stirring within, and then a further meeting."[18]

According to Leah, after several wordless "meetings" she asked some friends the name of the good-looking young man with the "chestnut hair and beautiful eyes." Then she approached the "terribly shy" youth who reminded her of the Bible's King David and asked, "Your

name is Yitzhak?" After his one-word answer–"Yes"–
she added, "And I'm Leah."[19]

Matters proceeded slowly from there, in part because Yitzhak rarely had time off from the Palmach. In
1945, Leah graduated from high school and herself joined
the Palmach. She served in the battalion of which Yitzhak
was the deputy commander, "one of the rare occasions
in our life together when *she* was under *my* command,"
Rabin noted wryly.[20]

By then World War II finally was over. By 1943,
however, the Jews of Palestine had already learned that
the Nazis were engaged in the mass murder of European Jews. Now their worst fears were confirmed as the
unimaginably horrible toll of the Holocaust became
widely known: the Nazis had murdered six million Jews
in their campaign of genocide. But the Jewish community of Palestine barely had time to mourn. It had to do
what it could to help the few survivors. And, as Rabin
had foreseen, it had to fight for its life.

CHAPTER THREE

"Our war is just beginning."

The defeat of Nazi Germany in May 1945 removed the common enemy that had prevented a direct confrontation between the British and the Yishuv. They immediately clashed over two questions, each of which was critical to whether the Jews would have a national home in Palestine. First, what level of Jewish immigration would the British permit while they still controlled Palestine? Second, would the Jewish community be allowed to establish an independent state when and if the British were to leave Palestine?

The question of Jewish immigration brought the relations between the Yishuv and the British to the breaking point. With the war over, and in light of the catastrophe that had befallen the Jews of Europe, the Jews in Palestine expected the British to lift their White Paper restrictions. By the summer of 1945, it was clear that the

British govenment intended no such thing. In Europe 250,000 desperate Jewish refugees, among them tens of thousands of orphaned children, were wandering from place to place or waiting in "displaced persons" (DP) camps in Europe with no place to go. Yet the British government, increasingly pro-Arab in its outlook, ignored the pleas of the Jewish community in Palestine. It also ignored the request of U.S. President Harry Truman in August 1945 and the recommendation of a joint American-British committee in March 1946 to immediately allow 100,000 refugees into Palestine.

The Yishuv therefore decided to take matters into its own hands. Rabin and his comrades in the Palmach found themselves carrying out some of the most dangerous actions associated with that decision.

Beginning in mid-1945, agents from the Yishuv moved thousands of Holocaust survivors from DP camps to the coast of France and Italy. After walking for hundreds of miles, they sailed in battered and unsafe old boats for Palestine. Between 1945 and 1948, sixty-three ships sailed from Europe with their cargo of refugees. Only five made it. The rest were intercepted by gunboats and warships of the British navy off the coast of Palestine, within sight of the Promised Land. Often the refugees on the boats fought the British boarding parties. As the British towed their boat into Haifa harbor, one group unfurled a defiant banner that read as follows:

*We survived Hitler. Death is no stranger to us.
Nothing can keep us from our Jewish homeland.
The blood be on your head if you fire on this
unarmed ship.*[1]

This Hagana ship was seized by British naval units while attempting to land on the Palestine coast. The refugees were deported to Cyprus.

Neither fists nor banners could stop the British, who deported and imprisoned thousands of refugees from Hitler's deadly concentration camps on the island of Cyprus, and even sent some back to Germany. It was to prevent deportation that the Palmach sent Rabin and his comrades to liberate refugees from the Atlit camp in October 1945. That raid made him a hero to Palestine's Jews. It also made him a wanted man to the British.

Jewish defiance of the British went beyond smuggling refugees through the blockade. By the fall of 1945 armed Jewish units were attacking British soldiers and bases. Some of the attacks were launched by the mainstream Jewish community using the Hagana and the Palmach. Two smaller and more extreme organizations also turned on the British. One was called the Irgun. It was led by Menachem Begin, a Polish-born Jew who reached Palestine during World War II. In 1977, Begin would become Israel's prime minister. Even more militant than the Irgun was a tiny organization called Lehi, which the British called the Stern Gang.

One major Hagana strike against the British took place in June 1946 after the British intercepted a ship carrying more than 1,700 men, women, and children. The Hagana attacked British police stations and other targets throughout the country. An attack that never took place nonetheless knocked Rabin out of action and put him in the hospital. He was supposed to lead an assault on an important British police station in the town of Jenin. However, during the planning process, while rushing on his motorcycle to a meeting with Yigal Allon, Rabin hit a truck and broke his leg. He spent three weeks in the hospital and then was "sent home, hobbling on crutches. All I could do was to follow Palmach operations from an armchair, cursing my fate."[2]

Menachem Begin in one of his first public appearances is shown here with his "adjutant," a man who dressed exactly like him presumably to foil would-be assassins. Begin was at this point the leader of the Irgun, a militant underground organization that broke away from the Hagana in the 1930s. He later became leader of the Likud party which was the leading opposition to the party in power, Labor, in which Rabin became a prominent figure after returning to Israel in 1973.

Rabin was not in his armchair for long. On June 18, the Palmach blew up most of the bridges linking Palestine with its neighbors. The infuriated British retaliated by arresting more than 3,000 Hagana members over a two-week period. The British raids began on Saturday (the Jewish sabbath), June 29, a date Jews in Palestine have since called "Black Sabbath." Among those arrested were Nehemiah and Yitzhak Rabin. While Rabin was in prison the cast on his leg was removed, and he began an intensive exercise program to restore his badly withered leg to health. Finally, in November the prisoners were released.

At this point Rabin had to make a decision about his future. In 1940 he had declined a chance to study water engineering at the University of California at Berkeley because he decided that his place during World War II was in Palestine. Once again Kadoorie's star graduate had a chance to go to Berkeley. A conversation with Allon, the Palmach's commander, ended that possibility. "The World War has ended, but our war is just beginning," Allon said.[3] Rabin agreed, and one week later he took command of the Palmach's Second Battalion. In October 1947, Allon appointed Rabin deputy commander of the Palmach.

Between mid-1946 and the fall of 1947 the situation in Palestine changed drastically. Britain, exhausted by World War II and unable to stem the Jewish resistance in Palestine that was taking a growing toll on British soldiers, decided to give up its mandate and leave the country. The decision on what to do with Palestine was turned over to the United Nations Special Committee on Palestine (UNSCOP). It recommended dividing the country into a Jewish state and an Arab state.

Jerusalem would become an international zone, not part of either state. On November 29, 1947, the UN General Assembly formally approved the recommendation. A few days later, Britain announced it would leave Palestine on May 15, 1948.

Arabs both inside and outside of Palestine bitterly opposed the UN decision and the idea of a Jewish state in any part of Palestine. "Any drawn line by the United Nations will be nothing but a line of blood and fire," one Arab representative to the UN announced.[4] The reaction among the Jews was quite different. They were overjoyed at the chance to finally build a national home free of British interference. At the same time, they knew that they would face bitter and violent Arab opposition, not just from inside Palestine but from several neighboring Arab countries.

The Jewish community was hardly ready to face such a threat. Its population of approximately 650,000 was about one-third of the total in Palestine. The Arabs controlled most of the country's high ground. They also controlled the territory between the main concentration of the Yishuv's population and Jerusalem, where over 90,000 Jews were almost isolated. In addition, the Arabs were much more heavily armed than the Jews. Behind them stood the armies and heavy weapons of at least five Arab countries poised to invade Palestine when the mandate ended. The Arabs also were favored by the British, who when they withdrew from strategically important points often turned them over to Arab soldiers.

Against this, in April 1947 the Hagana had an arsenal that totaled about 10,000 rifles, 1,900 submachine guns, and 444 light machine guns. As Rabin observed later, "It goes without saying that there was not a single cannon, heavy machine gun, or antitank or antiaircraft weapon, not to mention armor, air, or naval force."[5] The Palmach numbered barely 2,000 troops. Another 1,000 soldiers stood in reserve. The Hagana had over 30,000 other troops, but they were not nearly as well trained as the Palmach. The Irgun and Lehi also had small armies, but for much of the war they acted on their own rather than under Hagana command.

Nor were the Jews given time to prepare. In essence, the War of Independence, which officially dates from May 15, 1948, began in late 1947. By then, Jews in Arab countries throughout the Middle East were in danger. During 1947 and 1948 there were murderous pogroms in Syria, Egypt, Libya, Iraq, and several other countries. The Jews of Palestine came under attacks from Arab terrorists. In December, Arabs murdered thirty Jews in Haifa. The worst incident occurred in February 1948 in Jerusalem, where 54 people died when terrorists blew up several buildings in the center of the city. Much more important, Arab forces moved to cut off the Jews of Jerusalem from the main Jewish areas along the Mediterranean coast and the city of Tel Aviv. They also tried to isolate Jewish communities in the Negev desert in the south and the Galilee region in the north.

Under Ben-Gurion's leadership, the Yishuv tried to resupply Jerusalem by sending convoys of trucks along the main road from Tel Aviv to Jerusalem. Arab snipers hidden in the hills ambushed the convoys and killed many of the drivers. Unless the Jews in Jerusalem were resupplied, the city would fall to the Arabs. In March, Ben-Gurion ordered the Hagana to clear the road to Jerusalem. The campaign was called Operation Nachshon. By April 6, after taking heavy losses, Jewish soldiers held enough key points so a convoy was able to reach Jerusalem. The

Palmach then was given the job of completing Operation Nachshon. It created a new unit for the job, the Harel Brigade, with Rabin as its commander.

Over the next month the 1,500-man Harel Brigade was involved in desperate and bloody fighting along the Jerusalem road and in Jerusalem itself. After briefly keeping the road open, the brigade was moved to Jerusalem, where 2,500 Jews living in the Jewish Quarter of the Old City were cut off from the modern western part of the city beyond the walls, where most Jews lived. The Harel Brigade was fighting to hold open the Jerusalem road, defend the new city, and link up with the besieged Jewish Quarter in the Old City.

It turned out to be an impossible assignment. Rabin's forces could not take a police fortress along the Jerusalem road at Latrun, which the British earlier had turned over to the Arabs. They were, however, able to take control of the center of Jerusalem when the British evacuated the city on May 14. But the Harel Brigade could not rescue the Jewish Quarter. It was a difficult time for Rabin, who had disagreed with military decisions made by others that turned out to be disastrous. His men became angry about the high rate of casualties, which by early May reached 100 dead and 400 wounded and would later go even higher. Some of them blamed their commander, adding to Rabin's pain.

Elsewhere, the tide of battle favored Jewish forces, whose numbers grew as the Hagana expanded its ranks. During April they took Haifa with its port on the Mediterranean, the town of Acre a few miles to the north, and the city of Tiberias on Lake Kinerret. On May 9–10, in house-to-house fighting, troops led by Yigal Allon seized the key mountain town of Safed. On May 14, the town of Jaffa near Tel Aviv was taken. These victories dramatically strengthened the Jewish position in critical parts of Palestine. Meanwhile, some new weapons purchased from Czechoslovakia were arriving, as were Jewish volunteers with military experience from several foreign countries.

As the fighting raged, on May 14, 1948, at a meeting at the Tel Aviv Museum, David Ben-Gurion read an announcement proclaiming "the establishment of the Jewish state in Palestine—to be called Israel."[6] Ben-Gurion's words announcing the first independent Jewish state in almost 1,900 years were broadcast on radio to Israel and the world. In its first act, Israel's new government revoked the White Paper of 1939. Henceforth, any Jew could enter and live in the new state. The government's first meeting lasted barely half an hour, at which point Ben-Gurion announced simply, "The State of Israel has arisen. The meeting is ended." That same day word arrived that the United States had become the first country to officially recognize the new state.

In most of Israel joyful people celebrated in the streets. At a kibbutz a few miles outside Jerusalem, Rabin and his exhausted soldiers had no energy to celebrate. As Ben-Gurion's voice came over the radio one weary soldier asked, "Hey, guys, turn it off. I'm dying for some sleep. We can hear the fine words tomorrow." As for Rabin:

> *I was mute, stifling my own mixture of emotions. None of us had ever dreamed that this was how we should greet the birth of our state, but we were filled with an even stronger sense of determination now that the state existed.*[7]

Israeli state officials listen as Prime Minister David Ben-Gurion reads the "Declaration of Independence," and the nation of Israel is born. The joy Israel felt was quickly muted as the very next morning, at dawn, the new state's Arab neighbors declared war and attacked both the southern and northern borders.

The Israelis would need all their determination. The next day, May 15, the armies of five Arab countries—Egypt, Syria, Lebanon, Transjordan, and Iraq—stormed into Israel, determined to destroy the infant state in its cradle. Azzam Pasha, the head of the Arab League to which they all belonged, left no doubt about their intent:

> *This will be a war of extermination and a momentous massacre which will be spoken of like the Mongol massacres and the Crusades.*[8]

At the time, it looked as if Pasha's prediction would come true. The Jews still had no weapons to match the tanks, artillery, aircraft, ships, and other heavy weapons of the invading Arabs. A few months before the invasion, the commander of British forces in Palestine expressed the generally accepted assessment when he said that Arab armies "would have no trouble in taking over the whole country."[9]

At dawn on May 15, Egyptian planes bombed Tel Aviv while its army attacked Israel from the south. In the north the armies of Syria, Iraq, Transjordan, and Lebanon crossed Israel's borders. The existence of the Jewish state clearly was threatened.

In Jerusalem, the Palmach and Rabin struggled desperately against Transjordan's Arab Legion, led by British officers, to save the Jewish Quarter in the Old City. At one point Rabin's men broke through to the Old City and delivered supplies and ammunition to the starving residents. But they could not hold out against the overwhelming odds and had to retreat. On May 28, Rabin was at the Palmach's strong point on Mount Zion, just outside the city walls. From there he witnessed a "shattering scene":

> *A delegation was emerging from the Jewish*
> *Quarter bearing white flags. I was horrified*
> *to learn that it consisted of rabbis and other*
> *residents on their way to hear the legion's*
> *terms for their capitulation. That same*
> *night the Jewish Quarter surrendered to*
> *the Arab Legion.*[10]

With the fall of the Jewish Quarter, the Western Wall, the last remaining part of the Second Temple of the ancient Israelites and the holiest site in Judaism, fell under Arab control. No Jew, Israeli or otherwise, would be allowed to visit the site until 1967, when Israel's soldiers under Rabin's leadership retook the Old City.

Meanwhile, the Egyptian army reached within 25 miles (40 kilometers) of Tel Aviv, despite heroic resistance by several Jewish settlements along its route. The Syrians pushed into the Galilee region, and Jordanian and Iraqi troops each held several key towns in the north and center of the country. Among them was Lydda, the country's only international airport.

Late in May the UN Security Council called for a cease-fire. Israel agreed, but the Arabs did not. They demanded that Israel first renounce its independence. The Israelis, despite their military difficulties, told the Security Council:

> *If the Arab states want peace with Israel, they can*
> *have it. If they want war—they can have it too.*

*But whether they want peace or war, they can
have it only with the State of Israel.*[11]

By early June, Israel's resistance had stiffened and its
military situation, while still serious, stabilized. Most of
the Jewish settlements under attack had beaten off the
enemy. Jewish forces in the Galilee were pushing the
Arabs back. The Jewish state held most of the area assigned to it by the UN partition. Generally, Hagana
forces were better trained then their foes and much more
motivated. They were well aware, as Golda Meir put it,
that they had nowhere else to go if they lost this war.
Meanwhile, immigrants from the Cyprus detention
camps and experienced Jewish soldiers from other countries were arriving and joining Hagana units. New and
more powerful weapons purchased abroad also began
to arrive, including invaluable fighter aircraft from
Czechoslovakia.

On July 8, a day before the truce was scheduled to
Both sides then agreed to a truce, which took effect
on June 11. They used the truce to reinforce their military positions. During the truce the Israelis managed to
pave a path near the Tel Aviv-Jerusalem road that allowed them to bypass the Latrun fortress. Rabin had
learned of the path in May from one of his officers, who
claimed he could make it from Jerusalem to the coast
via a path that bypassed Latrun. Rabin sent three soldiers with the officer to test the route. When he was convinced it could be used, he suggested paving the route
instead of continuing the bloody and thus far futile attacks on Latrun. Once the path was paved, the route to
Jerusalem was secured permanently.

On July 8, a day before the truce was scheduled to
end, the Egyptian army resumed fighting. The Israelis

successfully struck back on several fronts. In a span of ten days they punched through Egyptian lines in the Negev, took the town of Nazareth in the Galilee, captured important towns near Tel Aviv, and seized territory near Jerusalem. They also used their new aircraft to bomb both Cairo and Damascus, the capitals of Egypt and Syria. On July 18, a second UN-sponsored truce began.

During the second truce the Israelis continued to reorganize and strengthen their position. Israel now had an official new army: the Israel Defense Forces (IDF). It was organized into four commands: the south, the coastal, Jerusalem, and the north.

Rabin also underwent what he called a "personal reorganization." On August 23, taking advantage of the respite provided by the second truce, he and Leah were married in Tel Aviv. The shy warrior, who had been fighting brutal battles for months, found the ceremony and formality of getting married nerve-wracking. When the rabbi scheduled to perform the ceremony was thirty minutes late, Rabin snapped, "This is the last time that *I'm* getting married."[12] It was, of course, as the marriage was a happy and fruitful partnership that lasted for the rest of Yitzhak's life.

A third round of fighting broke out in October 1948. It took place along the southern front commanded by Yigal Allon. The man he chose as his deputy commander was Yitzhak Rabin. The Israelis were looking for an excuse to fight. The Egyptian army was still in Palestine dangerously close to Tel Aviv and also positioned so that the Negev was virtually cut off from the rest of the country. The Egyptians gave them that excuse when they violated the truce by firing on an Israeli supply convoy. In

Yitzhak and Leah were married in the summer
of 1948 during the second truce in the War of
Independence. The young couple's new home
was a small room in the apartment of Leah's
parents in Tel Aviv.

seven days of hard fighting the Israelis opened the road to the Negev and captured its main town of Beersheba. They also forced the Egyptians to withdraw from territory along the Mediterranean coast back to what today is the Gaza Strip. However, powerful Egyptian forces still remained inside Palestine.

In December, Allon and Rabin again attacked the Egyptians. Advancing Israeli troops crossed into Egyptian territory in the Sinai Peninsula. They were on the verge of destroying the Egyptian forces facing them. But Allon and Rabin did not get to finish the job. International pressure caused Prime Minister Ben-Gurion to stop the Israeli offensive. Allon and Rabin were furious. They warned Ben-Gurion that allowing the Egyptians to escape with their forces intact and hold the Gaza Strip would trigger another war. Ben-Gurion stuck to his decision, and in early January a cease-fire took hold. In 1956 and again in 1967 events proved his two young officers to be right.

On January 13, 1949, Israel began armistice negotiations with Egypt on the island of Rhodes in the Mediterranean. An American diplomat, Dr. Ralph Bunche, took charge of the difficult negotiations, which began with the Egyptians refusing to meet with the Israelis face-to-face. Even when Bunche finally got the Egyptians into the same room with the Israelis, the Egyptians at first refused to speak directly with the Israelis. Rabin was part of the Israeli delegation, serving as an advisor to the Israeli diplomats who did the actual negotiating. Before he left, Allon told his deputy: "See to it that no agreement is reached which is less than peace. And don't agree to anything that gives us less than Gaza."[13]

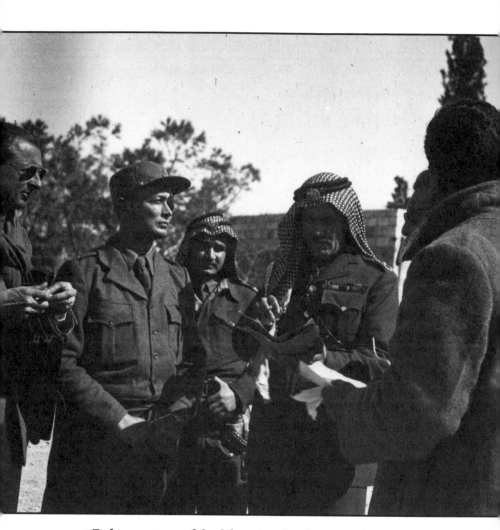

Rabin was part of the delegation that hammered out an armistice with Egypt, but he was not at all pleased with the final agreement, which he believed compromised Israeli security. Here Moshe Dayan stands by while a list of Egyptian prisoners to be repatriated is reviewed.

Rabin was unable to accomplish what Allon wanted. While at Rhodes he wrote to Allon that the Israeli diplomats were giving away too much. Rabin strongly disagreed with the Israeli decision to allow the Egyptians to remain in Gaza and the Jordanians in the mountain region south of Jerusalem. He disagreed with Israeli diplomats who thought that the agreements reached at Rhodes would lead to genuine peace talks. Rabin believed that they would lead to another war. Once again he was proven correct by subsequent events.

Rather less important but still annoying, while Rabin had "never worn a tie in my life" before leaving for Rhodes, ties were part of the expected attire at diplomatic negotiations. His efforts to learn how to tie one ended in failure. After someone tied it for him, Rabin learned how to loosen it enough to get it over his head without losing the knot. That way he could slip it back on when necessary. Somehow Rabin managed, although he remained "terrified at the prospect that the knot might come undone" during his entire stay at Rhodes.[14]

By the time the armistice agreement with Egypt was signed on February 24, Rabin was back in Israel. He participated in the very last part of the war against Jordanian forces, in which Israeli troops secured key parts of the Negev from the Dead Sea to the port of Eilat. Israel now held about 8,000 square miles (20,700 square kilometers) of Palestine, about 21 percent more than under the original UN partition plan. In March the new nation was admitted to the United Nations.

However, the Old City in Jerusalem, and with it the Western Wall, remained in Jordanian hands, while the Gaza Strip, dangerously close to Tel Aviv, was under Egyptian control. More than 6,000 Israelis, almost one percent of the total population, had died in the country's War of Independence. More than 30,000 had been wounded. Much of the country's best farmland, including many of its famous citrus groves, were damaged during the fighting. And the war had cost Israel more than $500 million dollars, which it did not have.

Yitzhak Rabin had played an important part in helping his country survive its stormy birth. He now had to decide what role he should play to help it grow and flourish.

CHAPTER FOUR

"We built a mighty army."

The victory in the War of Independence left the Israeli people and government no time to rest. Immense tasks of nation-building lay before them. The most immediate and urgent problem was bringing hundreds of thousands of refugees into the country, and once they were there, finding them homes and integrating them into Israeli society. The task was gigantic. Between 1948 and 1951, 687,000 immigrants arrived in Israel. They came from many different places and circumstances, almost all involving great hardship and suffering. Many were Holocaust survivors from DP camps in Europe. Others came from European countries like Bulgaria and Romania, where large numbers of Jews had survived the Holocaust, and non-Arab Muslim countries like Turkey and Iran.

In addition, Jews from Arab countries began their massive immigration to Israel. The Jews of Yemen and Iraq, the two oldest Jewish communities in the world outside of Israel, came in two remarkable airlifts. They left behind cruel persecution and all their property. They were soon followed by the majority of the Jewish communities of Egypt and the other Arab countries in North Africa, who had endured centuries of discrimination punctuated by periodic outbursts of violence. By 1953 the Jewish population in Israel had gone from its 1948 figure of 650,000 to almost 1.5 million.

The early days of independence were extremely difficult. Refugees with no education or property waited in tent camps while a frantic effort was made to build new housing, often entire settlements, help people find work, provide social services, and more. Economic conditions were hard for veteran Israelis as well.

Meanwhile, Israel remained surrounded by enemies determined to destroy it. None of Israel's Arab neighbors was willing to make peace. They sponsored terrorist raids across Israel's borders in which hundreds of civilians were murdered over the next several years. The Arab League vigorously enforced an economic boycott of Israel, while Egypt, in violation of international law, barred Israeli ships and cargoes from the Suez Canal. In another violation of international law, Egypt also blockaded the Straits of Tiran at the southern end of the Gulf of Aqaba (which the Israelis call the Gulf of Eilat). This prevented Israel from using its port at Eilat to trade with Asia and Africa. The prevailing Arab attitude toward Israel was summed up in 1954 by the Egyptian foreign minister:

The Arab people are not embarrassed to declare: We shall not be satisfied except by the obliteration of Israel from the map of the Middle East.[1]

Like many Israelis at this difficult time, Yitzhak Rabin stood "at a crossroads in my personal life." Once again he postponed, permanently as it turned out, his plans to go to the United States to study water engineering. Rabin felt what he called "a debt of honor toward the men whose courage and bodies had blocked the Arab advance." That is why he and other military officers made a commitment to "dedicate our lives to ensuring the State of Israel would never again be unprepared to meet aggression." While some Israeli leaders built up the new government and others provided vital social services, all accomplishing remarkable feats, none performed a more vital task for the new nation than Rabin and his comrades. As he put it, simply, "We built a mighty army."[2]

As he helped to build Israel's army, Rabin found out that political and personal conflicts often got in the way. The most important political issue for Rabin was the status of former Palmach officers such as himself. In 1948, Prime Minister Ben-Gurion had ordered the Palmach disbanded and its units integrated into the newly formed military command, the Israel Defense Forces (IDF). Ben-Gurion did not entirely trust the "Palmachniks," as they were called, because of their intense loyalties to each other and because many of them were associated with a different political party than the prime minister's. In October 1949 he even banned all IDF officers from attending a Palmach farewell rally. To keep Rabin from attending, Ben-Gurion invited him to his home, supposedly to discuss military matters. After several hours of discussions the prime minister even took the unusual step of inviting Rabin to stay for dinner. Rabin declined. After Yitzhak returned home and changed clothes, he and Leah rushed to the rally.

Rabin received an official reprimand for attending the rally, a much lighter punishment than he originally expected. He also received a personal scolding from the IDF's commanding officer, Chief of Staff Ya'akov Dori. Actually, Rabin's real punishment seems to have been meted out over the long term, in the form of delayed promotions and slower career advancement.

Still, Rabin did advance. The IDF, which was thrown together ad hoc during the War of Independence, was in the process of turning itself into a modern professional army. One of its most important priorities was training new officers. Rabin played a leading role in that project, and in 1950 he was promoted to the rank of colonel. In 1951 the new chief of staff Yigael Yadin, who also was a world-famous archaeologist, made Rabin head of the IDF's operations division. This appointment brought Rabin into the IDF's general staff, the top circle of officers that ran the army.

Rabin now was responsible for a wide variety of critical tasks in preparing the Israeli army for war. One such task was organizing the reserves. Because Israel had such a small population, it could not have a large standing army. Nonetheless, everyone who was able to do so served. All young people—men and women—entered the military at the age of eighteen. Young women served for a shorter period and did not go into combat. In addition, men remained in the reserves for many years after finishing their tour of duty, spending several weeks to a month in training each year. That way, if a war broke out, Israel could mobilize its reserves and immediately increase the size of its army by many times to face the far greater Arab standing armies. Rabin had the job of organizing this system that was so critical to the functioning of Israel's citizen army and its ability to assure the country's survival.

A year before becoming head of the operations division, Rabin took on another important job—that of father—when his daughter Dalia was born in 1950. In 1955, Leah and Yitzhak had a son, Yuval. In 1952 the Rabins moved to a modest home in Zahala, a suburb of Tel Aviv where many other military officers also chose to live. With the exception of a two-year stint as a teacher of English, Leah remained at home with the children. This was very important to Yitzhak. He wanted his children to have the full-time mother he had missed because of Rosa Cohen's many outside activities. Leah explained her decision:

> *I felt, though he never said it, that it was
> important for Yitzhak to know that I was
> home with the children, and that enabled him
> to throw himself body and soul into what-
> ever he was doing....I sensed that if anything
> compensated for his own childhood, and
> for the immense effort invested in what he did,
> it was the security of knowing that I was
> at home on a "full-time job."*[3]

During 1952–1953 the Rabins spent nine months in Britain, where Yitzhak studied at the British army's Royal Staff College in Camberley. Upon returning home he became the IDF's director of training. That position gave him his first chance to visit the United States to study American methods, which greatly impressed him. One American training method that Rabin adopted was to have all officers take either commando or paratroop training. However, when he followed his own regulations and took paratroop training, he had to keep his activities secret from his pregnant wife. With good reason he suspected that she would not approve of her husband jumping out of airplanes.

In 1954, Moshe Dayan, the new chief of staff, promoted Rabin to the rank of major-general. In 1956, Rabin moved from the general staff back into the field when he accepted the post as head of the northern command.

Rabin's new assignment made him responsible for dealing with the constant tension along the border with Syria. However, in 1956 the real action was in the south. Beginning in 1955, terrorist raids from the Egyptian-controlled Gaza Strip and Jordan increased dramatically. Many Israeli civilians were killed and wounded, and a great deal of property was destroyed. Retaliatory raids across the border by the Israeli army did not stop the terrorism, and Israeli complaints to the UN brought no relief.

Meanwhile, Egypt used its artillery at the Straits of Tiran to block all shipping to and from Eilat. Egypt's aggressive and vigorous new military dictator, Gamal Abdel Nasser, began buying new weapons from the Soviet bloc and openly threatening Israel with destruction. "There will be no peace on Israel's border," he warned in August 1955, "because we demand vengeance, and vengeance is Israel's death."[4]

As a result, Israel decided that it had no choice but to attack Egypt, wipe out the terrorist bases in Gaza and the Sinai, and end the illegal blockade at the Straits of Tiran that was choking its economy. The attack began on October 29, 1956. Israel acted in cooperation with Britain and France, who had their own disputes with Egypt over the Suez Canal. The Israeli army swept into the Sinai Desert, overwhelmed the Egyptian army, and occupied the Egyptian positions at the Straits of Tiran. However, heavy pressure from both the United States and the Soviet Union forced an Israeli withdrawal from the Sinai in 1957. But the Israelis did not return home empty-handed. A United Nations peace-keeping force was placed in the Sinai to keep the straits open and prevent terrorist attacks across the border. It fulfilled its mission for the next decade.

Rabin had no direct involvement with the Sinai campaign. After it was over he still had to deal with the Syrians, whose army looked down on northern Israel from a rocky ridge called the Golan Heights. The Syrians turned the Golan into a fortress, bristling with bunkers and artillery. While UN observers did nothing to stop them, the Syrians on the Golan shelled Israeli settlements at will, raining terror and destruction on the civilians below. In Rabin's account:

> *Exposed to Syrian artillery, our citizens were forced to build shelters, adapt buildings to wartime conditions, and disperse their homes, kindergartens, schools, and public buildings to diminish their vulnerability. Matters reached the point where we were forced to use armored tractors—often manned by soldiers—to cultivate the fields. We also had to deal with safeguarding our fishing rights…while the Syrian army harassed our fishing boats.*[5]

There also were several pitched battles between Israeli and Syrian army units.

By 1959, Rabin had been passed over for promotion several times and was questioning whether he should continue his army career. Then a major blunder during a national drill in calling up reserves–the public was not told it was only a drill and thought that Israel was on the brink of war–led to a shake-up of the IDF's top command. Rabin suddenly found himself as the IDF's second-ranking officer. He also received a promise from Ben-Gurion that he would be Israel's next chief of staff.

At about the same time, Rabin had what he considered his first clash with Shimon Peres, who was then deputy minister of defense. It was the beginning of a rivalry that often became personal and bitter and that would last for more than thirty years. In fact, the two men even disagreed about when they had their falling out: Rabin dated their conflict from the early 1960s, while Peres said the tension began in the 1970s. Ironically, it was not until the two strong-willed and ambitious Israelis combined to try to make peace between their country and the Arabs that they finally were able to make peace between themselves.

Late in 1963, David Ben-Gurion retired from public life. His successor was Levi Eshkol, who had served as Israel's finance minister under Ben-Gurion. One of Eshkol's first decisions was not to extend the term of the IDF chief of staff he inherited from Ben-Gurion. In his place he appointed forty-one-year-old Yitzhak Rabin. His term of office began on January 1, 1964. By the time it ended, he had emerged as one of his country's greatest heroes.

As chief of staff, Rabin focused on several issues. He had to deal with the Syrians, who "kept the border in turmoil by employing artillery and armor" against the Israelis.[6] Along with protecting Israeli civilians from attack, Rabin had to safeguard against sabotage Israel's massive project to pipe water from Lake Kinneret to the dry south. In January 1965 the Israelis thwarted an attempt to blow up one of the project's aqueducts.

Rabin also had to protect water flowing into Israel. In 1965, with Arab League backing, Syria began a project to divert tributaries of the Jordan River, a project that if completed would have left Israel without vital water resources. Rabin's job was to find a way to destroy the Syrian earthmoving equipment without the risk of setting off a war. He summoned Major-General Israel Tal and asked him if tanks shooting from the Israeli side of the border could hit the Syrian targets about a mile away. Tal, as Rabin recalled, "flung himself into the task" and concluded that it could be done.[7] When Rabin asked for a "guarantee" of success, Tal, a man of immense confidence as well as talent, replied: "The guarantee is that I will aim and fire the tank *personally*."[8] Tal was good to his word, and the Syrians had to abandon the diversion project.

Most immediately threatening, Syria and Egypt were buying huge quantities of modern Soviet arms, including tanks. Rabin knew the IDF would need the most modern weapons available so Israel's armed forces would have a "qualitative edge" against their far more numerous enemies. The Israelis already had purchased modern jets from France, but Rabin insisted that only arms from the United States could match what the Arabs were getting from the Soviets. Prime Minister Eshkol agreed. During Rabin's tenure as chief of staff Israel bought a variety of modern American weapons. The weapons included advanced tanks and, for the IDF air force, Skyhawk combat planes, which could carry four times the bomb load of French planes. The Israelis were very pleased with the purchase, although unhappy that the United States also decided to sell tanks to Jordan.

In light of the new weapons, Rabin restructured the IDF. He divided it into two sections, offensive and defensive, equipping each section according to its tasks. To increase speed and mobility, the IDF's offensive forces stressed armored and motorized units and paratroops, along with regular infantry. The air force was to focus first on gaining air superiority if war broke out, and then to support ground forces. Rabin's restructuring of the military and introduction of new weapons turned out to be the right moves at the right time.

The year 1966, however, brought Israel plenty of trouble. The Syrians increased the pace of border attacks involving sabotage and shootings. An IDF reprisal raid against a terrorist base inside Jordan turned into a major clash with Jordanian troops. One incident with Syria that did not involve shooting brought Rabin and two of his top commanders—chief of operations Ezer Weizman and head of the northern command David Elazar—almost face to face with the Syrians. They were at Lake Kinneret when an Israeli fishing boat ran aground near the eastern shore of the lake. Although the lake itself was in Israeli territory, Syrian-controlled territory began only a few yards from shore.

In typical Israeli fashion—officers are expected to lead their troops into battle, not just order them in—the three commanders mounted their own rescue effort. Their "disguise" in an operation that took them to within 50 yards (46 meters) of Syrian soldiers, who actually photographed them, was to shed their uniforms for bathing trunks. Why the Syrians did not open fire on the stranded Israelis and their would-be rescuers remains a mystery. In any event, the three Israeli generals were not successful. A navy ship had to be called to tow the fishing boat to safety.

By the 1960s it was customary for the IDF chief of staff to serve a three-year term, so 1966 could have been Rabin's last year at his post. However, Prime Minister Eshkol asked Rabin to serve another year. When Rabin agreed, his decision put squarely on his shoulders the burden of defending Israel against the greatest threat to its survival since the War of Independence.

The crisis began in mid-May, just over a month after an air battle in which Israeli planes shot down six Syrian Soviet-built MIG fighter aircraft. As the Syrians turned to Egypt for help, the Soviet Union passed on false information to the Arabs that Israel was about to attack Syria. Egypt's president, Gamal Abdel Nasser, determined to prove he could deal with Israel, responded with a series of steps. On May 14 he began sending tens of thousands of troops and hundreds of tanks into the Sinai Peninsula, heading for the Israeli border. He then demanded that the UN peace-keeping force along the Egyptian-Israeli border withdraw. As Rabin succinctly put it, "The chariots of war were beginning to roll."[9]

Much to everybody's shock, including Nasser's, UN Secretary-General U Thant agreed. UN troops abandoned their posts along the border, in the Gaza Strip, and at Sharm el-Sheikh, a fortified position overlooking the Straits of Tiran from which Egyptian guns had enforced the blockade of Eilat prior to 1956. The UN troops left on May 19th. Three days later, Nasser announced a renewal of the blockade, a step that Israel considered an act of war.

Thus began a nerve-wracking period in Israel known as the "Hamtana," or waiting period. Israel turned to the world for help: to the United States, which in 1957, in return for Israel's withdrawal from Sinai, had promised to take responsibility for keeping the Tiran Straits open; to France, its most important supplier of arms up to that point; and to the UN, which for ten years had helped prevent a new war in the region. It received no help from any of them: no help in opening the straits from the United States, no promised arms from France, and no decisive action from the UN.

The Israelis were in a bind. They had been taken by surprise, they had no outside help, and events were moving incredibly fast. They could not afford to let Egypt and Syria, possibly aided by Jordan, strike first. Tiny in area, only 9 miles (14 kilometers) wide at its narrowest point, and facing a war on three fronts, Israel would then become a battleground. Its civilians would suffer enormous casualties. Visions of the Holocaust haunted Israel. So did statements like the one that Nasser made in 1965, when he promised the Arab world: "We shall not enter Palestine with its soil covered in sand. We shall enter it with its soil saturated in blood." [10]

But if Israel struck first, how would the world react? The Soviet Union supported the Arabs and was hostile to Israel. The United States was friendly to Israel, but also was courting the oil-rich Arabs, and had taken a leading role in forcing Israel to leave the Sinai Peninsula in 1957. France already was turning against the Israelis.

Meanwhile, Rabin experienced his own personal crisis. He had been under tremendous pressure for over a week, especially since Prime Minister Levi Eshkol and other politicians running the country seemed indecisive.

They all seemed to be turning to him to make the key decisions. As he put it later: "I was put in a position where the Government was saying: 'What do you want us to do? You have to tell us.'"[11]

On May 23 the pressure became too great. Israel was mobilizing for war. Rabin returned home "in a state of physical and mental exhaustion."[12] He was plagued by doubt. Had he prepared the IDF sufficiently for this crisis? How many thousands of young men would be killed or wounded, even if Israel prevailed in the coming struggle? That night Rabin seems to have suffered a nervous collapse. When Ezer Weizman visited him at home Rabin asked, "Am I to blame? Should I relinquish my post?"[13] Weizman tried to calm his chief of staff, first warning him, "If you resign now, you'll be finished for the rest of your life." He then added, "You'll be the victorious chief of staff. You'll reach the Suez Canal and the Jordan."[14]

A doctor was called to the scene. He gave Rabin sleeping medication, and the chief of staff slept until 3 P.M. the next morning. Rabin awoke refreshed and by the next day had returned to full activity. He had a great deal to do.

While the military prepared, Israel's diplomats desperately struggled to find backing abroad that would lead to a peaceful solution to the crisis. Prime Minister Eshkol stated his policy: "The IDF will not attack before the political options are exhausted."[15] Meanwhile, Egyptian troops continued to pour into Sinai, Iraqi troops arrived in Syria, and the noose around Israel was tightening. Rabin and his generals warned that time was running out. The IDF's intelligence chief, Aharon Yariv, warned: "Every passing day lessens the chances of Israel attaining air superiority," which was vital for achieving victory.[16] At one meeting, where action was delayed yet again, one general angrily shouted at the politicians, "What are we waiting for?"[17]

On May 30, Jordan signed a military pact with Egypt, meaning that Israel faced a war on three fronts. Arab leaders from Cairo to Baghdad echoed Nasser, who announced the Arab goal was to "totally exterminate the State of Israel for all time."[18] In Cairo huge crowds shouted: "Nasser, Nasser, Nasser, we are behind you. We will slaughter them. We will destroy them. Slaughter, slaughter, slaughter."[19]

By May 31, Egypt had 100,000 men, 1,000 tanks, and 500 heavy guns along Israel's border. As June dawned, Arab forces massed along Israel's borders outnumbered its own army by three to one. With the drumbeat of Arab threats and hatred in their ears, amplified by the deafening silence of the international community, Israelis prepared to fight for their country's survival. On May 31, the leading opposition political parties joined the government, thereby creating a regime of national unity. It included Menachem Begin and, significantly, Moshe Dayan, the hero of the 1956 Sinai victory, who became minister of defense on June 1. That same day it became incontestably clear that all political options were exhausted. The word came from Washington that the United States, Israel's last hope, would not take decisive action. Israel stood alone. On June 4, the Israeli government made the final decision to strike.

The war known as the Six-Day War began at 7:45 A.M. on June 5, 1967. Wave after wave of Israeli planes attacked Egyptian air bases, destroying most of the air force of Israel's most powerful enemy on the ground.

This photo of Israeli infantrymen was taken on May 31, 1967, as they marched to defend their country. They were outnumbered three to one by Arab forces massed along Israel's borders.

Of Israel's 200 combat aircraft, only twelve remained behind to protect Israeli air space. In the words of air force chief Motti Hod, "We used all we had."[20] And they used it again and again. Israeli planes operated on a precise time table: 22.5 minutes to reach their Egyptian targets, 8 minutes to attack, 20 minutes to return to base, 7.5 minutes to rearm and refuel, and then back to phase one. That left exactly two minutes as a safety margin to correct for the unexpected.

The bold gamble paid off. Within three hours the attack on Egypt was completed. Israeli planes then bombed airfields in Jordan and Syria with similar success. As the air battle unfolded, Rabin studied Motti Hod, the man who had prepared the air force for this day and who had dared to take the risks and predict success:

> *Was he excited? Did his face show any…hint of*
> *"I told you so?" I was so pleased with him, and*
> *for him….But his features were rocklike in their*
> *impassivity; not a muscle moved. He gulped down*
> *incredible amounts of water and held his tongue.*[21]

Despite the brilliant air victory that decided the course of the war, Israel did not escape unscathed. On June 5 Syrian, Jordanian, and Iraqi planes bombed the country. Tel Aviv and Rabin's own neighborhood of Zahala were among the places shelled by artillery from the Jordanian-held town of Kalkilia, only 11 miles (18 kilometers) away. As he fled with his mother for shelter, young Yuval Rabin told her, "I want to be where my father is."[22] In the north, Syria's Soviet-built MIG fighters strafed Haifa. In the east, Jordanian infantry and tanks advanced in and around Jerusalem while its artillery pounded the city.

Meanwhile, Israeli troops, supported by the air force that attacked the Egyptian army from the air, swept into the Sinai. Their overwhelming victory in the desert sometimes has obscured the fact that the Israelis in the Sinai faced bitter fighting and suffered many casualties. General Ariel Sharon, by that time a hardened veteran of two wars, described a key battle and Israeli victory that took place on the fourth day of the war:

> *This was the Valley of Death. I came out of it an old man. Hundreds were killed. There were burning tanks everywhere. One had the feeling that man was nothing. A sandstorm had been churned up by our tanks. The noise was tremendous. Besides the din of tanks and guns, there was the roar of our aircraft...dropping supplies of water and ammunition by parachute, and of helicopters evacuating the wounded. The shooting and fighting continued, and vehicles loaded with fuel and ammunition were exploding all along the line.*[23]

On that day, Israeli forces reached the Suez Canal. Ironically, Sharm el-Sheikh, where the Egyptian blockade on Israeli shipping did so much to cause the war, fell without a single shot being fired. The Egyptians retreated from that post hours before the Israelis arrived there on June 7. Rabin was both surprised and delighted to hear from the Israeli commander on the spot: "There's no one to fight."[24]

Fighting in Jordanian-controlled territory known as the West Bank also was hard. As in Sinai, however, Israel's control of the air enabled its army to rout the

Jordanians. Much of the toughest fighting took place in the battle for Jerusalem's Old City. The Israelis first attacked Jordanian fortifications in East Jerusalem outside the Old City on June 6. Israeli paratroopers fought Jordanian soldiers hand-to-hand until those positions fell. On June 7 at 8:30 A.M. the Israelis broke into the Old City. Paratroopers under the command of Colonel Mordechai ("Motta") Gur, a future chief of staff, headed for the Temple Mount and its Western Wall. The Jordanians used one of the mosques on top of the Temple Mount as a sniping post, and had turned the Mount itself into an ammunition dump. About 10 A.M. Gur radioed back to his commanders: "The Temple Mount is in our hands."

Early that afternoon Rabin and Moshe Dayan arrived from Tel Aviv at the Lion's Gate, one of the entrances to the Old City. They marched together with General Uzi Narkiss, the overall commander of the Jerusalem operation, to the Western Wall. Rabin recalled the extraordinary experience:

> *As we made our way though the streets I remembered from childhood, pungent memories played on my emotions. The sheer excitement increased as we came closer to the Western Wall itself. It is still easy for me to conjure up the feelings that assaulted me, but it's very difficult to put them into words. The Wall was and is our national memento of the glories of Jewish independence in ancient times. Its stones have a power to speak to the hearts of Jews the world over, as if the historical memory of the Jewish people dwelled in the cracks between those ancient ashlars. For years I secretly harbored the dream that I might play a part not only in gaining Israel's independence but*

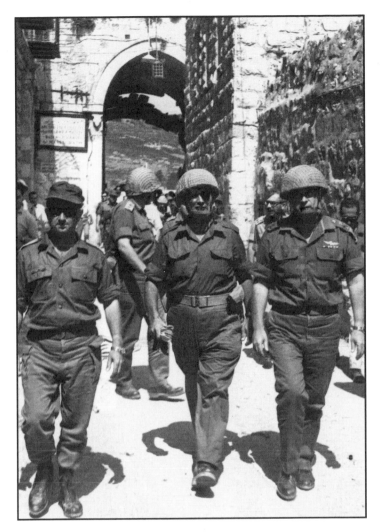

From left, General Uzi Narkiss, Defense Minister Moshe Dayan, and Chief of Staff Rabin march proudly through the Lion's Gate into the Old City. As Rabin recalled, "I knew that never again in my life would I experience quite the same peak of elation."

in restoring the Western Wall to the Jewish people....Now that dream had come true, and I suddenly wondered why I, of all men, should be so privileged.

When we reached the Western Wall I was breathless. It seemed as though all the tears of centuries were striving to break out of the men crowded in that narrow alley, while all the hopes of generations proclaimed, "This is no time for weeping! It is a time for redemption, for hope." Following an ancient custom, Dayan scrawled a wish on a piece of paper and pushed it between two of the stones. I felt truly shaken and stood there murmuring a prayer for peace. Motta Gur's paratroopers were struggling to reach the Wall and touch it. We stood among a tangle of rugged, battle-weary men who were unable to believe their eyes or restrain their emotions. Their eyes were moist with tears, their speech incoherent. The overwhelming desire was to cling to the Wall, to hold on to that great moment as long as possible.[25]

Yet there remained more fighting, especially in the north. The Golan Heights remained in Syrian hands, and the thousands of people from the Galilee region to the Jordan River valley who had lived for years under their murderous guns were demanding that their tormenters be dislodged. A delegation of Galilee residents came to Tel Aviv and told their national leaders:

The Syrians are riding on our backs. If the State of Israel is incapable of defending us, we're entitled to know. We should be told

*outright we are not part of this state, not
entitled to the protection of the IDF. We
should be told to leave our homes and flee
from this nightmare.*[26]

The government hesitated, primarily because some ministers were concerned that if Israel attacked Syria the Soviet Union would intervene in the war. However, most Israelis agreed that the situation in the north was intolerable. Therefore, having defeated the Egyptians and Jordanians, Israel's leaders ultimately decided to risk attacking the Syrians. On June 9, Israeli soldiers attacked the entrenched Syrians on the Golan Heights. The troops were skillfully led by General David ("Dado") Elazar. But the Syrians, with the advantage of the fortified high ground, fought back and the Israelis suffered many casualties, including more than 100 dead. By June 10 the Golan Heights was in Israeli hands. A cease-fire was in place. The Six-Day War was over.

The war yielded Israel enormous gains. The Israelis held all of Jerusalem, and annexed the Old City and the rest of East Jerusalem (as the part of the city formerly held by Jordan was called) on June 28. They also held the Golan Heights, the Gaza Strip, and the Sinai Peninsula. Altogether, the 1967 cease-fire lines put Israel in control of some 26,000 square miles (67,340 square kilometers), more than three times the territory it controlled before the war. In addition, the victory restored the country's confidence, which had been severely shaken in the weeks before the war.

Israel paid dearly for these gains. The IDF suffered at least 777 dead and 2,586 wounded, enormous figures for such a small country. Civilian casualties brought the total of dead and wounded to more than 800 to 3,000,

*Rabin and Dayan at the taking of the Golan Heights on the
last day of the Six-Day War. This final territorial gain was
very costly to Israel as the Syrians defending the Heights were
deeply entrenched, but it provided vital security for Israel's
northern settlements.*

respectively. And, as Rabin pointed out, Israeli gains brought with them enormous problems. Israel now ruled over one million hostile Arabs living in the West Bank and the Gaza Strip. Furthermore, Rabin understood that Israel would not be left in peace to deal with its territorial gains.

Rabin made all this clear when he accepted an honorary doctorate from the Hebrew University in Jerusalem on June 28. He felt awkward, as the IDF does not award decorations to its senior officers. However, Rabin decided to accept the honor so he could talk about the unique nature of Israel's citizen army:

> *The elation of victory has seized the whole nation. Yet among the soldiers themselves a curious phenomenon is to be observed. They cannot rejoice wholeheartedly. Their triumph is marred by grief and shock, and there are some who cannot rejoice at all. The men in the front lines saw with their own eyes not only the glory of victory, but also its cost: their comrades fallen beside them, soaked in blood. And I know that the terrible price the enemy paid has also deeply moved many of our men. Is it because neither their teaching nor their experience has ever accustomed the Jewish people to exult in conquest and victory, that they receive them with such mixed feelings?* [27]

Whatever his own ambivalent feelings, Rabin emerged from the Six-Day War as a hero to his country. At the same time, he knew that his term as chief of staff and therefore his military career was almost over. His mind turned to building a new civilian career that would permit him to continue serving his country.

CHAPTER FIVE

"You're no diplomat!"

E ven before the Six-Day War, Rabin was thinking about what to do when his term as IDF chief
of staff, and his military career, came to an end.
Rabin had a well-deserved reputation of being direct and
blunt. So when he suggested to Prime Minister Eshkol
that he be appointed Israel's next ambassador to the
United States, the response was a little less than encouraging. "Hold on to me, Yitzhak, or I'll fall out of my
chair," Eshkol blurted out, adding, "You're no diplomat!"[1] Nor was Rabin's command of English particularly good, especially compared with Israel's two
previous ambassadors to the United States, both of whom
were native English speakers born in South Africa.
Unfazed, Rabin renewed his efforts to be appointed to
the post after the war. Despite strong competition for the
desirable position, he was appointed and began preparing to take his post as of March 1968.

Before Rabin arrived in America, the diplomatic and political situation that he would face as a result of the Six-Day War was beginning to take shape. Within Israel, the overwhelming conviction was that the country could never return to the 1967 borders that had left it so insecure. Only two days after the war ended, Prime Minister Eshkol told Israel's parliament:

> *Let this be said—there should be no illusion*
> *that Israel is prepared to return to the conditions*
> *that existed a week ago—We have fought alone*
> *for our existence and our security, and we are*
> *therefore justified in deciding for ourselves what*
> *are the genuine and indispensable interests of*
> *our state, and how to guarantee its future.*[2]

At the same time, Israel hoped to be able to negotiate with its Arab neighbors to return much of the captured territory in exchange for peace. The Israelis insisted that this required direct negotiations between themselves and the Arabs and genuine peace treaties, not the indirect negotiations as in 1949 at Rhodes and the continued state of war and cease-fire that existed between 1949 and 1967.

One issue alone was not negotiable: Jerusalem would be united and under its rule. Moshe Dayan spoke for most of his countrymen when, entering the Old City flanked by Rabin and Uzi Narkiss, he announced, "We have returned to all that is holy in our land. We have returned never to be parted from it again."[3] What the Israelis found upon that return after being barred for nineteen years genuinely shocked them. The Jordanians had destroyed every Jewish house of worship in the Old City. They had even uprooted tombstones from Jewish graves in the ancient Mount of Olives cemetery and used them to pave army latrines. The Israelis pledged to allow Muslims and Christians to control their own holy sites. But the city itself would be united as the capital of Israel.

Given their overwhelming victory, the Israelis expected the Arabs finally would negotiate with them. As the saying went, they waited for a "phone call" from their neighbors. Instead of a phone call they received a rude awakening in August in the form of the infamous "three noes" announced at an Arab conference in Khartoum, Sudan: "No peace with Israel, no recognition of Israel, no negotiations with Israel."[4]

A more positive statement came from the United Nations Security Council on November 22. Its Resolution 242 called for Israel's withdrawal from "territories"– significantly, at the insistence of the United States, not *the* territories or *all* the territories–in return for a negotiated peace in which all nations in the region could live within secure and recognized boundaries. Israel, Egypt, and Jordan all accepted Resolution 242; Syria rejected it.

As Rabin was preparing for his new post in America, an important new player was emerging in the Arab-Israeli conflict: the Palestine Liberation Organization. The PLO was founded in 1964 on the initiative of the Arab League, when the West Bank, Gaza, and East Jerusalem all were under Arab rule. In its founding document, the Palestinian National Covenant, it called the establishment of Israel "null and void." In other words, the PLO denied Israel's right to exist, regardless of its borders. The PLO actually was an umbrella organization for a variety of feuding Palestinian groups united mainly by their determination to destroy Israel. After 1967 the most powerful group, known as Fatah, dominated the PLO, although it could not control the other groups that belonged to the organization. Fatah's leader, Yasir Arafat, an engineer who claimed he was born in Jerusalem but probably was born in Cairo, became the PLO chairman.

Over the next few years, Arafat's Fatah and other PLO groups committed hundreds of terrorist acts against Israeli civilians both inside and outside its borders, leaving many dead and wounded. Among the attacks that occurred while Rabin was in Washington was the mid-air bombing of a Swissair plane bound for Tel Aviv, killing all 47 people aboard. There also were several attacks on planes and passengers of Israel's El Al airline. On the ground, a May 1970 ambush of an Israeli school bus near the Lebanese border left twelve children and teachers dead. Perhaps the most publicized attack occurred during the 1972 Munich Olympic Games, when a PLO group closely tied to Fatah murdered eleven Israeli athletes.

Despite his inexperience and inadequate English, Rabin had an imposing agenda as he prepared to take his new post. A primary goal was to make sure that Israel could buy the arms it needed from the United States to balance arms the Arab states received from the Soviet Union. He had to secure American aid to cover at least some of these expensive purchases. Rabin also had to keep the United States sympathetic to Israel's approach for making peace. In particular, Israel insisted on direct negotiations with the Arabs, not a "solution" imposed on it by the American and Soviet superpowers, as the Arabs wanted. Israel also wanted the United States to support the idea that peace treaties should be negotiated *before* Israel withdrew from territories it held. This ran up against Arab and Soviet demands for the reverse: that Israel agree to a complete withdrawal prior to the start of peace negotiations. Israel also wanted the United States to prevent direct Soviet intervention on the Arab side if fighting broke out again in the turbulent Middle East.

Rabin's first difficulty actually emerged before he arrived in Washington. He and Leah agreed that their daughter Dalia would remain in Israel to complete her final year of high school. Then, like other Israeli eighteen-year-olds, she would enter the army. Although Dalia would be staying with Leah's sister and therefore was in "good hands," the parting was tearful for both mother and daughter. Yitzhak recalled:

> *I tried to remain stoic but I doubt I*
> *succeeded in hiding the ache that every*
> *father must feel when he sees his "little*
> *girl" going off into the world on her own.*[5]

Nor was it easy for him to accept, even as a former chief of staff, that he would be almost half a world away when his daughter was in the army.

When Rabin arrived in the United States in February 1968, he found a country in turmoil. The year 1968 marked the peak of the Vietnam War, which was increasingly unpopular with a large segment of the American population. Angry and sometimes violent demonstrations against the war were commonplace. Just after his arrival Rabin watched President Lyndon Johnson announce on television that he would not be a candidate for president in the upcoming November elections. Then came the assassination of Martin Luther King, Jr., on April 4. Rabin was stunned as he watched racial unrest turn into riots

Rabin, Israel's new Ambassador to the United States, presenting his credentials to President Johnson. Less than one month after this first meeting Martin Luther King, Jr. was assassinated. The riots and demonstrations growing out of anti-Vietnam war sentiments and the King assassination left Rabin deeply worried about the future of the country he called "this great democracy-the leader of the free world."[6]

and looting in several American cities, including Washington, D.C. To a "new and inexperienced ambassador, the situation looked depressingly grave."

On June 4, when Rabin was in New York, he was invited to meet with Robert F. Kennedy, who was campaigning for the Democratic party's presidential nomination. Tight scheduling prevented the meeting, which tragically never took place. The next day, the first anniversary of the outbreak of the Six-Day War, Kennedy was assassinated by a young Palestinian who was bitter about the senator's strong support for Israel.

As soon as he was settled, Rabin tried to convince the American government to sell Israel the ultramodern weapons it needed for defense. This was not an easy task. From the late 1940s until the late 1950s the Truman and Eisenhower administrations had refused to sell Israel any arms. Finally, in the late 1950s the Eisenhower administration sold Israel a few weapons. In the 1960s the Kennedy and then the Johnson administrations opened the arms spigot a bit more, but continued to refuse Israel's request for top-of-the-line fighter planes. Israel especially needed fifty American supersonic Phantom jets, the world's best and most powerful warplane. After long and complicated negotiations, a deal was reached in the fall of 1968. However, final approval from President Johnson did not come until January 1969, just a few days before he left office.

The campaign to get more American arms continued when Richard Nixon succeeded Johnson as president in 1969. Despite his characteristic bluntness, Rabin maintained good relations with many people in that administration, including Nixon himself, who was sympathetic toward Israel. It also helped that Nixon got along with Israeli Prime Minister Golda Meir, who succeeded Levi Eshkol at his death in early 1969. Also sympathetic was Joseph Sisco, a high State Department official, who appreciated that Rabin "says what he means and means what he says."[7] Rabin found additional support for Israel among leading Democrats such as Senators Henry Jackson of Washington and Stuart Symington of Missouri. He was especially fond of Jackson, an influential senator from a state with few Jewish voters, who stressed that "the American people support Israel."[8] Rabin said Jackson was "among my most—and Israel's most—cherished friends in the U.S. Senate."[9]

Rabin also developed an excellent relationship with Dr. Henry Kissinger, Nixon's national security advisor. Kissinger was a Jewish immigrant from Germany whose parents had fled the Nazis in the late 1930s. Many Israelis feared that precisely because he was Jewish, Kissinger would go overboard to prove his neutrality in the Arab-Israeli struggle, and therefore possibly favor the Arabs. Rabin found that not to be the case. With both Kissinger and Nixon, policy always was driven first and foremost by America's Cold War struggle with the Soviet Union, which included limiting Soviet influence in the Middle East. That required support for Israel, but also, Kissinger stressed to Rabin, strong U.S. ties with important Arab countries. Like Nixon, Kissinger was sympathetic toward Israel, but he was prepared to be very tough on Israel and pressure it to make concessions whenever it suited his overall Middle East strategy and American policy.

The two men developed a deep respect for one another. Rabin was extremely impressed by how Kissinger combined vast knowledge with a practical approach to problems, as well as the broad strategic

Prime Minister Rabin and Secretary of State Henry Kissinger had established a strong rapport ten years earlier when Rabin was the Israeli Ambassador to the United States. Their respect and admiration for each other's abilities seemed to be on both a personal and political level.

scope of his policies and diplomacy. Kissinger admired Rabin's integrity and noted that his "analytical brilliance in cutting to the core of a problem was awesome." Kissinger added, "I valued his judgment, often on matters unconnected with the Middle East."[10] However, neither man ever allowed personal respect to get in the way of national policy. Rabin experienced some of his most difficult moments in Washington, as well as some of his best, when dealing with Kissinger.

Rabin and Israel got much less sympathy from Nixon's secretary of state, William Rogers. Israel's ambassador also was confronted by the consistently pro-Arab outlook of several important officials within the State Department.

One problem that Rabin constantly faced was pressure from would-be mediators to get Israel to return all Arab land taken in 1967 before negotiations began. This was the approach of Gunnar Jarring, the UN diplomat in charge of promoting Arab-Israeli negotiations. Rabin, like most Israelis, had no faith in Jarring or in the UN, which Israelis believed had let them down time and again since independence. The numbers bear out Israeli suspicions. Between 1947 and 1989, the UN General Assembly passed 321 resolutions condemning Israel; the Security Council passed 49. During that period neither body passed a single resolution condemning any Arab state or the PLO. Rabin counted much more on the United States. That is why he was so disturbed when Secretary of State Rogers proposed his "Rogers Plan" in December 1969, which followed Jarring's approach. The Israeli government in Jerusalem and Rabin in Washington strongly criticized the plan, angering the Americans. However, the point became moot when the Egyptians also rejected the plan.

The Rogers Plan emerged during a tense period known as the "War of Attrition." In 1969, Egypt began bombarding Israeli positions on the east bank of the Suez Canal from its positions along the western bank. Its main goal was to cause as many Israeli casualties as possible and thereby force an Israeli withdrawal or other concessions. The fighting included continual hit-and-run attacks and aerial dogfights between warplanes. As their casualties mounted, Israel looked for ways to stop the Egyptian attacks.

Rabin recommended bombing raids on Egyptian military bases deep inside the country. Israel began these raids in January 1970, but the initial results were largely unfavorable. The Soviets responded by sending modern anti-aircraft missiles to Egypt, along with thousands of instructors and soldiers. Matters became worse when Soviet pilots began flying patrols near the Suez Canal and Soviet anti-aircraft missiles shot down several Israeli Phantoms. The tension came close to the boiling point on June 30, when Israeli fighters shot down four planes flown by Russian pilots. Both sides now drew back and a cease-fire took effect on August 7. Within days the Egyptians violated the cease-fire by moving Soviet anti-aircraft missiles up to the Suez Canal.

Within barely a month after the cease-fire a new Middle East crisis brought Israel and the United States closer than ever before. By 1970 the PLO had become so strong in Jordan that it threatened King Hussein's authority. In September, Hussein struck back furiously with his army to save his throne. In pitched battles thousands of Palestinians were killed. Some fled into Israel to escape the fury of the Jordanian wrath. The PLO itself relocated its headquarters to Lebanon. The Palestinians called this event "Black September." Meanwhile, to rescue the PLO, Syria sent 250 tanks across the Jordanian border. King Hussein suddenly had a far more serious threat on his hands.

At this point Rabin received an urgent call from Henry Kissinger. The United States was worried that if Syria toppled Hussein, Soviet influence in the Middle East would increase. Kissinger requested that Israel prepare to use its air force to save Hussein if that became necessary. Israel agreed, although it turned out that Jordan was able to drive the Syrian tanks back on its own. The entire matter was handled with great secrecy. Rabin used an obscure side entrance to the White House to avoid being seen when he delivered Israel's reply to Kissinger. This and other secret meetings with Kissinger led Rabin to observe:

> *In the course of scores of meetings with Kissinger,*
> *I must have become acquainted with every possible*
> *way of getting into the White House with the*
> *exception of sliding down the roof.* [11]

Israel came out of the crisis with new deals for additional American arms. They included Phantom and Skyhawk aircraft and modern M-60 tanks. The United States also increased its loans to Israel to help it pay for the expensive but vital new weapons. However, the flow of military technology was not all one way. For example, in 1969, Israeli forces along the Suez Canal captured an advanced Soviet radar station from the Egyptians. It was the same kind of radar being used in Vietnam to track and help shoot down American warplanes. The Israelis immediately sent the radar equipment to the United

States, so it could be studied and countermeasures developed to save the lives of American pilots.

Immediately after the Jordanian crisis, a new variable was thrown into the complex Middle East political equation. On September 28, 1970, Gamal Abdel Nasser, by far the Arab world's most important leader, suffered a heart attack and died. His successor was Egypt's little-known vice president, Anwar Sadat, whose policies were destined to surprise experts and politicians in capitals from Washington to Jerusalem to Moscow.

The Syrian-Jordanian confrontation was the last major crisis of Rabin's tenure in Washington. During the next two years, there were fruitless attempts to jump-start negotiations between Israel and Egypt. Both the Israeli government and Rabin himself have been criticized for missing a possible opportunity in 1971, when Egypt's President Sadat suggested reopening negotiations. In his memoirs, written after the fact, Rabin hints that he believed his government was being too rigid in responding to Sadat. In particular, Israel might have pulled back its troops a short distance from the Suez Canal to get negotiations started. He writes: "For a time I actually found myself in the rather unorthodox position of negotiating with my own government on a set of proposals for a partial agreement!"[12] In any event, 1971, which Sadat called the "year of decision," passed without any progress, as did 1972.

Still, the man who supposedly was "no diplomat" achieved a great deal as Israel's ambassador. Rabin was the first Israeli ambassador to Washington to gain access to the highest levels of the United States government on a regular basis. He played an important role in convincing the United States to sell Israel high-tech weapons.

He fostered ties between the Israeli and American military establishments. During his tenure, the United States came to view Israel as its only reliable partner in the Middle East.

Rabin also went beyond formal diplomacy. He reached out to non-Jewish audiences in the United States to present Israel's case. His varied contacts ranged from liberal labor leader George Meany to conservative religious leader Billy Graham. Rabin received invitations to lecture to groups all over the country and accepted as many as his schedule would allow.

The one arena where Rabin's outreach met difficulties was on the college campuses. Rabin understood that America's campuses were in turmoil because of opposition to the Vietnam War, but he was shocked and dismayed to find himself the target of extremist left-wing groups such as the Students for a Democratic Society and the Black Panthers. By the late 1960s they and similar radical groups were siding with the Arabs and viciously attacking Israel. When he spoke on college campuses Rabin was denounced as a murderer and worse. Tactics like heckling and fake bomb scares were used to disrupt his talks. Israel's ambassador was distressed that "in this greatest and proudest of democracies, young men and women were pouring so much energy into preventing a man from speaking his mind."

Even more painful was that in America's finest institutions of higher learning, "I was witnessing a self-righteous crusade based on sheer ignorance" of the history of Israel and the Jewish people. Rabin was especially disturbed because the accusation of "murderer" was "all too familiar in the annals of Jewish history." It was a "favorite anti-Semitic slander" used to turn people against the Jews "from the Dark Ages right through to modern times." Furthermore, "there was nothing new in turning on the Jews in times of crisis." Rabin wanted to tell his critics, "Read your history." But, as he wrote sadly in his memoirs, "they were too involved in their rage, and history was presumably irrelevant....They merely continued to hurl that age-old indictment at me in the ugly tradition of ignorance, prejudice, and hatred."[13]

In June 1972, Ambassador Rabin became embroiled in the upcoming American presidential election. While in Israel he indicated during a radio interview that he preferred the Republican candidate Richard Nixon to Democrat George McGovern. In truth, Rabin personally did prefer Nixon, since he thought McGovern's desire to cut the American defense budget and limit its worldwide commitments would hurt Israel. Rabin was accused of interfering in the American election. The *Washington Post* newspaper called him "Israel's undiplomatic diplomat." Rabin dismissed the charge by noting that the campaign had not yet begun and he was speaking to an Israeli audience that obviously was "not going to the [American] polls."[14]

Rabin's last day as ambassador was March 11, 1973. He was satisfied he had done his job well. As he left the United States he said, simply as usual but more diplomatically than usual, "I was happy to serve here and at the same time I'm happy to be going home."[15]

CHAPTER SIX

"The sons of the founding fathers have come of age."

W hen Rabin returned to Israel on March 11, 1973, he found a confident country. The economy was much stronger than in 1967. New immigrants in growing numbers were arriving from the Soviet Union, more than 30,000 in 1972 alone. Tens of thousands of new cars crowded Israel's narrow roads, while antennas sprouted like weeds to take advantage of television, introduced to the country after the Six-Day War. Israel's new borders, even if they were not permanent, at least appeared to give its people the safety they had never before enjoyed. Egypt's army was behind the Suez Canal, Syria's beyond the Golan Heights, and Jordan's across the Jordan River. Although tense, the borders were quiet. Like most Israelis, Rabin accepted the government's reassuring claim: "The lines are safe. The bridges are open. Jerusalem is united...and our political position is stable."[1] People were enjoying the peace; they gave little thought to war.

Rabin, at least personally, was a bit insecure; he was in the process of changing careers. After spending most of his adult life as a soldier, and then five years as a diplomat, he was about to enter the complex world of Israeli politics. Given his background as a socialist, it was natural that Rabin join Israel's political arena on the side of the Labor party, which was a combination of several socialist groups. Labor's main rival was Likud, a recently organized non-socialist party that itself was a combination of several political parties.

Under Israel's parliamentary system, voters traditionally cast their ballots for political parties rather than individuals. Each party received seats in the 120-member Knesset, or parliament, according to the percentage of votes it received. The seats were filled from a list that each party presented before the election, with the party leaders at the top of the list and lower-ranking members further down. The party with the most seats was then designated to form a government, and its leader became the country's prime minister. Israel also had a president, which was a largely ceremonial position.

This has always been a complicated process, because no single political party has yet succeeded in winning more than 50 percent of the vote in any parliamentary election. Forming a government, therefore, has always required a coalition of the victorious party with one or more smaller parties. In 1992 the electoral system was changed to allow direct election of the prime minister by the people.

Rabin clearly was popular with the Israeli public when he returned home, which is why the leaders of the

Labor party gave him the 20th place on their electoral list. Since the Labor party in its various forms had won every election in Israel's history, Rabin was assured a seat in the new Knesset.

By October the campaign was in full swing. Campaigning stopped for Yom Kippur, the Day of Atonement, the holiest day of the Jewish year. The holiday began at sundown on Friday, October 5, and lasted until sundown of October 6. But the election campaign would not begin again on October 7. On the afternoon of October 6, Egypt and Syria launched a massive air and ground attack on Israeli forces along the Suez Canal and on the Golan Heights. For the second time in barely six years, the Jewish state was fighting for its survival.

Unlike in 1967, Israel on Yom Kippur of 1973 was not prepared for war. The IDF had not taken into account the enormous amounts of ultramodern weapons, including antitank and anti-aircraft missiles, the Soviet Union had supplied to Egypt and Syria. Organization and discipline were not at the same high level as in 1967. Making matters worse, when the Israeli leadership finally realized on October 5 they were about to be attacked, they were unable, as in 1967, to strike first. If they did, the international community, swayed by its dependence on Arab oil, would come down very hard on Israel. The word from the United States, Israel's only reliable foreign friend, was blunt and unmistakable: "Don't preempt." In the tension-packed meetings just before the Egyptian/Syrian onslaught, Prime Minister Golda Meir and her cabinet rejected Chief of Staff David Elazar's urgent advice that Israel's air force attack the massing Arab troops. Meir explained her reasoning to the chief of staff in this way:

I know all the arguments in favor of a preemptive strike, but I am against it. We don't know, any of us, what the future will hold, but there is always the possibility that we will need help, and if we strike first, we will get nothing from anyone. I would like to say yes because I know what it would mean, but with a heavy heart I am going to say no.[2]

Israel and its soldiers paid a terrible price as a result.

As a retired general, Rabin found himself on the sidelines. He spent some time at the IDF headquarters in Tel Aviv at the start of the war, but did little as his successors ran the war. He accompanied Elazar on visits to the battlefront "and served as a sounding board whenever he asked me my opinion." Since he was not doing much, on the fourth day of the war he accepted an assignment to take charge of a war loan drive to raise money the government desperately needed. It was a task he "accepted without enthusiasm," but there was not much else he could do during this terrible time. As Rabin put it, during a war it "is difficult for a former chief of staff to put his mind to raising money."[3]

It took desperate fighting and extraordinary heroism to turn the tide of battle. The IDF's first priority was to stop the Syrians, whose advancing troops and tanks threatened to break into the Jordan Valley in northern Israel. In battles on the Golan Heights, Israeli tanks were outnumbered ten or twenty to one, and sometimes more. In one epic battle, the IDF's Seventh Armored Brigade, down to seven tanks from about one hundred, stopped a major Syrian advance. As the Syrians retreated on October 9, General Rafael ("Raful") Eitan, Israel's commander on the Golan, radioed a simple but chillingly accurate message to his exhausted men, "You have saved the people of Israel."[4]

Actually, more than two weeks of bitter fighting lay ahead. During the fighting the Soviet Union, which had encouraged Anwar Sadat and Syrian dictator Hafaz al-Assad to go to war, launched a huge airlift to resupply the Arab armies. A few days later, with Israel desperately short of weapons and ammunition, the United States began a massive airlift of its own that included everything from Phantom jets to artillery shells. However, not until the Israelis turned the tide of battle did the Soviet Union seek a cease-fire. The official cease-fire request came from United Nations Resolution 338, adopted on October 22, which also called for peace negotiations on the basis of UN Resolution 242. By then an Israeli army under General Ariel ("Arik") Sharon had fought its way across the Suez Canal, surrounding a major part of the Egyptian army. Three days later, with the Syrians routed, Egypt's army in a state of collapse, and Sadat in a state of panic, the shooting finally stopped.

Israel's price of victory in the Yom Kippur War was terrible. In a country of about 3 million, almost 3,000 soldiers were dead, the equivalent of almost 2.5 million dead for a country the size of the United States. Almost 9,000 soldiers were wounded. The war cost over $9 billion, more than Israel's entire gross national product for an entire year.

Israel, Egypt, and Syria were not the only countries to suffer from the war. Even as the fighting was going on, Saudi Arabia and other Arab oil producers declared a total oil embargo against the United States and several other countries for supporting Israel. The five-month-long oil boycott cost the United States 500,000 jobs and $10 to $20 billion in lost gross national product.

Still reeling from the war, Israelis went to the polls in December. Although Labor's strength declined, it remained the leading vote-getter. As Rabin recalled:

> *Considering they were exhausted, mourning their dead, and having difficulty digesting recent events or comprehending the significance of them, the voters were merciful to the Labor party.[5]*

However, the government formed by Golda Meir, which included Rabin as minister of labor, did not last long. There were angry protests against the leading figures in power before the war, especially Golda Meir and Defense Minister Moshe Dayan. In April a commission established to investigate Israel's failure to prepare for war issued its report. It put the blame on the military, especially Chief of Staff David Elazar. It was a conclusion that most citizens, Rabin included, did not accept. As Rabin saw it, "as soon as the government accepts the recommendations of the military, both share the consequences."[6] And that was the way it turned out. Elazar resigned, but the public uproar soon drove both Meir and Dayan into retirement. The Labor party had to find new leaders and organize a new government.

Although at first there appeared to be several candidates for the post of prime minister, the choice soon boiled down to Yitzhak Rabin and Shimon Peres. The contest was heated: According to Peres, the real origin of hostility between the two men was when "we ran against each other for the prime ministership and Labor party leadership in 1974."[7] Rabin was accused of profiting from his tour as Israeli ambassador by collecting $90,000 in lecture fees, a charge that fell flat when it was revealed that previous ambassadors had done the same thing. Far more serious, Ezer Weizman went public with the story of Rabin's emotional crises before the Six-Day War. Backed by strong support from Generals Sharon, Tal, and Yariv, Rabin survived that storm as well. In a close vote, on April 22, the Labor party's Central Committee selected him as party leader.

Now all Rabin had to do was form a government. That was not easy given the background of Labor's reduced strength in the Knesset and several intense personal rivalries within the Labor party leadership. At the same time, Rabin was involved in complicated and difficult negotiations to separate Israeli and Syrian forces on the Golan Heights. The negotiations were conducted by Henry Kissinger, who by now was the American secretary of state. In January 1974 he had come to the Middle East to arrange a separation of forces between Egyptian and Israeli troops in the Sinai. Because the Arabs would not meet the Israelis face to face, Kissinger "shuttled" between Cairo and Jerusalem until an agreement was reached. However, negotiations were more difficult with the Syrians, whose hatred of Israel was as strong as anywhere in the Arab world. Rabin had to twist his schedule to conform to Kissinger's as he conducted his "shuttle diplomacy" between Damascus and Jerusalem. "That left me little time for talks with possible coalition partners, though the construction of a government was not going to be a simple matter," Rabin remembered.[8]

Kissinger completed his mission successfully on May 31. On June 3, Rabin finally assembled his government. It had a precarious one-vote majority (61 seats) in the Knesset. The new government included Yigal Allon as foreign minister and deputy prime minister. Rabin yielded to political necessity—he had to take into account the Peres faction within the Labor party—and "with a heavy heart" appointed his rival to the post of defense minister.[9]

When Rabin became prime minister a new era began in Israel. Rabin was the first of his generation and the first native-born Israeli—or Sabra—to lead his country. As he put it in his acceptance speech to the Labor party leadership, "The sons of the founding fathers have come of age."[10] They had plenty of work ahead of them. The IDF had to be made more efficient and reinforced with new weapons. The new government also had to cope with economic problems caused by the war, and with a range of social problems as well.

Rabin decided he was strong enough to take several difficult but necessary economic steps after the National Religious party, with its ten seats in the Knesset, joined the government in October 1974. During 1974 and 1975 he reduced the government budget, devalued Israel's currency, and overhauled the tax system to cut loopholes and make it fairer. Determined to make the wealthy carry their share of the burden, he also banned imports of cars and other luxury products for six months. But Rabin's reforms could not prevent Israelis, with the country's huge defense budget, from being the highest-taxed people in the world. A wave of strikes and protests swept the country as Israel's working classes struggled to make ends meet.

On the security front, the Rabin government had to deal with growing terrorism by PLO groups. Just before Rabin became prime minister, two particularly vicious terrorist raids took place. On April 11, terrorists attacked the northern town of Kiryat Shmona and killed

18 people, including 8 children. An even worse attack took place on May 15 in the town of Ma'alot, where PLO terrorists seized a schoolhouse and held more than 100 children hostage. In the rescue attempt, 20 children died and 70 were wounded. More terrorist attacks followed, including one on July 4, 1975, in which a bomb hidden inside a refrigerator in downtown Jerusalem killed 14 and wounded 75 people.

With all this, and more, to deal with, Rabin's top priority was "to focus on moving away from war and toward some state of peace."[11] The separation of forces agreements of 1974 clearly were only temporary measures. They had to be reinforced and expanded to keep war from breaking out again. Rabin discussed both arms for the IDF and how to build on 1974 agreements with President Nixon during his June 1974 visit to Israel and during a meeting in the United States in September with Nixon's successor, Gerald Ford.

The meeting with Ford led to an unexpected crisis for which Rabin, usually a meticulous planner, was totally unprepared. At the conclusion of a state dinner, it was announced, to Rabin's dismay, that dancing would follow. Immediately, President Ford "bore down on Leah, bowed slightly, and swept her off to the brightly lit ballroom." Rabin was "on the spot."

> *If only I could dance—even poorly. If only someone would get in ahead of me and invite Mrs. Ford to the dance floor. But miracles of that nature do not happen at the White House. Deciding to adopt the tactics I followed in every sphere, I strode up to Mrs. Ford...swallowing hard, I explained, "I'm sorry, Mrs. Ford, but I simply don't know how to dance. Not a step."*

Rabin thought the "worst was over," until the smiling and gracious Mrs. Ford told him she had been a dance instructor as a young woman. Rabin found himself on the dance floor trying "to keep damage to a minimum." Finally Henry Kissinger "came to my rescue" and got Rabin off the dance floor. "If he had never done anything else for Israel, I would still be eternally grateful to Kissinger for that small mercy," Rabin remembered.[12]

Rabin soon was dealing with Kissinger on a more serious matter: maintaining the tenuous cease-fire in the Middle East. In March 1975, Kissinger arrived in the region for a new round of shuttle diplomacy. He did not find Rabin in a good mood. Just three days before Kissinger's arrival, a PLO terrorist attack on a seaside hotel in Tel Aviv had left eight Israelis dead. Rabin's angry response when he arrived at the scene was: "The only place we will meet the terrorists is on the battlefield."[13]

The talks bogged down immediately. Egypt demanded significant Israeli withdrawals in the Sinai that included the Abu Rudeis oil fields developed by Israel and the strategic Giddi and Mitla passes, the keys to the Sinai. In return, the Egyptians offered what Rabin considered only vague promises, what he told Kissinger were "words, words, words." Rabin could not convince Kissinger that his objections to the Egyptian terms were valid. Tempers rose and led to what Rabin called "the most painful conversation" the two men ever had.[14] Rabin was deeply concerned that the price of standing his ground would be high: a deterioration of Israeli-American relations. He was correct.

When the talks failed after ten days, President Ford announced a "reassessment" of American-Israeli relations. For six months the United States refused to sign new arms deals with Israel. Rabin worried not only about the arms but also how Israel's enemies would perceive and react to the apparent American-Israeli split. In September a new effort brought an agreement. Basically, a combination of Israeli concessions to American pressure and a complicated formula regarding control of the Mitla and Gidi passes broke the deadlock. Israel gave up the Abu Rudeis oil fields and retreated to the eastern end of the two passes. Egypt agreed to a pledge in which each side agreed not to "resort to the threat or use of force or military blockade" against the other.[15] The agreement was to last for three years. In letters from Ford and Kissinger to Rabin, the United States sweetened the deal by increasing both its arms supplies—including ultramodern F-16 fighter aircraft—and financial aid to Israel. The United States also agreed not to recognize the PLO unless it recognized Israel's right to exist and accepted UN Resolution 242. Rabin had succeeded in restoring American-Israeli relations to good health.

Despite Israel's improved relations with the United States, the Jewish state remained isolated in the international community. A combination of Arab oil money and Soviet-bloc influence had so biased the United Nations against Israel that it routinely and without cause passed anti-Israel resolutions. Some resolutions failed to be adopted only because the United States vetoed them in the Security Council. However, Israel's international standing improved briefly in mid-1976. The event responsible for this change took place not in the Middle East but in central Africa, at an airport in Uganda called Entebbe.

The chain of events that focused the world's attention on Entebbe began on June 27 when PLO terrorists hijacked an Air France aircraft just after it left Athens.

The flight had originated in Tel Aviv and was on its way to Paris. On board were 230 passengers, including 83 Israelis. The hijackers included Arabs and two Germans, a man and a woman. The plane ended up in Uganda, whose dictator, the notorious Idi Amin, collaborated with the hijackers. At that point the Israelis and other passengers with dual citizenship identified as Jews were separated from the other passengers. The hijackers demanded the release of over 50 terrorists imprisoned in several countries, including Israel. If their demands were not met, the hostages would be killed.

Israel had a policy of not negotiating with terrorists and using force to rescue hostages. But Entebbe was over 2,600 miles (4,100 kilometers) from Tel Aviv. In Jerusalem on June 29, Rabin asked Modechai Gur, the IDF chief of staff, if the military had a plan to rescue the hostages. Since at the time it did not, Rabin felt he had no choice but to negotiate, a decision on which he clashed with Defense Minister Shimon Peres, who opposed negotiations with terrorists regardless of the circumstances. As Rabin stalled for time with the terrorists, the IDF, pressed hard by Peres, worked furiously to come up with a workable plan.

Rabin was under enormous pressure. The families of the hostages, including one couple whom Leah knew personally, were demanding he make the terrorist/hostage exchange. He also knew a decision to launch a military rescue had to be made very soon, or it would be too late. Rabin stood his ground like a rock. He was well aware that whatever course he chose, he would "have to live with my conscience for the rest of my life." He did not want to give in to the terrorists, but, as always, he was unwilling to go ahead with a military operation until

These passengers were just released from the hijacked
Air France Airbus. The Israeli and other Jewish passengers
who continued to be held hostage were rescued in a
spectacular operation which was approved by Rabin
only when he felt the preparations met the highest possible
standards. He himself estimated 15-20 would die during
the rescue, but agreed with the IDF chief of staff that
the operation was "the right thing to do."

the preparations met the highest possible standards. He would not permit "a rescue operation with soldiers holding one-way tickets."[16]

The Israelis got a break when the terrorists made two errors. They extended their deadline until July 4, and they released their non-Jewish hostages. This gave the IDF more time. It also allowed Israeli intelligence officers to interview the former hostages and learn about the situation on the ground at Entebbe, such as the location of the captives, the hijackers, and Ugandan soldiers. On July 3, with time running out, Gur told the government that the IDF was ready. After being questioned by the cabinet about the risks, Gur said, "It's the right thing to do."[17] Fifteen minutes before the cabinet decided, four giant Hercules transport planes filled with equipment and Israeli paratroopers, and a Boeing 707 jet serving as the overall command plane, had taken off for Entebbe. The schedule was that tight. Had the cabinet voted no, the planes would have been recalled.

The overall commander of the operation was General Dan Shomron; he would be the first Israeli on the ground at Entebbe and the last to leave. The man in charge of the paratroopers assigned to liberate the hostages was Yonatan Netanyahu, a Harvard-educated officer and one of the IDF's outstanding soldiers. The operation was a stunning success. The lead Hercules landed undetected by flying in, according to plan, just behind a scheduled British flight. On the ground, surprise was maintained by hiding Israeli soldiers disguised as Ugandans inside a black Mercedes limousine and two jeeps, the exact vehicles Idi Amin used when he traveled. This allowed the paratroopers to reach the terminal where the hostages were being held without the hijackers knowing anything was happening. By then the paratroopers had removed their disguises—so they would not accidentally shoot at each other—and rushed into the terminal. The shooting inside the terminal lasted less than two minutes. Outside, another group of paratroopers destroyed eleven Ugandan military jet fighters on the ground to make sure they would not be used to shoot down any Israeli aircraft.

The first Hercules crammed with hostages took off 57 minutes after the first landing. The last Israeli aircraft followed 40 minutes later. Yet ultimate success did not prevent every one of those minutes from being harrowing. The last plane to leave just barely became airborne before reaching the end of a slick and muddy runway. Its pilot recalled his 90 minutes at Entebbe amid explosions and flying bullets, which at any moment could have disabled his plane:

> *I felt lonely and exposed, and each minute felt like a lifetime. It seemed a miracle that the preceding transports had escaped without incident. We planned a meticulous schedule. My head told me that everything was going according to plan, ticking like a well-oiled clock. But my belly told me: Everything can't be that perfect—you're the last one left.*[18]

Four hostages died at Entebbe, three at the airport and one who was in the hospital during the rescue and was later murdered by Ugandan soldiers. The rest were returned safely to Israel. All six hijackers guarding the hostages were killed. Israel suffered one military death when Netanyahu was shot in the back. In honor of the young hero the country affectionately called Yoni, Israelis named the Entebbe mission Operation Yonatan. Rabin personally felt each loss and wrote, "There can be no consolation for the bereaved families." Yet, he added, the losses were "smaller than I dared to hope."[19]

The success at Entebbe brought overwhelming joy to Israel. It boosted the country's confidence, still shaken by the Yom Kippur War. Entebbe also boosted Rabin's political standing when he needed it. Further afield, people all over the world reacted with enthusiasm and admiration for Israel, the only country that seemed willing or able to deal with the growing problem of international terrorism. And for a while, foreign governments seemed to have learned something; in several cases during the following few years they successfully used police or special antiterrorist units to end hijackings or hostage-taking incidents.

One of the most complex problems that Rabin faced as prime minister was how to deal with the territories conquered during the Six-Day War. Rabin always believed that Israel should be prepared to return territory for peace. At the same time, he was convinced that Israel could not go back to its dangerous 1967 borders. They had left the country with a narrow 9-mile (14-kilometer) waist near Tel Aviv, put its northern settlements under Syrian guns, and left Israeli towns near the Mediterranean coast only minutes away from the Egyptian army in the Gaza Strip. Israel had to retain some of the conquered territory in order to protect its security.

Aside from Jerusalem and its environs, Rabin believed that Israel had to hold part of the Golan Heights and certain parts of the West Bank, especially the thinly settled Jordan Valley. Here, Rabin and Labor disagreed with Menachem Begin and Likud, who opposed giving up any part of the West Bank, an area they referred to by its Biblical names of Judea (the southern part) and Samaria (the northern part). Rabin also believed that Israel's security required control of the Gaza Strip and Sharm el-Sheikh in the Sinai Peninsula. He did not want Israel to keep areas heavily populated by Arabs. Overall, his ideas were close to a 1967 proposal of his old mentor Yigal Allon, appropriately called the Allon Plan.

Rabin also agreed with most Israelis that under no circumstances should an independent Palestinian state be established on the Gaza Strip and West Bank. Such a state, they were convinced, would not be satisfied with anything less than the destruction of Israel. In any event, it would not solve the Arab-Israeli conflict. The core of that conflict, Rabin pointed out, was the refusal of all the Arab states to recognize Israel's right to exist. Under Rabin, Israel continued to refuse to recognize the PLO, which in any event also refused to recognize Israel's right to exist. He tried to reach an agreement with Jordan about how to divide the West Bank, and met secretly with King Hussein five times. Those meetings did not produce any results.

In the territories themselves, Rabin continued the policy of establishing and expanding Jewish settlements in strategically important areas away from centers of Arab population. These settlements were in the Jordan Valley, in parts of the Gaza Strip, and on the Golan Heights. However, the government was under pressure from certain religious and militant groups to place Jewish settlements in areas associated with ancient Jewish history and the Bible. The trouble was that most of these areas were centers of Arab population, such as the town of Hebron, where the patriarch Abraham, father of the Jewish people, is believed by many to be buried.

The best organized of the groups pressing for settlements in Biblical areas was called Gush Emunim (Community of the Believers). Its strategy was to begin settlements without government permission and exploit divisions within Israeli society and even within Rabin's cabinet to keep the government from evicting them. Between 1974 and 1977, the group was able to establish five settlements on the West Bank outside government-approved areas, including the town of Kiryat Arba near Hebron. The Likud party strongly supported these efforts.

By 1977 the ground was beginning to move under Rabin's feet. The United States had a new president, Jimmy Carter, about whom Rabin felt very uneasy. While visiting Washington in March, he was stunned when Carter told a press conference that Israel should withdraw to its 1967 borders, with slight modifications. Meanwhile, there were major problems at home. There was constant tension between Rabin and Peres. As Rabin put it, "It was no secret that there was a considerable degree of friction between the defense minister and myself."[20] In fact, in February, Peres challenged Rabin for the post of Labor party leader, losing in the party's Central Committee by a small margin.

The victory did Rabin little good. In mid-March, a story broke in the Israeli press that Mrs. Rabin had kept a bank account in the United States after Rabin's term as ambassador to the United States ended. Then it turned out that there were two accounts. Keeping such a foreign account was illegal under Israeli law at the time. Although most Israelis did not consider the offense to be a major one, the news was embarrassing, especially since

*In 1977, the Likud party won the election and Begin became
Prime Minister. The old hard-line politician then revealed
surprising flexibility which enabled him to reach a point
where successful negotiations with Anwar Sadat were
possible. This photograph shows a remarkable moment in the
history of Israel—Prime Minister Begin welcomes Egyptian
President Anwar Sadat to Israel.*

it came on the heels of several financial scandals involving other Labor politicians.

Rabin was adamant that he would share responsibility for the account with Leah. He decided he had no choice but to resign his office. Eventually a court fined Leah the huge amount of $27,000 (more money than was in the two accounts) for her violation of the law (which was later repealed). Yitzhak was fined a lesser amount ($1,600), because his name technically appeared on the accounts Leah had managed. Despite public sympathy, he was leaving office under a cloud.

Labor's fortunes also declined. In elections in May 1977, the Likud scored an enormous upset. Led by Menachem Begin, it soundly defeated Labor led by Peres. Israel not only would have a new prime minister, but for the first time since the founding of the state a new party would be in power. For Israel, and for Yitzhak Rabin, a new era had begun.

CHAPTER SEVEN

"Yet he strode like a soldier...."

B etween June 1977 and June 1984, Israel was governed by a coalition led by the Likud party. For most of that period the country's prime minister was Menachem Begin. Born in Poland, Begin belonged to the generation that had founded Israel. Most of his family had died in the Holocaust. He arrived in Palestine in 1942, after a harrowing roundabout journey that initially took him from Poland to a Soviet prison camp in Siberia. Begin then became the fiery underground leader of the Irgun in the struggle against the British prior to 1948. He was the leading opposition politician during the next 29 years when Labor governments ruled the country. After Begin retired from public life in 1983, Yitzhak Shamir, likewise a veteran underground leader born in Poland, took his place as Likud's leader and Israel's prime minister.

The Likud years were filled with important events, including Anwar Sadat's dramatic visit to Jerusalem in

1977 and Israel's momentous peace treaty with Egypt in 1979, the first ever with an Arab state. Yet, like Peres and the rest of the Labor leadership, Rabin had to view these historic events from the sidelines as a member of the main opposition party in the Knesset. Leah Rabin summed up her husband's mood during what may be considered the Begin era:

> He didn't enjoy those years from 1977 to 1984. He was bored to tears. He would call me three or four times a day, sometimes out of frustration and boredom. There was no action. He's basically a doer. He likes responsibility. But he didn't consider doing anything else outside of politics.[1]

By far the most important development that Rabin watched from the sidelines was the 1979 peace treaty. Menachem Begin and Anwar Sadat, the two men most responsible for making it happen, were unlikely partners. Begin was known as an unyielding hard-liner when dealing with the Arabs; Sadat's background included being imprisoned by the British during World War II for his pro-Nazi sympathies. Yet by 1977 both men believed that they had to leave at least part of the past behind. Sadat's own mistrust of Israel was reduced in mid-1977 when the Israelis warned him of an assassination plot against him, complete with names and addresses of the Palestinian assassins already in Cairo.

The first step had to come from Sadat, since for decades Egypt had refused to negotiate directly with Israel. On November 9, 1977, he told the Egyptian parliament that he was ready "to go to their own house, to the

Knesset" to talk to the Israelis.[2] Ten days later Sadat walked off an airplane at Israel's Ben-Gurion Airport. Rabin watched the "uniquely electric moment" from his place in the receiving line. He was impressed by how Sadat, "meeting all his former archenemies, one after another, in the space of seconds," somehow knew "exactly the right thing to say to each and every one of them."[3] Rabin also was impressed by Sadat's speech to the Knesset the next day, especially when he told the Israelis that he understood their need for security. As Rabin noted with some irony, "It was a statement we had never heard before—even from some of Israel's best friends."[4]

Yet long and difficult negotiations lay ahead. Finally, in September 1978, President Carter brought Begin and Sadat together in the United States where the three leaders hammered out a preliminary agreement called the Camp David Accords. The accords had two "frameworks." The first called for Israel, Egypt, Jordan, and undefined "representatives of the Palestinian people" to negotiate terms for limited Palestinian self-government in the West Bank and Gaza. It called for a five-year transition period, during which the parties would negotiate the final status of those territories. In effect, the Palestinian issue was put off so that Israel and Egypt could agree on the second "framework" dealing with a peace treaty between their two countries. On September 25, Rabin spoke in favor of the accords in the Knesset and joined an overwhelming majority of that body in approving them after an intense debate.

After more hard negotiations, an Israeli-Egyptian peace treaty was signed at the White House on March 26, 1979. At Begin's invitation, a pleased Yitzhak Rabin was present at the ceremony. Although Rabin had no role in the peace negotiations, he was convinced that his 1975 agreement with Egypt as well as later efforts until 1977 helped pave the way for the treaty signed in 1979. As he put it:

> *Mr. Begin was kind enough to invite me as a former prime minister and, I like to believe, in recognition of my contribution in paving the way for the final peace process.*[5]

The peace with Egypt came at a high price for Israel. Israel gave up the entire Sinai Peninsula, including Sharm el-Sheikh. Israel lost its important military bases in the Sinai, in which it had invested $10 billion. The cost of moving and building new bases was over $4 billion, only a quarter of which was covered by American aid. Additional billions invested in developing oil wells in the Sinai, which in 1979 were providing half of Israel's energy needs, also were forfeited. Begin also agreed to remove all Jewish settlements in the region, including the seaside town of Yamit, where he had hoped someday to retire. In return, Egypt accepted strict limits on the troops and weapons it could keep in the Sinai; in effect, a large part of the peninsula became a buffer zone between Israel and Egypt. Egypt pledged to allow Israeli ships through the Straits of Tiran and, for the first time, through the Suez Canal. Each side accepted the other's right to live at peace with "secure and recognized boundaries" and agreed to establish normal diplomatic, economic, and cultural ties.

In Israel the peace treaty was greeted with enthusiasm, although also with considerable caution. A minority opposed the agreement, mainly on security grounds.

While those fears proved to be unfounded, the treaty certainly did not produce the people-to-people ties that Israelis had wanted. The Egyptian government kept its relations with Israel strictly formal. There were few cultural or economic ties, and popular hostility to Israel among the Egyptian people remained intense and widespread. Borrowing from the language of the Cold War, Israelis referred to their relationship with Egypt as a "Cold Peace."

The Arab world outside of Egypt, from the PLO to the other Arab states, reacted to the peace treaty with fury. Within five days, nineteen of the Arab League's twenty-two members met in Baghdad, Iraq, and announced a series of sanctions against Egypt. Over the next two months most Arab countries broke diplomatic relations with Egypt. Egypt was suspended from the Arab League, expelled from the Islamic Conference, and thrown out of several other international Arab organizations. Two years later, Sadat was assassinated by Muslim extremists opposed to any peace with Israel.

Although the state of war between Israel and Egypt ended, the feud between Yitzhak Rabin and Shimon Peres continued. It was fueled by both political differences and personal rivalry. In the 1960s the two men had disagreed on several policy issues. In the 1970s two ambitious and highly capable men with very different styles—Rabin, the ex-general, direct and blunt; Peres, the intellectual career politician, smooth and subtle—were competing for their party's leadership and the country's top post. Not surprisingly, the feud did neither man any good and often angered other party leaders, who saw that the Rabin-Peres infighting was damaging Labor's chances to unseat Likud. Many of those leaders were especially upset by

Rabin's strident attacks on Peres in *The Rabin Memoirs*, published in 1979. It seemed hard to believe that the Peres pictured by Rabin was the same man who for many years had played such a critical role in developing Israel's defense capabilities and its nuclear research program. Rabin's use of his memoirs to attack Peres was not his finest hour. If anything, it undermined his position in the party. When he challenged Peres for the party leadership in December 1980, Rabin was soundly defeated. Peres received an overwhelming 70 percent of the Central Committee's votes.

Peres therefore led Labor in the 1981 campaign leading up to the elections on June 30. Likud actually struck its most powerful blow in the campaign 500 miles (800 kilometers) from Israel. On June 7, eight American-built F-16 fighter-bombers destroyed Iraq's Osiraq nuclear reactor, which was still under construction. It was a feat that rivaled the Entebbe mission. The planes had to fly to the very limit of their range over Jordanian and Saudi Arabian territory and take special precautions to avoid being detected by radar. The pilots then bombed their target with what one observer called "stupefying accuracy."[6] Begin had throttled the Iraqi nuclear weapons program. At the time, Israel was severely criticized by the international community, including the United States. Ten years later, when Americans and other soldiers faced the Iraqi army in Kuwait during operation Desert Storm, that criticism turned to belated praise.

Rabin supported the raid, saying "everything should be done" to postpone or prevent an Arab state from getting nuclear weapons.[7] The Israeli voters showed their support at the polls. Likud came from behind in the polls to narrowly win the election. Begin then put together a new Likud-led coalition government to govern the country for the next four years.

Begin was much less successful in another bold strike closer to home. In 1982, Israel invaded Lebanon. Lebanon was a weak and unstable country, divided into a variety of feuding Muslim and Christian groups. It was about half Christian, making it unique in the almost totally Muslim Arab world. For that reason, Israeli leaders thought it might be possible to make peace with Lebanon, despite its many internal divisions, if they could help the local Christians consolidate their power. As prime minister, Rabin also tried to play the Lebanon card. On one occasion he secretly sailed northward in a navy gunboat and met with the leader of one of the local Christian factions just off the Lebanese coast.

Since 1970 the PLO had built up a powerful presence in Lebanon, a veritable "state within a state." Southern Lebanon became a PLO base for attacking Israel. During 1981, PLO rocket attacks on settlements in northern Israel brought civilian activity in several areas to a halt. Begin was persuaded to invade Lebanon by Ariel Sharon, his new defense minister. The stated goal of the invasion was to drive the PLO from southern Lebanon and restore security to northern Israel. However, under Sharon's direction the invasion soon took on greater scope, as Israeli troops advanced to Beirut, Lebanon's capital. Sharon intended to drive the PLO from the country entirely, force Syrian forces out as well, and help create a Christian-dominated Lebanese government that would make peace with Israel.

At first Rabin supported both the invasion and Sharon. He even supported the IDF's siege of Beirut and visited the defense minister at the front lines several times. But Rabin became concerned as the invasion turned into an occupation. He doubted Israel's expanded goals in Lebanon could be achieved and, like other Israelis, was appalled at the IDF's mounting casualties. In 1983, Rabin warned against Israel getting stuck in the *botz ha'Levanoni*, or the Lebanese mud. As it turned out, he soon would be given the difficult job of getting Israel out of that mud.

In August 1983, Menachem Begin suddenly retired from public life. He gave no reason, but it appeared that the recent death of his wife and the growing cost of the fighting in Lebanon had taken their toll on him. Begin was succeeded by sixty-eight-year-old Yitzhak Shamir, a hard-liner who had opposed returning Sinai to Egypt. In June 1984, Israelis once again went to the polls. Their concern with losses in Lebanon, mounting inflation and other economic problems, and squabbling politicians showed in the election results. Both Labor and Likud lost strength, the former winning forty-four seats and the latter forty-one.

The result, after several months of political maneuvering, was a National Unity Government organized in September. The parties would share power according to a "rotation" plan. For the first two years Peres would be prime minister and Shamir foreign minister. Then they would switch posts. The two parties agreed that the other key post, defense minister, would be filled for the full four-year term by one man: Yitzhak Rabin. After seven years in the political wilderness, Rabin had returned to power. Leah Rabin was flushed with pride and joy for her husband:

Seventeen years after removing his uniform,
Yitzhak had returned to the defense establishment
as though coming home after a prolonged absence,
full of ups and downs in life. Seventeen years had
passed, his hair had turned grey and he was
wearing a suit in place of a uniform. Yet he strode
like a soldier, as in the past, his face not revealing
his inner feelings.[8]

Rabin's first task in his new post was to get the IDF out of Lebanon. This was urgent given the growing cost in Israeli lives, which passed 500 even before Rabin took office. One of the worst incidents took place just after Rabin became minister of defense. In November 1983, a booby-trapped truck blew up at an Israeli military checkpoint. It killed 29 soldiers and wounded many more. Debates within the government about how fast to withdraw took place during 1984. As frequently was the case, Rabin and Peres disagreed, Peres supporting an immediate full withdrawal and Rabin favoring one in stages. By then Israel's main goal was reduced to maintaining a security zone along the border free of both the PLO and the Syrians. What happened in the rest of Lebanon, Israel could not control. As Rabin told the American press, "I don't want to be the policeman of Lebanon."[9]

The withdrawal took place in stages as Rabin wanted and was completed by June 1985. Israel kept a small contingent of soldiers in Lebanon in a narrow "security zone" along Israel's northern border. It also backed a small militia of Lebanese Christians that operated in the zone to protect local Christian villages from the PLO and other armed Muslim groups. The Begin-Sharon invasion had destroyed the PLO's state-within-a-state in Lebanon. But the cost in lives and morale was terribly high, and the enterprise had not achieved any of Sharon's other goals or left Israel in a position to prevent the subsequent return of armed PLO forces to Lebanon.

Rabin's great challenge as minister of defense did not come from abroad. It came from an uprising that began in December 1987 in the Gaza Strip and quickly spread to the West Bank. Soon it took on a life and intensity that nobody expected. It would last almost six years and is known as the Intifada, an Arabic term that means "shaking off." The Intifada reflected the deep frustration and despair among Palestinians in the territories who lived under Israeli rule, especially young people who had been born and grown up under Israeli occupation. They hated the Israelis, but also felt deserted by the rest of the Arab world.

As minister of defense, Rabin was the man on the spot whose job was to stop the Intifada. He was in the United States at the time of the first riots and did not return home until the Intifada was two weeks old. Rabin therefore has been accused by Israelis of not recognizing quickly enough that something unprecedented in scope had broken out. If the criticism is valid, and it would seem to be, then Rabin was hardly the only person who should have been more in touch with the mood of Palestinians in the territories. From his headquarters in Tunisia, PLO chairman Yasir Arafat also mistakenly viewed the December rioting as something that he had seen before and would pass. That is why he described the incidents with the word "intifada," which in the past Arabs had applied to relatively limited outbursts.

The Intifada spread like wildfire and defied Rabin's attempts to control it. There were constant riots and attacks on Israeli settlers and soldiers. Israeli settlers were a prime target in part because after 1977 the Likud government had followed a policy of building new Jewish settlements anywhere on the West Bank, including areas near large Arab population centers. The attacks could be deadly, as the rioters not only threw stones but also gasoline-filled bottles called Molotov cocktails. When Israeli troops used force to quell the riots, people, often teenagers, were killed. The riots and the Israeli response was filmed by the press and watched by millions of people throughout the world. The news coverage created a public-relations disaster for the Jewish state. ⌐oreign television viewers usually were not aware that the PLO soon took control of many Intifada actions and used them for its own purposes. Nor did foreign viewers in Europe and the United States understand that Intifada activists had become skilled at manipulating and intimidating the foreign press to get the coverage they wanted.

Rabin's hard-line policy against the Intifada was called the "iron fist," a term that did little to improve Israel's public image. Even his attempts to reduce Palestinian casualties backfired. IDF troops were issued clubs and told to use them instead of firing their rifles whenever possible. As a result, the world saw television pictures of Israeli troops beating Palestinian youths, making Israel look even worse. Rabin admitted that he was "surprised to discover that the sensitivity of world opinion to blows and physical confrontation was greater than to that of shooting."[10]

During the first year of the Intifada, more than 150 Palestinians were killed and 11,500 were wounded. Part of the Israeli dilemma was summed up by General Dan Shomron, the leader of the Entebbe raid and the current IDF chief of staff:

> *People are constantly pressuring us to come down hard [on the Palestinians]. But I'm also thinking about the future, about the question of who will have to live here, and I'm trying not to burn our bridges.*[11]

As for Rabin, within a few months he admitted, "It is far easier to solve classic military problems" than to quell a mass uprising.[12]

The Intifada dragged on into the 1990s. Neither side was able get its way, and both sides were seeing consequences they did not like. The death toll, among both Palestinians and Israelis, was mounting. Within the Palestinian community, the constant closing of schools was depriving a generation of education. There was a general rise of lawlessness, as extremist elements and criminals used the cover of the uprising to take revenge on their opponents or rivals. It was enough to label someone an "Israeli collaborator," regardless of the facts, to put his life in grave danger. During 1992 and 1993, more Palestinians were killed by other Palestinians, often with great cruelty, than by Israeli troops. Meanwhile, Palestinian leaders could see that Israel was not disappearing, and was in fact growing stronger and larger as hundreds of thousands of immigrants continued to arrive, recently having been allowed to leave the Soviet Union and its successor states.

Nor could the Israelis find comfort in their frustrating struggle against the Intifada. Many Israelis were deeply troubled by the harsh measures that the IDF had to use to control Palestinian rioters. Parents who were prepared to see their sons at risk on a battlefield did not want them swinging clubs against teenagers in the territories. Meanwhile, the Intifada was undermining the morale of the IDF, which was supposed to defend the country against foreign armies, not chase gangs of youths in the streets and alleys of cities and towns. Time spent on the West Bank also took away from training exercises vital to battle readiness. Still another problem was that the Intifada boosted the influence of a fundamentalist Islamic organization called Hamas, which was more extreme than most of the factions in the PLO. Hamas rejected any thought of negotiations of peace with Israel or with Jews, whom Hamas called "the sons of monkeys and swines."[13]

As Israelis looked for a way out of the quagmire, some of them began to change their attitude toward the Palestinians. One person whose thinking was evolving was Yitzhak Rabin. Ironically, the Intifada improved his standing among the Israeli public, which generally saw him as a tough and uncomplaining soldier willing to take the heat to protect them. A poll in March 1988 showed Rabin more popular than either Peres or Shamir. Yet Rabin was becoming convinced that Israel could not continue to rule over a large and hostile Arab population. The use of force against the Intifada had reached a dead end. Only a political solution could end the violence. During the spring of 1988 and into 1989, in search of new ideas, he met secretly with Palestinian notables from the West Bank. Those discussions produced no concrete results, however.

In November 1988, national elections produced another virtual dead heat between Likud and Labor, with Likud edging out its rival by one seat, 40 to 39. Once again, the two parties formed a national-unity government with Shamir as prime minister. However, by 1990 the tension within the government had reached the breaking point over a new American peace initiative. The United States under President George Bush wanted to set up a peace conference that would include a delegation of Palestinian Arabs unaffiliated with the PLO. Shamir took a hard line on exactly which non-PLO Palestinians would be acceptable to Israel. Peres and his supporters within Labor wanted Israel to be more flexible. They accused Shamir of subverting the peace process, and he retorted that they were prepared to make unwise concessions. These differences were piled on top of the Labor-Likud disagreement about whether Israel should give up land for peace, which Labor favored and Likud opposed. Rabin, who had his problems with both Shamir and Peres, finally decided Shamir's stalling was unacceptable. With its two normally quarreling leaders in agreement, Labor quit the unity government, thereby bringing it down.

The next few months saw a swirl of political squabbling. Peres, as party leader, failed in his attempt to form a Labor government. For Peres, losing the chance to become prime minister was a deep personal disappointment and a severe political setback. Shamir then succeeded in getting several religious parties to join a Likud-led coalition. The Israeli public as a whole reacted angrily to the political wheeling and dealing it took to form a government. There were widespread demands for electoral reform that would reduce the influence of small political parties and strengthen the political center.

Rabin meanwhile took advantage of Peres's failure to challenge him for the Labor leadership. This time it was Rabin's turn to be disappointed. Although Rabin seemed to be the most popular politician in the country, Peres still held sway inside Labor's Central Committee. In July it again chose him over Rabin. However, Labor was listening to the popular outcry. Once the 1990 leadership battle was over, the committee voted to change its election system. Instead of the Central Committee deciding the matter, the party would hold an American-style primary and allow the membership to choose its leader.

In August 1990, one month after Rabin's unsuccessful challenge to Peres, almost everything in the Middle East was put on hold when Iraqi dictator Saddam Hussein invaded neighboring Kuwait. By seizing Kuwait and adding its vast oil reserves to those of Iraq, Hussein suddenly had control of almost 20 percent of the world's total supply. And next door for the taking was Saudi Arabia, with a quarter of the world's oil. The United States responded by forming a coalition of countries from around the world, including Egypt and Saudi Arabia, that drove Iraq from Kuwait in January 1991.

Israel's role, which it accepted reluctantly, was to stay out of the action and not retaliate against Iraqi missile attacks (using Soviet Scud missiles) on its cities. If Israel defended itself, the United States feared, the Arab states would defect from the coalition. After the war, when the full extent of Iraq's nuclear weapons and poison-gas programs became known, the wisdom of Israel's 1981 attack against Iraq's nuclear reactor received far greater recognition. A major loser in the Gulf War, aside from Iraq, was the PLO, which strongly supported the invasion of Kuwait and the missile attacks against Israel.

In the aftermath of the Gulf War the United States put new pressure on the Shamir government to come to a peace conference. The result was the Madrid Conference, which began on October 30, and was co-sponsored by the United States and the Soviet Union. It gave Israel a chance to negotiate directly with Lebanon, Jordan, and Syria on the basis of UN resolutions 242 and 338. The Palestinians were represented as part of a joint Jordanian-Palestinian delegation. This reflected Israel's steadfast refusal to negotiate with the PLO, whose covenant still called for Israel's destruction. Although the Madrid Conference yielded little concrete progress, in retrospect it was a step forward. For the first time, Israel was negotiating face-to-face with its front-line Arab adversaries: Syria, Lebanon, and a joint Jordanian-Palestinian delegation.

Back in Israel, Shamir's participation at Madrid appeared to be winning increased public support for Likud. The party looked to be in better shape than Labor for the coming elections in June. But the political ground was shifting fast in Israel. By the time it stopped moving, Labor would win a solid victory and Yitzhak Rabin would reclaim the office of prime minister.

CHAPTER EIGHT

"We must take risks."

I t took two changes in Israel's political alignment to bring Yitzhak Rabin to power as prime minister. First, Rabin had to capture the Labor party leadership from Peres; second, Labor had to defeat Likud in a general election.

The first change occurred when Labor selected its new leader and candidate for prime minister in Israel's first-ever primary election in February 1992. Two other candidates joined the perennial rivals Rabin and Peres in the primary. Labor's rules required that the winning candidate get over 40 percent of the vote. Otherwise, the two candidates with the most votes would compete in a runoff.

The primary took place on February 19. Rabin was cautiously optimistic, but hardly overconfident in a race that most people correctly rated a toss-up between him and Peres. As Leah recalled, Rabin "was under control.

I was going out of my mind."[1] When the ballots were counted, Rabin received 40.59 percent of the vote. It was not an overwhelming victory, but it was enough.

While Rabin was grasping the reigns of power inside the Labor party, Likud was losing its power in the country as a whole. A number of factors undermined the Shamir government. While it continued to invest huge sums in Jewish settlements on the West Bank, Shamir's government neglected the parts of Israel inside the 1967 borders where most of its citizens (over 96 percent) lived. By the spring of 1992 unemployment approached 12 percent, never a good sign for the future of any democratically elected government. Among the new immigrants, including the hundreds of thousands from the former Soviet Union, unemployment was a staggering 40 percent.

Shamir's refusal to slow down the settlement program on the West Bank or consider territorial compromise in negotiations with the Arabs strained relations with the United States, a development that worried Rabin as well as most Israelis. Following Begin's approach, the most that Shamir was willing to offer the Palestinians was local autonomy in their cities and towns; Israel would retain physical control of the region. By 1992, Shamir's hard line was losing its appeal at home, mainly because the public was weary of the unending stalemate. Israelis increasingly seemed to feel that Israel could do more to move peace negotiations forward without endangering its security.

Shamir's government collapsed in January 1992 when two small rightist parties walked out of the Likud-led coalition. As Likud entered the election campaign that followed, it was plagued by internal conflict between factions respectively led by Housing Minister Sharon, Foreign Minister David Levy, and Shamir. Meanwhile, Labor managed temporarily to circumvent its internal quarrels, including the usual Rabin-Peres tension, and unite behind Rabin.

A key factor in Rabin's victory over Peres in the Labor primary was that many party members believed that their best chance in the general election was with Rabin at the head of the ticket. The party's campaign reflected that sentiment. Labor muted its traditional socialist identity and went to the people as "Labor headed by Rabin." Instead of its trademark socialist red flag, the party shifted to blue, which is identified with Israel's blue-and-white flag and therefore with nationalist feelings. The main campaign slogans ran: "Israel is waiting for Rabin" and "Rabin is the only hope."[2]

Rabin meanwhile promised a new orientation. He said that a Labor government would no longer sink money into any and all settlements on the West Bank, many of which, he insisted, did nothing for Israel's security. Rather, his government would shift priorities from the territories to Israel proper, where, he charged, Likud's neglect had left everything from roads to schools to social programs in disrepair. As for peace negotiations, still the key issue, he pledged a new and more flexible effort to reach agreements with the Palestinians as well as with Jordan and Syria.

Rabin's reputation as Israel's "Mr. Security," earned from his military career and years as minister of defense fighting the Intifada, was crucial to Labor's chances in the election. That reputation counterbalanced the general public's view of Labor as dominated by leftist and dovish politicians, many associated with Peres, who would give away too much and compromise Israel's security in negotiations with the Arabs. Rabin's reputation allowed him to stake out a position that appeared to promise both flexibility and security. As he wrote on June 1, 1992, in an Israeli newspaper:

> *I am unwilling to give up a single inch of Israel's security, but I am willing to give up many inches of sentiments and territories—as well as 1,700,000 Arab inhabitants—for the sake of peace. That is the whole doctrine in a nutshell. We seek a territorial compromise which will bring peace and security. A lot of security.*[3]

Rabin stressed that "a lot of security" meant retaining territory around Jerusalem, the Jordan Valley south of Lake Kinneret, and the Golan Heights. On the other hand, it also meant that Israel could not continue to rule over 1.7 million hostile Arabs in the territories. In saying that, Rabin still firmly opposed an independent Palestinian state on the West Bank and Gaza. A Palestinian state, he warned, inevitably would fall under control of radical forces who would not be satisfied until they destroyed Israel. Any territories that Israel gave up would have to return to Jordanian control in one way or another. In a televised debate with Shamir a week before the election on June 23, Rabin summed up the "three points on which I will stand: no Palestinian state; no return to the 1967 borders; and a united Jerusalem under Israeli control."[4]

Labor's strategy paid off. With Rabin leading the charge, it defeated Likud by the decisive margin of 44 seats to 32. Actually, the large margin was due far more to Likud's losses (it fell from 40 to 32 seats) than Labor's gains (from 39 to 44). After fifteen years, Yitzhak Rabin once again was charged with putting together a coalition to govern Israel.

The job of assembling a coalition was easier than in 1977, mainly because of two new political parties. One was called Meretz. It was formed in 1992 when three small parties on the left that shared dovish views regarding negotiations with the Arabs merged. Meretz was eager to add its 12 seats to Labor's 44. Six more seats, putting Labor over the threshold of 60, came from a religious party called Shas, formed in 1984.

Rabin's goal, however, was to form a centrist coalition that could claim support across a wide arc of Israel's spectrum. During the election he had promised that his government would not tilt to the left or right. To keep that promise Rabin had to balance Meretz. The only available ballast on the right was yet another new party, called Tsomet, formed in 1988. It was led by Raphael Eitan, a former general and one of the heroes of the Yom Kippur War and a hard-liner on how to deal with the West Bank and Gaza. But efforts to bring Tsomet into Rabin's coalition failed, leaving Rabin with a government whose tilt away from the center of Israeli politics was deepened by a tactical alliance with five Arab members of the Knesset. Although not officially members of the government, they consistently sided with it in Knesset votes.

In his new government Rabin took on the post of defense minister as well as prime minister. Peres became foreign minister, a position that Rabin had to give his old rival because of his strong following in the Labor party. During the campaign, relations between the two men, as Peres put it, "were strained." After the election they met privately to establish a working relationship. Rabin already had made it clear that he intended to be in charge, a situation that Peres, swallowing his pride, had to accept. Yet both men were determined to subordinate everything, including their personal rivalry, to the greater goal of making peace. On that basis, and with time slowly healing old wounds, Peres could accurately say that "a close and fruitful working relationship between us evolved."[5]

Rabin presented his new government to the Knesset and the nation on July 13. With his wife and sister watching in the gallery, he delivered a direct and eloquent speech that left no doubt about how and where he intended to lead his country. "We are going to change the national order of priorities," he announced. While the prime minister mentioned dealing with unemployment, immigrant problems, and other social and economic issues, the government's "central goal" would be "to promote the making of peace and take vigorous steps that will lead to the end of the Arab-Israeli conflict." Rabin admitted to his people that the path he had chosen would involve "crises...disappointments, tears, and pain." But he reminded them that "this is a propitious hour, a time of great possibilities and opportunities" that Israel should not squander. "We do not intend to lose precious time," he said.

Then Rabin stopped talking to his people and in a remarkable and dramatic moment addressed their enemy and his, the Palestinians:

> *To you, the Palestinians in the territories, I wish to say from this rostrum: We have been fated to live together on this same patch of land, in the*

same country. We lead our lives with you, beside
you and against you. You have failed in the war
against us. One hundred years of your bloodshed
and terror against us have brought you only
suffering, humiliation, bereavement and pain.
…For forty-four years you have been living
under a delusion. Your leaders have led you
through lies and deceit. They have missed every
opportunity, rejected all the proposals for a
settlement, and have taken you from one
tragedy to another.

To you, Palestinians who live in the ter-
ritories…you who have never known a single
day of freedom and joy in your lives—listen to
us, if only this once. We offer you the fairest
and most viable proposal from our standpoint
today—autonomy, self-government—with all its
advantages and limitations. You will not get
everything you want. Perhaps neither will we.
So once and for all, take your destiny in your
own hands. Don't lose this opportunity that
may never return. Take our proposal serious-
ly—to avoid further suffering and grief; to end
the shedding of tears and of blood.[6]

Rabin then turned back to his own people. He promised
them that "when it comes to security, we will concede
nothing," adding that "security takes preference even over
peace." The new prime minister concluded by saying
that his entire policy could be summed up from a single
Biblical verse: "May the Lord give his people strength,
may the Lord bless his people with peace…."[7] Nobody
in the audience doubted that Israel would need all its
strength to achieve the peace Rabin sought.

Working up to sixteen hours a day, Rabin moved quickly on several fronts. In July he visited Egyptian President Hosni Mubarak in Cairo. He announced a slowdown in housing construction on the West Bank, a move that pleased the United States. A visit to the United States and President George Bush improved the strained relations with Israel's main ally. During 1993, government spending on roads and other public facilities inside the 1967 borders both improved overall living conditions and stimulated the economy.

One of Rabin's most important long-term domestic efforts involved education, an area considered vital to Israel's future. The school day was lengthened. Over several years the education budget was increased by 50 percent. While there were sweeping changes in all areas of education, special attention was devoted to improving the teaching of science and technology. The results were impressive. In 1995 a delegation of educators from the United States said that their country should copy Israel's reforms in science education, while in 1996 a UN education expert said Israel may be the world leader in science education.

Of course, none of this brought peace any closer. During 1992, negotiations in Washington conducted under the Madrid framework made no progress. Meanwhile, Israel was rocked by a series of bloody attacks against both soldiers and civilians by Hamas and another Islamic fundamentalist organization opposed to any peace with Israel, called Hezbollah. The death toll mounted, but despite angry reactions from the political opposition and many Israeli citizens, Rabin refused to stop the peace negotiations. He knew that was exactly

*A Hamas suicide terrorist caused the destruction of
these buses resulting in the deaths of five people
and the injuries of more than one hundred. As
Rabin's peace negotiations continued, so did the deaths of
both Israeli soldiers and civilians as Hamas and Hezbollah
violently opposed any peace at all with Israel.*

what Hamas and Hezbollah wanted. As he told the people in a television interview:

> *Why has there been an increase in shooting incidents in recent months? I have no doubt that those who propose action are, first and foremost, the ones who want to kill…the peace and the chance to achieve peace.*[8]

Yet pressure was growing for Rabin to do something to increase the country's security. On December 16, after Hamas terrorists kidnapped and murdered a 29-year-old border policeman, the prime minister took action. Israeli forces rounded up 415 Hamas activists and other terrorist suspects and expelled them to Lebanon. It was not the first time that Israel had expelled Palestinian terrorist suspects, nor was the expulsion necessarily permanent. Those involved had the right to appeal their expulsion within sixty days. Nonetheless, the expulsion led to extensive international criticism of Israel. Rabin held out against pressures to revoke the expulsion. To his foreign critics he said that the murdered Israeli "was not granted the right to appeal the brutal, bloody sentence passed on him. The Hamas deportees do get that right."[9] Only after lengthy negotiations did Israel agree to allow the expelled men to return to their homes during the course of 1993.

In Israel, the expulsion shored up Rabin's reputation for toughness. So did his sealing off of the territories in March 1993, after a series of stabbings and attacks took fifteen Israeli lives in one month. The closure prevented would-be terrorists from reaching their intended victims. However, it also prevented other Palestinians, including 100,000 commuting to their jobs, from cross-ing into Israel. In July, after Hezbollah forces killed several Israeli soldiers and hit several northern Israeli towns with rockets, Rabin further demonstrated his willingness to use strong measures for security when the IDF bombarded southern Lebanon for a week. Eitan Haber, one of Rabin's closest aides and friends, summed up the rationale behind these measures: "If you want to make drastic concessions on peace, you must first show the public you can take drastic measures for security."[10]

Ironically, the peace negotiations at which concessions were being made were unknown to the Israeli public, and even to most members of Rabin's government. They had started in December 1992 and were taking place in secret in Oslo, Norway. These talks began as strictly unofficial discussions between private citizens. They were the latest example of unofficial contacts between Palestinians and Israelis that went back nearly twenty years. At times this secret "citizen diplomacy" involved contacts between Israelis and people connected with the PLO. Private meetings took place over the years despite an Israeli law, in effect from 1986 to January 1993, that prohibited Israelis from speaking to PLO officials and, far more menacing, the murder of several participating Palestinians by extremists within their own camp.

The so-called Oslo talks actually began in London before they were moved to Norway. The participants were several PLO officials and two Israeli academicians. However, what gave these talks special significance was the involvement behind the scenes of people in powerful positions within the PLO leadership and the Israeli government. On the Israeli side, the key link to the government was Yossi Beilin, Israel's deputy foreign minister and a long-time associate of Foreign Minister Shimon Peres. The stage manager for the PLO was a moderate member of its executive committee named Mahmoud Abbas (Abu Mazen), a veteran of many earlier attempts at "citizen diplomacy."

Critical support for the entire effort came from Norway, a country far from the Middle East but one with a long-standing concern with solving the Arab-Israeli conflict. A Norwegian academic named Terje Larsen, who was well connected to government officials, helped to get the talks started, while the Norwegian foreign ministry, headed by Johan Jorgen Holst, provided essential help in keeping the negotiations going.

Mahmoud Abbas described the Norwegian contribution to the talks:

> *It was a difficult task that required absolute secrecy....It imposed on the Israelis and Palestinians complete secrecy of movement, but also burdened the Norwegians with the even greater responsibility of controlling these movements on their territory in order not to attract the attention of foreign embassies, the media and the various intelligence services. It was an apparently impossible mission, but it was accomplished. The Norwegians continually moved the...negotiations from one place to another, so that no two consecutive meetings were held in the same place. They also restricted the number of people who would be responsible for the whole operation, who concealed themselves behind a wall of mist to prevent leaks to other Norwegian Foreign Ministry staff.[11]*

The talks, in fact, were so secret that Rabin himself initially did not know about them. The main architect of the Oslo talks from the Israeli side was Foreign Minister Shimon Peres. He told Beilin to pursue the idea and see what happened. The Israeli negotiators reported to Beilin, who in turn reported to Peres. When the talks, to almost everyone's surprise, seemed to be making progress, Peres went to Rabin early in February 1993. Rabin, cautious as ever, was reluctant at first to use what was called the Oslo "back channel." Apparently, Peres convinced him to support the talks by pointing out that they provided information on what the PLO was thinking without obligating the Israelis to anything.

Why did Rabin go along with this rather irregular diplomacy, and why with the PLO, whom he had repeatedly rejected as a negotiating partner? The answer lies in Rabin's speech to the Knesset, when he told his people that the world was changing quickly. It was "our duty," said Rabin, to "see the new world as it is now," being careful to "discern its dangers," but also making sure to "explore its prospects."[12] And there were new prospects, for several reasons.

The collapse of the Soviet Union had deprived the Arab forces most opposed to a peace with Israel of their main military backer. The PLO was weakened in addition by its support of Iraq during the Gulf War. This meant that Arafat might be ready to compromise before his organization weakened further. Meanwhile, the Intifada and the lack of progress under the Madrid framework had convinced Rabin that no other organization had any power to speak for the Palestinians. Rabin and Peres, therefore, concluded that if Israel wanted to reach an agreement with their adversaries, it had to be with the

PLO. They also recognized that given the rise of Islamic fundamentalism, if Israel did not deal with the PLO it soon might have no one left to deal with but Hamas, an organization utterly opposed to any peace with Israel.

In short, new conditions caused Rabin to change his mind about the PLO. It was not an easy decision. As a close advisor to Peres noted, to change Rabin needed "indisputable evidence that he is wrong. However, if there is a brick missing from the wall, he tears down the whole thing."[13] In this case, it appeared to Rabin that the bricks, slowly and one-by-one, were being put into place in Oslo. Throughout his career Rabin was above all a pragmatist and realist. Therefore, Peres recalled, once Rabin was convinced the Oslo negotiations *might* lead to peace, despite his continued doubts "he gave me, and the talks, a chance."[14]

Having decided to go ahead, Rabin worked closely with Peres. It was during their many long meetings that the two adversaries, both aging (Rabin, at seventy, was a year older than Peres) and aware that their time at center stage was running out, finally managed to overcome their personal antagonisms. In fact they had to, for they were working under extreme secrecy and almost alone. Probably no more than seven Israelis, including the negotiators, knew what was going on in Oslo.

The Oslo system of using private individuals rather than professional negotiators to represent Israel was not without its flaws. Early in the negotiations, the two Israeli academicians made concessions that were unacceptable to their government. In May, Rabin and Peres sent two government experts to Oslo to join the negotiating team. They had to make concessions on other less important issues in order to revise the unacceptable terms agreed to by the academicians.

The negotiations finally were completed in mid-August. On August 20, what was called the Declaration of Principles (DOP) was initialed by Peres representing Israel and Abbas representing the PLO. As Rabin had predicted in his Knesset speech thirteen months earlier, neither the Palestinians nor Israel got everything they wanted. He was well aware he had made significant and painful concessions to an organization he once had said that Israel could only meet on the battlefield.

The Oslo agreement called for Israel to withdraw its military forces from most of the Gaza Strip and the West bank city of Jericho and its environs by April 1994. What were called "authorized Palestinians" would then take over most local governmental functions, including police protection. In the future, the complicated document provided for self-rule to be extended to most of the rest of the West Bank. However, while Arabs would have self-rule under an elected Palestinian Council, Israel would continue to control foreign affairs and defense and have authority over Jewish settlements throughout the territories. Many complex issues—including the timing and pace of additional withdrawals, security arrangements, final borders, the Israeli settlements, and Jerusalem—were left for future negotiations over a five-year period.

When the Oslo accord was made public, a clear majority of Israelis supported it. Still, there was strong opposition from many quarters in Israeli society. Likud's new leader, Benjamin Netanyahu, the younger brother of "Yoni" Netanyahu, warned that the Oslo accord would lead to a Palestinian state and represented the "start of the destruction of Israel in line with the PLO plan."[15] Thousands of Jewish settlers from the West Bank and other Israelis who supported them demonstrated in protest. Rabin himself openly admitted that he had doubts. He told his Labor colleagues that he had no illusions about the PLO:

> *They killed. They are murderers, but peace you make with your enemies, including despicable enemies. I'm not going to beautify them. I can't tell you that some formulas in the agreement don't give me stomach pains. I have such pains, but I have to see also the comprehensive picture. We have to take risks.[16]*

On September 9, Yasir Arafat wrote a letter to Rabin in which he explicitly stated for the first time that the PLO recognized Israel's right to exist and accepted UN Resolutions 242 and 338. The next day, Prime Minister Rabin sent Arafat a letter recognizing the PLO. On September 13, both men, along with Peres and Abbas, stood on the White House lawn in Washington, D.C., with President Bill Clinton for an official signing of the Oslo accord. Rabin was proud of his role in reaching an agreement that could provide the basis for an Israeli-Palestinian peace. He knew that the picture of him shaking hands with Arafat was considered by people across the globe as a historic breakthrough.

Yet the White House ceremony and especially the handshake with Arafat were very difficult for Rabin. He could barely contain the personal loathing he felt for the PLO chairman. An Israeli reporter observed:

> *Rabin's body language seemed to communicate virtual physical pain. He twisted and turned constantly and the expression on his face—*

Rabin, President Clinton and Yasir Arafat pose for photographers prior to signing the peace accord agreed to in Oslo. The ceremony was difficult for Rabin, as he weighed the realization that he had negotiated with the PLO, which he'd sworn never to do, against the hope of security and peace for Israel.

*particularly when he reached out to shake Arafat's
hand—remained an uncomfortable grimace
throughout the ceremony.*[17]

As Rabin put it later, "Of all the hands in the world, it
was not the hand I wanted or even dreamed of touching."[18] Yet he did so, because, as he told the small crowd
on the White House lawn and the world watching on
television, the time finally had come for "a new reckoning in the relations between peoples." In his short speech,
Rabin quoted the timeless words from the Biblical book
of Ecclesiastes:

> *To every thing there is a season and a time to every
> purpose under heaven. A time to be born and a
> time to die, a time to kill and a time to heal. A
> time to weep and a time to laugh. A time to love
> and a time to hate, a time of war and a time of
> peace.*

Then he added, "Ladies and gentlemen, the time for
peace has come."[19]

When he returned home, Rabin had to defend the
Oslo accord agreement in front of a divided Knesset,
where even some Labor members had serious doubts
about dealing with the PLO. Rabin rose to the occasion,
telling his colleagues:

> *Members of the Knesset, we cannot choose our
> neighbors, or our enemies, not even the cruelest
> among them. We only have what there is. The
> PLO has fought against us, and we have fought
> against them—and with them we are today seeking*

a path to peace.... We have the moral right not to sit at the negotiating table with the PLO...not to shake the hand that pulled the trigger. We have the power to reject with revulsion the PLO proposals— and then to be unwilling partners to the continuing cycle with which we have been forced to live until now: war, terrorism, and violence.[20]

After a heated debate the Knesset ratified the Oslo accord by a vote of 61 to 50, with nine members abstaining. The governing body of the PLO did likewise. Israeli-Palestinian relations were about to enter a new and promising, but also difficult and dangerous, era. Yitzhak Rabin personally was fated to do the same.

CHAPTER NINE

"I am not afraid."

The signing of the Oslo accord was only the beginning of what everyone involved knew would be a long and arduous peace process. Difficult negotiations lay ahead in order to resolve many thorny issues and implement the overall agreement. Rabin was well aware that the Oslo accord and future agreements would require Israel to make enormous concessions and take great risks. He also knew that he already had asked his people to accept conditions that he had emphatically rejected as recently as the election campaign of 1992. Not the least of them was the fact that he had negotiated with the PLO.

Rabin therefore knew it was crucial for the peace process that the PLO uphold its end of the bargain. Above all, Rabin and the Israeli public demanded an end to Palestinian terrorism that had taken so many lives. If the terrorism did not end, it would be extremely difficult for Rabin to get his people to go along with the peace process. Simply put, the peace process had to provide less violence and more peace.

During the following year the Oslo accord achieved nothing of the kind. In the last quarter of 1993 a wave of Hamas terror and murder left sixteen Israelis dead. Arafat and the PLO, who according to Oslo were supposed to represent and speak for the Palestinian people, seemed either unwilling or unable to control Hamas. The Israeli public reacted angrily. Support for the Oslo accord and for Rabin himself dropped noticeably.

On February 25, 1994, the peace process was nearly derailed by the mad act of an extremist Jewish settler from the town of Qiryat Arba near Hebron. Acting entirely on his own, the settler shot and killed 29 Muslims praying at the Tomb of the Patriarchs in Hebron, a site holy to both Jews and Muslims, and was himself beaten to death. Although Rabin and every leading Israeli politician denounced the crime in horror, the PLO suspended negotiations on implementing the Declaration of Principles (DOP) for a month.

Meanwhile, the Hamas-led wave of terror against Israel continued. By the end of 1994 the total number of bombing, shooting, and stabbing attacks exceeded 35. The worst occurred in October 1994 in Tel Aviv, when a suicide bomber blew himself up on a crowded morning rush-hour bus, killing 22 people and wounding 47. In January 1995, another suicide bomber killed 21 Israelis at a bus stop, most of them young soldiers. By then many Israelis agreed with President Ezer Weizman, a long-time advocate of peace negotiations, who said, "If the peace process is paved on the bodies of dead Jews, then I take it back."[1]

Nor did certain comments by Arafat help Rabin boost Israeli confidence in the peace process. In May 1994 a tape of Arafat speaking in a mosque became public. In his speech he called for a *jihad*–or holy war–for Jerusalem. Even more disconcerting, Arafat compared the Oslo accord to a truce that the prophet Mohammed had made with a Jewish tribe in Arabia early in the seventh century. From the start Mohammed considered the truce strictly a tactical maneuver until he could gain strength; he broke the truce ten years later and wiped out the Jewish tribe. Another serious problem for Rabin was the failure of Arafat and the PLO to honor their commitment to revise the PLO Covenant by eliminating the clauses calling for the destruction of Israel.

Rabin and Peres nonetheless held to their course. Echoing Ben-Gurion's words on the Yishuv's dual struggle with the British and the Nazis during World War II, Rabin said, "We shall fight the terror as if there were no peace talks, and we will conduct the peace talks as if there were no terror."[2]

Negotiations continued with the Palestinians on the specifics of the Israeli withdrawal from Gaza and Jericho. Rabin knew that despite support for the peace process, many Israelis remained skeptical and fearful. He was aware of the criticism that Peres and his dovish views played too large a role in the Oslo accord. He also was driven by his usual emphasis on security and the fact that he had more confidence in IDF officers than foreign ministry officials. Rabin therefore initially put top military officers in charge of the negotiations, although he later decided that Peres should lead the Israeli team. The result was an agreement completed in May 1994–five months behind schedule–more than 300 pages long (the

DOP was only 23 pages), filled with elaborate guarantees of military security even as Israel withdrew from Gaza and Jericho.

Rabin and Peres knew that in the wake of continued terrorist attacks they had to show results on several fronts to keep the peace process alive. October 1994 proved to be a good month for the Rabin-Peres team. The Nobel Prize selection committee in Oslo announced that the two men would share the 1994 Nobel Peace Prize with Arafat. (One of the committee's members resigned over the award to Arafat, citing the PLO leader's violent past.) Far more important, on October 26, Israel signed a peace treaty with Jordan. The treaty had been in the works for over a year, and was preceded by several preliminary agreements. Israel accepted a small change in the border in Jordan's favor and agreed to share more of the water from the Jordan and Yarmuk rivers with its eastern neighbor.

The actual signing of the peace treaty, in a dusty Jordanian border village just north of the Israeli town of Eilat and the Jordanian town of Aqaba, was a deeply emotional moment for both sides. It was not a gathering of strangers: Rabin, Peres, and other Israeli leaders had met with King Hussein many times over the years. In contrast to how he felt about Yasir Arafat, Rabin had both respect and genuine affection for Hussein. Rabin made this clear during his short speech when he addressed the king:

> *Your Majesty.....I have learned to know and admire the quiet and the smiling power with which you guard your nation and the courage with which you lead your people. It is not*

only...our states that are making peace with
each other today, not only our nations that are
shaking hands in peace here....You and I, Your
Majesty, are making peace here, our own peace,
the peace of soldiers and the peace of friends.[3]

Hussein expressed similar sentiments, both for Rabin and other Israeli leaders present such as Peres and Weizman, men he referred to as "colleagues and friends." The Jordanian king stressed that he envisioned the type of genuine peace that Israelis wanted to see. It would not be like the disappointing "Cold Peace" with Egypt, which the Egyptians had kept strictly limited to a formal relationship between governments with little contact between Egyptians and Israelis. Instead, said Hussein:

This is a peace of dignity. This is peace with
commitment. This is our gift to our peoples
and the generations to come. It will herald the
change in the quality of life of people. It will
not simply be a piece of paper ratified by those
responsible, blessed by the world. It will be real,
as we open our hearts and minds to each other,
as we discover a human face to everything that
has happened and to each other—for all of us
have suffered for too long.[4]

Virtually all Israelis agreed that the Jordanian treaty held great promise at an acceptable risk. Netanyahu and the Likud lined up behind the agreement. It passed the Knesset by an overwhelming vote of 105 to 3, with 6 abstentions. It was not easy to recall any issue that so united that generally contentious body.

Nevertheless, it did not take long until bitter divisions again plagued the peace process, especially as the terror continued and more Israelis died. By April 1995, less than half of all Israelis favored the peace process, and more supported Netanyahu for prime minister than supported Rabin. The language of Israeli politics, never restrained and sometimes unacceptably strident by American standards, grew increasingly heated. Those for and against the peace process hurled insults at each other, both from political platforms and in the streets. It seemed to many that the "peace process" was beginning to tear Israel apart.

Some of those who disagreed with Rabin came from the ranks of his own Labor party. They formed a new organization called The Third Way. This group—it was not a political party—positioned itself between Likud, which opposed all territorial concessions, and Labor, which clearly was preparing for extensive concessions in the West Bank and possibly a complete return of the Golan Heights to Syria in return for a peace treaty. (Israel was negotiating separately with Syria as well as with the PLO.) The Third Way was headed by Avigdor Kahalani, a Labor member of parliament and a military hero in both the Six-Day and Yom Kippur wars. Another leader was Dan Shomron, the overall commander at Entebbe and a former IDF chief of staff.

Still, negotiations with the PLO continued, this time with the goal of extending the Gaza-Jericho agreement and Palestinian self-rule to much of the West Bank. The terror bombings also continued, killing ten Israelis in two bus attacks in July and August. Finally, an agreement that has become known as Oslo II was reached. Its official signing took place on the White House lawn on September 28, 1995. Oslo II initially divided the West Bank into three zones. Area "A", about 3 percent of the land, included the region's major urban areas, where the Palestinians would be given full territorial and security control during late 1995 and early 1996. Area "B" included about 465 Palestinian villages and 27 percent of the land. Here Israel would turn over partial control to the Palestinians during 1996, but retain control of military security. The remainder of the West Bank (Area "C") would remain under Israeli control until a final settlement was reached. It included all the Israeli settlements and the uninhabited parts of the region, including the Jordan River valley.

Oslo II met with stiff opposition in Israel. The Knesset staged a marathon fifteen-hour debate, during which more than 100 of its 120 members spoke. Rabin vigorously defended the agreement, stressing its security arrangements. He also pointed out that Israel, a democratic society, could not continue to rule the large Arab population of the West Bank and Gaya:

> *We had to choose between a Greater Land of Israel, which means a binational state and whose population would comprise, as of today, 4.5 million Jews and more than 3 million Palestinians, which are a separate entity— religious, political and national—and a state smaller in area, but which would be a Jewish state. We chose a Jewish state.[5]*

Tempers flared, as Rabin, Netanyahu, and others angrily attacked each other. Critics said the agreement was paving the way for Israel's return virtually to its insecure

1967 borders and the creation of a Palestinian state. In the end, the Knesset approved Oslo II by the narrowest possible margin, 61 to 59. Among those voting no were Kahalani and another Labor member of The Third Way. Rabin's critics were quick to point out that 5 of his 61 votes came from Arab members of the Knesset. Among the Knesset's Jewish delegates, only 56 voted for Oslo II, while 59 voted against. Meanwhile, public-opinion polls showed continued confusion and doubt: support for the peace process but also a lack of confidence in the agreements reached with the PLO.

In the aftermath of the Oslo II vote, Israel's political atmosphere grew even more stormy. In many ways the angry divisions were reminiscent of what Rabin had seen and lamented as ambassador to the United States during the Vietnam War. About a week after the vote, he was invited to speak at a gathering of immigrants from English-speaking countries. Some people in the crowd shouted him down. Rabin was furious and told the crowd so. Meanwhile, at antigovernment rallies some angry protesters called Rabin a traitor. Concern spread among politicians on both sides that matters were getting out of hand. On several occasions Netanyahu criticized anti-Rabin protesters for going too far. "We'll win by the vote, not by violence," he told one crowd.[6] In the Labor camp, Rabin's advisors feared for his safety, but he refused to take precautions such as wearing a bulletproof vest. "I am not afraid personally," he said. "I will not run away and let them silence me."[7]

Like every democracy, Israel has its seething and hostile political fringe where fanatical people scheme to silence those with whom they disagree. In 1963 in the United States a fanatic assassinated President John F.

Kennedy; in 1968, Rabin's first year as ambassador, fanatics took the lives of Martin Luther King, Jr., and Senator Robert F. Kennedy. In Israel, small groups of Jewish extremist West Bank settlers and their supporters belonged to that violent fringe. In February 1994 one of them murdered the Arab worshippers in Hebron, an act that horrified virtually all Israelis. On November 4, 1995, another fanatic struck, this time against Prime Minister Yitzhak Rabin.

Rabin was assassinated at a huge rally organized by the Labor party to counter opposition rallies and to demonstrate support for the peace process. More than 100,000 people gathered in Tel Aviv's Kings of Israel Square to cheer for Rabin and Peres and their policies. It was an extraordinary event. Normally ill at ease in public, Rabin on this day was relaxed and clearly enjoying himself. Revitalized by a sense that the country indeed supported him, Rabin spoke passionately to the crowd. "This government, which I have the privilege to head with my friend Shimon Peres, decided to give peace a chance," he said.[8] After his speech, Rabin joined with his audience in singing the "Song of Peace," a hit from the 1970s that over the years had become one of the most popular songs in Israel. Then, standing on the platform with Peres, he put his arm around his old rival, who after decades of feuding he finally could call "my friend," and greeted well-wishers.

When the time came to leave, Rabin walked to a waiting car. A young Jewish law student named Yigal Amir waited in the shadows. Amir held extreme religious views; he later told police that he had "received instructions from God to kill Prime Minister Rabin."[9] After months of stalking the prime minister, Amir finally

Speaking at the giant peace demonstration on November 4, 1995, one hour before an assassin's bullet would take his life.

had slipped through the tight security net that surrounded his prey. It was 9:40 P.M. Shots rang out. One of Rabin's bodyguards immediately threw himself on the prime minister, stopping one of the bullets with his own body. Within seconds Rabin was in the car and within two minutes in a hospital. But it was too late. The two bullets that hit the prime minister did massive damage. Desperate efforts by doctors to save him failed. Yitzhak Rabin, who had survived so many battles, was dead.

The assassination stunned Israel and much of the world. Israeli life came to a stop. An entire nation stood as if in a daze. People hardly knew what to think or say. The nation mourned, both for its fallen leader and for itself. In this small country, under siege for its entire history, where all young people answered the call of national defense and no family could escape the pain of war and terror, people were used to mourning together, as a family, when others lost a loved one to enemy fire or bombs. Where else did national leaders regularly attend the funerals of fallen soldiers or victims of terror? Yet something had gone terribly wrong. The intensity of the debate had flared out of control and created an atmosphere of anger and intolerance in which extremists could unleash their fury. Over the years Israelis, and especially their politicians, certainly had their differences, but who could have believed that the divisions and anger would come to this?

On November 5, a million people, nearly one Israeli in five, filed past Rabin's simple pine coffin at the Knesset. Rabin was buried on Monday, November 6. Leaders from more than eighty countries attended the funeral. Yasir Arafat asked to attend, but was not permitted for security reasons. The ceremony was carried live

Rabin's assassination provoked deep anguish in people around the world. Here an Arab man cries at a roadside memorial.

on television in countries throughout the world. Israeli and foreign leaders spoke of Rabin with deep respect and affection. Shimon Peres, speaking for "a nation with tears in their eyes," grieved the loss of the "youngest among Israel's generals...the greatest of Israel's peace-makers" and a man he called "my eldest brother." King Hussein mourned "a brother, a colleague and friend" who "lived as a soldier and died as a soldier for peace." President Bill Clinton told the Israeli people that he joined them in mourning the loss of "my partner and friend." The American president added that "Israel's covenant with God—for freedom, for tolerance, for security for peace—that covenant must hold. That covenant was Prime Minister Rabin's life work, now we must make it his lasting legacy."[10]

The most moving eulogy came not from a world leader but from seventeen-year-old Noa Ben-Artzi Filosof, Yitzhak Rabin's granddaughter. Her freckled face and reddish-brown hair, as well as her self-control, could not help but evoke memories of a young Yitzhak Rabin. Noa apologized for not wanting to talk about peace; she wanted to talk about her *saba*, her grandfather. She recalled "the caresses of your warm soft hands...your warm embrace that was reserved only for us...your half smile that always told me so much, that same smile which is no longer." Struggling to hold back tears, she concluded: "I imagine angels are accompanying you now and I ask them to take care of you, because you deserve their protection."[11]

When Israel lost Yitzhak Rabin, it lost a soldier and a statesman. It lost a military hero who knew how to prepare for and fight wars, and who did so brilliantly. It lost a political leader who understood that no war is com-

*Rabin's granddaughter, Noa Ben-Artzi Filosof, weeps as she
delivers the eulogy not for Rabin the statesman and soldier,
but for Yitzhak Rabin, her grandfather.*

pletely won unless the victory leads to peace. It lost a patriot who when waging war or making peace was guided by a stern and consistent realism, an outlook that demanded caution in preparing for battles or negotiations but sanctioned taking risks when the situation demanded. It lost a prime minister prepared to make the hard decisions, capable of adjusting to new conditions, and fortified with the inner strength to see things through. And it lost a visionary who did not let his dream for peace make him lose sight of the reality that Israel always had to protect its security.

When Yitzhak Rabin died he was at the center of an emotional public debate. His popularity had declined since 1992, and it was not at all certain that he and Labor would win the upcoming elections in 1996. Israelis of goodwill and common sense who wanted peace could be found on both sides of the debate over the peace process, with strong arguments to support their positions. But despite Israel's divisions and disagreements, Rabin was convinced that he had compelling reasons to continue his policies. As he told the crowd in Tel Aviv only ninety minutes before his assassination:

> *I was a military man for twenty-seven years. I waged war as long as there was no chance for peace. I believe there is now a chance for peace, a great chance, and we must take advantage of it.*[12]

That job has now fallen to his successors.

CHRONOLOGY

1920   Nehemiah Rabin meets Rosa Cohen in
            Jerusalem after each rushes to the Old City
            to help protect local Jews under attack from
            Arab rioters.

1921   Rabin and Cohen are married.

1922   March 1: Yitzhak Rabin is born in Jerusalem.

1936   Arab Revolt in Palestine begins.

1937   October: Rabin enters the Kadoorie Agricul-
            tural High School.

            November: Rosa Cohen dies from heart
            disease.

1939   September: World War II begins.

1940   Rabin graduates from high school; declines opportunity to study water engineering at the University of California at Berkeley.

1941   Rabin joins the Palmach and takes part in sabotage mission in Lebanon.

1943   Rabin is promoted to platoon leader.

1944   Rabin meets Leah Schlossberg.

1945   May: World War II ends. The full extent of the Nazi genocide against the Jews becomes known. The Yishuv smuggles Jewish refugees into Palestine in defiance of the British.

        October: Rabin helps lead the Atlit raid.

1946   June: Rabin is arrested along with other Hagana activists, including his father. They are held until November.

        November: Rabin decides once again not to attend Berkeley. He takes command of the Palmach's Second Battalion instead.

1947   February: Britain decides to give up its mandate and leave Palestine.

        October: Yigal Allon appoints Rabin deputy commander of the Palmach.

        November 19: The UN General Assembly votes to divide Palestine into a Jewish state and an Arab state. The Jews accept the decision; the Arabs reject it. Arabs begin attacking Jews throughout Palestine.

1948	April: The Harel Brigade under Rabin's command fights to keep open the road to Jerusalem and defend the Jewish Quarter in the Old City. The battle continues into May.
	May 14: Israel officially declares its independence.
	May 15: Five Arab armies invade Israel. The War of Independence officially begins.
	May 28: The Jewish Quarter falls to the Arab Legion. Rabin watches the surrender take place from just outside the Old City walls.
	June-July: Israeli resistance stiffens, and the tide of battle turns in Israel's favor.
	August 23: Yitzhak Rabin and Leah Schlossberg are married.
	October-December: Israeli forces on the southern front, where Allon is commander and Rabin is deputy commander, win major victories.
1949	January: Armistice talks begin on Rhodes. Rabin is part of the Israeli delegation.
	February: Armistice agreement is signed.
	March: Israel is admitted to the United Nations.
1950	The Rabins' daughter, Dalia, is born. A son, Yuval, is born in 1955.
1951	Rabin becomes head of the IDF operations division. He is now on the IDF's general staff.

1952	The Rabins move to Zahala
1952-1953	Rabin studies at the British army's Royal Staff College in Camberley, England.
1954	Rabin is promoted to rank of major-general.
1956	Rabin is appointed commander of the Northern Command. October-November: The Sinai Campaign. Israel overruns the Gaza Strip and the Sinai Peninsula.
1957	Israel withdraws from Sinai. A UN peacekeeping force is positioned in the Sinai.
1959	Rabin becomes the IDF's second-ranking officer after a shake-up of its top command.
1964	January 1: Rabin becomes the IDF Chief of Staff. May: Palestine Liberation Organization is formed.
1965	The IDF destroys the Syrian project to divert tributaries of the Jordan River.
1966	Prime Minister Eshkol asks Rabin to serve another year as chief of staff.
1967	May: Egypt sends troops into the Sinai Peninsula. UN peace-keeping troops withdraw. Egypt blockades the Straits of Tiran. Arab troops mass along Israel's borders.

May 23–24: Rabin suffers from nervous exhaustion. He returns to work on May 25.

June 5: Israel attacks Egyptian airfields. The Six-Day War begins.

June 7: Israeli troops take the Old City and the Western Wall.

June 10: The Six-Day War ends. Israel controls the West Bank, the Gaza Strip, all of Jerusalem, and the Golan Heights.

November 22: The UN Security Council passes Resolution 242.

1968   March: Rabin begins his tour of duty as Israel's ambassador to the United States. He serves in that post until 1973.

1969   Golda Meir becomes prime minister.

1969-1970   The War of Attrition along the Suez Canal.

1970   September: "Black September" in Jordan. Israel responds to American request to aid Jordan in the face of Syrian tank incursion.

September 28: Gamal Abdel Nasser dies. He is succeeded as president of Egypt by Anwar Sadat.

1972   September: PLO terrorists murder eleven Israeli athletes at the Olympic Games at Munich.

1973   Rabin returns to Israel and enters politics as member of the Labor party.

October 6: Egypt and Syria attack Israel. The Yom Kippur War begins. Israel defeats the invaders but suffers very high casualties.

December: Labor wins elections. Rabin becomes minister of labor in Golda Meir's new cabinet.

1974   April: Meir and Defense Minister Moshe Dayan resign after public criticism of their failure to prepare Israel for war. Rabin defeats Shimon Peres for the post of leader of the Labor party.

June 3: Prime Minister Rabin presents his government to the Knesset. Peres becomes defense minister. The two men feud throughout Rabin's tenure as prime minister.

1975   April: PLO terrorists murder eighteen people in Kiryat Shmona.

May: PLO terrorist attack leaves twenty children dead in Ma'alot.

September: After long and tedious negotiations conducted by U.S. Secretary of State Henry Kissinger, a separation of forces agreement is reached between Israel and Egypt involving significant Israeli withdrawals in the Sinai.

1976   June–July: Arab and German terrorists hijack an Air France jet with many Israeli passengers to Entebbe, Uganda. The hostages are rescued in a daring raid mounted by the IDF.

1977	March: Scandal of Leah Rabin's U.S. bank account leads to Rabin's resignation as prime minister.
	May: Likud defeats labor in national elections. Menachem Begin becomes prime minister.
1977–1984	Rabin is an opposition member of the Knesset.
1977	November: Sadat comes to Jerusalem.
1978	September: Camp David Accords are signed.
1979	March: Israeli-Egyptian peace treaty is signed. The agreement with Egypt turns out to be a "Cold Peace."
1980	December: Peres defeats Rabin for post of Labor party leader.
1981	June: Israel bombs and destroys Iraq's nuclear reactor.
1982	June: Israel invades Lebanon to drive the PLO from the southern part of the country, but becomes bogged down there.
1983	August: Begin suddenly retires and is replaced as prime minister by Yitzhak Shamir.
1984	September: National Unity government is formed after deadlocked election. Rabin is named minister of defense.

1987	December: The Intifada begins. Rabin responds with "iron fist" policy, but cannot stop the uprising.
1988	November: Another dead-heat election. Unity government continues with Rabin still minister of defense.
1990	March: Labor quits the unity government.
	July: Peres again defeats Rabin for Labor party leadership.
1991	January: The Gulf War. United States-led coalition drives Iraqi forces from Kuwait. Israel is attacked by Iraqi Scud missiles but agrees not to respond to the attack.
	October: Madrid peace conference opens.
1992	February: Rabin defeats Peres for Labor party leadership.
	June: Labor defeats Likud in national elections.
	July: Rabin again becomes prime minister. Peres is foreign minister in the new Labor government.
	December: Israel deports more than 400 Hamas activists to Lebanon.
	December: Secret talks between Israelis and representatives of the PLO begin in London. They continue in Oslo, Norway.

1993   February: Rabin is informed of the Oslo talks and decides to pursue them.

March: Rabin seals off the West Bank and Gaza.

July: The IDF bombards Lebanon.

August: Oslo negotiations are completed, and a Declaration of Principles (DOP) is signed.

September 9–10: PLO recognizes Israel's right to exist and UN Resolution 242. Israel recognizes PLO.

September 13: Formal signing of DOP at the White House. Rabin and Arafat shake hands.

October: Knesset ratifies the Oslo accord.

1994   May: Agreement is reached on the details of Israel's withdrawal from Gaza and Jericho.

October: Announcement that Rabin, Peres, and Arafat will share the 1994 Nobel Peace Prize.

October 26: Peace treaty signed with Jordan.

1995   Hamas terrorist attacks continue to take many Israeli lives. Israel is deeply divided over the peace process.

September 28: Oslo II, which extends Palestinian self-rule to much of the West Bank, is signed at the White House.

1995   October: After heated debate, the Knesset approves Oslo II by a vote of 61 to 59. A majority of Jewish members of the Knesset oppose the agreement.

October: Rabin is heckled while trying to address a gathering of English-speaking immigrants.

November 4: Yitzhak Rabin is assassinated after speaking at a huge and enthusiastic peace rally in Tel Aviv.

NOTES

Chapter One

1. Yitzhak Rabin, *The Rabin Memoirs* (Boston: Little, Brown, 1979), p. 15.
2. Ibid.
3. Ibid. p. 16.
4. Ibid.
5. Ibid.
6. Ibid. p. 17.
7. Quoted in Robert Slater, *Rabin of Israel* (New York: St. Martin's Press, 1993), p. 57.

Chapter Two

1. *The Rabin Memoirs*, p. 3.
2. Ibid. p. 5.
3. Quoted in Abba Eban, *My Country: The Story of Modern Israel* (New York: Random House, 1972), p. 10.

4. *The Rabin Memoirs*, p. 6.
5. Ibid.
6. Quoted in Slater, *Rabin of Israel*, p. 28.
7. *The Rabin Memoirs*, p. 6.
8. Quoted in Slater, p. 29.
9. *The Rabin Memoirs*, p. 6.
10. Quoted in Slater, p. 41.
11. Quoted in Slater, p. 43.
12. Quoted in Conner Cruise O'Brien, *The Siege: The Story of Israel and Zionism* (London: Paladin, 1986), p. 233.
13. Quoted in O'Brien, pp. 242–243.
14. ABC News Documentary, "Rabin: Action Biography," April 15, 1975.
15. *The Rabin Memoirs*, pp. 11–12.
16. Ibid. p. 13
17. Ibid.
18. Ibid. p. 35.
19. Quoted in Slater, p. 51.
20. *The Rabin Memoirs*, p. 35.

Chapter Three

1. Quoted in Howard M. Sachar, *A History of Israel: From the Rise of Zionism to Our Time* (New York: Knopf, 1976), p. 270.
2. *The Rabin Memoirs*, p. 17.
3. Ibid. p. 19.
4. Quoted in Eban, *My Country: The Story of Modern Israel*, p. 48.
5. *The Rabin Memoirs*, p. 19.
6. Quoted in Eban, p. 9.
7. *The Rabin Memoirs*, p. 29.
8. Quoted in Eban, p. 12.
9. Quoted in Sachar, p. 297.
10. *The Rabin Memoirs*, p. 32.

11. Quoted in Eban, p. 57.
12. *The Rabin Memoirs*, p. 36.
13. Quoted in Slater, *Rabin of Israel: Warrior for Peace*, p. 82.
14. *The Rabin Memoirs*, p. 42.

Chapter Four

1. *Al-Misri*, April 12, 1954. (An Egyptian newspaper)
2. *The Rabin Memoirs*, p. 45.
3. Quoted in Slater, *Rabin of Israel: Warrior for Peace*, p. 104.
4. *Middle East Affairs*, December 1956, p. 461.
5. *The Rabin Memoirs*, p. 52.
6. Ibid. p. 62.
7. Ibid. p. 63.
8. Quoted in Slater, p. 112.
9. *The Rabin Memoirs*, p. 68.
10. Quoted in Sachar, *A History of Israel*, p. 616.
11. Quoted in Slater, p. 125.
12. *The Rabin Memoirs*, p. 81.
13. Ibid. p. 81.
14. Quoted in Slater, p. 130.
15. Quoted in *The Rabin Memoirs*, p. 87.
16. Quoted in Ian Black and Benny Morris, *Israel's Secret Wars: A History of Israel's Intelligence* (London: Futura, 1991), p. 220.
17. Ibid.
18. Quoted in Sachar, p. 633.
19. Quoted in Eban, p. 214.
20. Quoted in Nadav Safran, *From War to War: The Arab-Israeli Confrontation, 1948–1967* (New York: Pegasus, 1969), p. 324.
21. *The Rabin Memoirs*, p. 104.
22. Quoted in Slater, p. 139.

23. Quoted in Safran, p. 348.
24. Quoted in *The Rabin Memoirs*, p. 108.
25. *The Rabin Memoirs*, pp. 111–112.
26. Quoted in *The Rabin Memoirs*, p. 115.
27. Quoted in Slater, pp. 148–149.

Chapter Five

1. Quoted in *The Rabin Memoirs*, p. 122.
2. Quoted in Sachar, *A History of Israel*, p. 673.
3. Ibid.
4. "Resolutions of the Khartoum Conference," in Ian J. Bickerton and Carla L. Klausner, *A Concise History of the Arab-Israeli Conflict*, 2nd ed. (Englewood Cliffs, NJ: Prentice Hall, 1995), p. 157.
5. *The Rabin Memoirs*, p. 125.
6. Ibid. pp. 127–128.
7. Quoted in Slater, *Rabine of Israel*, p. 188.
8. Quoted in Yossi Melman and Dan Raviv, *Friends in Deed: Inside the U.S.-Israeli Alliance* (New York: Hyperion, 1994), p. 157.
9. *The Rabin Memoirs*, p. 231.
10. Henry Kissinger, *White House Years* (Boston: Little, Brown, 1979), p. 355.
11. *The Rabin Memoirs*, p. 169.
12. Ibid. p. 198.
13. Ibid. pp. 226–227.
14. Ibid. p. 232.
15. Quoted in Slater, p. 189.

Chapter Six

1. Quoted in Sachar, *A History of Israel*, p. 740.
2. Golda Meir, *My Life* (London: Weidenfeld and Nicolson, 1975), p. 359.

3. *The Rabin Memoirs*, pp. 235–236.
4. Quoted in Chaim Herzog, *The War of Atonement: October 1973* (Boston: Little, Brown, 1975), p. 113.
5. *The Rabin Memoirs*, p. 236.
6. Ibid. p. 238.
7. Shimon Peres, *Battling for Peace: A Memoir*, edited by David Landau (New York: Random House, 1995), p. 144.
8. Ibid. p. 240.
9. Ibid. p. 241
10. Quoted in Slater, *Rabin of Israel*, p. 219.
11. *The Rabin Memoirs.* p. 242.
12. Ibid. p. 247.
13. Quoted in Slater, p. 237.
14. *The Rabin Memoirs*, p. 256.
15. Quoted in Howard Sachar, *A History of Israel: Volume II, From the Aftermath of the Yom Kippur War* (New York and Oxford: Oxford University Press, 1987), p. 7.
16. Quoted in William Stevenson, *90 Minutes to Entebbe* (New York: Bantam Books, 1976), pp. 82–83.
17. Quoted in Slater, p. 252.
18. Quoted in Stevenson, pp. 121–122.
19. *The Rabin Memoirs*, p. 288.
20. Quoted in Sachar, *A History of Israel*, vol. II, p. 19.

Chapter Seven

1. Quoted in Slater, *Rabin of Israel*, p. 299.
2. Quoted in O'Connor, p. 574.
3. *The Rabin Memoirs*, pp. 322-323.
4. Ibid. p. 324.
5. Ibid. p. 329.
6. Quoted in Sachar, *A History of Israel*, vol. II, p. 127.
7. Quoted in Slater, p. 318.
8. Quoted in Slater, p. 325.

9. *Time*, February 2, 1985.
10. Quoted in Slater, p. 340.
11. Quoted in Ze'ev Schiff and Ehud Ya'ari, *Intifada: The Inside Story of the Uprising That Changed the Middle East Equation* (New York: Simon & Schuster, 1989), p.144.
12. Quoted in Slater, p. 342.
13. Quoted in Bickerton and Klausner, *A Concise History of the Arab-Israeli Conflict*, p. 229.

Chapter Eight

1. Quoted in Slater, *Rabin of Israel*, p. 377.
2. Quoted in Gideon Doron, "Labor's Return to Power in Israel." *Current History*, January 1993, p. 30.
3. *The Jerusalem Post*, June 1, 1992.
4. Quoted in Slater, p. 401.
5. *Battling for Peace*, p. 272.
6. Quoted in the preface to *The Rabin Memoirs*, 2nd ed. (Bnei Brak, Israel: Steimatsky Ltd., 1994), pp. v–vi.
7. Ibid. p. 9.
8. Quoted in Slater, p. 446.
9. Quoted in Slater, p. 448.
10. Quoted in David Makovsky, *Making Peace With the PLO: The Rabin Government's Road to the Oslo Accord* (Boulder, CO: Westview Press, 1996), p. 87.
11. Mahmoud Abbas (Abu Mazen), *Through Secret Channels*, pp. 103–104.
12. Quoted in *The Rabin Memoirs*, 2nd ed., p. v.
13. Quoted in Makovsky, p. 119.
14. *Battling for Peace*, p. 285.
15. Quoted in Bickerton and Klausner, p. 269.
16. Quoted in Robert Slater, *Rabin of Israel: Warrior for Peace* (New York: HarperCollins, 1996), p. 583. Note that all other Slater citations refer to 1993 edition cited in Chapter One, note 7.

17. Makovsky, p. 81.
18. *Time*, November 13, 1995, p. 71.
19. "Rabin Statement at Signing of Accord," in Bickerton and Klausner, p. 283.
20. Quoted in Howard M. Sachar, *A History of Israel From the Rise of Zionism to Our Time*, 2nd ed., revised and updated (New York: Knopf, 1996), p. 993.

Chapter Nine

1. Quoted in Slater, *Rabin of Israel*, p. 599.
2. Quoted in Slater, p. 588.
3. *The New York Times*, October 27, 1994, p. A12.
4. Ibid.
5. *The Jerusalem Post International Edition*, October 14, 1995, p. 2.
6. *The Jerusalem Post International Edition*, October 21, 1995, p. 4.
7. Ibid.
8. *The Jerusalem Post International Edition*, November 11, 1995, p. 3.
9. Ibid. p. 2.
10. *The New York Times*, November 7, 1995, p. A10.
11. Ibid. p. A11.
12. *The Jerusalem Post International Edition*, November 11, 1995, p. 3.

BIBLIOGRAPHY

Abbas, Mahmoud (Abu Mazen). *Through Secret Channels.* Reading, England: Garnett, 1995.

Bickerton, Ian J. and Carla L. Klausner. *A Concise History of the Arab-Israeli Conflict,* 2nd ed. Englewood Cliffs, NJ: Prentice Hall, 1995.

Black, Ian and Benny Morris. *Israel's Secret Wars: A History of Israel's Secret Services.* London: Futura, 1991.

Freedman, Robert O., editor. *Israel Under Rabin.* Boulder, CO: Westview, 1995.

Golan, Matti. *Shimon Peres.* New York: St. Martin's Press, 1982.

Herzog, Chaim. *The War of Atonement: October, 1973.* Boston: Little, Brown, 1975.

Katz, Samuel M. *Soldier Spies: Israeli Military Intelligence.* Novato, CA: Presidio, 1992.

Laqueur, Walter and Barry Rubin, editors. *The Israel-Arab Reader: A Documentary History of the Middle East Conflict,* 5th revised and updated edition. New York and London: Penguin, 1995.

Livingstone Neil C. and David Halevy. *Inside the PLO.* New York: William Morrow, 1990.

Makovsky, David. *Making Peace With the PLO: The Rabin Government's Road to the Oslo Accord.* Boulder, CO: Westview, 1996.

Melman, Yossi and Dan Raviv. *Friends in Deed: Inside the U.S.-Israel Alliance.* New York: Hyperion, 1994.

O'Brien, Conor Cruise. *The Siege: The Story of Israel and Zionism.* London: Paladin, 1988.

Peres, Shimon. *Battling for Peace: A Memoir.* New York: Random House, 1995.

Perlmutter, Amos. *Israel: The Partitioned State: A Political History Since 1900.* New York: Charles Scribner's Sons, 1985.

Rabin, Yitzhak. *The Rabin Memoirs.* Boston: Little, Brown, 1979.

Sachar, Howard M. *A History of Israel From the Rise of Zionism to Our Time.* New York: Knopf, 1976.

Sachar, Howard M. *A History of Israel: Volume II, From the Aftermath of the Yom Kippur War.* New York and Oxford: Oxford University Press, 1987.

Safran, Nadav. *From War to War: The Arab-Israeli Confrontation, 1948-1967.* New York: Pegasus, 1969.

Schiff, Ze'ev and Ehud Ya'ari. *Intifada: The Inside Story of the Palestinian Uprising That Changed the Middle East Equation.* New York: Simon & Schuster, 1989.

Slater, Robert. *Rabin of Israel.* New York: St. Martin's Press, 1993.

Stevenson, William. *90 Minutes at Entebbe.* New York: Bantam, 1976.

INDEX

Graham, Billy, 91
Great Britain, 11-15, 19, 20, 27, 28, 30, 31, 35, 36, 38, 40, 41
Gulf of Aqaba (Gulf of Eilat), 56
Gulf War, 118, 127, 141
Gur, Mordechai ("Motta"), 71, 104, 106
Gush Emunim (Community of the Believers), 110

Haber, Eitan, 139
Hagana, 12, 15, 23, 30, 33, 38, 41, 42, 47
Haifa, 43, 70
Hamas, 125, 136, 138, 142, 149
Hamtana, 67
Harel Brigade, 43
Hebrew University, 77
Hebron, 17, 110, 149, 156
Hezbollah, 136, 138-139
Hod, Motti, 70
Holocaust, 34
Holocaust survivors, 11-14, 36, 55
Holst, Johan Jorgen, 140
Hussein, King, 88, 89, 109, 151-152, 160
Hussein, Saddam, 127

Intifada, 122-125, 131, 141
Iraq, 20, 42, 45, 46, 55, 68, 70, 118, 127
Irgun, 38, 39, 42, 113
Islamic Conference, 117
Israel, establishment of, 44
Israel Defense Forces (IDF), 48, 57-60, 62-64, 66, 68, 75, 95, 96, 100, 104, 106, 119-121, 123, 124, 150

Jackson, Henry, 85
Jaffa, 43
Jarring, Gunnar, 87
Jericho, 143, 150, 151
Jerusalem, 17, 18, 21-22, 40-43, 45-47, 52, 70, 71, 75, 79-80, 108
Jewish Legion, 19, 22
Johnson, Lyndon, 82, *83*, 84
Jordan, 20, 46, 52, 60, 64, 67, 69-72, 75, 80, 88-90, 93, 109, 115, 118, 128, 151-152
Jordan River, 63, 93, 151
Jordan Valley, 108, 109, 132, 154
Judea, 17, 109

Kahalani, Avigdor, 153, 155

Oil boycott, 97-98
Operation Nashon, 42-43
Operation Yonatan, 103-
104, *105*, 106-108
Osiraq nuclear reactor, 18
Oslo accord, 139-144, *145*,
146-150
Oslo II, 153-155

Palestine Liberation
Organization (PLO),
80-81, 87-89, 100-103,
109, 117, 119, 121-123,
125-128, 139, 141-144,
146-150, 153, 155
Palestinian National
Covenant, 80
Palmach, 12, 13, 30-33, 36,
38, 40, 42, 45, 57
Pasha, Azzam, 45
Peres, Shimon, 62, 98,
100, 104, 110, 114, 120,
121, 125-127, 129, 131,
133-134, 141-144, 150,
151, 156, 160
Pogroms, 20, 21, 42

Rabin, Dalia, 59, 82
Rabin, Leah Schlossberg,
15, 33-34, 48, *49*, 57, 59,
70, 82, 101, 104, 110,
112, 114, 120-121, 129-
130, 134

Rabin, Nehemiah, 16, 18-
23, 26, 40
Rabin, Rachel, 22, 23, *24*
Rabin, Rosa Cohen (*see*
Cohen, Rosa)
Rabin, Yitzhak, *29*, *51*, *86*,
157
as ambassador to U.S.,
78, 80-82, *83*, 84-85,
86, 87, 90-92
assassination of, 156,
158
Atlit operation and, 13-
15, 38
in Begin era, 114-116
birth of, 22
childhood of, 23, *24*, 25
children of, 59
courtship of Leah, 33-
34
death of mother, 26-27
education of, 25-28
emotional crises, 68, 99
Entebbe mission and,
104, 106, 108
financial affairs of, 110,
112
funeral of, 158, 160
honorary doctorate, 77
imprisoned by British,
40
invasion of Lebanon,
119-120

BOOKS BY JAMES DASHNER

The Mortality Doctrine Series
The Eye of Minds

The Maze Runner Series
The Maze Runner
The Scorch Trials
The Death Cure
The Kill Order

The 13th Reality Series
The Journal of Curious Letters
The Hunt for Dark Infinity
The Blade of Shattered Hope
The Void of Mist and Thunder

THE MAZE RUNNER

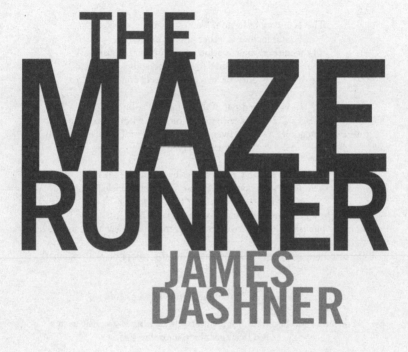

JAMES DASHNER

DELACORTE PRESS

Text copyright © 2009 by James Dashner
Cover images © 2014 Twentieth Century Fox Film Corporation
Interior photographs © 2014 Twentieth Century Fox Film Corporation
All rights reserved.

Published in the United States by Delacorte Press,
an imprint of Random House Children's Books,
a division of Random House LLC,
a Penguin Random House Company, New York.
Originally published in hardcover by Delacorte Press, New York, in 2009.

Delacorte Press is a registered trademark and the colophon is a trademark
of Random House LLC.

Visit us on the Web! randomhouseteens.com

Educators and librarians, for a variety of teaching tools, visit us at
RHTeachersLibrarians.com

Library of Congress Cataloging-in-Publication Data is available upon request.

ISBN 978-0-553-51153-6 (hc)
ISBN 978-0-385-38520-6 (tr. pbk.)

Printed in the United States of America

10 9 8 7 6 5 4 3 2 1

For Lynette. This book was a three-year journey,
and you never doubted.

CHAPTER 1

He began his new life standing up, surrounded by cold darkness and stale, dusty air.

Metal ground against metal; a lurching shudder shook the floor beneath him. He fell down at the sudden movement and shuffled backward on his hands and feet, drops of sweat beading on his forehead despite the cool air. His back struck a hard metal wall; he slid along it until he hit the corner of the room. Sinking to the floor, he pulled his legs up tight against his body, hoping his eyes would soon adjust to the darkness.

With another jolt, the room jerked upward like an old lift in a mine shaft.

Harsh sounds of chains and pulleys, like the workings of an ancient steel factory, echoed through the room, bouncing off the walls with a hollow, tinny whine. The lightless elevator swayed back and forth as it ascended, turning the boy's stomach sour with nausea; a smell like burnt oil invaded his senses, making him feel worse. He wanted to cry, but no tears came; he could only sit there, alone, waiting.

My name is Thomas, he thought.

That . . . that was the only thing he could remember about his life.

He didn't understand how this could be possible. His mind functioned without flaw, trying to calculate his surroundings and predicament. Knowledge flooded his thoughts, facts and images, memories and details of the world and how it works. He pictured snow on trees, running down a leaf-strewn road, eating a hamburger, the moon casting a pale glow on a grassy meadow, swimming in a lake, a busy city square with hundreds of people bustling about their business.

And yet he didn't know where he came from, or how he'd gotten inside the dark lift, or who his parents were. He didn't even know his last name. Images of people flashed across his mind, but there was no recognition, their faces replaced with haunted smears of color. He couldn't think of one person he knew, or recall a single conversation.

The room continued its ascent, swaying; Thomas grew immune to the ceaseless rattling of the chains that pulled him upward. A long time passed. Minutes stretched into hours, although it was impossible to know for sure because every second seemed an eternity. No. He was smarter than that. Trusting his instincts, he knew he'd been moving for roughly *half* an hour.

Strangely enough, he felt his fear whisked away like a swarm of gnats caught in the wind, replaced by an intense curiosity. He wanted to know where he was and what was happening.

With a groan and then a clonk, the rising room halted; the sudden change jolted Thomas from his huddled position and threw him across the hard floor. As he scrambled to his feet, he felt the room sway less and less until it finally stilled. Everything fell silent.

A minute passed. Two. He looked in every direction but saw only darkness; he felt along the walls again, searching for a way out. But there was nothing, only the cool metal. He groaned in frustration; his echo amplified through the air, like the haunted moan of death. It faded, and silence returned. He screamed, called for help, pounded on the walls with his fists.

Nothing.

Thomas backed into the corner once again, folded his arms and shivered, and the fear returned. He felt a worrying shudder in his chest, as if his heart wanted to escape, to flee his body.

2

"Someone . . . help . . . me!" he screamed; each word ripped his throat raw.

A loud clank rang out above him and he sucked in a startled breath as he looked up. A straight line of light appeared across the ceiling of the room, and Thomas watched as it expanded. A heavy grating sound revealed double sliding doors being forced open. After so long in darkness, the light stabbed his eyes; he looked away, covering his face with both hands.

He heard noises above—voices—and fear squeezed his chest.

"Look at that shank."

"How old is he?"

"Looks like a klunk in a T-shirt."

"You're the klunk, shuck-face."

"Dude, it smells like *feet* down there!"

"Hope you enjoyed the one-way trip, Greenie."

"Ain't no ticket back, bro."

Thomas was hit with a wave of confusion, blistered with panic. The voices were odd, tinged with echo; some of the words were completely foreign—others felt familiar. He willed his eyes to adjust as he squinted toward the light and those speaking. At first he could see only shifting shadows, but they soon turned into the shapes of bodies—people bending over the hole in the ceiling, looking down at him, pointing.

And then, as if the lens of a camera had sharpened its focus, the faces cleared. They were boys, all of them—some young, some older. Thomas didn't know what he'd expected, but seeing those faces puzzled him. They were just teenagers. Kids. Some of his fear melted away, but not enough to calm his racing heart.

Someone lowered a rope from above, the end of it tied into a big loop. Thomas hesitated, then stepped into it with his right foot and clutched the rope as he was yanked toward the sky. Hands reached down, lots of hands, grabbing him by his clothes, pulling him up. The world seemed to spin, a swirling mist of faces and color and light. A storm of emotions wrenched his gut, twisted and pulled; he wanted to scream, cry, throw up. The chorus of voices had grown silent, but someone spoke as they yanked him over the sharp edge of the dark box. And Thomas knew he'd never forget the words.

"Nice to meet ya, shank," the boy said. "Welcome to the Glade."

CHAPTER 2

The helping hands didn't stop swarming around him until Thomas stood up straight and had the dust brushed from his shirt and pants. Still dazzled by the light, he staggered a bit. He was consumed with curiosity but still felt too ill to look closely at his surroundings. His new companions said nothing as he swiveled his head around, trying to take it all in.

As he rotated in a slow circle, the other kids snickered and stared; some reached out and poked him with a finger. There had to be at least fifty of them, their clothes smudged and sweaty as if they'd been hard at work, all shapes and sizes and races, their hair of varying lengths. Thomas suddenly felt dizzy, his eyes flickering between the boys and the bizarre place in which he'd found himself.

They stood in a vast courtyard several times the size of a football field, surrounded by four enormous walls made of gray stone and covered in spots with thick ivy. The walls had to be hundreds of feet high and formed a perfect square around them, each side split in the exact middle by an opening as tall as the walls themselves that, from what Thomas could see, led to passages and long corridors beyond.

"Look at the Greenbean," a scratchy voice said; Thomas couldn't see who it came from. "Gonna break his shuck neck checkin' out the new digs." Several boys laughed.

"Shut your hole, Gally," a deeper voice responded.

Thomas focused back in on the dozens of strangers around him. He knew he must look out of it—he felt like he'd been drugged. A tall kid

5

with blond hair and a square jaw sniffed at him, his face devoid of expression. A short, pudgy boy fidgeted back and forth on his feet, looking up at Thomas with wide eyes. A thick, heavily muscled Asian kid folded his arms as he studied Thomas, his tight shirtsleeves rolled up to show off his biceps. A dark-skinned boy frowned—the same one who'd welcomed him. Countless others stared.

"Where am I?" Thomas asked, surprised at hearing his voice for the first time in his salvageable memory. It didn't sound quite right—higher than he would've imagined.

"Nowhere good." This came from the dark-skinned boy. "Just slim yourself nice and calm."

"Which Keeper he gonna get?" someone shouted from the back of the crowd.

"I told ya, shuck-face," a shrill voice responded. "He's a klunk, so he'll be a Slopper—no doubt about it." The kid giggled like he'd just said the funniest thing in history.

Thomas once again felt a pressing ache of confusion—hearing so many words and phrases that didn't make sense. *Shank. Shuck. Keeper. Slopper.* They popped out of the boys' mouths so naturally it seemed odd for him not to understand. It was as if his memory loss had stolen a chunk of his language—it was disorienting.

Different emotions battled for dominance in his mind and heart. Confusion. Curiosity. Panic. Fear. But laced through it all was the dark feeling of utter hopelessness, like the world had ended for him, had been wiped from his memory and replaced with something awful. He wanted to run and hide from these people.

The scratchy-voiced boy was talking. "—even do that much, bet my liver on it." Thomas still couldn't see his face.

"I said shut your holes!" the dark boy yelled. "Keep yapping and next break'll be cut in half!"

That must be their leader, Thomas realized. Hating how everyone gawked at him, he concentrated on studying the place the boy had called the Glade.

The floor of the courtyard looked like it was made of huge stone blocks, many of them cracked and filled with long grasses and weeds. An odd, dilapidated wooden building near one of the corners of the square contrasted greatly with the gray stone. A few trees surrounded it, their roots like gnarled hands digging into the rock floor for food. Another corner of the compound held gardens—from where he was standing Thomas recognized corn, tomato plants, fruit trees.

Across the courtyard from there stood wooden pens holding sheep and pigs and cows. A large grove of trees filled the final corner; the closest ones looked crippled and close to dying. The sky overhead was cloudless and blue, but Thomas could see no sign of the sun despite the brightness of the day. The creeping shadows of the walls didn't reveal the time or direction—it could be early morning or late afternoon. As he breathed in deeply, trying to settle his nerves, a mixture of smells bombarded him. Freshly turned dirt, manure, pine, something rotten and something sweet. Somehow he knew that these were the smells of a farm.

Thomas looked back at his captors, feeling awkward but desperate to ask questions. *Captors,* he thought. Then, *Why did that word pop into my head?* He scanned their faces, taking in each expression, judging them. One boy's eyes, flared with hatred, stopped him cold. He looked so angry, Thomas wouldn't have been surprised if the kid came at him with a knife. He had black hair, and when they made eye contact, the boy shook his head and turned away, walking toward a greasy iron pole with a wooden bench next to it. A multicolored flag hung limply at the top of the pole, no wind to reveal its pattern.

Shaken, Thomas stared at the boy's back until he turned and took a seat. Thomas quickly looked away.

7

Suddenly the leader of the group—perhaps he was seventeen—took a step forward. He wore normal clothes: black T-shirt, jeans, tennis shoes, a digital watch. For some reason the clothing here surprised Thomas; it seemed like everyone should be wearing something more menacing—like prison garb. The dark-skinned boy had short-cropped hair, his face clean shaven. But other than the permanent scowl, there was nothing scary about him at all.

"It's a long story, shank," the boy said. "Piece by piece, you'll learn—I'll be takin' you on the Tour tomorrow. Till then . . . just don't break anything." He held a hand out. "Name's Alby." He waited, clearly wanting to shake hands.

Thomas refused. Some instinct took over his actions and without saying anything he turned away from Alby and walked to a nearby tree, where he plopped down to sit with his back against the rough bark. Panic swelled inside him once again, almost too much to bear. But he took a deep breath and forced himself to try to accept the situation. *Just go with it,* he thought. *You won't figure out anything if you give in to fear.*

"Then tell me," Thomas called out, struggling to keep his voice even. "Tell me the long story."

Alby glanced at the friends closest to him, rolling his eyes, and Thomas studied the crowd again. His original estimate had been close—there were probably fifty to sixty of them, ranging from boys in their midteens to young adults like Alby, who seemed to be one of the oldest. At that moment, Thomas realized with a sickening lurch that he had no idea how old *he* was. His heart sank at the thought—he was so lost he didn't even know his own age.

"Seriously," he said, giving up on the show of courage. "Where am I?"

Alby walked over to him and sat down cross-legged; the crowd of boys followed and packed in behind. Heads popped up here and there, kids leaning in every direction to get a better look.

8

"If you ain't scared," Alby said, "you ain't human. Act any different and I'd throw you off the Cliff because it'd mean you're a psycho."

"The Cliff?" Thomas asked, blood draining from his face.

"Shuck it," Alby said, rubbing his eyes. "Ain't no way to start these conversations, you get me? We don't kill shanks like you here, I promise. Just try and avoid *being* killed, survive, whatever."

He paused, and Thomas realized his face must've whitened even more when he heard that last part.

"Man," Alby said, then ran his hands over his short hair as he let out a long sigh. "I ain't good at this—you're the first Greenbean since Nick was killed."

Thomas's eyes widened, and another boy stepped up and playfully slapped Alby across the head. "Wait for the bloody Tour, Alby," he said, his voice thick with an odd accent. "Kid's gonna have a buggin' heart attack, nothin' even been heard yet." He bent down and extended his hand toward Thomas. "Name's Newt, Greenie, and we'd all be right cheery if ya'd forgive our klunk-for-brains new leader, here."

Thomas reached out and shook the boy's hand—he seemed a lot nicer than Alby. Newt was taller than Alby too, but looked to be a year or so younger. His hair was blond and cut long, cascading over his T-shirt. Veins stuck out of his muscled arms.

"Pipe it, shuck-face," Alby grunted, pulling Newt down to sit next to him. "At least he can understand *half* my words." There were a few scattered laughs, and then everyone gathered behind Alby and Newt, packing in even tighter, waiting to hear what they said.

Alby spread his arms out, palms up. "This place is called the Glade, all right? It's where we live, where we eat, where we sleep—we call ourselves the Gladers. That's all you—"

"Who sent me here?" Thomas demanded, fear finally giving way to anger. "How'd—"

But Alby's hand shot out before he could finish, grabbing Thomas by the shirt as he leaned forward on his knees. "Get up, shank, get up!" Alby stood, pulling Thomas with him.

Thomas finally got his feet under him, scared all over again. He backed against the tree, trying to get away from Alby, who stayed right in his face.

"No interruptions, boy!" Alby shouted. "Whacker, if we told you everything, you'd die on the spot, right after you klunked your pants. Baggers'd drag you off, and you ain't no good to us then, are ya?"

"I don't even know what you're talking about," Thomas said slowly, shocked at how steady his voice sounded.

Newt reached out and grabbed Alby by the shoulders. "Alby, lay off a bit. You're hurtin' more than helpin', ya know?"

Alby let go of Thomas's shirt and stepped back, his chest heaving with breaths. "Ain't got time to be nice, Greenbean. Old life's over, new life's begun. Learn the rules quick, listen, don't talk. You get me?"

Thomas looked over at Newt, hoping for help. Everything inside him churned and hurt; the tears that had yet to come burned his eyes.

Newt nodded. "Greenie, you get him, right?" He nodded again.

Thomas fumed, wanted to punch somebody. But he simply said, "Yeah."

"Good that," Alby said. "First Day. That's what today is for you, shank. Night's comin', Runners'll be back soon. The Box came late to-day, ain't got time for the Tour. Tomorrow morning, right after the wake-up." He turned toward Newt. "Get him a bed, get him to sleep."

"Good that," Newt said.

Alby's eyes returned to Thomas, narrowing. "A few weeks, you'll be happy, shank. You'll be happy and helpin'. None of us knew jack on First Day, you neither. New life begins tomorrow."

Alby turned and pushed his way through the crowd, then headed for the slanted wooden building in the corner. Most of the kids wandered away then, each one giving Thomas a lingering look before they walked off.

Thomas folded his arms, closed his eyes, took a deep breath. Emptiness ate away at his insides, quickly replaced by a sadness that hurt his heart. It was all too much—where was he? What was this place? Was it some kind of prison? If so, why had he been sent here, and for how long? The language was odd, and none of the boys seemed to care whether he lived or died. Tears threatened again to fill his eyes, but he refused to let them come.

"What did I do?" he whispered, not really meaning for anyone to hear him. "What did I do—why'd they send me here?"

Newt clapped him on the shoulder. "Greenie, what you're feelin', we've all felt it. We've all had First Day, come out of that dark box. Things are bad, they are, and they'll get much worse for ya soon, that's the truth. But down the road a piece, you'll be fightin' true and good. I can tell you're not a bloody sissy."

"Is this a prison?" Thomas asked; he dug in the darkness of his thoughts, trying to find a crack to his past.

"Done asked four questions, haven't ya?" Newt replied. "No good answers for ya, not yet, anyway. Best be quiet now, accept the change—morn comes tomorrow."

Thomas said nothing, his head sunk, his eyes staring at the cracked, rocky ground. A line of small-leafed weeds ran along the edge of one of the stone blocks, tiny yellow flowers peeping through as if searching for the sun, long disappeared behind the enormous walls of the Glade.

"Chuck'll be a good fit for ya," Newt said. "Wee little fat shank, but nice sap when all's said and done. Stay here, I'll be back."

Newt had barely finished his sentence when a sudden, piercing scream ripped through the air. High and shrill, the barely human shriek echoed across the stone courtyard; every kid in sight turned to look toward the source. Thomas felt his blood turn to icy slush as he realized that the horrible sound came from the wooden building.

Even Newt had jumped as if startled, his forehead creasing in concern.

"Shuck it," he said. "Can't the bloody Med-jacks handle that boy for ten minutes without needin' my help?" He shook his head and lightly kicked Thomas on the foot. "Find Chuckie, tell him he's in charge of your sleepin' arrangements." And then he turned and headed in the direction of the building, running.

Thomas slid down the rough face of the tree until he sat on the ground again; he shrank back against the bark and closed his eyes, wishing he could wake up from this terrible, terrible dream.

CHAPTER 3

Thomas sat there for several moments, too overwhelmed to move. He finally forced himself to look over at the haggard building. A group of boys milled around outside, glancing anxiously at the upper windows as if expecting a hideous beast to leap out in an explosion of glass and wood.

A metallic clicking sound from the branches above grabbed his attention, made him look up; a flash of silver and red light caught his eyes just before disappearing around the trunk to the other side. He scrambled to his feet and walked around the tree, craning his neck for a sign of whatever he'd heard, but he saw only bare branches, gray and brown, forking out like skeleton fingers—and looking just as alive.

"That was one of them beetle blades," someone said.

Thomas turned to his right to see a kid standing nearby, short and pudgy, staring at him. He was young—probably the youngest of any in the group he'd seen so far, maybe twelve or thirteen years old. His brown hair hung down over his ears and neck, scraping the tops of his shoulders. Blue eyes shone through an otherwise pitiful face, flabby and flushed.

Thomas nodded at him. "A beetle what?"

"Beetle blade," the boy said, pointing to the top of the tree. "Won't hurt ya unless you're stupid enough to touch one of them." He paused. "Shank." He didn't sound comfortable saying the last word, as if he hadn't quite grasped the slang of the Glade.

Another scream, this one long and nerve-grinding, tore through the air and Thomas's heart lurched. The fear was like icy dew on his skin. "What's going on over there?" he asked, pointing at the building.

"Don't know," the chubby boy replied; his voice still carried the high pitch of childhood. "Ben's in there, sicker than a dog. *They* got him."

"They?" Thomas didn't like the malicious way the boy had said the word.

"Yeah."

"Who are *They?*"

"Better hope you never find out," the kid answered, looking far too comfortable for the situation. He held out his hand. "My name's Chuck. I was the Greenbean until you showed up."

This is my guide for the night? Thomas thought. He couldn't shake his extreme discomfort, and now annoyance crept in as well. Nothing made sense; his head hurt.

"Why is everyone calling me Greenbean?" he asked, shaking Chuck's hand quickly, then letting go.

"Cuz you're the newest Newbie." Chuck pointed at Thomas and laughed. Another scream came from the house, a sound like a starving animal being tortured.

"How can you be laughing?" Thomas asked, horrified by the noise. "It sounds like someone's dying in there."

"He'll be okay. No one dies if they make it back in time to get the Serum. It's all or nothing. Dead or not dead. Just hurts a lot."

This gave Thomas pause. "What hurts a lot?"

Chuck's eyes wandered as if he wasn't sure what to say. "Um, gettin' stung by the Grievers."

"Grievers?" Thomas was only getting more and more confused. *Stung. Grievers.* The words had a heavy weight of dread to them, and

14

he suddenly wasn't so sure he wanted to know what Chuck was talking about.

Chuck shrugged, then looked away, eyes rolling.

Thomas sighed in frustration and leaned back against the tree. "Looks like you barely know more than I do," he said, but he knew it wasn't true. His memory loss was strange. He mostly remembered the workings of the world—but emptied of specifics, faces, names. Like a book completely intact but missing one word in every dozen, making it a miserable and confusing read. He didn't even know his age.

"Chuck, how . . . old do you think I am?"

The boy scanned him up and down. "I'd say you're sixteen. And in case you were wondering, five foot nine . . . brown hair. Oh, and ugly as fried liver on a stick." He snorted a laugh.

Thomas was so stunned he'd barely heard the last part. Sixteen? He was *sixteen*? He felt much older than that.

"Are you serious?" He paused, searching for words. "How . . ." He didn't even know what to ask.

"Don't worry. You'll be all whacked for a few days, but then you'll get used to this place. I have. We live here, this is it. Better than living in a pile of klunk." He squinted, maybe anticipating Thomas's question. "*Klunk*'s another word for poo. Poo makes a klunk sound when it falls in our pee pots."

Thomas looked at Chuck, unable to believe he was having this conversation. "That's nice" was all he could manage. He stood up and walked past Chuck toward the old building; *shack* was a better word for the place. It looked three or four stories high and about to fall down at any minute—a crazy assortment of logs and boards and thick twine and windows seemingly thrown together at random, the massive, ivy-strewn stone walls rising up behind it. As he moved across the courtyard, the distinct smell of firewood and some kind of meat cooking

15

made his stomach grumble. Knowing now that it was just a sick kid do-ing the screaming made Thomas feel better. Until he thought about what had caused it . . .

"What's your name?" Chuck asked from behind, running to catch up.

"What?"

"Your *name*? You still haven't told us—and I know you remember that much."

"Thomas." He barely heard himself say it—his thoughts had spun in a new direction. If Chuck was right, he'd just discovered a link to the rest of the boys. A common pattern to their memory losses. They all remembered their names. Why not their parents' names? Why not a friend's name? Why not their *last* names?

"Nice to meet you, Thomas," Chuck said. "Don't you worry, I'll take care of you. I've been here a whole month, and I know the place inside and out. You can count on Chuck, okay?"

Thomas had almost reached the front door of the shack and the small group of boys congregating there when he was hit by a sudden and surprise rush of anger. He turned to face Chuck. "You can't even *tell* me anything. I wouldn't call that taking care of me." He turned back toward the door, intent on going inside to find some answers. Where this sudden courage and resolve came from, he had no idea.

Chuck shrugged. "Nothin' I say'll do you any good," he said. "I'm basically still a Newbie, too. But I can be your friend—"

"I don't need friends," Thomas interrupted.

He'd reached the door, an ugly slab of sun-faded wood, and he pulled it open to see several stoic-faced boys standing at the foot of a crooked staircase, the steps and railings twisted and angled in all direc-tions. Dark wallpaper covered the walls of the foyer and hallway, half of it peeling off. The only decorations in sight were a dusty vase on a three-legged table and a black-and-white picture of an ancient woman dressed in an old-fashioned white dress. It reminded Thomas of a haunted house from a movie or something. There were even planks of wood missing from the floor.

The place reeked of dust and mildew—a big contrast to the pleasant smells outside. Flickering fluorescent lights shone from the ceiling. He hadn't thought of it yet, but he had to wonder where the electricity came from in a place like the Glade. He stared at the old woman in the picture. Had she lived here once? Taken care of these people?

"Hey, look, it's the Greenbean," one of the older boys called out. With a start, Thomas realized it was the black-haired guy who'd given him the look of death earlier. He looked like he was fifteen or so, tall and skinny. His nose was the size of a small fist and resembled a deformed potato. "This shank probably klunked his pants when he heard old Benny baby scream like a girl. Need a new diaper, shuck-face?"

"My name's Thomas." He had to get away from this guy. Without another word, he made for the stairs, only because they were close, only because he had no idea what to do or say. But the bully stepped in front of him, holding a hand up.

"Hold on there, Greenie." He jerked a thumb in the direction of the upper floor. "Newbies aren't allowed to see someone who's been . . . *taken*. Newt and Alby won't allow it."

"What's your problem?" Thomas asked, trying to keep the fear out of his voice, trying not to think what the kid had meant by *taken*. "I don't even know where I am. All I want is some help."

"Listen to me, Greenbean." The boy wrinkled up his face, folded his arms. "I've seen you before. Something's fishy about you showing up here, and I'm gonna find out what."

A surge of heat pulsed through Thomas's veins. "I've never seen you before in my life. I have no idea who you are, and I couldn't care less," he spat. But really, how would he know? And how could this kid remember *him*?

The bully snickered, a short burst of laughter mixed with a phlegm-filled snort. Then his face grew serious, his eyebrows slanting inward. "I've . . . *seen* you, shank. Not too many in these parts can say they've been stung." He pointed up the stairs. "I have. I know what old Benny baby's going through. I've been there. And I saw *you* during the Changing."

He reached out and poked Thomas in the chest. "And I bet your first meal from Frypan that Benny'll say he's seen ya, too."

Thomas refused to break eye contact but decided to say nothing. Panic ate at him once again. Would things ever stop getting worse?

"Griever got ya wettin' yourself?" the boy said through a sneer. "A little scared now? Don't wanna get *stung*, do ya?"

There was that word again. *Stung.* Thomas tried not to think about it and pointed up the stairs, from where the moans of the sick kid echoed through the building. "If Newt went up there, then I wanna talk to him."

The boy said nothing, stared at Thomas for several seconds. Then he shook his head. "You know what? You're right, Tommy—I shouldn't be so mean to Newbies. Go on upstairs and I'm sure Alby and Newt'll fill you in. Seriously, go on. I'm sorry."

He lightly slapped Thomas's shoulder, then stepped back, gesturing up the stairs. But Thomas knew the kid was up to something. Losing parts of your memory didn't make you an idiot.

"What's your name?" Thomas asked, stalling for time while he tried to decide if he should go up after all.

"Gally. And don't let anyone fool you. I'm the real leader here, not the two geezer shanks upstairs. Me. You can call me Captain Gally if you want." He smiled for the first time; his teeth matched his disgusting nose. Two or three were missing, and not a single one approached anything close to the color white. His breath escaped just enough for Thomas to get a whiff, reminding him of some horrible memory that was just out of reach. It made his stomach turn.

"Okay," he said, so sick of the guy he wanted to scream, punch him in the face. "Captain Gally it is." He exaggerated a salute, feeling a rush of adrenaline, as he knew he'd just crossed a line.

A few snickers escaped the crowd, and Gally looked around, his face bright red. He peered back at Thomas, hatred furrowing his brow and crinkling his monstrous nose.

"Just go up the stairs," Gally said. "And stay away from me, you little slinthead." He pointed up again but didn't take his eyes off Thomas.

"Fine." Thomas looked around one more time, embarrassed, confused, angry. He felt the heat of blood in his face. No one made a move to stop him from doing as Gally asked, except for Chuck, who stood at the front door, shaking his head.

"You're not supposed to," the younger boy said. "You're a Newbie—you can't go up there."

"Go," said Gally with a sneer. "Go on up."

Thomas regretted having come inside in the first place—but he *did* want to talk to that Newt guy.

He started up the stairs. Each step groaned and creaked under his weight; he might've stopped for fear of falling through the old wood if he weren't leaving such an awkward situation below. Up he went, wincing at every splintered sound. The stairs reached a landing, turned left, then came upon a railed hallway leading to several rooms. Only one door had a light coming through the crack at the bottom.

"The Changing!" Gally shouted from below. "Look forward to it, shuck-face!"

As if the taunting gave Thomas a sudden burst of courage, he walked over to the lit door, ignoring the creaking floorboards and laughter downstairs—ignoring the onslaught of words he didn't understand, suppressing the dreadful feelings they induced. He reached down, turned the brass handle, and opened the door.

Inside the room, Newt and Alby crouched over someone lying on a bed.

Thomas leaned in closer to see what the fuss was all about, but when he got a clear look at the condition of the patient, his heart went cold. He had to fight the bile that surged up his throat.

The look was fast—only a few seconds—but it was enough to haunt him forever. A twisted, pale figure writhing in agony, chest bare and hideous. Tight, rigid cords of sickly green veins webbed across the boy's body and limbs, like ropes under his skin. Purplish bruises covered the kid, red hives, bloody scratches. His bloodshot eyes bulged, darting back and forth. The image had already burned into Thomas's mind before Alby jumped up, blocking the view but not the moans and screams, pushing Thomas out of the room, then slamming the door shut behind them.

"What're you doing up here, Greenie!" Alby yelled, his lips taut with anger, eyes on fire.

Thomas felt weak. "I . . . uh . . . want some answers," he murmured, but he couldn't put any strength in his words—felt himself give up inside. What was wrong with that kid? Thomas slouched against the railing in the hallway and stared at the floor, not sure what to do next.

"Get your runtcheeks down those stairs, right now," Alby ordered. "Chuck'll help you. If I see you again before tomorrow morning, you ain't reachin' another one alive. I'll throw you off the Cliff myself, you get me?"

Thomas was humiliated and scared. He felt like he'd shrunk to the size of a small rat. Without saying a word, he pushed past Alby and headed down the creaky steps, going as fast as he dared. Ignoring the gaping stares of everyone at the bottom—especially Gally—he walked out the door, pulling Chuck by the arm as he did so.

Thomas hated these people. He hated all of them. Except Chuck. "Get me away from these guys," Thomas said. He realized that Chuck might actually be his only friend in the world.

"You got it," Chuck replied, his voice chipper, as if thrilled to be needed. "But first we should get you some food from Frypan."

"I don't know if I can ever eat again." Not after what he'd just seen.

Chuck nodded. "Yeah, you will. I'll meet you at the same tree as before. Ten minutes."

Thomas was more than happy to get away from the house, and headed back toward the tree. He'd only known what it was like to be alive here for a short while and he already wanted it to end. He wished for all the world he could remember something about his previous life. Anything. His mom, his dad, a friend, his school, a hobby. A girl.

He blinked hard several times, trying to get the image of what he'd just seen in the shack out of his mind.

The Changing. Gally had called it the Changing.

It wasn't cold, but Thomas shuddered once again.

CHAPTER 4

Thomas leaned against the tree as he waited for Chuck. He scanned the compound of the Glade, this new place of nightmares where he seemed destined to live. The shadows from the walls had lengthened considerably, already creeping up the sides of the ivy-covered stone faces on the other side.

At least this helped Thomas know directions—the wooden building crouched in the northwest corner, wedged in a darkening patch of shadow, the grove of trees in the southwest. The farm area, where a few workers were still picking their way through the fields, spread across the entire northeast quarter of the Glade. The animals were in the southeast corner, mooing and crowing and baying.

In the exact middle of the courtyard, the still-gaping hole of the Box lay open, as if inviting him to jump back in and go home. Near that, maybe twenty feet to the south, stood a squat building made of rough concrete blocks, a menacing iron door its only entrance—there were no windows. A large round handle resembling a steel steering wheel marked the only way to open the door, just like something within a submarine. Despite what he'd just seen, Thomas didn't know which he felt more strongly—curiosity to know what was inside, or dread at finding out.

Thomas had just moved his attention to the four vast openings in the middle of the main walls of the Glade when Chuck arrived, a couple of sandwiches cradled in his arms, along with apples and two metal cups of water. The sense of relief that flooded through Thomas surprised him—he wasn't *completely* alone in this place.

"Frypan wasn't too happy about me invading his kitchen before suppertime," Chuck said, sitting down next to the tree, motioning to Thomas to do the same. He did, grabbed the sandwich, but hesitated, the writhing, monstrous image of what he'd seen in the shack popping back into his mind. Soon, though, his hunger won out and he took a huge bite. The wonderful tastes of ham and cheese and mayonnaise filled his mouth.

"Ah, man," Thomas mumbled through a mouthful. "I was starving."

"Told ya." Chuck chomped into his own sandwich.

After another couple of bites, Thomas finally asked the question that had been bothering him. "What's actually *wrong* with that Ben guy? He doesn't even look human anymore."

Chuck glanced over at the house. "Don't really know," he muttered absently. "I didn't see him."

Thomas could tell the boy was being less than honest but decided not to press him. "Well, you don't want to see him, trust me." He continued to eat, munching on the apples as he studied the huge breaks in the walls. Though it was hard to make out from where he sat, there was something odd about the stone edges of the exits to the outside corridors. He felt an uncomfortable sense of vertigo looking at the towering walls, as if he hovered above them instead of sitting at their base.

"What's out there?" he asked, finally breaking the silence. "Is this part of a huge castle or something?"

Chuck hesitated. Looked uncomfortable. "Um, I've never been outside the Glade."

Thomas paused. "You're hiding something," he finally replied, finishing off his last bite and taking a long swig of water. The frustration at getting no answers from anyone was starting to grind his nerves. It only made it worse to think that even if he *did* get answers, he wouldn't know if he'd be getting the truth. "Why are you guys so secretive?"

"That's just the way it is. Things are really weird around here, and most of us don't know everything. *Half* of everything."

It bothered Thomas that Chuck didn't seem to care about what he'd just said. That he seemed indifferent to having his life taken away from him. What was wrong with these people? Thomas got to his feet and started walking toward the eastern opening. "Well, no one said I couldn't look around." He needed to learn something or he was going to lose his mind.

"Whoa, wait!" Chuck cried, running to catch up. "Be careful, those puppies are about to close." He already sounded out of breath.

"Close?" Thomas repeated. "What are you talking about?"

"The Doors, you shank."

"Doors? I don't see any doors." Thomas knew Chuck wasn't just making stuff up—he knew he was missing something obvious. He grew uneasy and realized he'd slowed his pace, not so eager to reach the walls anymore.

"What do you call those big openings?" Chuck pointed up at the enormously tall gaps in the walls. They were only thirty feet away now.

"I'd call them *big openings*," Thomas said, trying to counter his discomfort with sarcasm and disappointed that it wasn't working.

"Well, they're *doors*. And they close up every night."

Thomas stopped, thinking Chuck had to have said something wrong. He looked up, looked side to side, examined the massive slabs of stone as the uneasy feeling blossomed into outright dread. "What do you mean, they *close*?"

"Just see for yourself in a minute. The Runners'll be back soon; then those big walls are going to *move* until the gaps are closed."

"You're jacked in the head," Thomas muttered. He couldn't see how the mammoth walls could possibly be mobile—felt so sure of it he relaxed, thinking Chuck was just playing a trick on him.

They reached the huge split that led outside to more stone pathways. Thomas gaped, his mind emptying of thought as he saw it all firsthand.

"This is called the East Door," Chuck said, as if proudly revealing a piece of art he'd created.

Thomas barely heard him, shocked by how much bigger it was up close. At least twenty feet across, the break in the wall went all the way to the top, far above. The edges that bordered the vast opening were smooth, except for one odd, repeating pattern on both sides. On the left side of the East Door, deep holes several inches in diameter and spaced a foot apart were bored into the rock, beginning near the ground and continuing all the way up.

On the right side of the Door, foot-long rods jutted out from the wall edge, also several inches in diameter, in the same pattern as the holes facing them on the other side. The purpose was obvious.

"Are you kidding?" Thomas asked, the dread slamming back into his gut. "You weren't playing with me? The walls really *move?*"

"What else would I have meant?"

Thomas had a hard time wrapping his mind around the possibility. "I don't know. I figured there was a door that swung shut or a little mini-wall that slid out of the big one. How could these walls move? They're huge, and they look like they've been standing here for a thousand years." And the idea of those walls closing and trapping him inside this place they called the Glade was downright terrifying.

Chuck threw his arms up, clearly frustrated. "I don't know, they just move. Makes one heck of a grinding noise. Same thing happens out in the Maze—those walls shift every night, too."

Thomas, his attention suddenly snapped up by a new detail, turned to face the younger boy. "What did you just say?"

"Huh?"

"You just called it a maze—you said, 'same thing happens out in the *maze.*'"

Chuck's face reddened. "I'm done with you. I'm done." He walked back toward the tree they'd just left.

Thomas ignored him, more interested than ever in the outside of the Glade. A *maze*? In front of him, through the East Door, he could make out passages leading to the left, to the right, and straight ahead. And the walls of the corridors were similar to those that surrounded the Glade, the ground made of the same massive stone blocks as in the courtyard. The ivy seemed even thicker out there. In the distance, more breaks in the walls led to other paths, and farther down, maybe a hundred yards or so away, the straight passage came to a dead end.

"Looks like a maze," Thomas whispered, almost laughing to himself. As if things couldn't have gotten any stranger. They'd wiped his memory and put him inside a gigantic maze. It was all so crazy it really did seem funny.

His heart skipped a beat when a boy unexpectedly appeared around a corner up ahead, entering the main passage from one of the offshoots to the right, running toward him and the Glade. Covered in sweat, his face red, clothes sticking to his body, the boy didn't slow, hardly glancing at Thomas as he went past. He headed straight for the squat concrete building located near the Box.

Thomas turned as he passed, his eyes riveted to the exhausted runner, unsure why this new development surprised him so much. Why *wouldn't* people go out and search the maze? Then he realized others were entering through the remaining three Glade openings, all of them running and looking as ragged as the guy who'd just whisked by him. There couldn't be much good about the maze if these guys came back looking so weary and worn.

He watched, curious, as they met at the big iron door of the small building; one of the boys turned the rusty wheel handle, grunting with the effort. Chuck had said something about runners earlier. What had they been doing out there?

The big door finally popped open, and with a deafening squeal of metal against metal, the boys swung it wide. They disappeared inside, pulling it shut behind them with a loud clonk. Thomas stared, his mind churning to come up with any possible explanation for what he'd just witnessed. Nothing developed, but something about that creepy old building gave him goose bumps, a disquieting chill.

Someone tugged on his sleeve, breaking him from his thoughts; Chuck had come back.

Before Thomas had a chance to think, questions were rushing out of his mouth. "Who are those guys and what were they doing? What's in that building?" He wheeled around and pointed out the East Door. "And why do you live inside a freaking maze?" He felt a rattling pressure of uncertainty, making his head splinter with pain.

"I'm not saying another word," Chuck replied, a new authority filling his voice. "I think you should get to bed early—you'll need your sleep. Ah"—he stopped, held up a finger, pricking up his right ear—"it's about to happen."

"What?" Thomas asked, thinking it kind of strange that Chuck was suddenly acting like an adult instead of the little kid desperate for a friend he'd been only moments earlier.

A loud boom exploded through the air, making Thomas jump. It was followed by a horrible crunching, grinding sound. He stumbled backward, fell to the ground. It felt as if the whole earth shook; he looked around, panicked. The walls were closing. The walls were *really* closing—trapping him inside the Glade. An onrushing sense of claustrophobia stifled him, compressed his lungs, as if water filled their cavities.

"Calm down, Greenie," Chuck yelled over the noise. "It's just the walls!"

Thomas barely heard him, too fascinated, too shaken by the closing of the Doors. He scrambled to his feet and took a few trembling steps back for a better view, finding it hard to believe what his eyes were seeing.

The enormous stone wall to the right of them seemed to defy every known law of physics as it slid along the ground, throwing sparks and dust as it moved, rock against rock. The crunching sound rattled his bones. Thomas realized that only *that* wall was moving, heading for its neighbor to the left, ready to seal shut with its protruding rods slipping into the drilled holes across from it. He looked around at the other openings. It felt like his head was spinning faster than his body, and his stomach flipped over with the dizziness. On all four sides of the Glade, only the right walls were moving, toward the left, closing the gap of the Doors.

Impossible, he thought. *How can they* do *that?* He fought the urge to run out there, slip past the moving slabs of rock before they shut, flee the Glade. Common sense won out—the maze held even more unknowns than his situation inside.

He tried to picture in his mind how the structure of it all worked. Massive stone walls, hundreds of feet high, moving like sliding glass doors—an image from his past life that flashed through his thoughts. He tried to grasp the memory, hold on to it, complete the picture with faces, names, a place, but it faded into obscurity. A pang of sadness pricked through his other swirling emotions.

He watched as the right wall reached the end of its journey, its connecting rods finding their mark and entering without a glitch. An echoing boom rumbled across the Glade as all four Doors sealed shut for the night. Thomas felt one final moment of trepidation, a quick slice of fear through his body, and then it vanished.

A surprising sense of calm eased his nerves; he let out a long sigh of relief. "Wow," he said, feeling dumb at such a monumental understatement.

"Ain't nothin', as Alby would say," Chuck murmured. "You kind of get used to it after a while."

Thomas looked around one more time, the *feel* of the place completely different now that all the walls were solid with no way out. He tried to imagine the purpose of such a thing, and he didn't know which guess was worse—that they were being sealed *in* or that they were being protected from something *out there*. The thought ended his brief moment of calm, stirring in his mind a million possibilities of what might live in the maze outside, all of them terrifying. Fear gripped him once again.

"Come *on*," Chuck said, pulling at Thomas's sleeve a second time. "Trust me, when nighttime strikes, you want to be in *bed*."

Thomas knew he had no other choice. He did his best to suppress everything he was feeling and followed.

CHAPTER 5

They ended up near the back of the Homestead—that was what Chuck called the leaning structure of wood and windows—in a dark shadow between the building and the stone wall behind it.

"Where are we going?" Thomas asked, still feeling the weight of seeing those walls close, thinking about the maze, the confusion, the fear. He told himself to stop or he'd drive himself crazy. Trying to grasp a sense of normalcy, he made a weak attempt at a joke. "If you're looking for a goodnight kiss, forget it."

Chuck didn't miss a beat. "Just shut up and stay close."

Thomas let out a big breath and shrugged before following the younger boy along the back of the building. They tiptoed until they came upon a small, dusty window, a soft beam of light shining through onto the stone and ivy. Thomas heard someone moving around inside.

"The bathroom," Chuck whispered.

"So?" A thread of unease stitched along Thomas's skin.

"I love doing this to people. Gives me great pleasure before bedtime."

"Doing what?" Something told Thomas Chuck was up to no good. "Maybe I should—"

"Just shut your mouth and watch." Chuck quietly stepped up onto a big wooden box that sat right under the window. He crouched so that his head was positioned just below where the person on the inside

30

would be able to see him. Then he reached up with his hand and lightly tapped on the glass.

"This is stupid," Thomas whispered. There couldn't possibly be a worse time to play a joke—Newt or Alby could be in there. "I don't wanna get in trouble—I just got here!"

Chuck suppressed a laugh by putting his hand over his mouth. Ignoring Thomas, he reached up and tapped the window again.

A shadow crossed the light; then the window slid open. Thomas jumped to hide, pressing himself against the back of the building as hard as he could. He just couldn't believe he'd been suckered into playing a practical joke on somebody. The angle of vision from the window protected him for the moment, but he knew he and Chuck would be seen if whoever was in there pushed his head outside to get a better look.

"Who's that!" yelled the boy from the bathroom, his voice scratchy and laced with anger. Thomas had to hold in a gasp when he realized it was Gally—he *knew* that voice already.

Without warning, Chuck suddenly popped his head up toward the window and screamed at the top of his lungs. A loud crash from inside revealed that the trick had worked—and the litany of swearwords following it let them know Gally was none too happy about it. Thomas was struck with an odd mix of horror and embarrassment.

"I'm gonna kill you, shuck-face!" Gally yelled, but Chuck was already off the box and running toward the open Glade. Thomas froze as he heard Gally open the door inside and run out of the bathroom.

Thomas finally snapped out of his daze and took off after his new—and only—friend. He'd just rounded the corner when Gally came screaming out of the Homestead, looking like a ferocious beast on the loose.

He immediately pointed at Thomas. "Come here!" he yelled.

Thomas's heart sank in surrender. Everything seemed to indicate

31

that he'd be getting a fist in the face. "It wasn't me, I swear," he said, though as he stood there, he sized the boy up and realized he shouldn't be so terrified after all. Gally wasn't that big—Thomas could actually take him if he had to.

"Wasn't you?" Gally snarled. He ambled up to Thomas slowly and stopped right in front of him. "Then how do you know there was something you didn't do?"

Thomas didn't say anything. He was definitely uncomfortable but not nearly as scared as a few moments earlier.

"I'm not a dong, Greenie," Gally spat. "I saw Chuck's fat face in the window." He pointed again, this time right at Thomas's chest. "But you better decide right quick who you want as your friends and enemies, hear me? One more trick like that—I don't care if it's your sissy idea or not—there'll be blood spilled. You got that, Newbie?" But before Thomas could answer Gally'd already turned to walk away.

Thomas just wanted this episode over. "Sorry," he muttered, wincing at how stupid it sounded.

"I know you," Gally added without looking back. "I saw you in the Changing, and I'm gonna figure out who you are."

Thomas watched as the bully disappeared back into the Homestead. He couldn't remember much, but something told him he'd never disliked someone so strongly. He was surprised by how much he truly hated the guy. He really, really hated him. He turned to see Chuck standing there, staring at the ground, clearly embarassed. "Thanks a lot, *buddy*."

"Sorry—if I'd known it was Gally, I never would've done it, I swear."

Surprising himself, Thomas laughed. An hour ago, he'd thought he'd never hear such a sound come out of his mouth again.

Chuck looked closely at Thomas and slowly broke into an uneasy grin. "What?"

Thomas shook his head. "Don't be sorry. The . . . shank deserved it, and I don't even know what a shank is. That was awesome." He felt much better.

A couple of hours later, Thomas was lying in a soft sleeping bag next to Chuck on a bed of grass near the gardens. It was a wide lawn that he hadn't noticed before, and quite a few of the group chose it as their bedtime spot. Thomas thought that was strange, but apparently there wasn't enough room inside the Homestead. At least it was warm. Which made him wonder for the millionth time *where* they were. His mind had a hard time grasping names of places, or remembering countries or rulers, how the world was organized. And none of the kids in the Glade had a clue, either—at least, they weren't sharing if they did.

He lay in silence for the longest time, looking at the stars and listening to the soft murmurs of various conversations drifting across the Glade. Sleep felt miles away, and he couldn't shake the despair and hopelessness that coursed through his body and mind—the temporary joy of Chuck's trick on Gally had long since faded away. It'd been one endless—and strange—day.

It was just so . . . weird. He remembered lots of little things about life—eating, clothes, studying, playing, general images of the makeup of the world. But any detail that would fill in the picture to create a true and complete memory had been erased somehow. It was like looking at an image through a foot of muddy water. More than anything else, perhaps, he felt . . . *sad*.

Chuck interrupted his thoughts. "Well, Greenie, you survived First Day."

"Barely." *Not now, Chuck*, he wanted to say. *I'm not in the mood.*

Chuck pulled himself up to lean on an elbow, looking at Thomas. "You'll learn a lot in the next couple of days, start getting used to things. Good that?"

"Um, yeah, good that, I guess. Where'd all these weird words and phrases come from, anyway?" It seemed like they'd taken some other language and melded it with his own.

Chuck flopped back down with a heavy flump. "I don't know—I've only been here a month, remember?"

Thomas wondered about Chuck, whether he knew more than he let on. He was a quirky kid, funny, and he seemed innocent, but who was to say? Really he was just as mysterious as everything else in the Glade.

A few minutes passed, and Thomas felt the long day finally catch up to him, the leaded edge of sleep crossing over his mind. But—like a fist had shoved it in his brain and let go—a thought popped into his head. One that he didn't expect, and he wasn't sure from where it came.

Suddenly, the Glade, the walls, the Maze—it all seemed . . . familiar. Comfortable. A warmth of calmness spread through his chest, and for the first time since he'd found himself there, he didn't feel like the Glade was the worst place in the universe. He stilled, felt his eyes widen, his breathing stop for a long moment. *What just happened?* he thought. *What changed?* Ironically, the feeling that things would be okay made him slightly uneasy.

Not quite understanding how, he knew what he needed to do. He didn't get it. The feeling—the epiphany—was a strange one, foreign and familiar at the same time. But it felt . . . right.

"I want to be one of those guys that goes out there," he said aloud, not knowing if Chuck was still awake. "Inside the Maze."

"Huh?" was the response from Chuck. Thomas could hear a tinge of annoyance in his voice.

"Runners," Thomas said, wishing he knew where this was coming from. "Whatever they're doing out there, I want in."

"You don't even know what you're talking about," Chuck grumbled, and rolled over. "Go to sleep."

Thomas felt a new surge of confidence, even though he truly *didn't* know what he was talking about. "I want to be a Runner."

Chuck turned back and got up on his elbow. "You can forget that little thought right now."

Thomas wondered at Chuck's reaction, but pressed on. "Don't try to—"

"Thomas. Newbie. My new friend. Forget it."

"I'll tell Alby tomorrow." *A Runner,* Thomas thought. *I don't even know what that* means. *Have I gone completely insane?*

Chuck lay down with a laugh. "You're a piece of klunk. Go to sleep."

But Thomas couldn't quit. "Something out there—it feels familiar."

"Go . . . to . . . sleep."

Then it hit Thomas—he felt like several pieces of a puzzle had been put together. He didn't know what the ultimate picture would be, but his next words almost felt like they were coming from someone else. "Chuck, I . . . I think I've *been* here before."

He heard his friend sit up, heard the intake of breath. But Thomas rolled over and refused to say another word, worried he'd mess up this new sense of being encouraged, eradicate the reassuring calm that filled his heart.

Sleep came much more easily than he'd expected.

CHAPTER 6

Someone shook Thomas awake. His eyes snapped open to see a too-close face staring down at him, everything around them still shadowed by the darkness of early morning. He opened his mouth to speak but a cold hand clamped down on it, gripping it shut. Panic flared until he saw who it was.

"Shh, Greenie. Don't wanna be wakin' Chuckie, now, do we?"

It was Newt—the guy who seemed to be second in command; the air reeked of his morning breath.

Though Thomas was surprised, any alarm melted away immediately. He couldn't help being curious, wondering what this boy wanted with him. Thomas nodded, doing his best to say yes with his eyes, until Newt finally took his hand away, then leaned back on his heels.

"Come on, Greenie," the tall boy whispered as he stood. He reached down and helped Thomas to his feet—he was so strong it felt like he could rip Thomas's arm off. "Supposed to show ya somethin' before the wake-up."

Any lingering haze of sleep had already vanished from Thomas's mind. "Okay," he said simply, ready to follow. He knew he should hold *some* suspicion, having no reason to trust anyone yet, but the curiosity won out. He quickly leaned over and slipped on his shoes. "Where are we going?"

"Just follow me. And stay close."

They snuck their way through the tightly strewn pack of sleeping bodies, Thomas almost tripping several times. He stepped on someone's hand, earning a sharp cry of pain in return, then a punch on the calf.

"Sorry," he whispered, ignoring a dirty look from Newt.

Once they left the lawn area and stepped onto the hard gray stone of the courtyard floor, Newt broke into a run, heading for the western wall. Thomas hesitated at first, wondering why he needed to run, but snapped out of it quickly and followed at the same pace.

The light was dim, but any obstructions loomed as darker shadows and he was able to make his way quickly along. He stopped when Newt did, right next to the massive wall towering above them like a skyscraper—another random image that floated in the murky pool of his memory wipe. Thomas noticed small red lights flashing here and there along the wall's face, moving about, stopping, turning off and on.

"What are those?" he whispered as loudly as he dared, wondering if his voice sounded as shaky as he felt. The twinkling red glow of the lights held an undercurrent of warning.

Newt stood just a couple of feet in front of the thick curtain of ivy on the wall. "When you bloody need to know, you'll know, Greenie."

"Well, it's kind of stupid to send me to a place where nothing makes sense and not answer my questions." Thomas paused, surprised at himself. *"Shank,"* he added, throwing all the sarcasm he could into the syllable.

Newt broke out in a laugh, but quickly cut it off. "I like you, Greenie. Now shut it and let me show ya somethin'."

Newt stepped forward and dug his hands into the thick ivy, spreading several vines away from the wall to reveal a dust-frosted window, a square about two feet wide. It was dark at the moment, as if it had been painted black.

"What're we looking for?" Thomas whispered.

"Hold your undies, boy. One'll be comin' along soon enough."

A minute passed, then two. Several more. Thomas fidgeted on his feet, wondering how Newt could stand there, perfectly patient and still, staring into nothing but darkness.

Then it changed.

Glimmers of an eerie light shone through the window; it cast a wavering spectrum of colors on Newt's body and face, as if he stood next to a lighted swimming pool. Thomas grew perfectly still, squinting, trying to make out what was on the other side. A thick lump grew in his throat. *What is that?* he thought.

"Out there's the Maze," Newt whispered, eyes wide as if in a trance. "Everything we do—our whole life, Greenie—revolves around the Maze. Every lovin' second of every lovin' day we spend in honor of the Maze, tryin' to solve somethin' that's not shown us it has a bloody solution, ya know? And we want to show ya why it's not to be messed with. Show ya why them buggin' walls close shut every night. Show ya why you should never, never find your butt out there."

Newt stepped back, still holding on to the ivy vines. He gestured for Thomas to take his place and look through the window.

Thomas did, leaning forward until his nose touched the cool surface of the glass. It took a second for his eyes to focus on the moving object on the other side, to look past the grime and dust and see what Newt wanted him to see. And when he did, he felt his breath catch in his throat, like an icy wind had blown down there and frozen the air solid.

A large, bulbous creature the size of a cow but with no distinct shape twisted and seethed along the ground in the corridor outside. It climbed the opposite wall, then leaped at the thick-glassed window with a loud thump. Thomas shrieked before he could stop himself, jerked away from the window—but the thing bounced backward, leaving the glass undamaged.

Thomas sucked in two huge breaths and leaned in once again. It was too dark to make out clearly, but odd lights flashed from an unknown source, revealing blurs of silver spikes and glistening flesh. Wicked instrument-tipped appendages protruded from its body like arms: a saw blade, a set of shears, long rods whose purpose could only be guessed.

The creature was a horrific mix of animal and machine, and seemed to realize it was being observed, seemed to know what lay inside the walls of the Glade, seemed to want to get inside and feast on human flesh. Thomas felt an icy terror blossom in his chest, expand like a tumor, making it hard to breathe. Even with the memory wipe, he felt sure he'd never seen something so truly awful.

He stepped back, the courage he'd felt the previous evening melting away.

"What is that thing?" he asked. Something shivered in his gut, and he wondered if he'd ever be able to eat again.

"Grievers, we call 'em," Newt answered. "Nasty bugger, eh? Just be glad the Grievers only come *out* at night. Be thankful for these walls."

Thomas swallowed, wondering how he could ever go out there. His desire to become a Runner had taken a major blow. But he had to do it. Somehow he *knew* he had to do it. It was such an odd thing to feel, especially after what he'd just seen.

Newt looked at the window absently. "Now you know what bloody lurks in the Maze, my friend. Now you know this isn't joke time. You've been sent to the Glade, Greenie, and we'll be expectin' ya to survive and help us do what we've been sent here to do."

"And what's that?" Thomas asked, even though he was terrified to hear the answer.

Newt turned to look him dead in the eye. The first traces of dawn had crept up on them, and Thomas could see every detail of Newt's face, his skin tight, his brow creased.

"Find our way out, Greenie," Newt said. "Solve the buggin' Maze and find our way home."

A couple of hours later, the doors having reopened, rumbling and grumbling and shaking the ground until they were finished, Thomas sat at a worn, tilted picnic table outside the Homestead. All he could think about was the Grievers, what their purpose could be, what they did out there during the night. What it would be like to be attacked by something so terrible.

He tried to get the image out of his head, move on to something else. The Runners. They'd just left without saying a word to anybody, bolting into the Maze at full speed and disappearing around corners. He pictured them in his mind as he picked at his eggs and bacon with a fork, speaking to no one, not even Chuck, who ate silently next to him. The poor guy had exhausted himself trying to start a conversation with Thomas, who'd refused to respond. All he wanted was to be left alone.

He just didn't get it; his brain was on overload trying to compute the sheer impossibility of the situation. How could a maze, with walls so massive and tall, be so big that dozens of kids hadn't been able to solve it after who knew how long trying? How could such a structure exist? And more importantly, *why?* What could possibly be the purpose of such a thing? Why were they all there? How *long* had they been there?

Try as he might to avoid it, his mind still kept wandering back to the image of the vicious Griever. Its phantom brother seemed to leap at him every time he blinked or rubbed his eyes.

Thomas knew he was a smart kid—he somehow felt it in his bones. But nothing about this place made any sense. Except for one thing. He was supposed to be a Runner. Why did he feel that so strongly? And even now, after seeing what lived in the maze?

A tap on his shoulder jarred him from his thoughts; he looked up to see Alby standing behind him, arms folded.

"Ain't you lookin' fresh?" Alby said. "Get a nice view out the window this morning?"

Thomas stood, hoping the time for answers had come—or maybe hoping for a distraction from his gloomy thoughts. "Enough to make me want to learn about this place," he said, hoping to avoid provoking the temper he'd seen flare in this guy the day before.

Alby nodded. "Me and you, shank. The Tour begins now." He started to move but then stopped, holding up a finger. "Ain't no questions till the end, you get me? Ain't got time to jaw with you all day."

"But . . ." Thomas stopped when Alby's eyebrows shot up. Why did the guy have to be such a jerk? "But tell me everything—I wanna know everything." He'd decided the night before not to tell anyone else how strangely familiar the place seemed, the odd feeling that he'd been there before—that he could *remember* things about it. Sharing that seemed like a very bad idea.

"I'll tell ya what I wanna tell ya, Greenie. Let's go."

"Can I come?" Chuck asked from the table.

Alby reached down and tweaked the boy's ear.

"Ow!" Chuck shrieked.

"Ain't you got a job, slinthead?" Alby asked. "Lots of sloppin' to do?"

Chuck rolled his eyes, then looked at Thomas. "Have fun."

"I'll try." He suddenly felt sorry for Chuck, wished people would treat the kid better. But there was nothing he could do about it—it was time to go.

He walked away with Alby, hoping the Tour had officially begun.

41

CHAPTER 7

They started at the Box, which was closed at the moment—double doors of metal lying flat on the ground, covered in white paint, faded and cracked. The day had brightened considerably, the shadows stretching in the opposite direction from what Thomas had seen yesterday. He still hadn't spotted the sun, but it looked like it was about to pop over the eastern wall at any minute.

Alby pointed down at the doors. "This here's the Box. Once a month, we get a Newbie like you, never fails. Once a *week,* we get supplies, clothes, some food. Ain't needin' a lot—pretty much run ourselves in the Glade."

Thomas nodded, his whole body itching with the desire to ask questions. *I need some tape to put over my mouth,* he thought.

"We don't know jack about the Box, you get me?" Alby continued. "Where it came from, how it gets here, who's in charge. The shanks that sent us here ain't told us nothin'. We got all the electricity we need, grow and raise most of our food, get clothes and such. Tried to send a slinthead Greenie back in the Box one time—thing wouldn't move till we took him out."

Thomas wondered what lay under the doors when the Box wasn't there, but held his tongue. He felt such a mixture of emotions—curiosity, frustration, wonder—all laced with the lingering horror of seeing the Griever that morning.

Alby kept talking, never bothering to look Thomas in the eye. "Glade's cut into four sections." He held up his fingers as he counted off the next four words. "Gardens, Blood House, Homestead, Deadheads. You got that?"

Thomas hesitated, then shook his head, confused.

Alby's eyelids fluttered briefly as he continued; he looked like he could think of a thousand things he'd rather be doing right then. He pointed to the northeast corner, where the fields and fruit trees were located. "Gardens—where we grow the crops. Water's pumped in through pipes in the ground—always has been, or we'd have starved to death a long time ago. Never rains here. Never." He pointed to the southeast corner, at the animal pens and barn. "Blood House— where we raise and slaughter animals." He pointed at the pitiful living quarters. "Homestead—stupid place is twice as big than when the first of us got here because we keep addin' to it when they send us wood and klunk. Ain't pretty, but it works. Most of us sleep outside anyway."

Thomas felt dizzy. So many questions splintered his mind he couldn't keep them straight.

Alby pointed to the southwest corner, the forest area fronted with several sickly trees and benches. "Call that the Deadheads. Graveyard's back in that corner, in the thicker woods. Ain't much else. You can go there to sit and rest, hang out, whatever." He cleared his throat, as if wanting to change subjects. "You'll spend the next two weeks working one day apiece for our different job Keepers—until we know what you're best at. Slopper, Bricknick, Bagger, Track-hoe—somethin'll stick, always does. Come on."

Alby walked toward the South Door, located between what he'd called the Deadheads and the Blood House. Thomas followed, wrinkling his nose up at the sudden smell of dirt and manure coming from the animal pens. *Graveyard?* he thought. *Why do they need a graveyard in a place full of teenagers?* That disturbed him even more than not knowing some of the words Alby kept saying—words like *Slopper* and *Bagger*—that didn't sound so good. He came as close to interrupting Alby as he'd done so far, but willed his mouth shut.

Frustrated, he turned his attention to the pens in the Blood House area.

Several cows nibbled and chewed at a trough full of greenish hay. Pigs lounged in a muddy pit, an occasionally flickering tail the only sign they were alive. Another pen held sheep, and there were chicken coops and turkey cages as well. Workers bustled about the area, looking as if they'd spent their whole lives on a farm.

Why do I remember these animals? Thomas wondered. Nothing about them seemed new or interesting—he knew what they were called, what they normally ate, what they looked like. Why was stuff like that still lodged in his memory, but not *where* he'd seen animals before, or with whom? His memory loss was baffling in its complexity.

Alby pointed to the large barn in the back corner, its red paint long faded to a dull rust color. "Back there's where the Slicers work. Nasty stuff, that. Nasty. If you like blood, you can be a Slicer."

Thomas shook his head. Slicer didn't sound good at all. As they kept walking, he focused his attention on the other side of the Glade, the section Alby had called the Deadheads. The trees grew thicker and denser the farther back in the corner they went, more alive and full of leaves. Dark shadows filled the depths of the wooded area, despite the time of day. Thomas looked up, squinting to see that the sun was finally visible, though it looked odd—more orange than it should be. It hit him that this was yet another example of the odd selective memory in his mind.

He returned his gaze to the Deadheads, a glowing disk still floating in his vision. Blinking to clear it away, he suddenly caught the red lights again, flickering and skittering about deep in the darkness of the woods. *What* are *those things?* he wondered, irritated that Alby hadn't answered him earlier. The secrecy was very annoying.

Alby stopped walking, and Thomas was surprised to see they'd reached the South Door; the two walls bracketing the exit towered above them. The thick slabs of gray stone were cracked and covered in ivy, as ancient as anything Thomas could imagine. He craned his neck to see the top of the walls far above; his mind spun with the odd sensation that he was looking *down*, not up. He staggered back a step, awed once again by the structure of his new home, then finally returned his attention to Alby, who had his back to the exit.

"Out there's the Maze." Alby jabbed a thumb over his shoulder, then paused. Thomas stared in that direction, through the gap in the walls that served as an exit from the Glade. The corridors out there looked much the same as the ones he'd seen from the window by the East Door early that morning. This thought gave him a chill, made him wonder if a Griever might come charging toward them at any minute. He took a step backward before realizing what he was doing. *Calm down,* he chided himself, embarrassed.

Alby continued. "Two years, I've been here. Ain't none been here longer. The few before me are already dead." Thomas felt his eyes widen, his heart quicken. "Two years we've tried to solve this thing, no luck. Shuckin' walls move out there at night just as much as these here doors. Mappin' it out ain't easy, ain't easy nohow." He nodded toward the concrete-blocked building into which the Runners had disappeared the night before.

Another stab of pain sliced through Thomas's head—there were too many things to compute at once. They'd been here two years? The walls moved out in the Maze? How many had died? He stepped forward, wanting to see the Maze for himself, as if the answers were printed on the walls out there.

Alby held out a hand and pushed Thomas in the chest, sent him stumbling backward. "Ain't no goin' out there, shank."

Thomas had to suppress his pride. "Why not?"

"You think I sent Newt to ya before the wake-up just for kicks? Freak, that's the Number One Rule, the only one you'll never be forgiven for breaking. Ain't nobody—*nobody*—allowed in the Maze except the Runners. Break that rule, and if you ain't killed by the Grievers, we'll kill you ourselves, you get me?"

Thomas nodded, grumbling inside, sure that Alby was exaggerating. Hoping that he was. Either way, if he'd had any doubt about what he'd told Chuck the night before, it had now completely vanished. He wanted to be a Runner. He *would* be a Runner. Deep inside he knew he had to go out there, into the Maze. Despite everything he'd learned and witnessed firsthand, it called to him as much as hunger or thirst.

A movement up on the left wall of the South Door caught his attention. Startled, he reacted quickly, looking just in time to see a flash of silver. A patch of ivy shook as the thing disappeared into it.

Thomas pointed up at the wall. "What was that?" he asked before he could be shut down again.

Alby didn't bother looking. "No questions till the end, shank. How many times I gotta tell ya?" He paused, then let out a sigh. "Beetle blades—it's how the Creators watch us. You better not—"

He was cut off by a booming, ringing alarm that sounded from all directions. Thomas clamped his hands to his ears, looking around as the siren blared, his heart about to thump its way out of his chest. But when he focused back on Alby, he stopped.

Alby wasn't acting scared—he appeared . . . confused. Surprised. The alarm clanged through the air.

"What's going on?" Thomas asked. Relief flooded his chest that his tour guide didn't seem to think the world was about to end—but even so, Thomas was getting tired of being hit by waves of panic.

"That's weird" was all Alby said as he scanned the Glade, squinting. Thomas noticed people in the Blood House pens glancing around, apparently just as confused. One shouted to Alby, a short, skinny kid drenched in mud.

"What's up with that?" the boy asked, looking to Thomas for some reason.

"I don't know," Alby murmured back in a distant voice.

But Thomas couldn't stand it anymore. "Alby! What's going on?"

"The Box, shuck-face, the Box!" was all Alby said before he set off for the middle of the Glade at a brisk pace that almost looked to Thomas like panic.

"What about it?" Thomas demanded, hurrying to catch up. *Talk to me!* he wanted to scream at him.

But Alby didn't answer or slow down, and as they got closer to the box Thomas could see that dozens of kids were running around the courtyard. He spotted Newt and called to him, trying to suppress his rising fear, telling himself things would be okay, that there had to be a reasonable explanation.

"Newt, what's going on!" he yelled.

Newt glanced over at him, then nodded and walked over, strangely calm in the middle of the chaos. He swatted Thomas on the back. "Means a bloody Newbie's comin' up in the Box." He paused as if expecting Thomas to be impressed. "Right *now*."

"So?" As Thomas looked more closely at Newt, he realized that what he'd mistaken for calm was actually disbelief—maybe even excitement.

"So?" Newt replied, his jaw dropping slightly. "Greenie, we've never had two Newbies show up in the same *month,* much less two days in a row."

And with that, he ran off toward the Homestead.

CHAPTER 8

The alarm finally stopped after blaring for a full two minutes. A crowd was gathered in the middle of the courtyard around the steel doors through which Thomas was startled to realize he'd arrived just yesterday. *Yesterday?* he thought. *Was that really just* yesterday?

Someone tapped him on the elbow; he looked over to see Chuck by his side again.

"How goes it, Greenbean?" Chuck asked.

"Fine," he replied, even though nothing could've been further from the truth. He pointed toward the doors of the Box. "Why is everyone freaking out? Isn't this how you all got here?"

Chuck shrugged. "I don't know—guess it's always been real regular-like. One a month, every month, same day. Maybe whoever's in charge realized you were nothing but a big mistake, sent someone to replace you." He giggled as he elbowed Thomas in the ribs, a high-pitched snicker that inexplicably made Thomas like him more.

Thomas shot his new friend a fake glare. "You're annoying. Seriously."

"Yeah, but we're buddies, now, right?" Chuck fully laughed this time, a squeaky sort of snort.

"Looks like you're not giving me much choice on that one." But truth was, he needed a friend, and Chuck would do just fine.

The kid folded his arms, looking very satisfied. "Glad that's settled, Greenie. Everyone needs a buddy in this place."

49

Thomas grabbed Chuck by the collar, joking around. "Okay, *buddy,* then call me by my name. Thomas. Or I'll throw you down the hole after the Box leaves." That triggered a thought in his head as he released Chuck. "Wait a minute, have you guys ever—"

"Tried it," Chuck interrupted before Thomas could finish.

"Tried what?"

"Going down in the Box after it makes a delivery," Chuck answered. "It won't do it. Won't go down until it's completely empty."

Thomas remembered Alby telling him that very thing. "I already knew that, but what about—"

"Tried it."

Thomas had to suppress a groan—this was getting irritating. "Man you're hard to talk to. Tried what?"

"Going through the hole *after* the Box goes down. Can't. Doors will open, but there's just emptiness, blackness, nothing. No ropes, nada. Can't do it."

How could that be possible? "Did you—"

"Tried it."

Thomas did groan this time. "Okay, what?"

"We threw some things into the hole. Never heard them land. It goes on for a long time."

Thomas paused before he replied, not wanting to be cut off again. "What are you, a mind reader or something?" He threw as much sarcasm as he could into the comment.

"Just brilliant, that's all." Chuck winked.

"Chuck, never wink at me again." Thomas said it with a smile. Chuck *was* a little annoying, but there was something about him that made things seem less terrible. Thomas took a deep breath and looked back toward the crowd around the hole. "So, how long until the delivery gets here?"

"Usually takes about half an hour after the alarm."

Thomas thought for a second. There *had* to be something they hadn't tried. "You're sure about the hole? Have you ever . . ." He paused, waiting for the interruption, but none came. "Have you ever tried making a rope?"

"Yeah, they did. With the ivy. Longest one they could possibly make. Let's just say that little experiment didn't go so well."

"What do you mean?" *What now?* Thomas thought.

"I wasn't here, but I heard the kid who volunteered to do it had only gone down about ten feet when something swooshed through the air and cut him clean in half."

"What?" Thomas laughed. "I don't believe that for a second."

"Oh, yeah, smart guy? I've seen the sucker's bones. Cut in half like a knife through whipped cream. They keep him in a box to remind future kids not to be so stupid."

Thomas waited for Chuck to laugh or smile, thinking it had to be a joke—who ever heard of someone being cut in half? But it never came. "You're serious?"

Chuck just stared back at him. "I don't lie, Gree—uh, Thomas. Come on, let's go over and see who's coming up. I can't believe you only have to be the Greenbean for one day. Klunkhead."

As they walked over, Thomas asked the one question he hadn't posed yet. "How do you know it's not just supplies or whatever?"

"The alarm doesn't go off when that happens," Chuck answered, simply. "The supplies come up at the same time every week. Hey, look." Chuck stopped and pointed to someone in the crowd. It was Gally, staring dead at them.

"Shuck it," Chuck said. "He does *not* like you, man."

"Yeah," Thomas muttered. "Figured that out already." And the feeling was mutual.

Chuck nudged Thomas with his elbow and the boys resumed their walk to the edge of the crowd, then waited in silence; any questions Thomas had were forgotten. He'd lost the urge to talk after seeing Gally.

Chuck apparently hadn't. "Why don't you go ask him what his problem is?" he asked, trying to sound tough.

Thomas wanted to think he was brave enough, but that currently sounded like the worst idea in history. "Well, for one, he has a lot more allies than I do. Not a good person to pick a fight with."

"Yeah, but you're smarter. And I bet you're quicker. You could take him and all his buddies."

One of the boys standing in front of them looked back over his shoulder, annoyance crossing his face.

Must be a friend of Gally's, Thomas thought. "Would you shut it?" he hissed at Chuck.

A door closed behind them; Thomas turned to see Alby and Newt heading over from the Homestead. They both looked exhausted.

Seeing them brought Ben back to his mind—along with the horrific image of him writhing in bed. "Chuck, man, you gotta tell me what this whole Changing business is. What have they been *doing* in there with that poor Ben kid?"

Chuck shrugged. "Don't know the details. The Grievers do bad things to you, make your whole body go through something awful. When it's over, you're . . . different."

Thomas sensed a chance to finally have a solid answer. "Different? What do you mean? And what does it have to do with the Grievers? Is that what Gally meant by 'being stung'?"

"Shh." Chuck held a finger to his mouth.

Thomas almost screamed in frustration, but he kept quiet. He resolved to make Chuck tell him later, whether the guy wanted to or not.

Alby and Newt had reached the crowd and pushed themselves to the front, standing right over the doors that led to the Box. Everyone quieted, and for the first time, Thomas noted the grinds and rattles of the rising lift, reminding him of his own nightmarish trip the day before. Sadness washed over him, almost as if he were reliving those few terrible minutes of awakening in darkness to the memory loss. He felt sorry for whoever this new kid was, going through the same things.

A muffled boom announced that the bizarre elevator had arrived.

Thomas watched in anticipation as Newt and Alby took positions on opposite sides of the shaft doors—a crack split the metal square right down the middle. Simple hook-handles were attached on both sides, and together they yanked them apart. With a metallic scrape the doors were opened, and a puff of dust from the surrounding stone rose into the air.

Complete silence settled over the Gladers. As Newt leaned over to get a better look into the Box, the faint bleating of a goat in the distance echoed across the courtyard. Thomas leaned forward as far as he possibly could, hoping to get a glance at the newcomer.

With a sudden jerk, Newt pushed himself back into an upright position, his face scrunched up in confusion. "Holy . . . ," he breathed, looking around at nothing in particular.

By this time, Alby had gotten a good look as well, with a similar reaction. "No way," he murmured, almost in a trance.

A chorus of questions filled the air as everyone began pushing forward to get a look into the small opening. *What do they see down there?* Thomas wondered. *What do they see!* He felt a sliver of muted fear, similar to what he'd experienced that morning when he stepped toward the window to see the Griever.

"Hold on!" Alby yelled, silencing everyone. "Just hold on!"

"Well, what's wrong?" someone yelled back.

Alby stood up. "Two Newbies in two days," he said, almost in a whisper. "Now this. Two years, nothing different, now this." Then, for some reason, he looked straight at Thomas. "What's goin' on here, Greenie?"

Thomas stared back, confused, his face turning bright red, his gut clenching. "How am I supposed to know?"

"Why don't you just tell us what the shuck is down there, Alby?" Gally called out. There were more murmurs and another surge forward.

"You shanks shut up!" Alby yelled. "Tell 'em, Newt."

Newt looked down in the Box one more time, then faced the crowd, gravely.

"It's a girl," he said.

Everyone started talking at once; Thomas only caught pieces here and there.

"A *girl*?"

"I got dibs!"

"What's she look like?"

"How old is she?"

Thomas was drowning in a sea of confusion. A *girl*? He hadn't even thought about why the Glade only had boys, no girls. Hadn't even had the chance to notice, really. *Who is she?* he wondered. *Why*—

Newt shushed them again. "That's not bloody half of it," he said, then pointed down into the Box. "I think she's dead."

A couple of boys grabbed some ropes made from ivy vines and lowered Alby and Newt into the Box so they could retrieve the girl's body. A mood of reserved shock had come over most of the Gladers, who were milling about with solemn faces, kicking loose rocks and not saying much at all. No one dared admit they couldn't wait to see the girl, but Thomas assumed they were all just as curious as he was.

Gally was one of the boys holding on to the ropes, ready to hoist her, Alby, and Newt out of the Box. Thomas watched him closely. His eyes were laced with something dark—almost a sick fascination. A gleam that made Thomas suddenly more scared of him than he'd been minutes earlier.

From deep in the shaft came Alby's voice shouting that they were ready, and Gally and a couple of others started pulling up on the rope. A few grunts later and the girl's lifeless body was dragged out, across the edge of the door and onto one of the stone blocks making up the ground of the Glade. Everyone immediately ran forward, forming a packed crowd around her, a palpable excitement hovering in the air. But Thomas stayed back. The eerie silence gave him the creeps, as if they'd just opened up a recently laid tomb.

Despite his own curiosity, Thomas didn't bother trying to force his way through to get a look—the bodies were too tightly squeezed together. But he *had* caught a glimpse of her before being blocked off. She was thin, but not too small. Maybe five and a half feet tall, from what he could tell. She looked like she could be fifteen or sixteen years old, and her hair was tar black. But the thing that had really stood out to him was her skin: pale, white as pearls.

Newt and Alby scrambled out of the Box after her, then forced their way through to the girl's lifeless body, the crowd re-forming behind to cut them off from Thomas's view. Only a few seconds later, the group parted again, and Newt was pointing straight at Thomas.

"Greenie, get over here," he said, not bothering to be polite about it.

Thomas's heart jumped into his throat; his hands started to sweat. What did they want him for? Things just kept getting worse and worse. He forced himself to walk forward, trying to seem innocent without acting like someone who was guilty who was trying to act innocent. *Oh, calm it,* he told himself. *You haven't done anything wrong.* But he had a strange feeling that maybe he had without realizing it.

The boys lining the path to Newt and the girl glared at him as he walked past, as if he were responsible for the entire mess of the Maze and the Glade and the Grievers. Thomas refused to make eye contact with any of them, afraid of looking guilty.

He approached Newt and Alby, who both knelt beside the girl. Thomas, not wanting to meet their stares, concentrated on the girl; despite her paleness, she was really pretty. More than pretty. Beautiful. Silky hair, flawless skin, perfect lips, long legs. It made him sick to think that way about a dead girl, but he couldn't look away. *Won't be that way for long,* he thought with a queasy twist in his stomach. *She'll start rotting soon.* He was surprised at having such a morbid thought.

"You know this girl, shank?" Alby asked, sounding ticked off.

Thomas was shocked by the question. "*Know* her? Of course I don't know her. I don't know anyone. Except for you guys."

"That's not . . . ," Alby began, then stopped with a frustrated sigh. "I meant does she look *familiar* at all? Any kind of feelin' you've seen her before?"

"No. Nothing." Thomas shifted, looked down at his feet, then back at the girl.

Alby's forehead creased. "You're sure?" He looked like he didn't believe a word Thomas said, seemed almost angry.

What could he possibly think I have to do with this? Thomas thought. He met Alby's glare evenly and answered the only way he knew how. "*Yes.* Why?"

"Shuck it," Alby muttered, looking back down at the girl. "Can't be a coincidence. Two days, two Greenies, one alive, one dead."

Then Alby's words started to make sense and panic flared in Thomas. "You don't think I . . ." He couldn't even finish the sentence.

"Slim it, Greenie," Newt said. "We're not sayin' you bloody killed the girl."

Thomas's mind was spinning. He was sure he'd never seen her before—but then the slightest hint of doubt crept into his mind. "I swear she doesn't look familiar at all," he said anyway. He'd had enough accusations.

"Are you—"

Before Newt could finish, the girl shot up into a sitting position. As she sucked in a huge breath, her eyes snapped open and she blinked, looking around at the crowd surrounding her. Alby cried out and fell backward. Newt gasped and jumped up, stumbling away from her. Thomas didn't move, his gaze locked on the girl, frozen in fear.

Burning blue eyes darted back and forth as she took deep breaths. Her pink lips trembled as she mumbled something over and over, indecipherable. Then she spoke one sentence—her voice hollow and haunted, but clear.

"Everything is going to change."

Thomas stared in wonder as her eyes rolled up into her head and she fell back to the ground. Her right fist shot into the air as she landed, staying rigid after she grew still, pointing toward the sky. Clutched in her hand was a wadded piece of paper.

Thomas tried to swallow but his mouth was too dry. Newt ran forward and pulled her fingers apart, grabbing the paper. With shaking hands he unfolded it, then dropped to his knees, spreading out the note on the ground. Thomas moved up behind him to get a look.

Scrawled across the paper in thick black letters were five words:

She's the last one.
Ever.

CHAPTER 9

An odd moment of complete silence hung over the Glade. It was as if a supernatural wind had swept through the place and sucked out all sound. Newt had read the message aloud for those who couldn't see the paper, but instead of erupting in confusion, the Gladers all stood dumbfounded.

Thomas would've expected shouts and questions, arguments. But no one said a word; all eyes were glued to the girl, now lying there as if asleep, her chest rising and falling with shallow breaths. Contrary to their original conclusion, she was very much alive.

Newt stood, and Thomas hoped for an explanation, a voice of reason, a calming presence. But all he did was crumple the note in his fist, veins popping from his skin as he squeezed it, and Thomas's heart sank. He wasn't sure why, but the situation made him very uneasy.

Alby cupped his hands around his mouth. "Med-jacks!"

Thomas wondered what that word meant—he knew he'd heard it before—but then he was abruptly knocked aside. Two older boys were pushing their way through the crowd—one was tall with a buzz cut, his nose the size of a fat lemon. The other was short and actually had gray hair already conquering the black on the sides of his head. Thomas could only hope they'd make some sense of everything.

"So what do we do with her?" the taller one asked, his voice much higher pitched than Thomas expected.

"How should I know?" Alby said. "You two shanks are the Med–jacks—figure it out."

Med-jacks, Thomas repeated in his head, a light going off. *They must be the closest thing they have to doctors.* The short one was already on the ground, kneeling beside the girl, feeling for her pulse and leaning over to listen to her heartbeat.

"Who said Clint had first shot at her?" someone yelled from the crowd. There were several barks of laughter. "I'm next!"

How can they joke around? Thomas thought. *The girl's half dead.* He felt sick inside.

Alby's eyes narrowed; his mouth pulled into a tight grin that didn't look like it had anything to do with humor. "If anybody touches this girl," Alby said, "you're gonna spend the night sleepin' with the Griev–ers in the Maze. Banished, no questions." He paused, turning in a slow circle as if he wanted every person to see his face. "Ain't nobody bet–ter touch her! Nobody!"

It was the first time Thomas had actually liked hearing something come out of Alby's mouth.

The short guy who'd been referred to as a Med-jack—*Clint,* if the spectator had been correct—stood up from his examination. "She seems fine. Breathing okay, normal heartbeat. Though it's a bit slow. Your guess is as good as mine, but I'd say she's in a coma. Jeff, let's take her to the Homestead."

His partner, Jeff, stepped over to grab her by the arms while Clint took hold of her feet. Thomas wished he could do more than watch—with every passing second, he doubted more and more that what he'd said earlier was true. She *did* seem familiar; he felt a connection to her, though it was impossible to grasp in his mind. The idea made him ner–vous, and he looked around, as if someone might've heard his thoughts.

"On the count of three," Jeff, the taller Med-jack, was saying, his tall frame looking ridiculous bent in half, like a praying mantis. "One . . . two . . . three!"

They lifted her with a quick jerk, almost throwing her up in the air—she was obviously a lot lighter than they'd thought—and Thomas almost shouted at them to be more careful.

"Guess we'll have to see what she does," Jeff said to no one in particular. "We can feed her soupy stuff if she doesn't wake up soon."

"Just watch her closely," Newt said. "Must be something special about her or they wouldn't have sent her here."

Thomas's gut clenched. He knew that he and the girl were connected somehow. They'd come a day apart, she seemed familiar, he had a consuming urge to become a Runner despite learning so many terrible things. . . . What did it all mean?

Alby leaned over to look in her face once more before they carried her off. "Put her next to Ben's room, and keep a watch on her day and night. Nothin' better happen without me knowing about it. I don't care if she talks in her sleep or takes a klunk—you come tell me."

"Yeah," Jeff muttered; then he and Clint shuffled off to the Homestead, the girl's body bouncing as they went, and the other Gladers finally started to talk about it, scattering as theories bubbled through the air.

Thomas watched all this in mute contemplation. This strange connection he felt wasn't his alone. The not-so-veiled accusations thrown at him only a few minutes before proved that the others suspected something, too, but what? He was already completely confused—being blamed for things only made him feel worse. As if reading his thoughts, Alby walked over and grabbed him by the shoulder.

"You ain't never seen her before?" he asked.

Thomas hesitated before he answered. "Not . . . no, not that I remember." He hoped his shaky voice didn't betray his doubts. What if he *did* know her somehow? What would that mean?

"You're sure?" Newt prodded, standing right behind Alby.

"I . . . no, I don't think so. Why are you grilling me like this?" All Thomas wanted right then was for night to fall, so he could be alone, go to sleep.

Alby shook his head, then turned back to Newt, releasing his grip on Thomas's shoulder. "Something's whacked. Call a Gathering."

He said it quietly enough that Thomas didn't think anyone else heard, but it sounded ominous. Then the leader and Newt walked off, and Thomas was relieved to see Chuck coming his way.

"Chuck, what's a Gathering?"

He looked proud to know the answer. "It's when the Keepers meet—they only call one when something weird or terrible happens."

"Well, I guess today fits both of those categories pretty well." Thomas's stomach rumbled, interrupting his thoughts. "I didn't finish my breakfast—can we get something somewhere? I'm starving."

Chuck looked up at him, his eyebrows raised. "Seeing that chick wig out made you hungry? You must be more psycho than I thought."

Thomas sighed. "Just get me some food."

The kitchen was small but had everything one needed to make a hearty meal. A big oven, a microwave, a dishwasher, a couple of tables. It seemed old and run-down but clean. Seeing the appliances and the familiar layout made Thomas feel as if memories—real, solid memories—were right on the edge of his mind. But again, the essential parts were missing—names, faces, places, events. It was maddening.

"Take a seat," Chuck said. "I'll get you something—but I swear this is the last time. Just be glad Frypan isn't around—he hates it when we raid his fridge."

Thomas was relieved they were alone. As Chuck fumbled about with dishes and things from the fridge, Thomas pulled out a wooden chair from a small plastic table and sat down. "This is crazy. How can this be for real? Somebody sent us here. Somebody evil."

Chuck paused. "Quit complaining. Just accept it and don't think about it."

"Yeah, right." Thomas looked out a window. This seemed a good time to bring up one of the million questions bouncing through his brain. "So where does the electricity come from?"

"Who cares? I'll take it."

What a surprise, Thomas thought. *No answer.*

Chuck brought two plates with sandwiches and carrots over to the table. The bread was thick and white, the carrots a sparkling, bright orange. Thomas's stomach begged him to hurry; he picked up his sandwich and started devouring it.

"Oh, man," he mumbled with a full mouth. "At least the food is good."

Thomas was able to eat the rest of his meal without another word from Chuck. And he was lucky that the kid didn't feel like talking, because despite the complete weirdness of everything that had happened within Thomas's known reach of memory, he felt calm again. His stomach full, his energy replenished, his mind thankful for a few moments of silence, he decided that from then on he'd quit whining and deal with things.

After his last bite, Thomas sat back in his chair. "So, Chuck," he said as he wiped his mouth with a napkin. "What do I have to do to become a Runner?"

"Not that again." Chuck looked up from his plate, where he'd been picking at the crumbs. He let out a low, gurgly burp that made Thomas cringe.

"Alby said I'd start my trials soon with the different Keepers. So, when do I get a shot with the Runners?" Thomas waited patiently to get some sort of actual information from Chuck.

Chuck rolled his eyes dramatically, leaving no doubt as to how stupid an idea he thought that would be. "They should be back in a few hours. Why don't you ask *them?*"

Thomas ignored the sarcasm, digging deeper. "What do they do when they get back every night? What's up with the concrete building?"

"Maps. They meet right when they get back, before they forget anything."

Maps? Thomas was confused. "But if they're trying to make a map, don't they have paper to write on while they're out there?" Maps. This intrigued him more than anything else he'd heard in a while. It was the first thing suggesting a potential solution to their predicament.

"Of course they do, but there's still stuff they need to talk about and discuss and analyze and all that klunk. Plus"—the boy rolled his eyes—"they spend most of their time running, not writing. That's why they're called *Runners.*"

Thomas thought about the Runners and the maps. Could the Maze really be so massively huge that even after two years they still hadn't found a way out? It seemed impossible. But then, he remembered what Alby said about the moving walls. What if all of them were sentenced to live here until they died?

Sentenced. The word made him feel a rush of panic, and the spark of hope the meal had brought him fizzled with a silent hiss.

"Chuck, what if we're all criminals? I mean—what if we're murderers or something?"

"Huh?" Chuck looked up at him as if he were a crazy person. "Where did that happy thought come from?"

"Think about it. Our memories are wiped. We live inside a place that seems to have no way out, surrounded by bloodthirsty monster-guards. Doesn't that sound like a prison to you?" As he said it out loud, it sounded more and more possible. Nausea trickled into his chest.

"I'm probably twelve years old, dude." Chuck pointed to his chest. "At the most, thirteen. You really think I did something that would send me to prison for the rest of my life?"

"I don't care what you did or didn't do. Either way, you *have* been sent to a prison. Does this seem like a vacation to you?" *Oh, man,* Thomas thought. *Please let me be wrong.*

Chuck thought for a moment. "I don't know. It's better than—"

"Yeah, I know, living in pile of klunk." Thomas stood up and pushed his chair back under the table. He liked Chuck, but trying to have an intelligent conversation with him was impossible. Not to mention frustrating and irritating. "Go make yourself another sandwich— I'm going exploring. See ya tonight."

He stepped out of the kitchen and into the courtyard before Chuck could offer to join him. The Glade had gone back to business as usual— people working the jobs, the doors of the Box closed, sun shining down. Any signs of a crazed girl bearing notes of doom had disappeared.

Having had his tour cut short, he decided to take a walk around the Glade on his own and get a better look and feel for the place. He headed out for the northeast corner, toward the big rows of tall green cornstalks that looked ready to harvest. There was other stuff, too: tomatoes, lettuce, peas, a lot more that Thomas didn't recognize.

He took a deep breath, loving the fresh whiff of dirt and growing plants. He was almost positive the smell would bring back some sort of pleasant memory, but nothing came. As he got closer, he saw that several boys were weeding and picking in the small fields. One waved at him with a smile. An actual smile.

Maybe this place won't be so bad after all, Thomas thought. *Not everyone here could be a jerk.* He took another deep breath of the pleasant air and pulled himself out of his thoughts—there was a lot more he wanted to see.

Next was the southeast corner, where shabbily built wooden fences held in several cows, goats, sheep, and pigs. No horses, though. *That sucks,* Thomas thought. *Riders* would definitely be faster than *Runners.* As he approached, he figured he must've dealt with animals in his life before the Glade. Their smell, their sound—they seemed very familiar to him.

The smell wasn't quite as nice as the crops, but still, he imagined it could've been a lot worse. As he explored the area, he realized more and more how well the Gladers kept up the place, how clean it was. He was impressed by how organized they must be, how hard they all must work. He could only imagine how truly horrific a place like this could be if everyone went lazy and stupid.

Finally, he made it to the southwest quarter, near the forest.

He was approaching the sparse, skeletal trees in front of the denser woods when he was startled by a blur of movement at his feet, followed by a hurried set of clacking sounds. He looked down just in time to see the sun flash off something metallic—a toy rat—scurrying past him and toward the small forest. The thing was already ten feet away by the time he realized it wasn't a rat at all—it was more like a lizard, with at least six legs scuttling the long silver torso along.

A beetle blade. *It's how they watch us,* Alby had said.

He caught a gleam of red light sweeping the ground in front of the creature as if it came from its eyes. Logic told him it had to be his mind playing tricks on him, but he swore he saw the word *WICKED* scrawled down its rounded back in large green letters. Something so strange had to be investigated.

Thomas sprinted after the scurrying spy, and in a matter of seconds he entered the thick copse of trees and the world became dark.

CHAPTER 10

He couldn't believe how quickly the light disappeared. From the Glade proper, the forest didn't look that big, maybe a couple of acres. Yet the trees were tall with sturdy trunks, packed tightly together, the canopy up above thick with leaves. The air around him had a greenish, muted hue, as if only several minutes of twilight remained in the day.

It was somehow beautiful and creepy, all at once.

Moving as fast as he could, Thomas crashed through the heavy foliage, thin branches slapping at his face. He ducked to avoid a low-hanging limb, almost falling. Reaching out, he caught hold of a branch and swung himself forward to regain his balance. A thick bed of leaves and fallen twigs crunched underneath him.

All the while, his eyes stayed riveted on the beetle blade scuttling across the forest floor. Deeper it went, its red light glowing brighter as the surroundings darkened.

Thomas had charged thirty or forty feet into the woods, dodging and ducking and losing ground with every second, when the beetle blade jumped onto a particularly large tree and scooted up its trunk. But by the time Thomas reached the tree, any sign of the creature had vanished. It had disappeared deep within the foliage—almost as if it had never existed.

He'd lost the sucker.

"Shuck it," Thomas whispered, almost as a joke. Almost. As strange as it seemed, the word felt natural on his lips, like he was already morphing into a Glader.

A twig snapped somewhere to his right and he jerked his head in that direction. He stilled his breath, listened.

Another snap, this time louder, almost like someone had broken a stick over their knee.

"Who's there?" Thomas yelled out, a tingle of fear shooting across his shoulders. His voice bounced off the canopy of leaves above him, echoing through the air. He stayed frozen, rooted to the spot as all grew silent, except for the whistling song of a few birds in the distance. But no one answered his call. Nor did he hear any more sounds from that direction.

Without really thinking it through, Thomas headed toward the noise he'd heard. Not bothering to hide his progress, he pushed aside branches as he walked, letting them whip back to position when he passed. He squinted, willed his eyes to work in the growing darkness, wishing he had a flashlight. He thought about flashlights and his memory. Once again, he remembered a tangible thing from his past, but couldn't assign it to any specific time or place, couldn't associate it with any other person or event. Frustrating.

"Anybody there?" he asked again, feeling a little calmer since the noise hadn't repeated. It was probably just an animal, maybe another beetle blade. Just in case, he called out, "It's me, Thomas. The new guy. Well, second-newest guy."

He winced and shook his head, hoping now that no one *was* there. He sounded like a complete idiot.

Again, no reply.

He stepped around a large oak and pulled up short. An icy shiver ran down his back. He'd reached the graveyard.

The clearing was small, maybe thirty square feet, and covered with a thick layer of leafy weeds growing close to the ground. Thomas could see several clumsily prepared wooden crosses poking through this growth, their horizontal pieces lashed to the upright ones with a splintery twine. The grave markers had been painted white, but by someone in an obvious hurry—gelled globs covered them and bare streaks of wood showed through. Names had been carved into the wood.

Thomas stepped up, hesitantly, to the closest one and knelt down to get a look. The light was so dull now that he almost felt as if he were looking through black mist. Even the birds had quieted, like they'd gone to bed for the night, and the sound of insects was barely noticeable, or at least much less than normal. For the first time, Thomas realized how humid it was in the woods, the damp air already beading sweat on his forehead, the backs of his hands.

He leaned closer to the first cross. It looked fresh and bore the name Stephen—the *n* extra small and right at the edge because the carver hadn't estimated well how much room he'd need.

Stephen, Thomas thought, feeling an unexpected but detached sorrow. *What's your story? Chuck annoy you to death?*

He stood and walked over to another cross, this one almost completely overgrown with weeds, the ground firm at its base. Whoever it was, he must've been one of the first to die, because his grave looked the oldest. The name was George.

Thomas looked around and saw there were a dozen or so other graves. A couple of them appeared to be just as fresh as the first one he'd examined. A silvery glint caught his attention. It was different from the scuttling beetle that had led him to the forest, but just as odd. He moved through the markers until he got to a grave covered with a sheet of grimy plastic or glass, its edges slimed with filth. He squinted, trying to make out what was on the other side, then gasped when it came into focus. It was a window into another grave—one that had the dusty remnants of a rotting body.

Completely creeped out, Thomas leaned closer to get a better look anyway, curious. The tomb was smaller than usual—only the top *half* of the deceased person lay inside. He remembered Chuck's story about the boy who'd tried to rappel down the dark hole of the Box after it had descended, only to be cut in two by something slicing through the air. Words were etched on the glass; Thomas could barely read them:

Let this half-shank be a warning to all:
You can't escape through the Box Hole.

Thomas felt the odd urge to snicker—it seemed too ridiculous to be true. But he was also disgusted with himself for being so shallow and glib. Shaking his head, he had stepped aside to read more names of the dead when another twig broke, this time straight in front of him, right behind the trees on the other side of the graveyard.

Then another snap. Then another. Coming closer. And the darkness was thick.

"Who's out there?" he called, his voice shaky and hollow—it sounded as if he were speaking inside an insulated tunnel. "Seriously, this is stupid." He hated to admit to himself just how terrified he was.

Instead of answering, the person gave up all pretense of stealth and started running, crashing through the forest line around the clearing of the graveyard, circling toward the spot where Thomas stood. He froze, panic overtaking him. Now only a few feet away, the visitor grew louder and louder until Thomas caught a shadowed glimpse of a skinny boy limping along in a strange, lilting run.

"Who the he—"

The boy burst through the trees before Thomas could finish. He saw only a flash of pale skin and enormous eyes—the haunted image of an apparition—and cried out, tried to run, but it was too late. The figure leaped into the air and was on top of him, slamming into his shoulders, gripping him with strong hands. Thomas crashed to the ground; he felt a grave marker dig into his back before it snapped in two, burning a deep scratch along his flesh.

He pushed and swatted at his attacker, a relentless jumble of skin and bones cavorting on top of him as he tried to gain purchase. It seemed like a monster, a horror from a nightmare, but Thomas knew it had to be a Glader, someone who'd completely lost his mind. He heard teeth snapping open and closed, a horrific clack, clack, clack. Then he felt the jarring dagger of pain as the boy's mouth found a home, bit deeply into Thomas's shoulder.

Thomas screamed, the pain like a burst of adrenaline through his blood. He planted the palms of his hands against his attacker's chest and pushed, straightening his arms until his muscles strained against the struggling figure above him. Finally the kid fell back; a sharp crack filled the air as another grave marker met its demise.

Thomas squirmed away on his hands and feet, sucking in breaths of air, and got his first good look at the crazed attacker.

It was the sick boy.

It was Ben.

CHAPTER 11

It looked as if Ben had recovered only slightly since Thomas had seen him in the Homestead. He wore nothing but shorts, his whiter-than-white skin stretched across his bones like a sheet wrapped tightly around a bundle of sticks. Ropelike veins ran along his body, pulsing and green—but less pronounced than the day before. His bloodshot eyes fell upon Thomas as if he were seeing his next meal.

Ben crouched, ready to spring for another attack. At some point a knife had made an appearance, gripped in his right hand. Thomas was filled with a queasy fear, disbelief that this was happening at all.

"Ben!"

Thomas looked toward the voice, surprised to see Alby standing at the edge of the graveyard, a mere phantom in the fading light. Relief flooded Thomas's body—Alby held a large bow, an arrow cocked for the kill, pointed straight at Ben.

"Ben," Alby repeated. "Stop right now, or you ain't gonna see to-morrow."

Thomas looked back at Ben, who stared viciously at Alby, his tongue darting between his lips to wet them. *What could possibly be wrong with that kid?* Thomas thought. The boy had turned into a monster. Why?

"If you kill me," Ben shrieked, spittle flying from his mouth, far enough to hit Thomas in the face, "you'll get the wrong guy." He snapped his gaze back to Thomas. "He's the shank you wanna kill." His voice was full of madness.

"Don't be stupid, Ben," Alby said, his voice calm as he continued to aim the arrow. "Thomas just got here—ain't nothing to worry about. You're still buggin' from the Changing. You should've never left your bed."

"He's not one of us!" Ben shouted. "I saw him—he's . . . he's bad. We have to kill him! Let me gut him!"

Thomas took an involuntary step backward, horrified by what Ben had said. What did he mean, he'd seen him? Why did he think Thomas was bad?

Alby hadn't moved his weapon an inch, still aiming for Ben. "You leave that to me and the Keepers to figure out, shuck-face." His hands were perfectly steady as he held the bow, almost as if he had propped it against a branch for support. "Right now, back your scrawny butt down and get to the Homestead."

"He'll wanna take us home," Ben said. "He'll wanna get us out of the Maze. Better we all jumped off the Cliff! Better we tore each other's guts out!"

"What are you talking—" Thomas began.

"Shut your face!" Ben screamed. "Shut your ugly, traitorous face!"

"Ben," Alby said calmly. "I'm gonna count to three."

"He's bad, he's bad, he's bad . . . ," Ben was whispering now, almost chanting. He swayed back and forth, switching the knife from hand to hand, eyes glued on Thomas.

"One."

"Bad, bad, bad, bad, bad . . ." Ben smiled; his teeth seemed to glow, greenish in the pale light.

Thomas wanted to look away, get out of there. But he couldn't move; he was too mesmerized, too scared.

"Two." Alby's voice was louder, filled with warning.

"Ben," Thomas said, trying to make sense of it all. "I'm not . . . I don't even know what—"

Ben screamed, a strangled gurgle of madness, and leaped into the air, slashing out with his blade.

"*Three!*" Alby shouted.

There was the sound of snapping wire. The *whoosh* of an object slicing through the air. The sickening, wet *thunk* of it finding a home.

Ben's head snapped violently to the left, twisting his body until he landed on his stomach, his feet pointed toward Thomas. He made no sound.

Thomas jumped to his feet and stumbled forward. The long shaft of the arrow stuck from Ben's cheek, the blood surprisingly less than Thomas had expected, but seeping out all the same. Black in the darkness, like oil. The only movement was Ben's right pinky finger, twitching. Thomas fought the urge to puke. Was Ben dead because of him? Was it his fault?

"Come on," Alby said. "Baggers'll take care of him tomorrow."

What just happened here? Thomas thought, the world tilting around him as he stared at the lifeless body. *What did I ever do to this kid?*

He looked up, wanting answers, but Alby was already gone, a trembling branch the only sign he'd ever stood there in the first place.

Thomas squeezed his eyes against the blinding light of the sun as he emerged from the woods. He was limping, his ankle screaming in pain, though he had no memory of hurting it. He held one hand carefully over the area where he'd been bitten; the other clutched his stomach as if that would prevent what Thomas now felt was an inevitable barf. The image of Ben's head popped into his mind, cocked at an unnatural angle, blood running down the shaft of the arrow until it collected, dripped, splattered on the ground. . . .

The image of it was the last straw.

He fell to his knees by one of the scraggly trees on the outskirts of the forest and threw up, retching as he coughed and spat out every last morsel of the acidic, nasty bile from his stomach. His whole body shook, and it seemed like the vomiting would never end.

And then, as if his brain were mocking him, trying to make it worse, he had a thought.

He'd now been at the Glade for roughly twenty-four hours. One full day. That was it. And look at all the things that had happened. All the terrible things.

Surely it could only get better.

That night, Thomas lay staring at the sparkling sky, wondering if he'd ever sleep again. Every time he closed his eyes, the monstrous image of Ben leaping at him, the boy's face set in lunacy, filled his mind. Eyes opened or not, he could swear he kept hearing the moist thunk of the arrow slamming into Ben's cheek.

Thomas knew he'd never forget those few terrible minutes in the graveyard.

"Say something," Chuck said for the fifth time since they'd set out their sleeping bags.

"No," Thomas replied, just as he had before.

"Everyone knows what happened. It's happened once or twice— some Griever-stung shank flipped out and attacked somebody. Don't think you're special."

For the first time, Thomas thought Chuck's personality had gone from mildly irritating to intolerable. "Chuck, be glad I'm not holding Alby's bow right about now."

"I'm just play—"

"Shut up, Chuck. Go to sleep." Thomas just couldn't handle it right then.

Eventually, his "buddy" did doze off, and based on the rumble of snores across the Glade, so did everyone else. Hours later, deep in the night, Thomas was still the only one awake. He wanted to cry, but didn't. He wanted to find Alby and punch him, for no reason whatsoever, but didn't. He wanted to scream and kick and spit and open up the Box and jump into the blackness below. But he didn't.

He closed his eyes and forced the thoughts and dark images away and at some point he fell asleep.

Chuck had to drag Thomas out of his sleeping bag in the morning, drag him to the showers, and drag him to the dressing rooms. The whole time, Thomas felt mopey and indifferent, his head aching, his body wanting more sleep. Breakfast was a blur, and an hour after it was over, Thomas couldn't remember what he'd eaten. He was so tired, his brain felt like someone had gone in and stapled it to his skull in a dozen places. Heartburn ravaged his chest.

But from what he could tell, naps were frowned upon in the giant working farm of the Glade.

He stood with Newt in front of the barn of the Blood House, getting ready for his first training session with a Keeper. Despite the rough morning, he was actually excited to learn more, and for the chance to get his mind off Ben and the graveyard. Cows mooed, sheep bleated, pigs squealed all around him. Somewhere close by, a dog barked, making Thomas hope Frypan didn't bring new meaning to the word *hot dog. Hot dog,* he thought. *When's the last time I had a hot dog? Who did I eat it with?*

"Tommy, are you even listening to me?"

Thomas snapped out of his daze and focused on Newt, who'd been talking for who knew how long; Thomas hadn't heard a word of it. "Yeah, sorry. Couldn't sleep last night."

Newt attempted a pathetic smile. "Can't blame ya there. Went through the buggin' ringer, you did. Probably think I'm a slinthead shank for gettin' you ready to work your butt off today after an episode the likes of that."

Thomas shrugged. "Work's probably the best thing I could do. Anything to get my mind off it."

Newt nodded, and his smile became more genuine. "You're as smart as you look, Tommy. That's one of the reasons we run this place all nice and busylike. You get lazy, you get sad. Start givin' up. Plain and simple."

Thomas nodded, absently kicking a loose rock across the dusty, cracked stone floor of the Glade. "So what's the latest on that girl from yesterday?" If anything had penetrated the haze of his long morning, it had been thoughts of her. He wanted to know more about her, understand the odd connection he felt to her.

"Still in a coma, sleepin'. Med-jacks are spoon-feeding her whatever soups Frypan can cook up, checking her vitals and such. She seems okay, just dead to the world for now."

"That was just plain weird." If it hadn't been for the whole Ben-in-the-graveyard incident, Thomas was sure she would've been all he'd thought about last night. Maybe he wouldn't have been able to sleep for an entirely different reason. He wanted to know who she was and if he really did know her somehow.

"Yeah," Newt said. "*Weird*'s as good a word as any, I 'spect."

Thomas looked over Newt's shoulder at the big faded-red barn, pushing thoughts of the girl aside. "So what's first? Milk cows or slaughter some poor little pigs?"

Newt laughed, a sound Thomas realized he hadn't heard much since he'd arrived. "We always make the Newbies start with the bloody Slicers. Don't worry, cuttin' up Frypan's victuals ain't but a part. Slicers do anything and everything dealin' with the beasties."

"Too bad I can't remember my whole life. Maybe I love killing animals." He was just joking, but Newt didn't seem to get it.

Newt nodded toward the barn. "Oh, you'll know good and well by the time sun sets tonight. Let's go meet Winston—he's the Keeper."

Winston was an acne-covered kid, short but muscular, and it seemed to Thomas the Keeper liked his job way too much. *Maybe he was sent here for being a serial killer,* he thought.

Winston showed Thomas around for the first hour, pointing out which pens held which animals, where the chicken and turkey coops were, what went where in the barn. The dog, a pesky black Lab named Bark, took quickly to Thomas, hanging at his feet the entire tour. Wondering where the dog came from, Thomas asked Winston, who said Bark had just always been there. Luckily, he seemed to have gotten his name as a joke, because he was pretty quiet.

The second hour was spent actually working with the farm animals— feeding, cleaning, fixing a fence, scraping up klunk. *Klunk.* Thomas found himself using the Glader terms more and more.

The third hour was the hardest for Thomas. He had to watch as Winston slaughtered a hog and began preparing its many parts for future eating. Thomas swore two things to himself as he walked away for lunch break. First, his career would not be with the animals; second, he'd never again eat something that came out of a pig.

Winston had said for him to go on alone, that he'd hang around the

Blood House, which was fine with Thomas. As he walked toward the East Door, he couldn't stop picturing Winston in a dark corner of the barn, gnawing on raw pigs' feet. The guy gave him the willies.

Thomas was just passing the Box when he was surprised to see someone enter the Glade from the Maze, through the West Door, to his left—an Asian kid with strong arms and short black hair, who looked a little older than Thomas. The Runner stopped three steps in, then bent over and put his hands on his knees, gasping for breath. He looked like he'd just run twenty miles, face red, skin covered in sweat, clothes soaked.

Thomas stared, overcome with curiosity—he'd yet to see a Runner up close or talk to one. Plus, based on the last couple of days, the Runner was home hours early. Thomas stepped forward, eager to meet him and ask questions.

But before he could form a sentence, the boy collapsed to the ground.

CHAPTER 12

Thomas didn't move for a few seconds. The boy lay in a crumpled heap, barely moving, but Thomas was frozen by indecision, afraid to get involved. What if something was seriously wrong with this guy? What if he'd been . . . *stung*? What if—

Thomas snapped out of it—the Runner obviously needed help.

"Alby!" he shouted. "Newt! Somebody get them!"

Thomas sprinted to the older boy and knelt down beside him. "Hey—you okay?" The Runner's head rested on outstretched arms as he panted, his chest heaving. He was conscious, but Thomas had never seen someone so exhausted.

"I'm . . . fine," he said between breaths, then looked up. "Who the klunk are you?"

"I'm new here." It hit Thomas then that the Runners were out in the Maze during the day and hadn't witnessed any of the recent events firsthand. Did this guy even know about the girl? Probably— surely someone had told him. "I'm Thomas—been here just a couple of days."

The Runner pushed himself up into a sitting position, his black hair matted to his skull with sweat. "Oh, yeah, Thomas," he huffed. "Newbie. You and the chick."

Alby jogged up then, clearly upset. "What're you doin' back, Minho? What happened?"

"Calm your wad, Alby," the Runner replied, seeming to gain

strength by the second. "Make yourself useful and get me some water—I dropped my pack out there somewhere."

But Alby didn't move. He kicked Minho in the leg—too hard to be playful. "What *happened*?"

"I can barely talk, shuck-face!" Minho yelled, his voice raw. "Get me some water!"

Alby looked over at Thomas, who was shocked to see the slightest hint of a smile flash across his face before vanishing in a scowl. "Minho's the only shank who can talk to me like that without getting his butt kicked off the Cliff."

Then, surprising Thomas even more, Alby turned and ran off, presumably to get Minho some water.

Thomas turned toward Minho. "He lets you boss him around?"

Minho shrugged, then wiped fresh beads of sweat off his forehead. "You scared of that pip-squeak? Dude, you got a lot to learn. Freakin' Newbies."

The rebuke hurt Thomas far more than it should have, considering he'd known this guy all of three minutes. "Isn't he the leader?"

"Leader?" Minho barked a grunt that was probably supposed to be a laugh. "Yeah, call him leader all you want. Maybe we should call him El Presidente. Nah, nah—Admiral Alby. There you go." He rubbed his eyes, snickering as he did so.

Thomas didn't know what to make of the conversation—it was hard to tell when Minho was joking. "So who *is* the leader if he isn't?"

"Greenie, just shut it before you confuse yourself more." Minho sighed as if bored, then muttered, almost to himself, "Why do you shanks always come in here asking stupid questions? It's really annoying."

"What do you expect us to do?" Thomas felt a flush of anger. *Like you were any different when you first came,* he wanted to say.

"Do what you're told, keep your mouth shut. That's what I expect."

Minho had looked him square in the face for the first time with that last sentence, and Thomas scooted back a few inches before he could stop himself. He realized immediately he'd just made a mistake—he couldn't let this guy think he could talk to him like that.

He pushed himself back up onto his knees so he was looking down at the older boy. "Yeah, I'm sure that's exactly what you did as a Newbie."

Minho looked at Thomas carefully. Then, again staring straight in his eyes, said, "I was one of the first Gladers, slinthead. Shut your hole till you know what you're talking about."

Thomas, now slightly scared of the guy but mostly fed up with his attitude, moved to get up. Minho's hand snapped out and grabbed his arm.

"Dude, sit down. I'm just playin' with your head. It's too much fun—you'll see when the next Newbie . . ." He trailed off, a perplexed look wrinkling his eyebrows. "Guess there won't *be* another Newbie, huh?"

Thomas relaxed, returned to a sitting position, surprised at how easily he'd been put back at ease. He thought of the girl and the note saying she was the last one ever. "Guess not."

Minho squinted slightly, as if he was studying Thomas. "You saw the chick, right? Everybody says you probably know her or something."

Thomas felt himself grow defensive. "I saw her. Doesn't really look familiar at all." He felt immediately guilty for lying—even if it was just a little lie.

"She hot?"

Thomas paused, not having thought of her in that way since she'd freaked out and delivered the note and her one-liner—*Everything is going to change*. But he remembered how beautiful she was. "Yeah, I guess she's hot."

Minho leaned back until he lay flat, eyes closed. "Yeah, you guess. If you got a thing for chicks in comas, right?" He snickered again.

"Right." Thomas was having the hardest time figuring out if he liked Minho or not—his personality seemed to change every minute. After a long pause, Thomas decided to take a chance. "So . . . ," he asked cautiously, "did you find anything today?"

Minho's eyes opened wide; he focused on Thomas. "You know what, Greenie? That's usually the dumbest shuck-faced thing you could ask a Runner." He closed his eyes again. "But not today."

"What do you mean?" Thomas dared to hope for information. *An answer,* he thought. *Please just give me an answer!*

"Just wait till the fancy admiral gets back. I don't like saying stuff twice. Plus, he might not want you to hear it anyway."

Thomas sighed. He wasn't in the least bit surprised at the non-answer. "Well, at least tell me why you look so tired. Don't you run out there every day?"

Minho groaned as he pulled himself up and crossed his legs under him. "Yeah, Greenie, I run out there every day. Let's just say I got a little excited and ran extra fast to get my bee-hind back here."

"Why?" Thomas desperately wanted to hear about what happened out in the Maze.

Minho threw his hands up. "Dude. I told you. Patience. Wait for General Alby."

Something in his voice lessened the blow, and Thomas made his decision. He liked Minho. "Okay, I'll shut up. Just make sure Alby lets me hear the news, too."

Minho studied him for a second. "Okay, Greenie. You da boss."

Alby walked up a moment later with a big plastic cup full of water and handed it to Minho, who gulped down the whole thing without stopping once for breath.

"Okay," Alby said, "out with it. What happened?"

Minho raised his eyebrows and nodded toward Thomas.

"He's fine," Alby replied. "I don't care what this shank hears. Just talk!"

Thomas sat quietly in anticipation as Minho struggled to stand up, wincing with every move, his whole demeanor just *screaming* exhaustion. The Runner balanced himself against the wall, gave both of them a cold look. "I found a dead one."

"Huh?" Alby asked. "A dead what?"

Minho smiled. "A dead Griever."

CHAPTER 13

Thomas was fascinated at the mention of a Griever. The nasty creature was terrifying to think about, but he wondered why finding a dead one was such a big deal. Had it never happened before?

Alby looked like someone had just told him he could grow wings and fly. "Ain't a good time for jokes," he said.

"Look," Minho answered, "I wouldn't believe me if I were you, either. But trust me, I did. Big fat nasty one."

It's definitely never happened before, Thomas thought.

"You found a *dead* Griever," Alby repeated.

"*Yes,* Alby," Minho said, his words laced with annoyance. "A couple of miles from here, out near the Cliff."

Alby looked out at the Maze, then back at Minho. "Well . . . why didn't you bring it back with you?"

Minho laughed again, a half-grunt, half-giggle. "You been drinkin' Frypan's saucy-sauce? Those things must weigh half a ton, dude. Plus, I wouldn't touch one if you gave me a free trip out of this place."

Alby persisted with the questions. "What did it look like? Were the metal spikes in or out of its body? Did it move at all—was its skin still moist?"

Thomas was bursting with questions—*Metal spikes? Moist skin? What in the world?*—but held his tongue, not wanting to remind them he was there. And that maybe they should talk in private.

"Slim it, man," Minho said. "You gotta see it for yourself. It's . . . weird."

"Weird?" Alby looked confused.

"Dude, I'm exhausted, starving, and sun-sick. But if you wanna haul it right now, we could probably make it there and back before the walls shut."

Alby looked at his watch. "Better wait till the wake-up tomorrow."

"Smartest thing you've said in a week." Minho righted himself from leaning on the wall, hit Alby on the arm, then started walking toward the Homestead with a slight limp. He spoke over his shoulder as he shuffled away—it looked like his whole body was in pain. "I should go back out there, but screw it. I'm gonna go eat some of Frypan's nasty casserole."

Thomas felt a wash of disappointment. He had to admit Minho did look like he deserved a rest and a bite to eat, but he wanted to learn more.

Then Alby turned to Thomas, surprising him. "If you know something and ain't tellin' me . . ."

Thomas was sick of being accused of knowing things. Wasn't that the problem in the first place? He *didn't* know anything. He looked at the boy square in the face and asked, simply, "Why do you hate me so much?"

The look that came over Alby's face was indescribable—part confusion, part anger, part shock. "*Hate* you? Boy, you ain't learned nothin' since showing up in that Box. This ain't got nothin' to do with no hate or like or love or friends or anything. All we care about is surviving. Drop your sissy side and start using that shuck brain if you got one."

Thomas felt like he'd been slapped. "But . . . why do you keep accusing—"

"Cuz it can't be a coincidence, slinthead! You pop in here, then we get us a girl Newbie the next *day*, a crazy note, Ben tryin' to bite ya, dead Grievers. Something's goin' on and I ain't restin' till I figure it out."

"I don't *know* anything, Alby." It felt good to put some heat into his words. "I don't even know where I *was* three days ago, much less why this Minho guy would find a dead thing called a Griever. So back off!"

Alby leaned back slightly, stared absently at Thomas for several seconds. Then he said, "Slim it, Greenie. Grow up and start thinkin'. Ain't got nothin' to do with accusing nobody of nothin'. But if you remember anything, if something even *seems* familiar, you better start talking. Promise me."

Not until I have a solid memory, Thomas thought. *Not unless I want to share.* "Yeah, I guess, but—"

"Just promise!"

Thomas paused, sick of Alby and his attitude. "Whatever," he finally said. "I promise."

At that Alby turned and walked away, not saying another word.

Thomas found a tree in the Deadheads, one of the nicer ones on the edge of the forest with plenty of shade. He dreaded going back to work with Winston the Butcher and knew he needed to eat lunch, but he didn't want to be near anybody for as long as he could get away with it. Leaning back against the thick trunk, he wished for a breeze but didn't get one.

He'd just felt his eyelids droop when Chuck ruined his peace and quiet.

"Thomas! Thomas!" the boy shrieked as he ran toward him, pumping his arms, his face lit up with excitement.

Thomas rubbed his eyes and groaned; he wanted nothing in the world more than a half-hour nap. It wasn't until Chuck stopped right in front of him, panting to catch his breath, that he finally looked up. "What?"

Words slowly fell from Chuck, in between his gasps for breath. "Ben . . . Ben . . . he isn't . . . dead."

All signs of fatigue catapulted out of Thomas's system. He jumped up to stand nose to nose with Chuck. *"What?"*

"He . . . isn't dead. Baggers went to get him . . . arrow missed his brain . . . Med-jacks patched him up."

Thomas turned away to stare into the forest where the sick boy had attacked him just the night before. "You gotta be kidding. I saw him. . . ." He wasn't dead? Thomas didn't know what he felt most strongly: confusion, relief, fear that he'd be attacked again . . .

"Well, so did I," Chuck said. "He's locked up in the Slammer, a huge bandage covering half his head."

Thomas spun to face Chuck again. "The Slammer? What do you mean?"

"The Slammer. It's our jail on the north side of the Homestead." Chuck pointed in that direction. "They threw him in it so fast, the Med-jacks had to patch him up in there."

Thomas rubbed his eyes. Guilt consumed him when he realized how he truly felt—he'd been relieved that Ben was dead, that he didn't have to worry about facing him again. "So what are they gonna do with him?"

"Already had a Gathering of the Keepers this morning—made a unanimous decision by the sounds of it. Looks like Ben'll be wishing that arrow had found a home inside his shuck brain after all."

Thomas squinted, confused by what Chuck had said. "What are you talking about?"

"He's being Banished. Tonight, for trying to kill you."

"Banished? What does *that* mean?" Thomas had to ask, though he knew it couldn't be good if Chuck thought it was worse than being dead.

And then Thomas saw perhaps the most disturbing thing he'd seen since he'd arrived at the Glade. Chuck didn't answer; he only smiled. *Smiled,* despite it all, despite the sinister sound of what he'd just announced. Then he turned and ran, maybe to tell someone else the exciting news.

That night, Newt and Alby gathered every last Glader at the East Door about a half hour before it closed, the first traces of twilight's dimness creeping across the sky. The Runners had just returned and entered the mysterious Map Room, clanging the iron door shut; Minho had already gone in earlier. Alby told the Runners to hurry about their business—he wanted them back out in twenty minutes.

It still bothered Thomas how Chuck had smiled when breaking the news about Ben being Banished. Though he didn't know exactly what it meant, it certainly didn't sound like a good thing. Especially since they were all standing so close to the Maze. *Are they going to put him out there?* he wondered. *With the Grievers?*

The other Gladers murmured their conversations in hushed tones, an intense feeling of dreadful anticipation hanging over them like a patch of thick fog. But Thomas said nothing, standing with arms folded, waiting for the show. He stood quietly until the Runners finally came out of their building, all of them looking exhausted, their faces pinched from deep thinking. Minho had been the first to exit, which made Thomas wonder if he was the Keeper of the Runners.

"Bring him out!" Alby shouted, startling Thomas out of his thoughts.

His arms fell to his sides as he turned, looking around the Glade for a sign of Ben, trepidation building within him as he wondered what the boy would do when he saw him.

From around the far side of the Homestead, three of the bigger boys appeared, literally dragging Ben along the ground. His clothes were tattered, barely hanging on; a bloody, thick bandage covered half his head and face. Refusing to put his feet down or help the progress in any way, he seemed as dead as the last time Thomas had seen him. Except for one thing.

His eyes were open, and they were wide with terror.

"Newt," Alby said in a much quieter voice; Thomas wouldn't have heard him if he hadn't been standing just a few feet away. "Bring out the Pole."

Newt nodded, already on the move toward a small tool shed used for the Gardens; he'd clearly been waiting for the order.

Thomas turned his focus back to Ben and the guards. The pale, miserable boy still made no effort to resist, letting them drag him across the dusty stone of the courtyard. When they reached the crowd, they pulled Ben to his feet in front of Alby, their leader, where Ben hung his head, refusing to make eye contact with anyone.

"You brought this on yourself, Ben," Alby said. Then he shook his head and looked toward the shack to which Newt had gone.

Thomas followed his gaze just in time to see Newt walk though the slanted door. He was holding several aluminum poles, connecting the ends to make a shaft maybe twenty feet long. When he was finished, he grabbed something odd-shaped on one of the ends and dragged the whole thing along toward the group. A shiver ran up Thomas's spine at the metallic scrape of the pole on the stone ground as Newt walked.

Thomas was horrified by the whole affair—he couldn't help feeling responsible even though he'd never done anything to provoke Ben.

How was any of this his fault? No answer came to him, but he felt the guilt all the same, like a disease in his blood.

Finally, Newt stepped up to Alby and handed over the end of the pole he was holding. Thomas could see the strange attachment now. A loop of rough leather, fastened to the metal with a massive staple. A large button snap revealed that the loop could be opened and closed, and its purpose became obvious.

It was a collar.

CHAPTER 14

Thomas watched as Alby unbuttoned the collar, then wrapped it around Ben's neck; Ben finally looked up just as the loop of leather snapped closed with a loud pop. Tears glistened in his eyes; dribbles of snot oozed from his nostrils. The Gladers looked on, not a word from any of them.

"Please, Alby," Ben pleaded, his shaky voice so pathetic that Thomas couldn't believe it was the same guy who'd tried to bite his throat off the day before. "I swear I was just sick in the head from the Changing. I never would've killed him—just lost my mind for a second. Please, Alby, *please*."

Every word from the kid was like a fist punching Thomas in the gut, making him feel more guilty and confused.

Alby didn't respond to Ben; he pulled on the collar to make sure it was both firmly snapped and solidly attached to the long pole. He walked past Ben and along the pole, picking it up off the ground as he slid its length through his palm and fingers. When he reached the end, he gripped it tightly and turned to face the crowd. Eyes bloodshot, face wrinkled in anger, breathing heavily—to Thomas, he suddenly looked evil.

And it was an odd sight on the other side: Ben, trembling, crying, a roughly cut collar of old leather wrapped around his pale, scrawny neck, attached to a long pole that stretched from him to Alby, twenty feet away. The shaft of aluminum bowed in the middle, but only a little. Even from where Thomas was standing, it looked surprisingly strong.

Alby spoke in a loud, almost ceremonious voice, looking at no one and everyone at the same time. "Ben of the Builders, you've been sentenced to Banishment for the attempted murder of Thomas the Newbie. The Keepers have spoken, and their word ain't changing. And you ain't coming back. Ever." A long pause. "Keepers, take your place on the Banishment Pole."

Thomas hated that his link to Ben was being made public—hated the responsibility he felt. Being the center of attention again could only bring more suspicion about him. His guilt transformed into anger and blame. More than anything, he just wanted Ben gone, wanted it all to be over.

One by one, boys were stepping out of the crowd and walking over to the long pole; they grabbed it with both hands, gripped it as if readying for a tug-of-war match. Newt was one of them, as was Minho, confirming Thomas's guess that he was the Keeper of the Runners. Winston the Butcher also took up a position.

Once they were all in place—ten Keepers spaced evenly apart between Alby and Ben—the air grew still and silent. The only sounds were the muffled sobs of Ben, who kept wiping at his nose and eyes. He was looking left and right, though the collar around his neck prevented him from seeing the pole and Keepers behind him.

Thomas's feelings changed again. Something was obviously wrong with Ben. Why did he deserve this fate? Couldn't something be done for him? Would Thomas spend the rest of his days feeling responsible? *Just end,* he screamed in his head. *Just be over!*

"Please," Ben said, his voice rising in desperation. *"Plllleeeeeeeeease!* Somebody, help me! You can't do this to me!"

"Shut up!" Alby roared from behind.

But Ben ignored him, pleading for help as he started to pull on the leather looped around his neck. "Someone stop them! Help me!

Please!" He glanced from boy to boy, begging with his eyes. Without fail, everyone looked away. Thomas quickly stepped behind a taller boy to avoid his own confrontation with Ben. *I can't look into those eyes again,* he thought.

"If we let shanks like you get away with that stuff," Alby said, "we never would've survived this long. Keepers, get ready."

"No, no, no, no, no," Ben was saying, half under his breath. "I swear I'll do anything! I swear I'll never do it again! *Plllleeeeeee—*"

His shrill cry was cut off by the rumbling crack of the East Door beginning to close. Sparks flew from the stone as the massive right wall slid to the left, groaning thunderously as it made its journey to close off the Glade from the Maze for the night. The ground shook beneath them, and Thomas didn't know if he could watch what he knew was going to happen next.

"Keepers, *now!*" Alby shouted.

Ben's head snapped back as he was jerked forward, the Keepers pushing the pole toward the Maze outside the Glade. A strangling cry erupted from Ben's throat, louder than the sounds of the closing Door. He fell to his knees, only to be jerked back to his feet by the Keeper in front, a thick guy with black hair and a snarl on his face.

"*Noooooooooo!*" Ben screamed, spit flying from his mouth as he thrashed about, tearing at the collar with his hands. But the combined strength of the Keepers was way too much, forcing the condemned boy closer and closer to the edge of the Glade, just as the right wall was almost there. *"Noooo!"* he screamed again, and then again.

He tried to plant his feet at the threshold, but it only lasted for a split second; the pole sent him into the Maze with a lurch. Soon he was fully four feet outside the Glade, jerking his body from side to side as he tried to escape his collar. The walls of the Door were only seconds from sealing shut.

With one last violent effort, Ben was finally able to twist his neck in the circle of leather so that his whole body turned to face the Gladers. Thomas couldn't believe he was still looking upon a human being—the madness in Ben's eyes, the phlegm flying from his mouth, the pale skin stretched taut across his veins and bones. He looked as alien as anything Thomas could imagine.

"*Hold!*" Alby shouted.

Ben screamed then, without pause, a sound so piercing that Thomas covered his ears. It was a bestial, lunatic cry, surely ripping the boy's vocal cords to shreds. At the last second, the front Keeper somehow loosened the larger pole from the piece attached to Ben and yanked it back into the Glade, leaving the boy to his Banishment. Ben's final screams were cut off when the walls closed with a terrible boom.

Thomas squeezed his eyes shut and was surprised to feel tears trickling down his cheeks.

CHAPTER 15

For the second night in a row, Thomas went to bed with the haunted image of Ben's face burned into his mind, tormenting him. How different would things be right now if it weren't for that one boy? Thomas could almost convince himself he'd be completely content, happy and excited to learn his new life, aim for his goal of being a Runner. Almost. Deep down he knew that Ben was only part of his many problems.

But now he was gone, Banished to the world of the Grievers, taken to wherever they took their prey, victim to whatever was done there. Though he had plenty of reasons to despise Ben, he mostly felt sorry for him.

Thomas couldn't imagine going out that way, but based on Ben's last moments, psychotically thrashing and spitting and screaming, he no longer doubted the importance of the Glade rule that no one should enter the Maze except Runners, and then only during the day. Somehow Ben had already been stung once, which meant he knew better than perhaps anyone just exactly what lay in store for him.

That poor guy, he thought. *That poor, poor guy.*

Thomas shuddered and rolled over on his side. The more he thought about it, being a Runner didn't sound like such a great idea. But, inexplicably, it still called to him.

The next morning, dawn had barely touched the sky before the working sounds of the Glade wakened Thomas from the deepest slumber since he'd arrived. He sat up, rubbing his eyes, trying to shake the heavy grogginess. Giving up, he lay back down, hoping no one would bother him.

It didn't last a minute.

Someone tapped his shoulder and he opened his eyes to see Newt staring down at him. *What now?* he thought.

"Get up, ya lug."

"Yeah, good morning to you, too. What time is it?"

"Seven o'clock, Greenie," Newt said with a mocking smile. "Figured I'd let ya sleep in after such a rough couple days."

Thomas rolled into a sitting position, hating that he couldn't just lie there for another few hours. "Sleep in? What are you guys, a bunch of farmers?" Farmers—how did he remember so much about them? Once again his memory wipe baffled him.

"Uh . . . yeah, now that ya mention it." Newt plopped down beside Thomas and folded his legs up under himself. He sat quietly for a few moments, looking out at all the hustle-bustle starting to whip up across the Glade. "Gonna put ya with the Track-hoes today, Greenie. See if that suits your fancy more than slicin' up bloody piggies and such."

Thomas was sick of being treated like a baby. "Aren't you supposed to quit calling me that?"

"What, bloody piggies?"

Thomas forced a laugh and shook his head. "No, *Greenie.* I'm not really the newest Newbie anymore, right? The girl in the coma is. Call *her* Greenie—my name's Thomas." Thoughts of the girl crashed around his mind, made him remember the connection he felt. A sadness washed over him, as if he missed her, wanted to see her. *That doesn't make sense,* he thought. *I don't even know her name.*

Newt leaned back, eyebrows raised. "Burn me—you grew some right nice-sized eggs over night, now didn't ya?"

Thomas ignored him and moved on. "What's a Track-hoe?"

"It's what we call the guys workin' their butts off in the Gardens—tilling, weeding, planting and such."

Thomas nodded in that direction. "Who's the Keeper?"

"Zart. Nice guy, s'long as you don't sluff on the job, that is. He's the big one that stood in front last night."

Thomas didn't say anything to that, hoping that somehow he could go through the entire day without talking about Ben and the Banishment. The subject only made him sick and guilty, so he moved on to something else. "So why'd you come wake me up?"

"What, don't like seein' my face first thing on the wake-up?"

"Not especially. So—" But before he could finish his sentence the rumble of the walls opening for the day cut him off. He looked toward the East Door, almost expecting to see Ben standing there on the other side. Instead, he saw Minho stretching. Then Thomas watched as he walked over and picked something up.

It was the section of pole with the leather collar attached to it. Minho seemed to think nothing of it, throwing it to one of the other Runners, who went and put it back in the tool shed near the Gardens.

Thomas turned back to Newt, confused. How could Minho act so nonchalant about it all? "What the—"

"Only seen three Banishments, Tommy. All as nasty as the one you peeped on last night. But every buggin' time, the Grievers leave the collar on our doorstep. Gives me the willies like nothin' else."

Thomas had to agree. "What do they *do* with people when they catch them?" Did he really want to know?

Newt just shrugged, his indifference not very convincing. More likely he didn't want to talk about it.

"So tell me about the Runners," Thomas said suddenly. The words seemed to pop out of nowhere. But he remained still, despite an odd urge to apologize and change the subject; he wanted to know every-thing about them. Even after what he'd seen last night, even after wit-nessing the Griever through the window, he wanted to know. The *pull* to know was strong, and he didn't quite understand why. Becoming a Runner just felt like something he was born to do.

Newt had paused, looking confused. "The Runners? Why?"

"Just wondering."

Newt gave him a suspicious look. "Best of the best, those guys. Have to be. Everything depends on them." He picked up a loose rock and tossed it, watching it absently as it bounced to a stop.

"Why aren't you one?"

Newt's gaze returned to Thomas, sharply. "Was till I hurt my leg few months back. Hasn't been the bloody same since." He reached down and rubbed his right ankle absently, a brief look of pain flashing across his face. The look made Thomas think it was more from the memory, not any actual physical pain he still felt.

"How'd you do it?" Thomas asked, thinking the more he could get Newt to talk, the more he'd learn.

"Runnin' from the buggin' Grievers, what else? Almost got me." He paused. "Still gives me the chills thinkin' I might have gone through the Changing."

The Changing. It was the one topic that Thomas thought might lead him to answers more than anything else. "What *is* that, anyway? What changes? Does everyone go psycho like Ben and start trying to kill people?"

"Ben was way worse than most. But I thought you wanted to talk about the Runners." Newt's tone warned that the conversation about the Changing was over.

This made Thomas even more curious, though he was just fine go-ing back to the subject of Runners. "Okay, I'm listening."

"Like I said, best of the best."

"So what do you do? Test everybody to see how fast they are?"

Newt gave Thomas a disgusted look, then groaned. "Show me some smarts, Greenie, Tommy, whatever ya like. How fast you can bloody run is only part of it. A very small part, actually."

This piqued Thomas's interest. "What do you mean?"

"When I say best of the best, I mean at everything. To survive the buggin' Maze, you gotta be smart, quick, strong. Gotta be a decision maker, know the right amount of risk to take. Can't be reckless, can't be timid, either." Newt straightened his legs and leaned back on his hands. "It's bloody awful out there, ya know? I don't miss it."

"I thought the Grievers only came out at night." Destiny or not, Thomas didn't want to run into one of those things.

"Yeah, usually."

"Then why is it so terrible out there?" What *else* didn't he know about?

Newt sighed. "Pressure. Stress. Maze pattern different every day, tryin' to picture things in your mind, tryin' to get us out of here. Worryin' about the bloody Maps. Worst part, you're always scared you might not make it back. A normal maze'd be hard enough—but when it *changes* every night, couple of mental mistakes and you're spendin' the night with vicious beasts. No room or time for dummies or brats."

Thomas frowned, not quite understanding the drive inside him, urging him on. Especially after last night. But he still felt it. Felt it all over.

"Why all the interest?" Newt asked.

Thomas hesitated, thinking, scared to say it out loud again. "I want to be a Runner."

Newt turned and looked him in the eye. "Haven't been here a week, shank. Little early for death wishes, don't ya think?"

"I'm serious." It barely made sense even to Thomas, but he felt it deeply. In fact, the desire to become a Runner was the only thing driving him on, helping him accept his predicament.

Newt didn't break his gaze. "So am I. Forget it. No one's ever become a Runner in their first month, much less their first week. Got a lot of provin' to do before we'll recommend you to the Keeper."

Thomas stood and started folding up his sleeping gear. "Newt, I mean it. I can't pull weeds all day—I'll go nuts. I don't have a clue what I did before they shipped me here in that metal box, but my gut tells me that being a Runner is what I'm supposed to do. I can do it."

Newt still sat there, staring up at Thomas, not offering to help. "No one said you couldn't. But give it a rest for now."

Thomas felt a surge of impatience. "But—"

"Listen, trust me on this, Tommy. Start stompin' around this place yappin' about how you're too good to work like a peasant, how you're all nice and ready to be a Runner—you'll make plenty of enemies. Drop it for now."

Making enemies was the last thing Thomas wanted, but still. He decided on another direction. "Fine, I'll talk to Minho about it."

"Good try, ya buggin' shank. The Gathering elects Runners, and if you think *I'm* tough, they'd laugh in your face."

"For all you guys know, I could be really good at it. It's a waste of time to make me wait."

Newt stood to join Thomas and jabbed a finger in his face. "You listen to me, Greenie. You listenin' all nice and pretty?"

Thomas surprisingly didn't feel that intimidated. He rolled his eyes, but then nodded.

"You better stop this nonsense, before others hear about it. That's not how it works around here, and our whole existence depends on things *working*."

He paused, but Thomas said nothing, dreading the lecture he knew was coming.

"Order," Newt continued. "Order. You say that bloody word over and over in your shuck head. Reason we're all sane around here is 'cause we work our butts off and maintain order. Order's the reason we put Ben out—can't very well have loonies runnin' around tryin' to kill people, now can we? *Order*. Last thing we need is you screwin' that up."

The stubbornness washed out of Thomas. He knew it was time to shut up. "Yeah" was all he said.

Newt slapped him on the back. "Let's make a deal."

"What?" Thomas felt his hopes rise.

"You keep your mouth shut about it, and I'll put you on the list of potential trainees as soon as you show some clout. *Don't* keep your trap shut, and I'll bloody make sure ya never see it happen. Deal?"

Thomas hated the idea of waiting, not knowing how long it might be. "That's a sucky deal."

Newt raised his eyebrows.

Thomas finally nodded. "Deal."

"Come on, let's get us some grub from Frypan. And hope we don't bloody choke."

That morning, Thomas finally met the infamous Frypan, if only from a distance. The guy was too busy trying to feed breakfast to an army of starving Gladers. He couldn't have been more than sixteen years old, but he had a full beard and hair sticking out all over the rest of his body, as if each follicle were trying to escape the confines of his food-smeared clothes. Didn't seem like the most sanitary guy in the world to oversee all the cooking, Thomas thought. He made a mental note to watch out for nasty black hairs in his meals.

He and Newt had just joined Chuck for breakfast at a picnic table right outside the Kitchen when a large group of Gladers got up and ran toward the West Door, talking excitedly about something.

"What's going on?" Thomas asked, surprising himself at how nonchalantly he said it. New developments in the Glade had just become a part of life.

Newt shrugged as he dug into his eggs. "Just seein' off Minho and Alby—they're going to look at the buggin' dead Griever."

"Hey," Chuck said. A small piece of bacon flew out of his mouth when he spoke. "I've got a question about that."

"Yeah, Chuckie?" Newt asked, somewhat sarcastically. "And what's your bloody question?"

Chuck seemed deep in thought. "Well, they found a dead Griever, right?"

"Yeah," Newt replied. "Thanks for that bit of news."

Chuck absently tapped his fork against the table for a few seconds. "Well, then who *killed* the stupid thing?"

Excellent question, Thomas thought. He waited for Newt to answer, but nothing came. He obviously didn't have a clue.

CHAPTER 16

Thomas spent the morning with the Keeper of the Gardens, "working his butt off," as Newt would've said. Zart was the tall, black-haired kid who'd stood at the front of the pole during Ben's Banishment, and who for some odd reason smelled like sour milk. He didn't say much, but showed Thomas the ropes until he could start working on his own. Weeding, pruning an apricot tree, planting squash and zucchini seeds, picking veggies. He didn't love it, and mostly ignored the other boys working alongside him, but he didn't hate it nearly as much as what he'd done for Winston at the Blood House.

Thomas and Zart were weeding a long row of young corn when Thomas decided it was a good time to start asking questions. This Keeper seemed a lot more approachable.

"So, Zart," he said.

The Keeper glanced up at him, then resumed his work. The kid had droopy eyes and a long face—for some reason he looked as bored as humanly possible. "Yeah, Greenie, what you want?"

"How many Keepers total are there?" Thomas asked, trying to act casual. "And what are the job options?"

"Well, you got the Builders, the Sloppers, Baggers, Cooks, Map-makers, Med-jacks, Track-Hoes, Blood Housers. The Runners, of course. I don't know, a few more, maybe. Pretty much keep to myself and my own stuff."

Most of the words were self-explanatory, but Thomas wondered about a couple of them. "What's a Slopper?" He knew that was what Chuck did, but the boy never wanted to talk about it. Refused to talk about it.

"That's what the shanks do that can't do nothin' else. Clean toilets, clean the showers, clean the kitchen, clean up the Blood House after a slaughter, everything. Spend one day with them suckers—that'll cure any thoughts of goin' that direction, I can tell ya that."

Thomas felt a pang of guilt over Chuck—felt sorry for him. The kid tried so hard to be everyone's friend, but no one seemed to like him or even pay attention to him. Yeah, he was a little excitable and talked too much, but Thomas was glad enough to have him around.

"What about the Track-hoes?" Thomas asked as he yanked out a huge weed, clumps of dirt swaying on the roots.

Zart cleared his throat and kept on working as he answered. "They're the ones take care of all the heavy stuff for the Gardens. Trenching and whatnot. During off times they do other stuff round the Glade. Actually, a lot of Gladers have more than one job. Anyone tell you that?"

Thomas ignored the question and moved on, determined to get as many answers as possible. "What about the Baggers? I know they take care of dead people, but it can't happen *that* often, can it?"

"Those are the creepy fellas. They act as guards and poh-lice, too. Everyone just likes to call 'em Baggers. Have fun that day, brother." He snickered, the first time Thomas had heard him do so—there was something very likable about it.

Thomas had more questions. Lots more. Chuck and everyone else around the Glade never wanted to give him the answers to anything. And here was Zart, who seemed perfectly willing. But suddenly Thomas didn't feel like talking anymore. For some reason the girl had popped into his head again, out of the blue, and then thoughts of Ben, and the dead Griever, which should have been a good thing but every-one acted as if it were anything but.

His new life pretty much sucked.

He drew a deep, long breath. *Just work,* he thought. And he did.

By the time midafternoon arrived, Thomas was ready to collapse from exhaustion—all that bending over and crawling around on your knees in the dirt was the pits. Blood House, Gardens. Two strikes.

Runner, he thought as he went on break. *Just let me be a Runner.* Once again he thought about how absurd it was that he wanted it so badly. But even though he didn't understand it, or where it came from, the desire was undeniable. Just as strong were thoughts of the girl, but he pushed them aside as much as possible.

Tired and sore, he headed to the Kitchen for a snack and some wa-ter. He could've eaten a full-blown meal despite having had lunch just two hours earlier. Even pig was starting to sound good again.

He bit into an apple, then plopped on the ground beside Chuck. Newt was there, too, but sat alone, ignoring everybody. His eyes were bloodshot, his forehead creased with heavy lines. Thomas watched as Newt chewed his fingernails, something he hadn't seen the older boy do before.

Chuck noticed and asked the question that was on Thomas's mind. "What's wrong with him?" the boy whispered. "Looks like you did when you popped out of the Box."

"I don't know," Thomas replied. "Why don't you go ask him."

"I can hear every bloody word you guys are saying," Newt called in a loud voice. "No wonder people hate sleepin' next to you shanks."

Thomas felt like he'd been caught stealing, but he was genuinely concerned—Newt was one of the few people in the Glade he actually liked.

"What *is* wrong with you?" Chuck asked. "No offense, but you look like klunk."

"Every lovin' thing in the universe," he replied, then fell silent as he stared off into space for a long moment. Thomas almost pushed him with another question, but Newt finally continued. "The girl from the Box. Keeps groanin' and saying all kinds of weird stuff, but won't wake up. Med-jacks're doing their best to feed her, but she's eatin' less each time. I'm tellin' ya, something's very bad about that whole bloody thing."

Thomas looked down at his apple, then took a bite. It tasted sour now—he realized he was worried about the girl. Concerned for her welfare. As if he knew her.

Newt let out a long sigh. "Shuck it. But that's not what really has me buggin'."

"Then what does?" Chuck asked.

Thomas leaned forward, so curious he was able to put the girl out of his mind.

Newt's eyes narrowed as he looked out toward one of the entrances to the Maze. "Alby and Minho," he muttered. "They should've come back hours ago."

Before Thomas knew it he was back at work, pulling up weeds again, counting down the minutes until he'd be done with the Gardens. He glanced constantly at the West Door, looking for any sign of Alby and Minho, Newt's concern having rubbed off on him.

Newt had said they were supposed to have come back by noon, just enough time for them to get to the dead Griever, explore for an hour or two, then return. No wonder he'd looked so upset. When Chuck offered up that maybe they were just exploring and having some fun, Newt had given him a stare so harsh Thomas thought Chuck might spontaneously combust.

He'd never forget the next look that had come over Newt's face. When Thomas asked why Newt and some others didn't just go into the Maze and search for their friends, Newt's expression had changed to outright horror—his cheeks had *shrunk* into his face, becoming sallow and dark. It gradually passed, and he'd explained that sending out search parties was forbidden, lest even more people be lost, but there was no mistaking the fear that had crossed his face.

Newt was terrified of the Maze.

Whatever had happened to him out there—maybe even related to his lingering ankle injury—had been truly awful.

Thomas tried not to think about it as he put his focus back on yanking weeds.

That night dinner proved to be a somber affair, and it had nothing to do with the food. Frypan and his cooks served up a grand meal of steak, mashed potatoes, green beans and hot rolls. Thomas was quickly learning that jokes about Frypan's cooking were just that—jokes. Everyone gobbled up his food and usually begged for more. But tonight, the Gladers ate like dead men resurrected for one last meal before being sent to live with the devil.

The Runners had returned at their normal time, and Thomas had grown more and more upset as he watched Newt run from Door to Door as they entered the Glade, not bothering to hide his panic. But Alby and Minho never showed up. Newt forced the Gladers to go on and get some of Frypan's hard-earned dinner, but he insisted on standing watch for the missing duo. No one said it, but Thomas knew it wouldn't be long before the Doors closed.

Thomas reluctantly followed orders like the rest of the boys and was sharing a picnic table on the south side of the Homestead with

Chuck and Winston. He'd only been able to eat a few bites when he couldn't take it anymore.

"I can't stand sitting here while they're out there missing," he said as he dropped his fork on the plate. "I'm going over to watch the Doors with Newt." He stood up and headed out to look.

Not surprisingly, Chuck was right behind him.

They found Newt at the West Door, pacing, running his hands through his hair. He looked up as Thomas and Chuck approached.

"Where *are* they?" Newt said, his voice thin and strained.

Thomas was touched that Newt cared so much about Alby and Minho—as if they were his own kin. "Why don't we send out a search party?" he suggested again. It seemed so stupid to sit here and worry themselves to death when they could go out there and *find* them.

"Bloody he—" Newt started before stopping himself; he closed his eyes for a second and took a deep breath. "We can't. Okay? Don't say it again. One hundred percent against the rules. Especially with the buggin' Doors about to close."

"But why?" Thomas persisted, in disbelief at Newt's stubbornness. "Won't the Grievers get them if they stay out there? Shouldn't we do something?"

Newt turned on him, his face flushed red, his eyes flamed with fury.

"Shut your hole, Greenie!" he yelled. "Not a bloody week you've been here! You think I wouldn't risk my life in a second to save those lugs?"

"No . . . I . . . Sorry. I didn't mean . . ." Thomas didn't know what to say—he was just trying to help.

Newt's face softened. "You don't get it yet, Tommy. Going out there at night is beggin' for death. We'd just be throwin' more lives away. If those shanks don't make it back . . ." He paused, seeming hesitant to say what everyone was thinking. "Both of 'em swore an oath, just like I did. Like we all did. You, too, when you go to your first Gathering and get chosen by a Keeper. Never go out at night. No matter what. Never."

Thomas looked over at Chuck, who seemed as pale-faced as Newt.

"Newt won't say it," the boy said, "so I will. If they're not back, it means they're dead. Minho's too smart to get lost. Impossible. They're dead."

Newt said nothing, and Chuck turned and walked back toward the Homestead, his head hanging low. *Dead?* Thomas thought. The situation had become so grave he didn't know how to react, felt a pit of emptiness in his heart.

"The shank's right," Newt said solemnly. "That's why we can't go out. We can't afford to make things bloody worse than they already are."

He put his hand on Thomas's shoulder, then let it slump to his side. Tears moistened Newt's eyes, and Thomas was sure that even within the dark chamber of memories that were locked away, out of his reach, he'd never seen someone look so sad. The growing darkness of twilight was a perfect fit for how grim things felt to Thomas.

"The Doors close in two minutes," Newt said, a statement so succinct and final it seemed to hang in the air like a burial shroud caught in a puff of wind. Then he walked away, hunched over, quiet.

Thomas shook his head and looked back into the Maze. He barely knew Alby and Minho. But his chest ached at the thought of them out there, killed by the horrendous creature he'd seen through the window his first morning in the Glade.

A loud boom sounded from all directions, startling Thomas out of his thoughts. Then came the crunching, grinding sound of stone against stone. The Doors were closing for the night.

The right wall rumbled across the ground, spitting dirt and rocks as it moved. The vertical row of connecting rods, so many they seemed to reach the sky far above, slid toward their corresponding holes on the left wall, ready to seal shut until the morning. Once again, Thomas looked in awe at the massive moving wall—it defied any sense of physics. It seemed impossible.

Then a flicker of movement to the left caught his eyes.

Something stirred inside the Maze, down the long corridor in front of him.

At first, a shot of panic raced through him; he stepped back, worried it might be a Griever. But then two forms took shape, stumbling along the alley toward the Door. His eyes finally focused through the initial blindness of fear, and he realized it was Minho, with one of Alby's arms draped across his shoulders, practically dragging the boy along behind him. Minho looked up, saw Thomas, who knew his eyes must be bulging out of his head.

"They got him!" Minho shouted, his voice strangled and weak with exhaustion. Every step he took seemed like it could be his last.

Thomas was so stunned by the turn of events, it took a moment for him to act. "Newt!" he finally screamed, forcing his gaze away from Minho and Alby to face the other direction. "They're coming! I can see 'em!" He knew he should run into the Maze and help, but the rule about not leaving the Glade was seared into his mind.

Newt had already made it back to the Homestead, but at Thomas's cry he immediately spun around and broke into a stuttering run toward the Door.

Thomas turned to look back into the Maze and dread washed

through him. Alby had slipped out of Minho's clutches and fallen to the ground. Thomas watched as Minho tried desperately to get him back on his feet, then, finally giving up, started to drag the boy across the stone floor by the arms.

But they were still a hundred feet away.

The right wall was closing fast, seeming to quicken its pace the more Thomas willed it to slow down. There were only seconds left until it shut completely. They had no chance of making it in time. No chance at all.

Thomas turned to look at Newt: limping along as well as he could, he'd only made it halfway to Thomas.

He looked back into the Maze, at the closing wall. Only a few feet more and it'd be over.

Minho stumbled up ahead, fell to the ground. They weren't going to make it. Time was up. That was it.

Thomas heard Newt scream something from behind him.

"Don't do it, Tommy! Don't you bloody do it!"

The rods on the right wall seemed to reach like stretched-out arms for their home, grasping for those little holes that would serve as their resting place for the night. The crunching, grinding sound of the Doors filled the air, deafening.

Five feet. Four feet. Three. Two.

Thomas knew he had no choice. He *moved*. Forward. He squeezed past the connecting rods at the last second and stepped into the Maze.

The walls slammed shut behind him, the echo of its boom bouncing off the ivy-covered stone like mad laughter.

CHAPTER 17

For several seconds, Thomas felt like the world had frozen in place. A thick silence followed the thunderous rumble of the Door closing, and a veil of darkness seemed to cover the sky, as if even the sun had been frightened away by what lurked in the Maze. Twilight had fallen, and the mammoth walls looked like enormous tombstones in a weed-infested cemetery for giants. Thomas leaned back against the rough rock, overcome by disbelief at what he had just done.

Filled with terror at what the consequences might be.

Then a sharp cry from Alby up ahead snapped Thomas to attention; Minho was moaning. Thomas pushed himself away from the wall and ran to the two Gladers.

Minho had pulled himself up and was standing once again, but he looked terrible, even in the pale light still available—sweaty, dirty, scratched-up. Alby, on the ground, looked worse, his clothes ripped, his arms covered with cuts and bruises. Thomas shuddered. Had Alby been attacked by a Griever?

"Greenie," Minho said, "if you think that was brave comin' out here, listen up. You're the shuckiest shuck-faced shuck there ever was. You're as good as dead, just like us."

Thomas felt his face heat up—he'd expected at least a little gratitude. "I couldn't just sit there and leave you guys out here."

"And what good are you with us?" Minho rolled his eyes. "Whatever, dude. Break the Number One Rule, kill yourself, whatever."

"You're welcome. I was just trying to help." Thomas felt like kicking him in the face.

Minho forced a bitter laugh, then knelt back on the ground beside Alby. Thomas took a closer look at the collapsed boy and realized just how bad things were. Alby looked on the edge of death. His usually dark skin was losing color fast and his breaths were quick and shallow.

Hopelessness rained down on Thomas. "What happened?" he asked, trying to put aside his anger.

"Don't wanna talk about it," Minho said as he checked Alby's pulse and bent over to listen to his chest. "Let's just say the Grievers can play dead really well."

This statement took Thomas by surprise. "So he was . . . bitten? Stung, whatever? Is he going through the Changing?"

"You've got a lot to learn," was all Minho would say.

Thomas wanted to scream. He knew he had a lot to learn—that was why he was asking questions. "Is he going to die?" he forced himself to say, cringing at how shallow and empty it sounded.

"Since we didn't make it back before sunset, probably. Could be dead in an hour—I don't know how long it takes if you don't get the Serum. Course, we'll be dead, too, so don't get all weepy for him. Yep, we'll all be nice and dead soon." He said it so matter-of-factly, Thomas could hardly process the meaning of the words.

But fast enough, the dire reality of the situation began to hit Thomas, and his insides turned to rot. "We're really going to die?" he asked, unable to accept it. "You're telling me we have no chance?"

"None."

Thomas was annoyed at Minho's constant negativity. "Oh, come on—there has to be something we can do. How many Grievers'll come at us?" He peered down the corridor that led deeper into the Maze, as

114

if expecting the creatures to arrive then, summoned by the sound of their name.

"I don't know."

A thought sprang into Thomas's mind, giving him hope. "But . . . what about Ben? And Gally, and others who've been stung and survived?"

Minho glanced up at him with a look that said he was dumber than cow klunk. "Didn't you hear me? They made it back before sunset, you dong. Made it back and got the Serum. All of them."

Thomas wondered about the mention of a serum, but had too many other questions to get out first. "But I thought the Grievers only came out at night."

"Then you were *wrong*, shank. They *always* come out at night. That doesn't mean they never show up during the day."

Thomas wouldn't allow himself to give in to Minho's hopelessness—he didn't want to give up and die just yet. "Has anyone ever been caught outside the walls at night and lived through it?"

"Never."

Thomas scowled, wishing he could find one little spark of hope. "How many have died, then?"

Minho stared at the ground, crouched with one forearm on a knee. He was clearly exhausted, almost in a daze. "At least twelve. Haven't you been to the graveyard?"

"Yeah." *So that's how they died,* he thought.

"Well, those are just the ones we *found*. There are more whose bodies never showed up." Minho pointed absently back toward the sealed-off Glade. "That freaking graveyard's back in the woods for a reason. Nothing kills happy time more than being reminded of your slaughtered friends every day."

Minho stood and grabbed Alby's arms, then nodded toward his feet. "Grab those smelly suckers. We gotta carry him over to the Door. Give 'em one body that's easy to find in the morning."

Thomas couldn't believe how *morbid* a statement that was. "How can this be happening!" he screamed to the walls, turning in a circle. He felt close to losing it once and for all.

"Quit your crying. You should've followed the rules and stayed inside. Now come on, grab his legs."

Wincing at the growing cramps in his gut, Thomas walked over and lifted Alby's feet as he was told. They half carried, half dragged the almost-lifeless body a hundred feet or so to the vertical crack of the Door, where Minho propped Alby up against the wall in a semi-sitting position. Alby's chest rose and fell with struggled breaths, but his skin was drenched in sweat; he looked like he wouldn't last much longer.

"Where was he bitten?" Thomas asked. "Can you see it?"

"They don't freaking *bite* you. They prick you. And no, you can't see it. There could be dozens all over his body." Minho folded his arms and leaned against the wall.

For some reason, Thomas thought the word *prick* sounded a lot worse than *bite*. "Prick you? What does that mean?"

"Dude, you just have to see them to know what I'm talking about."

Thomas pointed at Minho's arms, then his legs. "Well, why didn't the thing *prick* you?"

Minho held his hands out. "Maybe it did—maybe I'll collapse any second."

"They . . . ," Thomas began, but didn't know how to finish. He couldn't tell if Minho had been serious.

"There was no *they,* just the one we thought was dead. It went nuts and stung Alby, but then ran away." Minho looked back into the Maze, which was now almost completely dark with nighttime. "But I'm sure

116

it and a whole bunch of them suckers'll be here soon to finish us off with their needles."

"Needles?" Things just kept sounding more and more disturbing to Thomas.

"Yeah, needles." He didn't elaborate, and his face said he didn't plan to.

Thomas looked up at the enormous walls covered in thick vines—desperation had finally clicked him into problem-solving mode. "Can't we climb this thing?" He looked at Minho, who didn't say a word. "The *vines*—can't we climb them?"

Minho let out a frustrated sigh. "I swear, Greenie, you must think we're a bunch of idiots. You really think we've never had the ingenious thought of climbing the freaking *walls*?"

For the first time, Thomas felt anger creeping in to compete with his fear and panic. "I'm just trying to help, man. Why don't you quit moping at every word I say and *talk* to me?"

Minho abruptly jumped at Thomas and grabbed him by the shirt. "You don't *understand,* shuck-face! You don't know anything, and you're just making it worse by trying to have hope! We're dead, you hear me? Dead!"

Thomas didn't know which he felt more strongly at that moment—anger at Minho or pity for him. He was giving up too easily.

Minho looked down at his hands clasped to Thomas's shirt and shame washed across his face. Slowly, he let go and backed away. Thomas straightened his clothes defiantly.

"Ah, man, oh man," Minho whispered, then crumpled to the ground, burying his face in clenched fists. "I've never been this scared before, dude. Not like this."

Thomas wanted to say something, tell him to grow up, tell him to *think,* tell him to explain everything he knew. Something!

He opened his mouth to speak, but closed it quickly when he heard the *noise*. Minho's head popped up; he looked down one of the darkened stone corridors. Thomas felt his own breath quicken.

It came from deep within the Maze, a low, haunting sound. A constant whirring that had a metallic ring every few seconds, like sharp knives rubbing against each other. It grew louder by the second, and then a series of eerie clicks joined in. Thomas thought of long fingernails tapping against glass. A hollow moan filled the air, and then something that sounded like the clanking of chains.

All of it, together, was horrifying, and the small amount of courage Thomas had gathered began to slip away.

Minho stood, his face barely visible in the dying light. But when he spoke, Thomas imagined his eyes wide with terror. "We have to split up—it's our only chance. Just keep moving. Don't stop moving!"

And then he turned and ran, disappearing in seconds, swallowed by the Maze and darkness.

CHAPTER 18

Thomas stared at the spot where Minho had vanished.

A sudden dislike for the guy swelled up inside him. Minho was a veteran in this place, a Runner. Thomas was a Newbie, just a few days in the Glade, a few minutes in the Maze. Yet of the two of them, Minho had broken down and panicked, only to run off at the first sign of trouble. *How could he leave me here?* Thomas thought. *How could he do that!*

The noises grew louder. The roar of engines interspersed with rolling, cranking sounds like chains hoisting machinery in an old, grimy factory. And then came the smell—something burning, oily. Thomas couldn't begin to guess what was in store for him; he'd seen a Griever, but only a glimpse, and through a dirty window. What would they do to him? How long would he last?

Stop, he told himself. He had to quit wasting time waiting for them to come and end his life.

He turned and faced Alby, still propped against the stone wall, now only a mound of shadow in the darkness. Kneeling on the ground, Thomas found Alby's neck, then searched for a pulse. Something there. He listened at his chest like Minho had done.

buh-bump, buh-bump, buh-bump

Still alive.

Thomas rocked back on his heels, then ran his arm across his forehead, wiping away the sweat. And at that moment, in the space of only a few seconds, he learned a lot about himself. About the Thomas that was *before*.

He couldn't leave a friend to die. Even someone as cranky as Alby.

He reached down and grabbed both of Alby's arms, then squatted into a sitting position and wrapped the arms around his neck from behind. He pulled the lifeless body onto his back and pushed with his legs, grunting with the effort.

But it was too much. Thomas collapsed forward onto his face; Alby sprawled to the side with a loud flump.

The frightening sounds of the Grievers grew closer by the second, echoing off the stone walls of the Maze. Thomas thought he could see bright flashes of light far away, bouncing off the night sky. He didn't want to meet the source of those lights, those sounds.

Trying a new approach, he grabbed Alby's arms again and started dragging him along the ground. He couldn't believe how *heavy* the boy was, and it took only ten feet or so for Thomas to realize that it just wasn't going to work. Where would he take him, anyway?

He pushed and pulled Alby back over to the crack that marked the entrance to the Glade, and propped him once more into a sitting position, leaning against the stone wall.

Thomas sat back against it himself, panting from exertion, thinking. As he looked into the dark recesses of the Maze, he searched his mind for a solution. He could hardly see anything, and he knew, despite what Minho had said, that it'd be stupid to run even if he *could* carry Alby. Not only was there the chance of getting lost, he could actually find himself running toward the Grievers instead of away from them.

He thought of the wall, the ivy. Minho hadn't explained, but he had made it sound as if climbing the walls was impossible. Still . . .

A plan formed in his mind. It all depended on the unknown abilities of the Grievers, but it was the best thing he could come up with.

Thomas walked a few feet along the wall until he found a thick growth of ivy covering most of the stone. He reached down and grabbed one of the vines that went all the way to the ground and wrapped his hand around it. It felt thicker and more solid than he would've imagined, maybe a half-inch in diameter. He pulled on it, and with the sound of thick paper ripping apart, the vine came unattached from the wall—more and more as Thomas stepped away from it. When he'd moved back ten feet, he could no longer see the end of the vine way above; it disappeared in the darkness. But the trailing plant had yet to fall free, so Thomas knew it was still attached up there somewhere.

Hesitant to try, Thomas steeled himself and pulled on the vine of ivy with all his strength.

It held.

He yanked on it again. Then again, pulling and relaxing with both hands over and over. Then he lifted his feet and hung onto the vine; his body swung forward.

The vine held.

Quickly, Thomas grabbed other vines, ripping them away from the wall, creating a series of climbing ropes. He tested each one, and they all proved to be as strong as the first. Encouraged, he went back to Alby and dragged him over to the vines.

A sharp crack echoed from within the Maze, followed by the horrible sound of crumpling metal. Thomas, startled, swung around to look, his mind so concentrated on the vines that he'd momentarily shut out the Grievers; he searched all three directions of the Maze. He couldn't see anything coming, but the sounds were louder—the whirring, the groaning, the clanging. And the air had brightened ever so slightly; he could make out more of the details of the Maze than he'd been able to just minutes before.

He remembered the odd lights he'd observed through the Glade window with Newt. The Grievers were close. They had to be.

Thomas pushed aside the swelling panic and set himself to work.

He grabbed one of the vines and wrapped it around Alby's right arm. The plant would only reach so far, so he had to prop Alby up as much as he could to make it work. After several wraps, he tied the vine off. Then he took another vine and put it around Alby's left arm, then both of his legs, tying each one tightly. He worried about the Glader's circulation getting cut off, but decided it was worth the risk.

Trying to ignore the doubt that was seeping into his mind about the plan, Thomas continued on. Now it was his turn.

He snatched a vine with both hands and started to climb, directly over the spot where he'd just tied up Alby. The thick leaves of the ivy served well as handholds, and Thomas was elated to find that the many cracks in the stone wall were perfect supports for his feet as he climbed. He began to think how easy it would be without . . .

He refused to finish the thought. He couldn't leave Alby behind.

Once he reached a point a couple of feet above his friend, Thomas wrapped one of the vines around his own chest, around and around several times, snug against his armpits for support. Slowly, he let himself sag, letting go with his hands but keeping his feet planted firmly in a large crack. Relief filled him when the vine held.

Now came the really hard part.

The four vines tied to Alby below hung tautly around him. Thomas took hold of the one attached to Alby's left leg, and pulled. He was only able to get it up a few inches before letting go—the weight was too much. He couldn't do it.

He climbed back down to the Maze floor, decided to try *pushing* from below instead of *pulling* from above. To test it, he tried raising Alby only a couple of feet, limb by limb. First, he pushed the left leg up, then tied a new vine around it. Then the right leg. When both were secure, Thomas did the same to Alby's arms—right, then left.

He stepped back, panting, to take a look.

Alby hung there, seemingly lifeless, now three feet higher than he'd been five minutes earlier.

Clangs from the Maze. Whirrs. Buzzes. Moans. Thomas thought he saw a couple of red flashes to his left. The Grievers were getting closer, and it was now obvious that there were more than one.

He got back to work.

Using the same method of pushing each of Alby's arms and legs up two or three feet at a time, Thomas slowly made his way up the stone wall. He climbed until he was right below the body, wrapped a vine around his own chest for support, then pushed Alby up as far as he could, limb by limb, and tied them off with ivy. Then he repeated the whole process.

Climb, wrap, push up, tie off.

Climb, wrap, push up, tie off. The Grievers at least seemed to be moving slowly through the Maze, giving him time.

Over and over, little by little, up they went. The effort was exhausting; Thomas heaved in every breath, felt sweat cover every inch of his skin. His hands began to slip and slide on the vines. His feet ached from pressing into the stone cracks. The sounds grew louder—the awful, awful sounds. Still Thomas worked.

When they'd reached a spot about thirty feet off the ground, Thomas stopped, swaying on the vine he'd tied around his chest. Using his drained, rubbery arms, he turned himself around to face the Maze.

An exhaustion he'd not known possible filled every tiny particle of his body. He ached with weariness; his muscles screamed. He couldn't push Alby up another inch. He was done.

This was where they'd hide. Or make their stand.

He'd known they couldn't reach the top—he only hoped the Grievers couldn't or wouldn't look above them. Or, at the very least, Thomas hoped he could fight them off from high up, one by one, instead of being overwhelmed on the ground.

He had no idea what to expect; he didn't know if he'd see tomorrow. But here, hanging in the ivy, Thomas and Alby would meet their fate.

A few minutes passed before Thomas saw the first glimmer of light shine off the Maze walls up ahead. The terrible sounds he'd heard escalate for the last hour took on a high-pitched, mechanical squeal, like a robotic death yell.

A red light to his left, on the wall, caught his attention. He turned and almost screamed out loud—a beetle blade was only a few inches from him, its spindly legs poking through the ivy and somehow sticking to the stone. The red light of its eye was like a little sun, too bright to look at directly. Thomas squinted and tried to focus on the beetle's body.

The torso was a silver cylinder, maybe three inches in diameter and ten inches long. Twelve jointed legs ran along the length of its bottom, spread out, making the thing look like a sleeping lizard. The head was impossible to see because of the red beam of light shining right at him, though it seemed small, vision its only purpose, perhaps.

But then Thomas saw the most chilling part. He thought he'd seen it before, back in the Glade when the beetle blade had scooted past him and into the woods. Now it was confirmed: the red light from its eye cast a creepy glow on six capital letters smeared across the torso, as if they had been written with blood:

Thomas couldn't imagine why that one word would be stamped on the beetle blade, unless for the purpose of announcing to the Gladers that it was evil. Wicked.

He knew it had to be a spy for whoever had sent them here—Alby had told him as much, saying the beetles were how the Creators watched them. Thomas stilled himself, held his breath, hoping that maybe the beetle only detected movement. Long seconds passed, his lungs screaming for air.

With a click and then a clack, the beetle turned and scuttled off, disappearing into the ivy. Thomas sucked in a huge gulp of air, then another, feeling the pinch of the vines tied around his chest.

Another mechanical squeal screeched through the Maze, close now, followed by the surge of revved machinery. Thomas tried to imitate Alby's lifeless body, hanging limp in the vines.

And then something rounded the corner up ahead, and came toward them.

Something he'd seen before, but through the safety of thick glass.

Something unspeakable.

A Griever.

CHAPTER 19

Thomas stared in horror at the monstrous thing making its way down the long corridor of the Maze.

It looked like an experiment gone terribly wrong—something from a nightmare. Part animal, part machine, the Griever rolled and clicked along the stone pathway. Its body resembled a gigantic slug, sparsely covered in hair and glistening with slime, grotesquely pulsating in and out as it breathed. It had no distinguishable head or tail, but front to end it was at least six feet long, four feet thick.

Every ten to fifteen seconds, sharp metal spikes popped through its bulbous flesh and the whole creature abruptly curled into a ball and spun forward. Then it would settle, seeming to gather its bearings, the spikes receding back through the moist skin with a sick slurping sound. It did this over and over, traveling just a few feet at a time.

But hair and spikes were not the only things protruding from the Griever's body. Several randomly placed mechanical arms stuck out here and there, each one with a different purpose. A few had bright lights attached to them. Others had long, menacing needles. One had a three-fingered claw that clasped and unclasped for no apparent reason. When the creature rolled, these arms folded and maneuvered to avoid being crushed. Thomas wondered what—or who—could create such frightening, disgusting creatures.

The source of the sounds he'd been hearing made sense now. When the Griever rolled, it made the metallic whirring sound, like the spinning blade of a saw. The spikes and the arms explained the creepy clicking sounds, metal against stone. But nothing sent chills up and down Thomas's spine like the haunted, deathly moans that somehow escaped the creature when it sat still, like the sound of dying men on a battlefield.

Seeing it all now—the beast matched with the sounds—Thomas couldn't think of any nightmare that could equal this hideous thing coming toward him. He fought the fear, forced his body to remain perfectly still, hanging there in the vines. He was sure their only hope was to avoid being noticed.

Maybe it won't see us, he thought. *Just maybe.* But the reality of the situation sank like a stone in his belly. The beetle blade had already revealed his exact position.

The Griever rolled and clicked its way closer, zigzagging back and forth, moaning and whirring. Every time it stopped, the metal arms unfolded and turned this way and that, like a roving robot on an alien planet looking for signs of life. The lights cast eerie shadows across the Maze. A faint memory tried to escape the locked box within his mind—shadows on the walls when he was a kid, scaring him. He longed to be back to wherever that was, to run to the mom and dad he hoped still lived, somewhere, missing him, searching for him.

A strong whiff of something burnt stung his nostrils; a sick mixture of overheated engines and charred flesh. He couldn't believe people could create something so horrible and send it after kids.

Trying not to think about it, Thomas closed his eyes for a moment and concentrated on remaining still and quiet. The creature kept coming.

whirrrrrrrrrrrrrrr
click-click-click
whirrrrrrrrrrrrrrr

click-click-click

Thomas peeked down without moving his head—the Griever had finally reached the wall where he and Alby hung. It paused by the closed Door that led into the Glade, only a few yards to Thomas's right.

Please go the other way, Thomas pleaded silently.

Turn.

Go.

That way.

Please!

The Griever's spikes popped out; its body rolled toward Thomas and Alby.

whirrrrrrrrrrrrrrr

click-click-click

It came to a stop, then rolled once more, right up to the wall.

Thomas held his breath, not daring to make the slightest sound. The Griever now sat directly below them. Thomas wanted to look down so badly, but knew any movement might give him away. The beams of light from the creature shone all over the place, completely random, never settling in one spot.

Then, without warning, they went out.

The world turned instantly dark and silent. It was as if the creature had turned *off*. It didn't move, made no sound—even the haunting groans had stopped completely. And with no more lights, Thomas couldn't see a single thing.

He was blind.

He took small breaths through his nose; his pumping heart needed oxygen desperately. Could it hear him? Smell him? Sweat drenched his hair, his hands, his clothes, everything. A fear he had never known filled him to the point of insanity.

Still, nothing. No movement, no light, no sound. The anticipation of trying to guess its next move was killing Thomas.

Seconds passed. Minutes. The ropy plant dug into Thomas's flesh—his chest felt numb. He wanted to scream at the monster below him: *Kill me or go back to your hiding hole!*

Then, in a sudden burst of light and sound, the Griever came back to life, whirring and clicking.

And then it started to climb the wall.

CHAPTER 20

The Griever's spikes tore into the stone, throwing shredded ivy and rock chips in every direction. Its arms shifted about like the legs of the beetle blade, some with sharp picks that drove into the stone of the wall for support. A bright light on the end of one arm pointed directly at Thomas, only this time, the beam didn't move away.

Thomas felt the last drop of hope drain from his body.

He knew the only option left was to run. *I'm sorry, Alby,* he thought as he unraveled the thick vine from his chest. Using his left hand to hold tight to the foliage above him, he finished unwrapping himself and prepared to move. He knew he couldn't go up—that would bring the Griever across the path of Alby. Down, of course, was only an option if he wanted to die as quickly as possible.

He had to go to the side.

Thomas reached out and grabbed a vine two feet to the left of where he hung. Wrapping it around his hand, he yanked on it with a sharp tug. It held true, just like all the others. A quick glance below revealed that the Griever had already halved the distance between them, and it was moving faster yet, no more pauses or stops.

Thomas let go of the rope he'd used around his chest and heaved his body to the left, scraping along the wall. Before his pendulum swing took him back toward Alby, he reached out for another vine, catching a nice thick one. This time he grabbed it with both hands and turned to plant the bottom of his feet on the wall. He shuffled his body to the right as far as the plant would let him, then let go and grabbed another one. Then another. Like some tree-climbing monkey, Thomas found he could move more quickly than he ever could've hoped.

The sounds of his pursuer went on relentlessly, only now with the bone-shuddering addition of cracking and splitting rock joined in. Thomas swung to the right several more times before he dared to look back.

The Griever had altered its course from Alby to head directly for Thomas. *Finally,* Thomas thought, *something went right.* Pushing off with his feet as strongly as he could, swing by swing, he fled the hideous thing.

Thomas didn't need to look behind him to know the Griever was gaining on him with every passing second. The sounds gave it away. Somehow, he had to get back to the ground, or it would all end quickly.

On the next switch, he let his hand slip a bit before clasping tightly. The ivy-rope burned his palm, but he'd slipped several feet closer to the ground. He did the same with the next vine. And the next. Three swings later he'd made his way halfway to the Maze floor. Scorching pain flared up both his arms; he felt the sting of raw skin on his hands. The adrenaline rushing through his body helped push away his fear—he just kept moving.

On his next swing, the darkness prevented Thomas from seeing a new wall looming in front of him until it was too late; the corridor ended and turned to the right.

He slammed into the stone ahead, losing his grip on the vine. Throwing his arms out, Thomas flailed, reaching and grabbing to stop his plunge to the hard stone below. At the same instant, he saw the Griever out of the corner of his left eye. It had altered its course and was almost on him, reaching out with its clasping claw.

Thomas found a vine halfway to the ground and grasped it, his arms almost ripping out of their sockets at the sudden stop. He pushed off the wall with both feet as hard as he could, swinging his body away from it just as the Griever charged in with its claw and needles. Thomas kicked out with his right leg, connecting with the arm attached to the claw. A sharp crack revealed a small victory, but any elation ended when he realized that the momentum of his swing was now pulling him back down to land right on top of the creature.

Pulsing with adrenaline, Thomas drew his legs together and pulled them tight against his chest. As soon as he made contact with the Griever's body, disgustingly sinking inches into its gushy skin, he kicked out with both feet to push off, squirming to avoid the swarm of needles and claws coming at him from all directions. He swung his body out and to the left; then he jumped toward the wall of the Maze, trying to grab another vine; the Griever's vicious tools snapped and clawed at him from behind. He felt a deep scratch on his back.

Flailing once again, Thomas found a new vine and clutched it with both hands. He gripped the plant just enough to slow him down as he slid to the ground, ignoring the horrible burn. As soon as his feet hit the solid stone floor, he took off, running despite the scream of exhaustion from his body.

A booming crash sounded behind him, followed by the rolling, cracking, whirring of the Griever. But Thomas refused to look back, knowing every second counted.

He rounded a corner of the Maze, then another. Pounding the stone with his feet, he fled as fast as he possibly could. Somewhere in his mind he tracked his own movements, hoping he'd live long enough to use the information to return to the Door again.

Right, then left. Down a long corridor, then right again. Left. Right. Two lefts. Another long corridor. The sounds of pursuit from behind didn't relent or fade, but he wasn't *losing* ground, either.

On and on he ran, his heart ready to blow its way out of his chest. With great, sucking heaves of breath, he tried to get oxygen in his lungs, but he knew he couldn't last much longer. He wondered if it'd just be easier to turn and fight, get it over with.

When he rounded the next corner, he skidded to a halt at the sight in front of him. Panting uncontrollably, he stared.

Three Grievers were up ahead, rolling along as they dug their spikes into the stone, coming directly toward him.

CHAPTER 21

Thomas turned to see his original pursuer still coming, though it had slowed a bit, clasping and unclasping a metal claw as if mocking him, laughing.

It knows I'm done, he thought. After all that effort, here he was, surrounded by Grievers. It was over. Not even a week of salvageable memory, and his life was over.

Almost consumed by grief, he made a decision. He'd go down fighting.

Much preferring one over three, he ran straight toward the Griever that had chased him there. The ugly thing retracted just an inch, stopped moving its claw, as if shocked at his boldness. Taking heart at the slight falter, Thomas started screaming as he charged.

The Griever came to life, spikes popping out of its skin; it rolled forward, ready to collide head-on with its foe. The sudden movement almost made Thomas stop, his brief moment of insane courage washing away, but he kept running.

At the last second before collision, just as he got a close look at the metal and hair and slime, Thomas planted his left foot and dove to the right. Unable to stop its momentum, the Griever zoomed straight past him before it shuddered to a halt—Thomas noticed the thing was moving a lot faster now. With a metallic howl, it swiveled and readied to pounce on its victim. But now, no longer surrounded, Thomas had a clear shot away, back down the path.

He scrambled to his feet and sprinted forward. Sounds of pursuit, this time from all four Grievers, followed close behind. Sure that he was pushing his body beyond its physical limits, he ran on, trying to rid himself of the hopeless feeling that it was only a matter of time before they got him.

Then, three corridors down, two hands suddenly reached out and yanked him into the adjoining hallway. Thomas's heart leaped into his throat as he struggled to free himself. He stopped when he realized it was Minho.

"What—"

"Shut up and follow me!" Minho yelled, already dragging Thomas away until he was able to get his feet under him.

Without a moment to think, Thomas collected himself. Together, they ran through corridors, taking turn after turn. Minho seemed to know exactly what he was doing, where he was going; he never paused to think about which way they should run.

As they rounded the next corner, Minho attempted to speak. Between heaving breaths, he gasped, "I just saw . . . the dive move you did . . . back there . . . gave me an idea . . . we only have to last . . . a little while longer."

Thomas didn't bother wasting his own breath on questions; he just kept running, following Minho. Without having to look behind him, he knew the Grievers were gaining ground at an alarming rate. Every inch of his body hurt, inside and out; his limbs cried for him to quit running. But he ran on, hoped his heart didn't quit pumping.

A few turns later, Thomas saw something ahead of them that didn't register with his brain. It seemed . . . wrong. And the faint light emanating from their pursuers made the oddity up ahead all the more apparent.

The corridor didn't end in another stone wall.

It ended in blackness.

Thomas narrowed his eyes as they ran toward the wall of darkness, trying to comprehend what they were approaching. The two ivy-covered walls on either side of him seemed to intersect with nothing but sky up ahead. He could see stars. As they got closer, he finally realized that it was an opening—the Maze ended.

How? he wondered. *After years of searching, how did Minho and I find it this easily?*

Minho seemed to sense his thoughts. "Don't get excited," he said, barely able to get the words out.

A few feet before the end of the corridor, Minho pulled up, holding his hand out over Thomas's chest to make sure he stopped, too. Thomas slowed, then walked up to where the Maze opened out into open sky. The sounds of the onrushing Grievers grew closer, but he had to see.

They had indeed reached a way out of the Maze, but like Minho had said, it was nothing to get excited about. All Thomas could see in every direction, up and down, side to side, was empty air and fading stars. It was a strange and unsettling sight, like he was standing at the edge of the universe, and for a brief moment he was overcome by vertigo, his knees weakening before he steadied himself.

Dawn was beginning to make its mark, the sky seeming to have lightened considerably even in the last minute or so. Thomas stared in complete disbelief, not understanding how it could all be possible. It was like somebody had built the Maze and then set it afloat in the sky to hover there in the middle of nothing for the rest of eternity.

"I don't get it," he whispered, not knowing if Minho could even hear him.

"Careful," the Runner replied. "You wouldn't be the first shank to fall off the Cliff." He grabbed Thomas's shoulder. "Did you forget something?" He nodded back toward the inside of the Maze.

Thomas remembered hearing the word *Cliff* before, but couldn't place it at the moment. Seeing the vast, open sky in front of and below him had put him into some kind of hypnotized stupor. He shook himself back to reality and turned to face the oncoming Grievers. They were now only dozens of yards away, single file, charging in with a vengeance, moving surprisingly fast.

Everything clicked, then, even before Minho explained what they were going to do.

"These things may be vicious," Minho said, "but they're dumb as dirt. Stand here, close to me, facing—"

Thomas cut him off. "I know. I'm ready."

They shuffled their feet until they stood scrunched up together in front of the drop-off at the very middle of the corridor, facing the Grievers. Their heels were only inches from the edge of the Cliff behind them, nothing but air waiting after that.

The only thing left for them was courage.

"We need to be in sync!" Minho yelled, almost drowned out by the earsplitting sounds of the thundering spikes rolling along the stone. "On my mark!"

Why the Grievers had lined up single file was a mystery. Maybe the Maze proved just narrow enough to make it awkward for them to travel side by side. But one after the other, they rolled down the stone hallway, clicking and moaning and ready to kill. Dozens of yards had become dozens of feet, and the monsters were only seconds away from crashing into the waiting boys.

"Ready," Minho said steadily. "Not yet . . . not yet . . ."

Thomas hated every millisecond of waiting. He just wanted to close his eyes and never see another Griever again.

"Now!" screamed Minho.

Just as the first Griever's arm extended out to nip at them, Minho

137

and Thomas dove in opposite directions, each toward one of the outer walls of the corridor. The tactic had worked for Thomas earlier, and judging by the horrible screeching sound that escaped the first Griever, it had worked again. The monster flew off the edge of the Cliff. Oddly, its battle cry cut off sharply instead of fading as it plummeted to the depths beyond.

Thomas landed against the wall and spun just in time to see the second creature tumble over the edge, not able to stop itself. The third one planted a heavily spiked arm into the stone, but its momentum was too much. The nerve-grinding squeal of the spike cutting through the ground sent a shiver up Thomas's spine, though a second later the Griever tumbled into the abyss. Again, neither of them made a sound as they fell—as if they'd disappeared instead of falling.

The fourth and final approaching creature was able to stop in time, teetering on the very edge of the cliff, a spike and a claw holding it in place.

Instinctively Thomas knew what he had to do. Looking to Minho, he nodded, then turned. Both boys ran in at the Griever and jumped feetfirst at the creature, kicking out at the last second with every waning bit of strength. They both connected, sending the last monster plummeting to its death.

Thomas quickly scrambled to the edge of the abyss, poking his head over to see the falling Grievers. But impossibly, they were gone—not even a sign of them in the emptiness that stretched below. Nothing.

His mind couldn't process the thought of where the Cliff led or what had happened to the terrible creatures. His last ounce of strength disappeared, and he curled into a ball on the ground.

Then, finally, came the tears.

CHAPTER 22

A half hour passed.

Neither Thomas nor Minho had moved an inch.

Thomas had finally stopped crying; he couldn't help wondering what Minho would think of him, or if he'd tell others, calling him a sissy. But there wasn't a shred of self-control left in him; he couldn't have prevented the tears, he knew that. Despite his lack of memory, he was sure he'd just been through the most traumatic night of his life. And his sore hands and utter exhaustion didn't help.

He crawled to the edge of the Cliff once more, stuck his head over again to get a better look now that dawn was in full force. The open sky in front of him was a deep purple, slowly fading into the bright blue of day, with tinges of orange from the sun on a distant, flat horizon.

He stared straight down, saw that the stone wall of the Maze went toward the ground in a sheer cliff until it disappeared into whatever lay far, far below. But even with the ever-increasing light, he still couldn't tell what was down there. It seemed as if the Maze was perched on a structure several miles above the ground.

But that was impossible, he thought. *It can't be. Has to be an illusion.*

He rolled over onto his back, groaning at the movement. Things seemed to hurt on him and inside him that he'd never known existed before. At least the Doors would be opening soon, and they could return to the Glade. He looked over at Minho, huddled against the hall of the corridor. "I can't believe we're still alive," he said.

Minho said nothing, just nodded, his face devoid of expression.

"Are there more of them? Did we just kill them all?"

Minho snorted. "Somehow we made it to sunrise, or we would've had ten more on our butts before long." He shifted his body, wincing and groaning. "I can't believe it. Seriously. We made it through the whole night—never been done before."

Thomas knew he should feel proud, brave, something. But all he felt was tired and relieved. "What did we do differently?"

"I don't know. It's kind of hard to ask a dead guy what he did wrong."

Thomas couldn't stop wondering about how the Grievers' enraged cries had ended as they fell from the Cliff, and how he hadn't been able to see them plummeting to their deaths. There was something very strange and unsettling about it. "Seems like they disappeared or something after they went over the edge."

"Yeah, that was kinda psycho. Couple of Gladers had a theory that other things had disappeared, but we proved 'em wrong. Look."

Thomas watched as Minho tossed a rock over the Cliff, then followed its path with his eyes. Down and down it went, not leaving his sight until it grew too small to see. He turned back toward Minho. "How does that prove them wrong?"

Minho shrugged. "Well, the rock didn't disappear, now, did it?"

"Then what do you think happened?" There was something significant here, Thomas could feel it.

Minho shrugged again. "Maybe they're magic. My head hurts too much to think about it."

With a jolt, all thoughts of the Cliff were forgotten. Thomas remembered Alby. "We have to get back." Straining, he forced himself to get to his feet. "Gotta get Alby off the wall." Seeing the look of confusion on Minho's face, he quickly explained what he'd done with the ropes of ivy.

Minho looked down, his eyes dejected. "No way he's still alive."

Thomas refused to believe it. "How do you know? Come on." He started limping back along the corridor.

"Because no one's ever made it . . ."

He trailed off, and Thomas knew what he was thinking. "That's because they've always been killed by the Grievers by the time you found them. Alby was only stuck with one of those needles, right?"

Minho stood up and joined Thomas in his slow walk back toward the Glade. "I don't know, I guess this has never happened before. A few guys have been stung by the needles during the day. And those are the ones who got the Serum and went through the Changing. The poor shanks who got stuck out in the Maze all night weren't found until later—days later, sometimes, if at all. And all of them were killed in ways you don't wanna hear about."

Thomas shuddered at the thought. "After what we just went through, I think I can imagine."

Minho looked up, surprise transforming his face. "I think you just figured it out. We've been wrong—well, *hopefully* we've been wrong. Because no one who'd been stung and *didn't* make it back by sunset has ever survived, we just assumed that was the point of no return—when it's too late to get the Serum." He seemed excited by his line of thinking.

They turned yet another corner, Minho suddenly taking the lead. The boy's pace was picking up, but Thomas stayed on his heels, surprised at how familiar he felt with the directions, usually even leaning into turns before Minho showed the way.

"Okay—this Serum," Thomas said. "I've heard that a couple of times now. What *is* that? And where does it come from?"

"Just what it sounds like, shank. It's a serum. The Grief Serum."

Thomas forced out a pathetic laugh. "Just when I think I've learned everything about this stupid place. Why is it called that? And why are Grievers called Grievers?"

Minho explained as they continued through the endless turns of the Maze, neither one of them leading now. "I don't know where we got the names, but the Serum comes from the Creators—or that's what we call them, at least. It's with the supplies in the Box every week, always has been. It's a medicine or antidote or something, already inside a medical syringe, ready to use." He made a show of sticking a needle in his arm. "Stick that sucker in someone who's been stung and it saves 'em. They go through the Changing—which sucks—but after that, they're healed."

A minute or two passed in silence as Thomas processed the information; they made a couple more turns. He wondered about the Changing, and what it meant. And for some reason, he kept thinking of the girl.

"Weird, though," Minho finally continued. "We've never talked about this before. If he's still alive, there's really no reason to think Alby can't be saved by the Serum. We somehow got it into our klunk heads that once the Doors closed, you were done—end of story. I gotta see this hanging-on-the-wall thing myself—I think you're shuckin' me."

The boys kept walking, Minho almost looking happy, but something was nagging at Thomas. He'd been avoiding it, denying it to himself. "What if another Griever got Alby after I diverted the one chasing me?"

Minho looked over at him, a blank expression on his face.

"Let's just hurry, is all I'm saying," Thomas said, hoping all that effort to save Alby hadn't been wasted.

They tried to pick up the pace, but their bodies hurt too much and they settled back into a slow walk despite the urgency. The next time they rounded a corner, Thomas faltered, his heart skipping a beat when he saw movement up ahead. Relief washed through him an instant later when he realized it was Newt and a group of Gladers. The West Door to the Glade towered over them and it was open. They'd made it back.

At the boys' appearance, Newt limped over to them. "What happened?" he asked; he sounded almost angry. "How in the bloody—"

"We'll tell you later," Thomas interrupted. "We have to save Alby."

Newt's face went white. "What do you mean? He's alive?"

"Just come here." Thomas headed to the right, craning his neck to look high up at the wall, searching along the thick vines until he found the spot where Alby hung by his arms and legs far above them. Without saying anything, Thomas pointed up, not daring to be relieved yet. He was still there, and in one piece, but there was no sign of movement.

Newt finally saw his friend hanging in the ivy, and looked back at Thomas. If he'd seemed shocked before, now he looked completely bewildered. "Is he . . . alive?"

Please let him be, Thomas thought. "I don't know. Was when I left him up there."

"When *you* left him . . ." Newt shook his head. "You and Minho get your butts inside, get yourselves checked by the Med-jacks. You look bloody awful. I want the whole story when they're done and you're rested up."

Thomas wanted to wait and see if Alby was okay. He started to speak but Minho grabbed him by the arm and forced him to walk toward the Glade. "We need sleep. And bandages. *Now.*"

And Thomas knew he was right. He relented, glancing back up at Alby, then followed Minho out and away from the Maze.

The walk back into the Glade and then to the Homestead seemed endless, a row of Gladers on both sides gawking at them. Their faces showed complete awe, as if they were watching two ghosts strolling through a graveyard. Thomas knew it was because they'd accomplished something never done before, but he was embarrassed by the attention.

He almost stopped walking altogether when he spotted Gally up ahead, arms folded and glaring, but he kept moving. It took every ounce of his willpower, but he looked directly into Gally's eyes, never breaking contact. When he got to within five feet, the other boy's stare fell to the ground.

It almost disturbed Thomas how good that felt. Almost.

The next few minutes were a blur. Escorted into the Homestead by a couple of Med-jacks, up the stairs, a glimpse through a barely ajar door of someone feeding the comatose girl in her bed—he felt an incredibly strong urge to go see her, to check on her—into their own rooms, into bed, food, water, bandages. Pain. Finally, he was left alone, his head resting on the softest pillow his limited memory could recall.

But as he fell asleep, two things wouldn't leave his mind. First, the word he'd seen scrawled across the torso of both beetle blades—WICKED—ran through his thoughts again and again.

The second thing was the girl.

Hours later—days for all he knew—Chuck was there, shaking him awake. It took several seconds for Thomas to get his bearings and see straight. He focused in on Chuck, groaned. "Let me sleep, you shank."

"I thought you'd want to know."

Thomas rubbed his eyes and yawned. "Know what?" He looked at Chuck again, confused by his big smile.

"He's alive," he said. "Alby's okay—the Serum worked."

Thomas's grogginess instantly washed away, replaced with relief—it surprised him how much joy the information brought. But then Chuck's next words made him reconsider.

"He just started the Changing."

As if brought on by the words, a blood-chilling scream erupted from a room down the hall.

CHAPTER 23

Thomas wondered long and hard about Alby. It'd seemed such a victory just to save his life, bring him back from a night in the Maze. But had it been worth it? Now the boy was in intense pain, going through the same things as Ben. And what if he became as psychotic as Ben? Troubling thoughts all around.

Twilight fell upon the Glade and Alby's screams continued to haunt the air. It was impossible to escape the terrible sound, even after Thomas finally talked the Med-jacks into letting him go—weary, sore, bandaged, but tired of the piercing, agonized wails of their leader. Newt had adamantly refused when Thomas asked to see the person he'd risked his life for. *It'll only make it worse*, he'd said, and would not be swayed.

Thomas was too tired to put up a fight. He'd had no idea it was possible to feel so exhausted, despite the few hours of sleep he'd gotten. He'd hurt too much to do anything after that, and had spent most of the day on a bench on the outskirts of the Deadheads, wallowing in despair. The elation of his escape had faded rapidly, leaving him with pain and thoughts of his new life in the Glade. Every muscle ached; cuts and bruises covered him from head to toe. But even that wasn't as bad as the heavy emotional weight of what he'd been through the previous night. It seemed as if all the realities of living there had finally settled in his mind, like hearing a final diagnosis of terminal cancer.

How could anyone ever be happy in a life like this? he thought. Then,

How could anyone be evil enough to do this to us? He understood more than ever the passion the Gladers felt for finding their way out of the Maze. It wasn't just a matter of escape. For the first time, he felt a hunger to get revenge on the people responsible for sending him there.

But those thoughts just led back to the hopelessness that had filled him so many times already. If Newt and the others hadn't been able to solve the Maze after two *years* of searching, it seemed impossible there could actually *be* a solution. The fact that the Gladers hadn't given up said more about these people than anything else.

And now he was one of them.

This is my life, he thought. *Living in a giant maze, surrounded by hideous beasts.* Sadness filled him like a heavy poison. Alby's screams, now distant but still audible, only made it worse. He had to squeeze his hands to his ears every time he heard them.

Eventually, the day dragged to a close, and the setting of the sun brought the now-familiar grinding of the four Doors closing for the night. Thomas had no memory of his life before the Box, but he was positive he'd finished the worst twenty-four hours of his existence.

Just after dark, Chuck brought him some dinner and a big glass of cold water.

"Thanks," Thomas said, feeling a burst of warmth for the kid. He scooped the beef and noodles off the plate as fast as his aching arms could move. "I so needed this," he mumbled through a huge bite. He took a big swig of his drink, then went back to attacking the food. He hadn't realized how hungry he was until he'd started eating.

"You're disgusting when you eat," Chuck said, sitting on the bench next to him. "It's like watching a starving pig eat his own klunk."

"That's funny," Thomas said, sarcasm lacing his voice. "You should go entertain the Grievers—see if they laugh."

A quick expression of hurt flashed across Chuck's face, making

Thomas feel bad, but vanished almost as fast as it had appeared. "That reminds me—you're the talk of the town."

Thomas sat up straighter, not sure how he felt about the news. "What's *that* supposed to mean?"

"Oh, gee, let me think. First, you go out in the Maze when you're not supposed to, at night. Then you turn into some kind of freaky jungle dude, climbing vines and tying people up on walls. Next, you become one of the first people ever to survive an entire night outside the Glade, and to top it all off you kill four Grievers. Can't imagine what those shanks are talking about."

A surge of pride filled Thomas's body, then fizzled. Thomas was sickened by the happiness he'd just felt. Alby was still in bed, screaming his head off in pain—probably *wishing* he were dead. "Tricking them to go over the Cliff was Minho's idea, not mine."

"Not according to him. He saw you do the wait-and-dive thingy, then had the idea to do the same thing at the Cliff."

"The 'wait-and-dive thingy'?" Thomas asked, rolling his eyes. "Any idiot on the planet would've done that."

"Don't get all humbly bumbly on us—what you did is freaking unbelievable. You and Minho, both."

Thomas tossed the empty plate on the ground, suddenly angry. "Then why do I feel so crappy, Chuck? Wanna answer me that?"

Thomas searched Chuck's face for an answer, but by the looks of it he didn't have one. The boy just sat clasping his hands as he leaned forward on his knees, head hanging. Finally, half under his breath, he murmured, "Same reason we all feel crappy."

They sat in silence until, a few minutes later, Newt walked up, looking like death on two feet. He sat on the ground in front of them, as sad and worried as any person could possibly appear. Still, Thomas was glad to have him around.

"I think the worst part's over," Newt said. "The bugger should be sleepin' for a couple of days, then wake up okay. Maybe a little screaming now and then."

Thomas couldn't imagine how bad the whole ordeal must be—but the whole process of the Changing was still a mystery to him. He turned to the older boy, trying his best to be casual. "Newt, what's he going through up there? Seriously, I don't get what this Changing thing is."

Newt's response startled Thomas. "You think *we* do?" he spat, throwing his arms up, then slapping them back down on his knees. "All we bloody know is if the Grievers sting you with their nasty needles, you inject the Grief Serum or you die. If you do get the Serum, then your body wigs out and shakes and your skin bubbles and turns a freaky green color and you vomit all over yourself. Enough explanation for ya there, Tommy?"

Thomas frowned. He didn't want to make Newt any more upset than he already was, but he needed answers. "Hey, I know it sucks to see your friend go through that, but I just want to know what's really happening up there. Why do you call it the Changing?"

Newt relaxed, seemed to shrink, even, and sighed. "It brings back memories. Just little snippets, but definite memories of before we came to this horrible place. Anyone who goes through it acts like a bloody psycho when it's over—although usually not as bad as poor Ben. Anyway, it's like being given your old life back, only to have it snatched away again."

Thomas's mind was churning. "Are you sure?" he asked.

Newt looked confused. "What do you mean? Sure about what?"

"Are they *changed* because they want to go back to their old life, or is it because they're so depressed at realizing their old life was no better than what we have now?"

149

Newt stared at him for a second, then looked away, seemingly deep in thought. "Shanks who've been through it'll never really talk about it. They get . . . different. Unlikable. There's a handful around the Glade, but I can't stand to be around them." His voice was distant, his eyes having strayed to a certain blank spot in the woods. Thomas knew he was thinking about how Alby might never be the same again.

"Tell me about it," Chuck chimed in. "Gally's the worst of 'em all."

"Anything new on the girl?" Thomas asked, changing the subject. He was in no mood to talk about Gally. Plus, his thoughts kept going back to her. "I saw the Med-jacks feeding her upstairs."

"No," Newt answered. "Still in the buggin' coma, or whatever it is. Every once in a while she'll mumble something—nonsense, like she's dreaming. She takes the food, seems to be doing all right. It's kind of weird."

A long pause followed, as if the three of them were trying to come up with an explanation for the girl. Thomas wondered again about his inexplicable feeling of connection with her, though it *had* faded a little—but that could have been because of everything else occupying his thoughts.

Newt finally broke the silence. "Anyway, next up—figure out what we do with Tommy here."

Thomas perked up at that, confused by the statement. "*Do* with me? What're you talking about?"

Newt stood, stretched his arms. "Turned this whole place upside down, you bloody shank. Half the Gladers think you're God, the other half wanna throw your butt down the Box Hole. Lotta stuff to talk about."

"Like what?" Thomas didn't know which was more unsettling—that people thought he was some kind of hero, or that some wished he didn't exist.

"Patience," Newt said. "You'll find out after the wake-up."

"Tomorrow? Why?" Thomas didn't like the sound of this.

"I've called a Gathering. And you'll be there. You're the only buggin' thing on the agenda."

And with that, he turned and walked away, leaving Thomas to wonder why in the world a Gathering was needed just to talk about *him*.

CHAPTER 24

The next morning, Thomas found himself sitting in a chair, worried and anxious, sweating, facing eleven other boys. They were seated in chairs arranged in a semicircle around him. Once settled, he realized they were the Keepers, and to his chagrin that meant Gally was among them. One chair directly in front of Thomas stood empty—he didn't need to be told that it was Alby's.

They sat in a large room of the Homestead that Thomas hadn't been in before. Besides the chairs, there was no other furniture except for a small table in the corner. The walls were made of wood, as was the floor, and it didn't look like anyone had ever attempted to make the place look inviting. There were no windows; the room smelled of mildew and old books. Thomas wasn't cold, but shivered all the same.

He was at least relieved that Newt was there. He sat in the chair to the right of Alby's empty seat. "In place of our leader, sick in bed, I declare this Gathering begun," he said, with a subtle roll of his eyes as if he hated anything approaching formality. "As you all know, the last few days have been bloody crazy, and quite a bit seems centered around our Greenbean, Tommy, seated before us."

Thomas's face flushed with embarrassment.

"He's not the Greenie anymore," Gally said, his scratchy voice so low and cruel it was almost comical. "He's just a rule breaker now."

This started off a rumbling of murmurs and whispers, but Newt shushed them. Thomas suddenly wanted to be as far from that room as possible.

"Gally," Newt said, "try to keep some buggin' order, here. If you're gonna blabber your shuck mouth every time I say something, you can go ahead and bloody leave, because I'm not in a very cheerful mood."

Thomas wished he could cheer at that.

Gally folded his arms and leaned back in his chair, the scowl on his face so forced that Thomas almost laughed out loud. He was having a harder and harder time believing he'd been terrified of this guy just a day earlier—he seemed silly, even pathetic now.

Newt gave Gally a hard stare, then continued. "Glad we got that out of the way." Another roll of the eyes. "Reason we're here is because almost every lovin' kid in the Glade has come up to me in the last day or two either boohooing about Thomas or beggin' to take his bloody hand in marriage. We need to decide what we're gonna do with him."

Gally leaned forward, but Newt cut him off before he could say anything.

"You'll have your chance, Gally. One at a time. And Tommy, you're not allowed to say a buggin' thing until we ask you to. Good that?" He waited for a nod of consent from Thomas—who gave it reluctantly—then pointed to the kid in the chair on the far right. "Zart the Fart, you start."

There were a few snickers as Zart, the quiet big guy who watched over the Gardens, shifted in his seat. He looked to Thomas more out of place than a carrot on a tomato plant.

"Well," Zart began, his eyes darting around almost like he was waiting for someone else to tell him what to say. "I don't know. He broke one of our most important rules. We can't just let people think that's okay." He paused and looked down at his hands, rubbing them together. "But then again, he's . . . changed things. Now we know we can survive out there, and that we can beat the Grievers."

Relief flooded Thomas. He had someone else on his side. He made a promise to himself to be extra nice to Zart.

"Oh, give me a break," Gally spurted. "I bet Minho's the one who actually got rid of the stupid things."

"Gally, shut your hole!" Newt yelled, standing for effect this time; once again Thomas felt like cheering. "I'm the bloody Chair right now, and if I hear one more buggin' word out of turn from you, I'll be arrangin' another Banishing for your sorry butt."

"Please," Gally whispered sarcastically, the ridiculous scowl returning as he slouched back into his chair again.

Newt sat down and motioned to Zart. "Is that it? Any official recommendations?"

Zart shook his head.

"Okay. You're next, Frypan."

The cook smiled through his beard and sat up straighter. "Shank's got more guts than I've fried up from every pig and cow in the last year." He paused, as if expecting a laugh, but none came. "How stupid is this—he saves Alby's life, kills a couple of Grievers, and we're sitting here yappin' about what to do with him. As Chuck would say, this is a pile of klunk."

Thomas wanted to walk over and shake Frypan's hand—he'd just said exactly what Thomas himself had been thinking about all of this.

"So what're ya recommendin'?" Newt asked.

Frypan folded his arms. "Put him on the freaking Council and have him train us on everything he did out there."

Voices erupted from every direction, and it took Newt half a minute to calm everyone down. Thomas winced; Frypan had gone too

154

far with that recommendation, almost invalidating his well-stated opinion of the whole mess.

"All right, writin' her down," Newt said as he did just that, scribbling on a notepad. "Now everyone keep their bloody mouths shut, I mean it. You know the rules—no idea's unacceptable—and you'll all have your say when we vote on it." He finished writing and pointed to the third member of the Council, a kid Thomas hadn't met yet with black hair and a freckly face.

"I don't really have an opinion," he said.

"What?" Newt asked angrily. "Lot of good it did to choose you for the Council, then."

"Sorry, I honestly don't." He shrugged. "If anything, I agree with Frypan, I guess. Why punish a guy for saving someone's life?"

"So you do have an opinion—is that it?" Newt insisted, pencil in hand.

The kid nodded and Newt scribbled a note. Thomas was feeling more and more relieved—it seemed like most of the Keepers were for him, not against him. Still, he was having a hard time just sitting there; he desperately wanted to speak on his own behalf. But he forced himself to follow Newt's orders and keep quiet.

Next was acne-covered Winston, Keeper of the Blood House. "I think he should be punished. No offense, Greenie, but Newt, you're the one always harping about *order*. If we don't punish him, we'll set a bad example. He broke our Number One Rule."

"Okay," Newt said, writing on his pad. "So you're recommendin' punishment. What kind?"

"I think he should be put in the Slammer for a week with only bread and water—and we need to make sure everyone knows about it so they don't get any ideas."

Gally clapped, earning a scowl from Newt. Thomas's heart fell just a bit.

Two more Keepers spoke, one for Frypan's idea, one for Winston's. Then it was Newt's turn.

"I agree with the lot of ya. He should be punished, but then we need to figure out a way to use him. I'm reservin' my recommendation until I hear everyone out. Next."

Thomas hated all this talk about punishment, even more than he hated having to keep his mouth shut. But deep inside he couldn't bring himself to disagree—as odd as it seemed after what he'd accomplished, he *had* broken a major rule.

Down the line they went. Some thought he should be praised, some thought he should be punished. Or both. Thomas could barely listen anymore, anticipating the comments from the last two Keepers, Gally and Minho. The latter hadn't said a word since Thomas had entered the room; he just sat there, drooped in his chair, looking like he hadn't slept in a week.

Gally went first. "I think I've made my opinions pretty clear already."

Great, Thomas thought. *Then just keep your mouth shut.*

"Good that," Newt said with yet another roll of the eyes. "Go on, then, Minho."

"No!" Gally yelled, making a couple of Keepers jump in their seats. "I still wanna say something."

"Then bloody say it," Newt replied. It made Thomas feel a little better that the temporary Council Chair despised Gally almost as much as he did. Though Thomas wasn't that afraid of him anymore, he still hated the guy's guts.

"Just think about it," Gally began. "This slinthead comes up in the Box, acting all confused and scared. A few days later, he's running around the Maze with Grievers, acting like he owns the place."

156

Thomas shrank into his chair, hoping that others hadn't been thinking anything like that.

Gally continued his rant. "I think it was all an act. How could he have done what he did out there after just a few days? I ain't buyin' it."

"What're you tryin' to say, Gally?" Newt asked. "How 'bout having a bloody *point*?"

"I think he's a spy from the people who put us here."

Another uproar exploded in the room; Thomas could do nothing but shake his head—he just didn't get how Gally could come up with all these ideas. Newt finally calmed everyone down again, but Gally wasn't finished.

"We can't trust this shank," he continued. "Day after he shows up, a psycho girl comes, spoutin' off that things are gonna change, clutching that freaky note. We find a dead Griever. Thomas conveniently finds himself in the Maze for the night, then tries to convince everyone he's a hero. Well, neither Minho nor anyone else actually *saw* him do anything in the vines. How do we know it was the Greenie who tied Alby up there?"

Gally paused; no one said a word for several seconds, and panic rose inside Thomas's chest. Could they actually believe what Gally was saying? He was anxious to defend himself and almost broke his silence for the first time—but before he could get a word in, Gally was talking again.

"There's too many weird things going on, and it all started when this shuck-face Greenie showed up. And he just happens to be the first person to survive a night out in the Maze. Something ain't right, and until we figure it out, I officially recommend that we lock his butt in the Slammer—for a month, and then have another review."

More rumblings broke out, and Newt wrote something on his pad, shaking his head the whole time—which gave Thomas a tinge of hope.

"Finished, Captain Gally?" Newt asked.

"Quit being such a smart aleck, Newt," he spat, his face flushing red. "I'm dead serious. How can we trust this shank after less than a week? Quit voting me down before you even *think* about what I'm saying."

For the first time, Thomas felt a little empathy for Gally—he did have a point about how Newt was treating him. Gally was a Keeper, after all. *But I still hate him*, Thomas thought.

"Fine, Gally," Newt said. "I'm sorry. We heard you, and we'll all consider your bloody recommendation. Are you done?"

"Yes, I'm done. And I'm *right*."

With no more words for Gally, Newt pointed at Minho. "Go ahead, last but not least."

Thomas was elated that it was finally Minho's turn; surely he'd defend him to the end.

Minho stood quickly, taking everyone off guard. "I was out there; I saw what this guy did—he stayed strong while I turned into a panty-wearin' chicken. No blabbin' on and on like Gally. I want to say my recommendation and be done with it."

Thomas held his breath, wondering what he'd say.

"Good that," Newt said. "Tell us, then."

Minho looked at Thomas. "I nominate this shank to replace me as Keeper of the Runners."

CHAPTER 25

Complete silence filled the room, as if the world had been frozen, and every member of the Council stared at Minho. Thomas sat stunned, waiting for the Runner to say he'd been kidding.

Gally finally broke the spell, standing up. "That's ridiculous!" He faced Newt and pointed back at Minho, who had taken his seat again. "He should be kicked off the Council for saying something so stupid."

Any pity Thomas had felt for Gally, however remote, completely vanished at that statement.

Some Keepers seemed to actually agree with Minho's recommendation—like Frypan, who clapped to drown out Gally, clamoring to take a vote. Others didn't. Winston shook his head adamantly, saying something that Thomas couldn't quite make out. When everyone started talking at once, Thomas put his head in his hands to wait it out, terrified and awed at the same time. Why had Minho said that? *Has to be a joke*, he thought. *Newt said it takes forever just to become a Runner, much less the Keeper.* He looked back up, wishing he were a thousand miles away.

Finally, Newt put his notepad down and stepped out from the semicircle, screaming at people to shut up. Thomas watched on as at first no one seemed to hear or notice Newt at all. Gradually, though, order was restored and everyone sat down.

"Shuck it," Newt said. "I've never seen so many shanks acting like teat-suckin' babies. We may not look it, but around these parts we're adults. Act like it, or we'll disband this bloody Council and start from scratch." He walked from end to end of the curved row of sitting Keepers, looking each of them in the eye as he spoke. "Are we clear?"

Quiet had swept across the group. Thomas expected more outbursts, but was surprised when everyone nodded their consent, even Gally.

"Good that." Newt walked back to his chair and sat down, putting the pad in his lap. He scratched out a few lines on the paper, then looked up at Minho. "That's some pretty serious klunk, brother. Sorry, but you need to talk it up to move it forward."

Thomas couldn't help feeling eager to hear the response.

Minho looked exhausted, but he started defending his proposal. "It's sure easy for you shanks to sit here and talk about something you're stupid on. I'm the only Runner in this group, and the only other one here who's even *been* out in the Maze is Newt."

Gally interjected: "Not if you count the time I—"

"I don't!" Minho shouted. "And believe me, you or nobody else has the slightest clue what it's like to be out there. The only reason you were stung is because you broke the same rule you're blaming Thomas for. That's called *hypocrisy,* you shuck-faced piece of—"

"Enough," Newt said. "Defend your proposal and be done with it."

The tension was palpable; Thomas felt like the air in the room had become glass that could shatter at any second. Both Gally and Minho looked as if the taut, red skin of their faces was about to burst—but they finally broke their stare.

"Anyway, listen to me," Minho continued as he took his seat. "I've never seen anything like it. He didn't panic. He didn't whine and cry, never seemed scared. Dude, he'd been here for just a few days. Think about what we were all like in the beginning. Huddling in corners, disoriented, crying every hour, not trusting anybody, refusing to do anything. We were all like that, for weeks or months, till we had no choice but to shuck it and live."

Minho stood back up, pointed at Thomas. "Just a few days after this guy shows up, he steps out in the Maze to save two shanks he hardly knows. All this klunk about him breaking a rule is just beyond stupid. He didn't get the rules yet. But plenty of people had told him what it's like in the Maze, especially at night. And he still stepped out there, just as the Door was closing, only caring that two people needed help." He took a deep breath, seeming to gain strength the more he spoke.

"But that was just the beginning. After that, he saw me give up on Alby, leave him for dead. And I was the veteran—the one with all the experience and knowledge. So when Thomas saw me give up, he shouldn't have questioned it. But he did. Think about the willpower and strength it took him to push Alby up that wall, inch by inch. It's psycho. It's freaking crazy.

"But that wasn't it. Then came the Grievers. I told Thomas we had to split up and I started the practiced evasive maneuvers, running in the patterns. Thomas, when he should've been wettin' his pants, took control, defied all laws of physics and gravity to get Alby up onto that wall, diverted the Grievers away from him, beat one off, found—"

"We get the point," Gally snapped. "Tommy here is a lucky shank."

Minho rounded on him. "No, you worthless shuck, you *don't* get it! I've been here two years, and I've never seen anything like it. For you to say anything . . ."

Minho paused, rubbing his eyes, groaning in frustration. Thomas realized his own mouth had dropped wide open. His emotions were scattered: appreciation for Minho standing up to everybody on his behalf, disbelief at Gally's continuous belligerence, fear of what the final decision would be.

"Gally," Minho said in a calmer voice, "you're nothing but a sissy who has never, not once, asked to be a Runner or tried out for it. You don't have the right to talk about things you don't understand. So shut your mouth."

Gally stood up again, fuming. "Say one more thing like that and I'll break your neck, right here in front of everybody." Spit flew from his mouth as he spoke.

Minho laughed, then raised the palm of his hand and shoved Gally in the face. Thomas half stood as he watched the Glader crash down into his chair, tipping it over backward, cracking it in two pieces. Gally sprawled across the floor, then scrambled to stand up, struggling to get his hands and feet under him. Minho stepped closer and stomped the bottom of his foot down on Gally's back, driving his body flat to the ground.

Thomas plopped back into his seat, stunned.

"I swear, Gally," Minho said with a sneer, "don't ever threaten me again. Don't ever *speak* to me again. Ever. If you do, I'll break *your* shuck neck, right after I'm done with your arms and legs."

Newt and Winston were on their feet and grabbing Minho before Thomas even knew what was going on. They pulled him away from Gally, who jumped up, his face a ruddied mask of rage. But he made no move toward Minho; he just stood there with his chest out, heaving ragged breaths.

Finally Gally backed away, half stumbling toward the exit behind him. His eyes darted around the room, lit with a burning hatred. Thomas had the sickening thought that Gally looked like someone about to commit murder. He backed toward the door, reached behind him to grab the handle.

"Things are different now," he said, spitting on the floor. "You shouldn't have done that, Minho. You should *not* have done that." His maniacal gaze shifted to Newt. "I know you hate me, that you've always hated me. You should be Banished for your embarrassing inability to lead this group. You're shameful, and any one of you who stays here is no better. Things are going to change. This, I promise."

Thomas's heart sank. As if things hadn't been awkward enough already.

Gally yanked the door open and stepped out into the hall, but before anyone could react, he popped his head back in the room. "And you," he said, glaring at Thomas, "the *Greenbean* who thinks he's friggin' God. Don't forget I've seen you before—I've *been* through the Changing. What these guys decide doesn't mean jack."

He paused, looking at each person in the room. When his malicious stare fell back on Thomas, he had one last thing to say. "Whatever you came here for—I swear on my life I'm gonna stop it. Kill you if I have to."

Then he turned and left the room, slamming the door behind him.

CHAPTER 26

Thomas sat frozen in his chair, a sickness growing in his stomach like an infestation. He'd been through the whole gamut of emotions in the short time since he'd arrived at the Glade. Fear, loneliness, desperation, sadness, even the slightest hint of joy. But this was something new—to hear a person say they hate you enough that they want to kill you.

Gally's crazy, he told himself. *He's completely insane.* But the thought only increased his worries. Insane people could really be capable of anything.

The Council members stood or sat in silence, seemingly as shocked as Thomas at what they'd just seen. Newt and Winston finally let go of Minho; all three of them sullenly walked to their chairs and sat down.

"He's finally whacked for good," Minho said, almost in a whisper. Thomas couldn't tell if he'd meant for the others to hear him.

"Well, you're not the bloody saint in the room," Newt said. "What were you *thinking*? That was a little overboard, don't ya think?"

Minho squinched up his eyes and pulled his head back, as if he were baffled by Newt's question. "Don't give me that garbage. Every one of you loved seeing that slinthead get his dues, and you know it. It's about time someone stood up to his klunk."

"He's on the Council for a reason," Newt said.

"Dude, he threatened to break my neck and kill Thomas! The guy is mentally whacked, and you better send someone right now to throw him in the Slammer. He's dangerous."

Thomas couldn't have agreed more and once again almost broke his order to stay quiet, but stopped himself. He didn't want to get in any more trouble than he was already in—but he didn't know how much longer he could last.

"Maybe he had a good point," Winston said, almost too quietly.

"What?" Minho asked, mirroring Thomas's thoughts exactly.

Winston looked surprised at the acknowledgment that he'd said anything. His eyes darted around the room before he explained. "Well . . . he *has* been through the Changing—Griever stung him in the middle of the day just outside the West Door. That means he has *memories,* and he said the Greenie looks familiar. Why would he make that up?"

Thomas thought about the Changing, and the fact that it brought back memories. The idea hadn't occurred to him before, but would it be worth it to get stung by the Grievers, go through that horrible process, just to remember something? He pictured Ben writhing in bed and remembered Alby's screams. *No way,* he thought.

"Winston, did you *see* what just happened?" Frypan asked, looking incredulous. "Gally's psycho. You can't put too much stock in his rambling nonsense. What, you think Thomas here is a Griever in disguise?"

Council rules or no Council rules, Thomas had finally had enough. He couldn't stay silent another second.

"Can I say something now?" he asked, frustration raising the volume of his voice. "I'm sick of you guys talking about me like I'm not here."

Newt glanced up at him and nodded. "Go ahead. This bloody meetin' can't be much more screwed up."

Thomas quickly gathered his thoughts, grasping for the right words inside the swirling cloud of frustration, confusion and anger in his mind. "I don't know why Gally hates me. I don't care. He seems psychotic to me. As for who I *really* am, you all know just as much as I do.

But if I remember correctly, we're here because of what I did out in the Maze, not because some idiot thinks I'm evil."

Someone snickered and Thomas quit talking, hoping he'd gotten his point across.

Newt nodded, looking satisfied. "Good that. Let's get this meeting over with and worry about Gally later."

"We can't vote without all the members here," Winston insisted. "Unless they're really sick, like Alby."

"For the love, Winston," Newt replied. "I'd say Gally's a wee bit ill today, too, so we continue without him. Thomas, defend yourself and then we'll take the vote on what we should do with you."

Thomas realized his hands were squeezed up into fists on his lap. He relaxed them and wiped his sweaty palms on his pants. Then he began, not sure of what he'd say before the words came out.

"I didn't do anything wrong. All I know is I saw two people struggling to get inside these walls and they couldn't make it. To ignore that because of some stupid rule seemed selfish, cowardly, and . . . well, stupid. If you want to throw me in jail for trying to save someone's life, then go ahead. Next time I promise I'll point at them and laugh, then go eat some of Frypan's dinner."

Thomas wasn't trying to be funny. He was just dumbfounded that the whole thing could even be an issue.

"Here's my recommendation," Newt said. "You broke our bloody Number One Rule, so you get one day in the Slammer. That's your punishment. I also recommend we elect you as a Runner, effective the second this meeting's over. You've proven more in one night than most trainees do in weeks. As for you being the buggin' Keeper, forget it." He looked over at Minho. "Gally was right on that count—stupid idea."

The comment hurt Thomas's feelings, even though he couldn't disagree. He looked to Minho for his reaction.

The Keeper didn't seem surprised, but argued all the same. "Why? He's the best we have—I swear it. The best should be the Keeper."

"Fine," Newt responded. "If that's true, we'll make the change later. Give it a month and see if he proves himself."

Minho shrugged. "Good that."

Thomas quietly sighed in relief. He still wanted to be a Runner— which surprised him, considering what he'd just gone through out in the Maze—but becoming the Keeper right away sounded ridiculous.

Newt glanced around the room. "Okay, we had several recommendations, so let's give it a go-round—"

"Oh, come on," Frypan said. "Just vote. I vote for yours."

"Me too," Minho said.

Everyone else chimed in their approval, filling Thomas with relief and a sense of pride. Winston was the only one to say no.

Newt looked at him. "We don't need your vote, but tell us what's bonkin' around your brain."

Winston gazed at Thomas carefully, then back to Newt. "It's fine with me, but we shouldn't totally ignore what Gally said. Something about it—I don't think he just made it up. And it's true that ever since Thomas got here, everything's been shucked and screwy."

"Fair enough," Newt said. "Everyone put some thought into it— maybe when we get right nice and bored we can have another Gathering to talk about it. Good that?"

Winston nodded.

Thomas groaned at how invisible he'd become. "I love how you guys are just talking about me like I'm not here."

"Look, Tommy," Newt said. "We just elected you as a buggin' Runner. Quit your cryin' and get out of here. Minho has a lot of training to give you."

It hadn't really hit Thomas until then. He was going to be a *Runner,* explore the Maze. Despite everything, he felt a shiver of excitement; he was sure they could avoid getting trapped out there at night again. Maybe he'd had his one and only turn of bad luck. "What about my punishment?"

"Tomorrow," Newt answered. "The wake-up till sunset."

One day, Thomas thought. *That won't be so bad.*

The meeting was dismissed and everyone except Newt and Minho left the room in a hurry. Newt hadn't moved from his chair, where he sat jotting notes. "Well, that was good times," he murmured.

Minho walked over and playfully punched Thomas in the arm. "It's all this shank's fault."

Thomas punched him back. "Keeper? You want me to be Keeper? You're nuttier than Gally by a long shot."

Minho faked an evil grin. "Worked, didn't it? Aim high, hit low. Thank me later."

Thomas couldn't help smiling at the Keeper's clever ways. A knock on the opened door grabbed his attention—he turned to see who it was. Chuck stood there, looking like he'd just been chased by a Griever. Thomas felt the grin fade from his face.

"What's wrong?" Newt asked, standing up. The tone of his voice only heightened Thomas's concern.

Chuck was wringing his hands. "Med-jacks sent me."

"Why?"

"I guess Alby's thrashing around and acting all crazy, telling them he needs to talk to somebody."

Newt made for the door, but Chuck held up his hand. "Um . . . he doesn't want you."

"What do you mean?"

Chuck pointed at Thomas. "He keeps asking for him."

CHAPTER 27

For the second time that day, Thomas was shocked into silence.

"Well, come on," Newt said to Thomas as he grabbed his arm. "No way I'm not going with ya."

Thomas followed him, with Chuck right behind, as they left the Council room and went down the hall toward a narrow, spiraling staircase that he hadn't noticed before. Newt took the first step, then gave Chuck a cold glare. "You. Stay."

For once, Chuck simply nodded and said nothing. Thomas figured that something about Alby's behavior had the kid's nerves on edge.

"Lighten up," Thomas said to Chuck as Newt headed up the staircase. "They just elected me a Runner, so you're buddies with a stud now." He was trying to make a joke, trying to deny that he was terrified to see Alby. What if he made accusations like Ben had? Or worse?

"Yeah, right," Chuck whispered, staring at the wooden steps in a daze.

With a shrug Thomas began climbing the stairs. Sweat slicked his palms, and he felt a drop trickle down his temple. He did *not* want to go up there.

Newt, all grim and solemn, was waiting for Thomas at the top of the stairwell. They stood at the opposite end of the long, dark hallway from the usual staircase, the one Thomas had climbed on his very first day to see Ben. The memory made him queasy; he hoped Alby was completely healed from the ordeal so he didn't have to witness something like that again—the sickly skin, the veins, the thrashing. But he expected the worst, and braced himself.

He followed Newt to the second door on the right and watched as the older boy knocked lightly; a moan sounded in reply. Newt pushed open the door, the slight creak once again reminding Thomas of some vague childhood memory of haunted-house movies. There it was again—the smallest glimpse at his past. He could remember movies, but not the actors' faces or with whom he'd watched them. He could remember theaters, but not what any specific one *looked* like. It was impossible to explain how that felt, even to himself.

Newt had stepped into the room and was motioning for Thomas to follow. As he entered, he prepared himself for the horror that might await. But when his eyes lifted, all he saw was a very weak-looking teenage boy lying in his bed, eyes closed.

"Is he asleep?" Thomas whispered, trying to avoid the real question that had popped in his mind: *He's not dead, is he?*

"I don't know," Newt said quietly. He walked over and sat in a wooden chair next to the bed. Thomas took a seat on the other side.

"Alby," Newt whispered. Then more loudly: "Alby. Chuck said you wanted to talk to Tommy."

Alby's eyes fluttered open—bloodshot orbs that glistened in the light. He looked at Newt, then across at Thomas. With a groan he shifted in the bed and sat up, his back against the headboard. "Yeah," he muttered, a scratchy croak.

"Chuck said you were thrashin' around, acting like a loonie." Newt leaned forward. "What's wrong? You still sick?"

Alby's next words came out in a wheeze, as if every one of them would take a week off his life. "Everything's . . . gonna change. . . . The girl . . . Thomas . . . I saw them . . ." His eyelids flickered closed, then open again; he sank back to a flat position on the bed, stared at the ceiling. "Don't feel so good."

"What do you mean, you saw—" Newt began.

"I wanted Thomas!" Alby yelled, with a sudden burst of energy that Thomas would've thought impossible a few seconds earlier. "I didn't ask for you, Newt! Thomas! I asked for freaking Thomas!"

Newt looked up, questioned Thomas with a raising of his eyebrows. Thomas shrugged, feeling sicker by the second. What did Alby want *him* for?

"Fine, ya grouchy shuck," Newt said. "He's right here—talk to him."

"Leave," Alby said, his eyes closed, his breathing heavy.

"No way—I wanna hear."

"Newt." A pause. "Leave. Now." Thomas felt incredibly awkward, worried about what Newt was thinking and dreading what Alby wanted to say to him.

"But—" Newt protested.

"Out!" Alby sat up as he yelled, his voice cracking with the strain of it. He scooted himself back to lean against the headboard again. "Get out!"

Newt's face sank in obvious hurt—Thomas was surprised to see no anger there. Then, after a long, tense moment, Newt stood from his chair and walked over to the door, opened it. *He's really going to leave?* Thomas thought.

"Don't expect me to kiss your butt when you come sayin' sorry," he said, then stepped into the hallway.

"Close the door!" Alby shouted, one final insult. Newt obeyed, slamming it shut.

Thomas's heart rate quickened—he was now alone with a guy

who'd had a bad temper *before* getting attacked by a Griever and going through the Changing. He hoped Alby would say what he wanted and be done with it. A long pause stretched into several minutes, and Thomas's hands shook with fear.

"I know who you are," Alby said finally, breaking the silence.

Thomas couldn't find words to reply. He tried; nothing came out but an incoherent mumble. He was utterly confused. And scared.

"I know who you are," Alby repeated slowly. "Seen it. Seen everything. Where we came from, who you are. Who the *girl* is. I remember the Flare."

The Flare? Thomas forced himself to talk. "I don't know what you're talking about. What did you see? I'd love to know who I am."

"It ain't pretty," Alby answered, and for the first time since Newt had left, Alby looked up, straight at Thomas. His eyes were deep pockets of sorrow, sunken, dark. "It's horrible, ya know. Why would those shucks want us to remember? Why can't we just live here and be happy?"

"Alby . . ." Thomas wished he could take a peek in the boy's mind, see what he'd seen. "The Changing," he pressed, "what happened? What came back? You're not making sense."

"You—" Alby started, then suddenly grabbed his own throat, making gurgly choking sounds. His legs kicked out and he rolled onto his side, thrashing back and forth as if someone *else* were trying to strangle him. His tongue stuck out of his mouth; he bit it over and over.

Thomas stood up quickly, stumbled backward, horrified—Alby struggled as if he was having a seizure, his legs kicking in every direction. The dark skin of his face, which had been oddly pale just a minute earlier, had turned purple, his eyes rolled up so far in their sockets they looked like glowing white marbles.

"Alby!" Thomas yelled, not daring to reach down and grab him.

172

"Newt!" he screamed, cupping his hands around his mouth. "Newt, get in here!"

The door was flung open before he'd finished his last sentence.

Newt ran to Alby and grabbed him by the shoulders, pushing with his whole body to pin the convulsing boy to the bed. "Grab his legs!"

Thomas moved forward, but Alby's legs kicked and flailed out, making it impossible to get any closer. His foot hit Thomas in the jaw; a lance of pain shot through his whole skull. He stumbled backward again, rubbing the sore spot.

"Just bloody do it!" Newt yelled.

Thomas steeled himself, then jumped on top of Alby's body, grabbing both legs and pinning them to the bed. He wrapped his arms around the boy's thighs and squeezed while Newt put a knee on one of Alby's shoulders, then grabbed at Alby's hands, still clasped around his own neck in a chokehold.

"Let go!" Newt yelled as he tugged. "You're bloody killin' yourself!"

Thomas could see the muscles in Newt's arms flexing, veins popping out as he pulled at Alby's hands, until finally, inch by inch, he was able to pry them away. He pushed them tightly against the struggling boy's chest. Alby's whole body jerked a couple of times, his midsection thrusting up and away from the bed. Then, slowly, he calmed, and a few seconds later he lay still, his breath evening; his eyes glazed over.

Thomas held firm to Alby's legs, afraid to move and set the boy off again. Newt waited a full minute before he slowly let go of Alby's hands. Then another minute before he pulled his knee back and stood up. Thomas took that as his cue to do the same, hoping the ordeal had truly ended.

Alby looked up, eyes droopy, as if he was on the edge of slipping into a deep sleep. "I'm sorry, Newt," he whispered. "Don't know what happened. It was like . . . something was controlling my body. I'm sorry. . . ."

Thomas took a deep breath, sure he'd never experience something so disturbing and uncomfortable again. He hoped.

"Sorries, nothin'," Newt replied. "You were trying to bloody kill yourself."

"Wasn't me, I swear," Alby murmured.

Newt threw his hands up. "What do you mean it wasn't you?" he asked.

"I don't know. . . . It . . . it wasn't me." Alby looked just as confused as Thomas felt.

But Newt seemed to think it wasn't worth trying to figure out. At least at the moment. He grabbed the blankets that had fallen off the bed in Alby's struggle and pulled them atop the sick boy. "Get your butt to sleep and we'll talk about it later." He patted him on the head, then added, "You're messed up, shank."

But Alby was already drifting off, nodding slightly as his eyes closed.

Newt caught Thomas's gaze and gestured for the door. Thomas had no problem leaving that crazy house—he followed Newt out and into the hall. Then, just as they stepped through the doorway, Alby mumbled something from his bed.

Both boys stopped in their tracks. "What?" Newt asked.

Alby opened his eyes for a brief moment, then repeated what he'd said, a little more loudly. "Be careful with the girl." Then his eyes slid shut.

There it was again—the girl. Somehow things always led back to the girl. Newt gave Thomas a questioning look, but Thomas could only return it with a shrug. He had no idea what was going on.

"Let's go," Newt whispered.

174

"And Newt?" Alby called again from the bed, not bothering to open his eyes.

"Yeah?"

"Protect the Maps." Alby rolled over, his back telling them he'd finally finished speaking.

Thomas didn't think that sounded very good. Not good at all. He and Newt left the room and softly closed the door.

CHAPTER 28

Thomas followed Newt as he hurried down the stairs and out of the Homestead into the bright light of midafternoon. Neither boy said a word for a while. For Thomas, things just seemed to be getting worse and worse.

"Hungry, Tommy?" Newt asked when they were outside.

Thomas couldn't believe the question. "Hungry? I feel like puking after what I just saw—no, I'm not hungry."

Newt only grinned. "Well, I am, ya shank. Let's go look for some leftovers from lunch. We need to talk."

"Somehow I knew you were going to say something like that." No matter what he did, he was becoming more and more entwined in the dealings of the Glade. And he was growing to expect it.

They made their way directly to the kitchen, where, despite Frypan's grumbling, they were able to get cheese sandwiches and raw vegetables. Thomas couldn't ignore the way the Keeper of the cooks kept giving him a weird look, eyes darting away whenever Thomas returned the stare.

Something told him this sort of treatment would now be the norm. For some reason, he was different from everyone else in the Glade. He felt like he'd lived an entire lifetime since awakening from his memory wipe, but he'd only been there a week.

The boys decided to take their lunches to eat outside, and a few minutes later they found themselves at the west wall, looking out at the many work activities going on throughout the Glade, their backs up against a spot of thick ivy. Thomas forced himself to eat; the way things were going, he needed to make sure he'd have strength to deal with whatever insane thing came his way next.

"Ever seen that happen before?" Thomas asked after a minute or so.

Newt looked at him, his face suddenly somber. "What Alby just did? No. Never. But then again, no one's ever tried to tell us what they remembered during the Changing. They always refuse. Alby tried to—must be why he went nuts for a while."

Thomas paused in the middle of chewing. Could the people behind the Maze *control* them somehow? It was a terrifying thought.

"We have to find Gally," Newt said through a bite of carrot, changing the subject. "Bugger's gone off and hid somewhere. Soon as we're done eating, I need to find him and throw his butt in jail."

"Serious?" Thomas couldn't help feeling a shot of pure elation at the thought. He'd be happy to slam the door closed and throw away the key himself.

"That shank threatened to kill you and we have to make bloody sure it never happens again. That shuck-face is gonna pay a heavy price for acting like that—he's lucky we don't Banish him. Remember what I told you about order."

"Yeah." Thomas's only concern was that Gally would just hate him all the more for being thrown in jail. *I don't care,* he thought. *I'm not scared of that guy anymore.*

"Here's how it'll play out, Tommy," Newt said. "You're with me the rest of today—we need to figure things. Tomorrow, the Slammer. Then you're Minho's, and I want you to stay away from the other shanks for a while. Got it?"

Thomas was more than happy to oblige. Being mostly alone sounded like a great idea. "Sounds beautiful. So Minho's going to train me?"

"That's right—you're a Runner now. Minho'll teach ya. The Maze, the Maps, everything. Lots to learn. I expect you to work your butt off."

Thomas was shocked that the idea of entering the Maze again didn't frighten him all that much. He resolved to do just as Newt said, hoping it would keep his mind off things. Deeper down, he hoped to get out of the Glade as much as possible. Avoiding other people was his new goal in life.

The boys sat in silence, finishing their lunches, until Newt finally got to what he really wanted to talk about. Crumpling his trash into a ball, he turned and looked straight at Thomas.

"Thomas," he began, "I need you to accept something. We've heard it too many times now to deny it, and it's time to discuss it."

Thomas knew what was coming, but was startled. He dreaded the words.

"Gally said it. Alby said it. Ben said it," Newt continued, "the girl, after we took her out of the Box—she said it."

He paused, perhaps expecting Thomas to ask what he meant. But Thomas already knew. "They all said things were going to change."

Newt looked away for a moment, then turned back. "That's right. And Gally, Alby and Ben claim they saw you in their memories after the Changing—and from what I gather, you weren't plantin' flowers and helpin' old ladies cross the street. According to Gally, there's somethin' rotten enough about ya that he wants to kill ya."

"Newt, I don't know—" Thomas started, but Newt didn't let him finish.

"I know you don't remember anything, Thomas! Quit sayin' that—don't ever say it again. None of us remember anything, and we're bloody sick of you reminding us. The point is there's something different about you, and it's time we figured it out."

Thomas was overwhelmed by a surge of anger. "Fine, so how do we do it? I want to know who I am just as much as anyone else. *Obviously.*"

"I need you to open your mind. Be honest if anything—anything at all—seems familiar."

"Nothing—" Thomas started, but stopped. So much had happened since arriving, he'd almost forgotten how familiar the Glade had felt to him that first night, sleeping next to Chuck. How comfortable and *at home* he'd felt. A far cry from the terror he should've experienced.

"I can see your wheels spinnin'," Newt said, quietly. "Talk."

Thomas hesitated, scared of the consequences of what he was about to say. But he was tired of keeping secrets. "Well . . . I can't put my finger on anything specific." He spoke slowly, carefully. "But I did feel like I'd been here before when I first got here." He looked at Newt, hoping to see some sort of recognition in his eyes. "Anyone else go through that?"

But Newt's face was blank. He simply rolled his eyes. "Uh, no, Tommy. Most of us spent a week klunkin' our pants and bawlin' our eyes out."

"Yeah, well." Thomas paused, upset and suddenly embarrassed. What did it all mean? Was he different from everyone else somehow? Was something wrong with him? "It all seemed familiar to me, and I knew I wanted to be a Runner."

"That's bloody interesting." Newt examined him for a second, not hiding his obvious suspicion. "Well, keep lookin' for it. Strain your mind, spend your free time wanderin' your thoughts, and *think* about this place. Delve inside that brain of yours, and seek it out. *Try,* for all our sakes."

"I will." Thomas closed his eyes, started searching the darkness of his mind.

"Not now, you dumb shuck." Newt laughed. "I just meant do it from now *on*. Free time, meals, goin' to sleep at night, as you walk

179

around, train, work. Tell me anything that seems even remotely familiar. Got it?"

"Yeah, got it." Thomas couldn't help worrying that he'd thrown up
some red flags for Newt, and that the older boy was just hiding his concern.

"Good that," Newt said, looking almost too agreeable. "To begin,
we better go see someone."

"Who?" Thomas asked, but knew the answer as soon as he spoke.
Dread filled him again.

"The girl. I want you to look at her till your eyes bleed, see if
somethin' gets triggered in that shuck brain of yours." Newt gathered
his lunch trash and stood up. "Then I want you to tell me every single
word Alby said to you."

Thomas sighed, then got to his feet. "Okay." He didn't know if he
could bring himself to tell the complete truth about Alby's accusations,
not to mention how he felt about the girl. It looked like he wasn't done
keeping secrets after all.

The boys walked back toward the Homestead, where the girl still
lay in a coma. Thomas couldn't stifle his worry about what Newt was
thinking. He'd opened himself up, and he really *liked* Newt. If Newt
turned on him now, Thomas didn't know if he could handle it.

"If all else fails," Newt said, interrupting Thomas's thoughts, "we'll
send ya to the Grievers—get ya stung so you can go through the
Changing. We *need* your memories."

Thomas barked a sarcastic laugh at the idea, but Newt wasn't smiling.

The girl seemed to be sleeping peacefully, like she'd wake up at any
minute. Thomas had almost expected the skeletal remnant of a
person—someone on the verge of death. But her chest rose and fell
with even breaths; her skin was full of color.

One of the Med-jacks was there, the shorter one—Thomas couldn't remember his name—dropping water into the comatose girl's mouth a few drips at a time. A plate and bowl on the bedside table had the remains of her lunch—mashed potatoes and soup. They were doing everything possible to keep her alive and healthy.

"Hey, Clint," Newt said, sounding comfortable, like he'd stopped by to visit many times before. "She surviving?"

"Yeah," Clint answered. "She's doing fine, though she talks in her sleep all the time. We think she'll come out of it soon."

Thomas felt his hackles rise. For some reason, he'd never really considered the possibility that the girl might wake up and be okay. That she might talk to people. He had no idea why that suddenly made him so nervous.

"Have you been writin' down every word she says?" Newt asked.

Clint nodded. "Most of it's impossible to understand. But yeah, when we can."

Newt pointed at a notepad on the nightstand. "Give me an example."

"Well, the same thing she said when we pulled her out of the Box, about things changing. Other stuff about the Creators and how 'it all has to end.' And, uh . . ." Clint looked at Thomas as if he didn't want to continue in his company.

"It's okay—he can hear whatever I hear," Newt assured him.

"Well . . . I can't make it all out, but . . ." Clint looked at Thomas again. "She keeps saying *his* name over and over."

Thomas almost fell down at this. Would the references to him never end? How did he know this girl? It was like a maddening itch inside his skull that wouldn't go away.

"Thanks, Clint," Newt said in what sounded to Thomas like an obvious dismissal. "Get us a report of all that, okay?"

"Will do." The Med-jack nodded at both of them and left the room.

"Pull up a chair," Newt said as he sat on the edge of the bed. Thomas, relieved that Newt still hadn't erupted into accusations, grabbed the one from the desk and placed it right next to where the girl's head lay; he sat down, leaning forward to look at her face.

"Anything ring a bell?" Newt asked. "Anything at all?"

Thomas didn't respond, kept looking, willing his mind to break down the memory barrier and seek out this girl from his past. He thought back to those brief moments when she'd opened her eyes right after being pulled out of the Box.

They'd been blue, richer in color than the eyes of any other person he could remember seeing before. He tried to picture those eyes on her now as he looked at her slumbering face, melding the two images in his mind. Her black hair, her perfect white skin, her full lips. . . . As he stared at her, he realized once more how truly beautiful she was.

Stronger recognition briefly tickled the back of his mind—a flutter of wings in a dark corner, unseen but there all the same. It lasted only an instant before vanishing into the abyss of his other captured memories. But he had *felt* something.

"I do know her," he whispered, leaning back in his chair. It felt good to finally admit it out loud.

Newt stood up. "What? Who is she?"

"No idea. But something clicked—I know her from somewhere." Thomas rubbed his eyes, frustrated that he couldn't solidify the link.

"Well, keep bloody thinking—don't lose it. Concentrate."

"I'm trying, so shut up." Thomas closed his eyes, searched the darkness of his thoughts, seeking her face in that emptiness. Who *was* she? The irony of the question struck him—he didn't even know who *he* was.

He leaned forward in his chair and took a deep breath, then looked at Newt, shaking his head in surrender. "I just don't—"

Teresa.

Thomas jolted up from the chair, knocked it backward, spun in a circle, searching. He had heard . . .

"What's wrong?" Newt asked. "Did ya remember somethin'?"

Thomas ignored him, looked around the room in confusion, knowing he'd heard a voice, then back at the girl.

"I . . ." He sat back down, leaned forward, staring at the girl's face. "Newt, did you just say something before I stood up?"

"No."

Of course not. "Oh. I just thought I heard something . . . I don't know. Maybe it was in my head. Did . . . *she* say anything?"

"Her?" Newt asked, his eyes lit up. "No. Why? What did you hear?"

Thomas was scared to admit it. "I . . . I swear I heard a name. Teresa."

"Teresa? No, I didn't hear that. Must've sprung loose from your bloody memory blocks! That's her name, Tommy. Teresa. Has to be."

Thomas felt . . . odd—an uncomfortable feeling, like something supernatural had just occurred. "It was . . . I swear I *heard* it. But in my mind, man. I can't explain it."

Thomas.

This time he jumped from the chair and scrambled as far from the bed as possible, knocking over the lamp on the table; it landed with the crash of broken glass. A voice. A girl's voice. Whispery, sweet, confident. He'd heard it. He *knew* he'd heard it.

"What's bloody wrong with you?" Newt asked.

Thomas's heart was racing. He felt the thumps in his skull. Acid boiled in his stomach. "She's . . . she's freakin' *talking* to me. In my head. She just said my name!"

"What?"

"I swear!" The world spun around him, pressed in, crushing his mind. "I'm . . . hearing her voice in my head—or something . . . it's not really a voice. . . ."

"Tommy, sit your butt down. *What* are you bloody talking about?"

"Newt, I'm serious. It's . . . not really a voice . . . but it *is*."

Tom, we're the last ones. It'll end soon. It has to.

The words echoed in his mind, touched his eardrums—he could *hear* them. Yet they didn't sound like they were coming from the room, from outside his body. They were literally, in every way, *inside* his mind.

Tom, don't freak out on me.

He put his hands up to his ears, squeezed his eyes shut. It was too strange; he couldn't bring his rational mind to accept what was happening.

My memory's fading already, Tom. I won't remember much when I wake up. We can pass the Trials. It has to end. They sent me as a trigger.

Thomas couldn't take it anymore. Ignoring Newt's questions, he stumbled to the door and yanked it open, stepped into the hall, ran. Down the stairs, out the front door, he ran. But it did nothing to shut her up.

Everything is going to change, she said.

He wanted to scream, run until he could run no more. He made it to the East Door and sprinted through it, out of the Glade. Kept going, through corridor after corridor, deep into the heart of the Maze, rules or no rules. But he still couldn't escape the voice.

It was you and me, Tom. We did this to them. To us.

CHAPTER 29

Thomas didn't stop until the voice had gone for good.

It shocked him when he realized he'd been running for almost an hour—the shadows of the walls ran long toward the east, and soon the sun would set for the night and the Doors would close. He had to get back. It only peripherally hit him then that without thinking he'd recognized the direction and the time. That his instincts were strong.

He had to get back.

But he didn't know if he could face her again. The voice in his head. The strange things she'd said.

He had no choice. Denying the truth would solve nothing. And as bad—as weird—as the invasion of his mind had been, it beat another date with the Grievers any day.

As he ran toward the Glade, he learned a lot about himself. Without meaning to or realizing it, he'd pictured in his mind his exact route through the Maze as he escaped the voice. Not once did he falter on his return, turning left and right and running down long corridors in reverse of the way he had come. He knew what it meant.

Minho had been right. Soon, Thomas would be the best Runner.

The second thing he learned about himself, as if the night in the Maze hadn't proved it already, was that his body was in perfect shape. Just a day earlier he'd been at the end of his strength and sore from top to bottom. He'd recovered quickly, and ran now with almost no effort, despite nearing the end of his second hour of running. It didn't take a math genius to calculate that his speed and time combined meant he'd run roughly half a marathon by the time he returned to the Glade.

Never before had the sheer size of the Maze truly hit him. Miles and miles and miles. With its walls that moved, every night, he finally understood why the Maze was so hard to solve. He'd doubted it until now, wondered how the Runners could be so inept.

On he ran, left and right, straight, on and on. By the time he'd crossed the threshold into the Glade, the Doors were only minutes away from closing for the night. Exhausted, he headed straight for the Deadheads, went deep into the forest until he reached the spot where the trees crowded against the southwest corner. More than anything, he wanted to be alone.

When he could hear only the sounds of distant Glader conversations, as well as faint echoes of bleating sheep and snorting pigs, his wish was granted; he found the junction of the two giant walls and collapsed into the corner to rest. No one came, no one bothered him. The south wall eventually moved, closing for the night; he leaned forward until it stopped. Minutes later, his back once again comfortably pressed against thick layers of ivy, he fell asleep.

The next morning, someone gently shook him awake.

"Thomas, wake up." It was Chuck—the kid seemed to be able to find him anywhere.

Groaning, Thomas leaned forward, stretched out his back and arms. A couple of blankets had been placed over him during the night—someone playing the Glade Mother.

"What time is it?" he asked.

"You're almost too late for breakfast." Chuck tugged on his arm. "Come on, get up. You need to start acting normal or things'll just get worse."

Dylan O'Brien as Thomas

Ki Hong Lee as Minho

Blake Cooper as Chuck

Thomas Brodie-Sangster as Newt

Will Poulter as Gally

Aml Ameen as Alby

Dexter Darden as Frypan

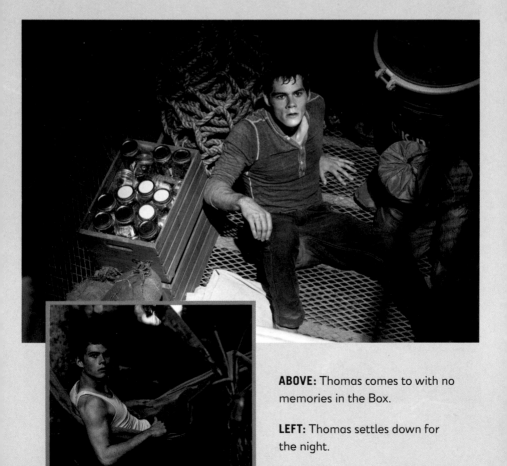

ABOVE: Thomas comes to with no memories in the Box.

LEFT: Thomas settles down for the night.

The Gladers are surprised by a new Box arrival.

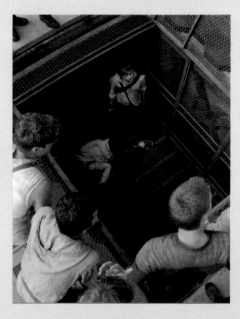

A girl arrives in the Box.

Kaya Scodelario as Teresa

LEFT: Ben faces the Keepers.

MIDDLE: Thomas comforts Chuck.

BOTTOM: The Gladers look into the Maze.

ABOVE: Minho, Thomas, and Alby are locked in the Maze overnight.

LEFT: Minho and Thomas run from Grievers in the Maze.

BELOW: Gally accuses Thomas of knowing more than he's letting on.

Minho, Thomas, and Newt contemplate what to do next.

Teresa and Thomas search for answers.

ABOVE: Minho shows Thomas the model of the Maze.

RIGHT: Thomas prepares for battle against the Grievers.

BELOW: The Maze door opens.

The Gladers arm themselves to escape.

The Gladers fight for their lives.

The events of the previous day came crashing into Thomas's mind, and his stomach seemed to twist inside out. *What are they going to do to me?* he thought. *Those things she said. Something about me and her doing this to them. To us. What did that* mean?

Then it hit him that maybe he was crazy. Maybe the stress of the Maze had driven him insane. Either way, only *he* had heard the voice inside his head. No one else knew the weird things Teresa had said, or accused him of. They didn't even know that she had told him her name. Well, no one except Newt.

And he would keep it that way. Things were bad enough—no way he'd make it worse by telling people about voices in his head. The only problem was Newt. Thomas would have to convince him somehow that stress had finally overwhelmed him and a good night's rest had solved everything. *I'm not crazy,* Thomas told himself. Surely he wasn't.

Chuck was looking at him with eyebrows raised.

"Sorry," Thomas said as he stood up, acting as normal as he could. "Just thinking. Let's eat, I'm starving."

"Good that," Chuck said, slapping Thomas on the back.

They headed for the Homestead, Chuck yapping the whole time. Thomas wasn't complaining—it was the closest thing to normal in his life.

"Newt found you last night and told everyone to let you sleep. *And* he told us what the Council decided about you—one day in the cell, then you'll enter the Runner training program. Some shanks grumbled, some cheered, most acted like they couldn't care less. As for me, I think it's pretty awesome." Chuck paused to take a breath, then kept going. "That first night, when you were bragging about being a Runner and all that klunk—shuck it, I was laughing inside so hard. I kept telling myself, this sucker's in for a rude awakening. Well, you proved *me* wrong, huh?"

But Thomas didn't feel like talking about it. "I just did what anyone else would've done. It's not my fault Minho and Newt want me to be a Runner."

"Yeah, right. Quit being modest."

Being a Runner was the last thing on Thomas's mind. What he couldn't stop thinking about was Teresa, the voice in his head, what she'd *said*. "I guess I'm a little excited." Thomas forced a grin, though he cringed at the thought of hanging out in the Slammer by himself all day before he got to start.

"We'll see how you feel after running your guts out. Anyway, as long as you know old Chucky is proud of you."

Thomas smiled at his friend's enthusiasm. "If only you were my mom," Thomas murmured, "life'd be a peach." *My mom*, he thought. The world seemed to darken for a moment—he couldn't even remember his own mother. He pushed the thought away before it consumed him.

They made it to the kitchen and grabbed a quick breakfast, taking two empty seats at the big table inside. Every Glader going in and out the door gave Thomas a stare; a few came up and offered congratulations. Other than a sprinkling of dirty looks here and there, most people seemed to be on his side. Then he remembered Gally.

"Hey, Chuck," he asked after taking a bite of eggs, trying to sound casual. "Did they ever find Gally?"

"No. I was gonna tell you—someone said they saw him run out into the Maze after he left the Gathering. Hasn't been seen since."

Thomas dropped his fork, not knowing what he'd expected or hoped for. Either way, the news stunned him. "What? You're serious? He went into the Maze?"

"Yeah. Everyone knows he went nuts—some shank even accused you of killing him when you ran out there yesterday."

"I can't believe . . ." Thomas stared at his plate, trying to under-stand why Gally would do that.

"Don't worry about it, dude. No one liked him except for his few shuck cronies. They're the ones accusing you of stuff."

Thomas couldn't believe how casually Chuck spoke about it. "Ya know, the guy is probably dead. You're talking about him like he went on vacation."

A contemplative look came over Chuck. "I don't think he's dead."

"Huh? Then where is he? Aren't Minho and I the only ones who've survived a night out there?"

"That's what I'm saying. I think his buddies are hiding him inside the Glade somewhere. Gally was an idiot, but he couldn't possibly be stupid enough to stay out in the Maze all night. Like you."

Thomas shook his head. "Maybe that's *exactly* why he stayed out there. Wanted to prove he could do anything I can do. The guy hates me." A pause. "Hated me."

"Well, whatever." Chuck shrugged as if they were arguing over what to have for breakfast. "If he's dead, you guys'll probably find him eventually. If not, he'll get hungry and show up to eat. I don't care."

Thomas picked up his plate and took it to the counter. "All I want is one normal day—one day to relax."

"Then your bloody wish is granted," said a voice from the kitchen door behind him.

Thomas turned to see Newt there, smiling. That grin sent a wave of reassurance through Thomas, as if he were finding out the world was okay again.

"Come on, ya buggin' jailbird," Newt said. "You can take it easy while you're hangin' in the Slammer. Let's go. Chucky'll bring ya some lunch at noon."

Thomas nodded and headed out the door, Newt leading the way. Suddenly a day in prison sounded excellent. A day to just sit and relax.

Though something told him there was a better chance of Gally bringing him flowers than of passing a day in the Glade with nothing strange happening.

CHAPTER 30

The Slammer stood in an obscure place between the Homestead and the north Glade wall, hidden behind thorny, ragged bushes that looked like they hadn't been trimmed in ages. It was a big block of roughly cut concrete, with one tiny, barred window and a wooden door that was locked with a menacing rusty metal latch, like something out of the Dark Ages.

Newt took out a key and opened it up, then motioned for Thomas to enter. "There's only a chair in there and nothin' at all for ya to do. Enjoy yourself."

Thomas groaned inwardly as he stepped inside and saw the one piece of furniture—an ugly, rickety chair with one leg obviously shorter than the rest, probably on purpose. Didn't even have a cushion.

"Have fun," Newt said before closing the door. Thomas turned back to his new home and heard the latch close and the lock click behind him. Newt's head appeared at the little glassless window, looking through the bars, a smirk on his face. "Nice reward for breakin' the rules. You saved some lives, Tommy, but ya still need to learn—"

"Yeah, I know. *Order.*"

Newt smiled. "You're not half bad, shank. But friends or no, gotta run things properly, keep us buggers alive. Think about that while ya sit here and stare at the bloody walls."

And then he was gone.

★ ★ ★

The first hour passed, and Thomas felt boredom creep in like rats under the door. By hour number two, he wanted to bang his head against the wall. Two hours after that he started to think having dinner with Gally and the Grievers would beat sitting inside that stupid Slammer. He sat and tried to bring back memories, but every effort evaporated into oblivious mist before anything formed.

Thankfully, Chuck arrived with lunch at noon, relieving Thomas from his thoughts.

After passing some pieces of chicken and a glass of water through the window, he took up his usual role of talking Thomas's ear off.

"Everything's getting back to normal," the boy announced. "The Runners are out in the Maze, everyone's working—maybe we'll survive after all. Still no sign of Gally—Newt told the Runners to come back lickety-splickety if they found his body. And, oh, yeah—Alby's up and around. Seems fine—and Newt's glad he doesn't have to be the big boss anymore."

The mention of Alby pulled Thomas's attention from his food. He pictured the older boy thrashing around, choking himself the day before. Then he remembered that no one else knew what Alby had said after Newt left the room—before the seizure. But that didn't mean Alby would keep it between them now that he was up and walking around.

Chuck continued talking, taking a completely unexpected turn. "Thomas, I'm kinda messed up, man. It's weird to feel sad and homesick, but have no idea what it is you wish you could go back to, ya know? All I know is I don't want to be here. I want to go back to my family. Whatever's there, whatever I was taken from. I wanna *remember*."

Thomas was a little surprised. He'd never heard Chuck say something so deep and so true. "I know what you mean," he murmured.

Chuck was too short for his eyes to reach where Thomas could see them as he spoke, but from his next statement, Thomas imagined them filling with a bleak sadness, maybe even tears. "I used to cry. Every night."

This made thoughts of Alby leave Thomas's mind. "Yeah?"

"Like a pants-wettin' baby. Almost till the day you got here. Then I just got used to it, I guess. This became home, even though we spend every day hoping to get out."

"I've only cried once since showing up, but that was after almost getting eaten alive. I'm probably just a shallow shuck-face." Thomas might not have admitted it if Chuck hadn't opened up.

"You cried?" he heard Chuck say through the window. "Then?"

"Yeah. When the last one finally fell over the Cliff, I broke down and sobbed till my throat and chest hurt." Thomas remembered all too well. "Everything crushed in on me at once. Sure made *me* feel better—don't feel bad about crying. Ever."

"Kinda *does* make ya feel better, huh? Weird how that works."

A few minutes passed in silence. Thomas found himself hoping Chuck wouldn't leave.

"Hey, Thomas?" Chuck asked.

"Still here."

"Do you think I have parents? *Real* parents?"

Thomas laughed, mostly to push away the sudden surge of sadness the statement caused. "Of course you do, shank. You need me to explain the birds and bees?" Thomas's heart hurt—he could remember getting that lecture but not who'd given it to him.

"That's not what I meant," Chuck said, his voice completely devoid of cheer. It was low and bleak, almost a mumble. "Most of the

193

guys who've gone through the Changing remember terrible things they won't even talk about, which makes me doubt I have anything good back home. So, I mean, you think it's really possible I have a mom and a dad out in the world somewhere, missing me? Do you think *they* cry at night?"

Thomas was completely shocked to realize his eyes had filled with tears. Life had been so crazy since he'd arrived, he'd never really thought of the Gladers as real people with real families, missing them. It was strange, but he hadn't even really thought of himself that way. Only about what it all meant, who'd sent them there, how they'd ever get out.

For the first time, he felt something for Chuck that made him so angry he wanted to kill somebody. The boy should be in school, in a home, playing with neighborhood kids. He deserved to go home at night to a family who loved him, worried about him. A mom who made him take a shower every day and a dad who helped him with homework.

Thomas hated the people who'd taken this poor, innocent kid from his family. He hated them with a passion he didn't know a human could feel. He wanted them dead, tortured, even. He wanted Chuck to be happy.

But happiness had been ripped from their lives. *Love* had been ripped from their lives.

"Listen to me, Chuck." Thomas paused, calming down as much as he could, making sure his voice didn't crack. "I'm sure you have parents. I know it. Sounds terrible, but I bet your mom is sitting in your room right now, holding your pillow, looking out at the world that stole you from her. And yeah, I bet she's crying. Hard. Puffy-eyed, snotty-nosed crying. The real deal."

Chuck didn't say anything, but Thomas thought he heard the slightest of sniffles.

"Don't give up, Chuck. We're gonna solve this thing, get out of here. I'm a Runner now—I promise on my life I'll get you back to that room of yours. Make your mom quit crying." And Thomas meant it. He felt it *burn* in his heart.

"Hope you're right," Chuck said with a shaky voice. He showed a thumbs-up sign in the window, then walked away.

Thomas stood up to pace around the little room, fuming with an intense desire to keep his promise. "I swear, Chuck," he whispered to no one. "I swear I'll get you back home."

CHAPTER 31

Just after Thomas heard the grind and rumble of stone against stone announce the closing of the Doors for the day, Alby showed up to release him, which was a huge surprise. The metal of key and lock jingled; then the door to the cell swung wide open.

"Ain't dead, are ya, shank?" Alby asked. He looked so much better than the day before, Thomas couldn't help staring at him. His skin was back to full color, his eyes no longer crisscrossed with red veins; he seemed to have gained fifteen pounds in twenty-four hours.

Alby noticed him goggling. "Shuck it, boy, what you lookin' at?"

Thomas shook his head slightly, feeling like he'd been in a trance. His mind was racing, wondering what Alby remembered, what he knew, what he might say about him. "Wha—Nothing. Just seems crazy you healed so quickly. You're fine now?"

Alby flexed his right bicep. "Ain't never been better—come on out."

Thomas did, hoping his eyes weren't flickering, making his concern obvious.

Alby closed the Slammer door and locked it, then turned to face him. "Actually, nothin' but a lie. I feel like a piece of klunk twice crapped by a Griever."

"Yeah, you looked it yesterday." When Alby glared, Thomas hoped it was in jest and quickly clarified. "But today you look brand-new. I swear."

Alby put the keys in his pocket and leaned back against the Slammer's door. "So, quite the little talk we had yesterday."

Thomas's heart pounded. He had no idea what to expect from Alby at that point. "Uh . . . yeah, I remember."

"I saw what I saw, Greenie. It's kinda fadin', but I ain't never gonna forget. It was terrible. Tried to talk about it, somethin' starts choking me. Now the images are gettin' up and gone, like that same somethin' don't like me remembering."

The scene from the day before flashed in Thomas's mind. Alby thrashing, trying to strangle himself—Thomas wouldn't have believed it had happened if he hadn't seen it himself. Despite fearing an answer, he knew he had to ask the next question. "What was it about me—you kept saying you saw me. What was I doing?"

Alby stared at an empty space in the distance for a while before answering. "You were with the . . . Creators. Helping them. But that ain't what got me shook up."

Thomas felt like someone had just rammed their fist in his abdomen. *Helping them?* He couldn't form the words to ask what that meant.

Alby continued. "I hope the Changing doesn't give us real memories—just plants fake ones. Some suspect it—I can only hope. If the world's the way I saw it . . ." He trailed off, leaving an ominous silence.

Thomas was confused, but pressed on. "Can't you tell me what you saw about me?"

Alby shook his head. "No way, shank. Ain't gonna risk stranglin' myself again. Might be something they got in our brains to control us—just like the memory wipe."

"Well, if I'm evil, maybe you should leave me locked up." Thomas half meant it.

"Greenie, you ain't evil. You might be a shuck-faced slinthead, but you ain't evil." Alby showed the slightest hint of a smile, a bare crack in his usually hard face. "What you did—riskin' your butt to save me and Minho—that ain't no evil I've ever heard of. Nah, just makes me think the Grief Serum and the Changing got somethin' fishy about 'em. For your sake and mine, I hope so."

Thomas was so relieved that Alby thought he was okay, he only heard about half of what the older boy had just said. "How bad *was* it? Your memories that came back."

"I remembered things from growin' up, where I lived, that sort of stuff. And if God himself came down right now and told me I could go back home . . ." Alby looked to the ground and shook his head again. "If it was real, Greenie, I swear I'd go shack up with the Grievers before goin' back."

Thomas was surprised to hear it was so bad—he wished Alby would give details, describe something, anything. But he knew the choking was still too fresh in Alby's mind for him to budge. "Well, maybe they're not real, Alby. Maybe the Grief Serum is some kind of psycho drug that gives you hallucinations." Thomas knew he was grasping at straws.

Alby thought for a minute. "A drug . . . hallucinations . . ." Then he shook his head. "Doubt it."

It had been worth a try. "We still have to escape this place."

"Yeah, thanks, Greenie," Alby said sarcastically. "Don't know what we'd do without your pep talks." Again, the almost-smile.

Alby's change of mood broke Thomas out of his gloom. "Quit calling me Greenie. The girl's the Greenie now."

"Okay, Greenie." Alby sighed, clearly done with the conversation. "Go find some dinner—your terrible prison sentence of *one day* is over."

"One was plenty." Despite wanting answers, Thomas was ready to get away from the Slammer. Plus, he was starving. He grinned at Alby, then headed straight for the kitchen and food.

Dinner was awesome.

Frypan had known Thomas would be coming late, so he'd left a plate full of roast beef and potatoes; a note announced there were cookies in the cupboard. The Cook seemed fully intent on backing up the support he'd shown for Thomas in the Gathering. Minho joined Thomas as he ate, prepping him a little before his first big day of Runner training, giving him a few stats and interesting facts. Things for him to think about as he went to sleep that night.

When they were finished, Thomas headed back to the secluded place where he'd slept the night before, in the corner behind the Deadheads. He thought about his conversation with Chuck, wondered how it would feel to have parents say good night to you.

Several boys milled about the Glade that night, but for the most part it was quiet, like everyone just wanted to go to sleep, end the day and be done with it. Thomas didn't complain—that was exactly what he needed.

The blankets someone had left for him the night before still lay there. He picked them up and settled in, snuggling up against the comforting corner where the stone walls met in a mass of soft ivy. The mixed smells of the forest greeted him as he took his first deep breath, trying to relax. The air felt perfect, and it made him wonder again about the weather of the place. Never rained, never snowed, never got too hot or too cold. If it weren't for the little fact they were torn apart from friends and families and trapped in a Maze with a bunch of monsters, it could be paradise.

Some things here were too perfect. He knew that, but had no explanation.

His thoughts drifted to what Minho had told him at dinner about the size and scale of the Maze. He believed it—he'd realized the massive scale when he'd been to the Cliff. But he just couldn't fathom how such a structure could have been built. The Maze stretched for miles and miles. The Runners had to be in almost superhuman shape to do what they did every day.

And yet they'd *never* found an exit. And despite that, despite the utter hopelessness of the situation, they still hadn't given up.

At dinner Minho had told him an old story—one of the bizarre and random things he remembered from before—about a woman trapped in a maze. She escaped by never taking her right hand off the walls of the maze, sliding it along as she walked. In doing so, she was forced to turn right at every turn, and the simple laws of physics and geometry ensured that eventually she found the exit. It made sense.

But not here. Here, all paths led back to the Glade. They had to be missing *something*.

Tomorrow, his training would begin. Tomorrow, he could start helping them find that missing something. Right then Thomas made a decision. Forget all the weird stuff. Forget all the bad things. Forget it all. He wouldn't quit until he'd solved the puzzle and found a way home.

Tomorrow. The word floated in his mind until he finally fell asleep.

CHAPTER 32

Minho woke Thomas before dawn, motioning with a flashlight to follow him back to the Homestead. Thomas easily shook off his morning grogginess, excited to begin his training. He crawled out from under his blanket and eagerly followed his teacher, winding his way through the crowd of Gladers who slept on the lawn, their snores the only sign they weren't dead. The slightest glow of early morning illuminated the Glade, turning everything dark blue and shadowed. Thomas had never seen the place look so peaceful. A cock crowed in the Blood House.

Finally, in a crooked cranny near a back corner of the Homestead, Minho pulled out a key and opened up a shabby door leading to a small storage closet. Thomas felt a shiver of anticipation, wondering what was inside. He caught glimpses of ropes and chains and other odds and ends as Minho's flashlight crisscrossed the closet. Eventually, it fell on an open box full of running shoes. Thomas almost laughed, it seemed so ordinary.

"That right there's the number one supply we get," Minho announced. "At least for us. They send new ones in the Box every so often. If we had bad shoes, we'd have feet that look like freaking Mars." He bent over and rummaged through the pile. "What size you wear?"

"Size?" Thomas thought for a second. "I . . . don't know." It was so odd sometimes what he could and couldn't remember. He reached down and pulled off a shoe he'd worn since coming to the Glade and took a look inside. "Eleven."

"Geez, shank, you got big feet." Minho stood up holding a pair of

201

sleek silver ones. "But looks like I've got some—man, we could go canoeing in these things."

"Those are fancy." Thomas took them and walked out of the closet to sit on the ground, eager to try them on. Minho grabbed a few more things before coming out to join him.

"Only Runners and Keepers get these," Minho said. Before Thomas could look up from tying his shoes, a plastic wristwatch dropped into his lap. It was black and very simple, its face showing only a digital display of the time. "Put it on and never take it off. Your life might depend on it."

Thomas was glad to have it. Though the sun and the shadows had seemed plenty to let him know roughly what time it was up to that point, being a Runner probably required more precision. He buckled the watch onto his wrist and then returned to fitting on his shoes.

Minho continued talking. "Here's a backpack, water bottles, lunch pack, some shorts and T-shirts, other stuff." He nudged Thomas, who looked up. Minho was holding out a couple of pairs of tightly cut underwear, made from a shiny white material. "These bad boys're what we call Runnie-undies. Keeps you, um, nice and comfy."

"Nice and comfy?"

"Yeah, ya know. Your—"

"Yeah, got it." Thomas took the underwear and other stuff. "You guys really have this all thought out, don't you?"

"Couple of years runnin' your butt off every day, you figure out what you need and ask for it." He started stuffing things into his own backpack.

Thomas was surprised. "You mean, you can make requests? Supplies you want?" Why would the people who'd sent them there help so much?

"Of course we can. Just drop a note in the Box, and there she goes.

Doesn't mean we always get what we want from the Creators. Sometimes we do, sometimes we don't."

"Ever asked for a map?"

Minho laughed. "Yeah, tried that one. Asked for a TV, too, but no luck. I guess those shuck-faces don't want us seeing how wonderful life is when you don't live in a freaking maze."

Thomas felt a trickle of doubt that life was so great back home—what kind of world allowed people to make kids live like this? The thought surprised him, as if its source had been founded in actual memory, a wisp of light in the darkness of his mind. But it was already gone. Shaking his head, he finished lacing up his shoes, then stood up and jogged around in circles, jumping up and down to test them out. "They feel pretty good. I guess I'm ready."

Minho was still crouched over his backpack on the ground; he glanced up at Thomas with a look of disgust. "You look like an idiot, prancin' around like a shuck ballerina. Good luck out there with no breakfast, no packed lunch, no weapons."

Thomas had already stopped moving, felt an icy chill. "Weapons?"

"Weapons." Minho stood and walked back to the closet. "Come here, I'll show ya."

Thomas followed Minho into the small room and watched as he pulled a few boxes away from the back wall. Underneath lay a small trapdoor. Minho lifted it to reveal a set of wooden stairs leading into blackness. "Keep 'em down in the basement so shanks like Gally can't get to them. Come on."

Minho went first. The stairs creaked with every shift of weight as they descended the dozen or so steps. The cool air was refreshing, despite the dust and the strong scent of mildew. They hit a dirt floor, and Thomas couldn't see a thing until Minho turned on a single lightbulb by pulling a string.

The room was larger than Thomas had expected, at least thirty feet square. Shelves lined the walls, and there were several blocky wooden tables; everything in sight was covered with all manner of junk that gave him the creeps. Wooden poles, metal spikes, large pieces of mesh—like what covers a chicken coop—rolls of barbed wire, saws, knives, swords. One entire wall was dedicated to archery: wooden bows, arrows, spare strings. The sight of it immediately brought back the memory of Ben getting shot by Alby in the Deadheads.

"Wow," Thomas murmured, his voice a dull thump in the enclosed place. At first he was terrified that they needed so many weapons, but he was relieved to see that the vast majority of it was covered with a thick layer of dust.

"Don't use most of it," Minho said. "But ya never know. All we usually take with us is a couple of sharp knives."

He nodded toward a large wooden trunk in the corner, its top open and leaning against the wall. Knives of all shapes and sizes were stacked haphazardly all the way to the top.

Thomas just hoped the room was kept secret from most of the Gladers. "Seems kind of dangerous to have all this stuff," he said. "What if Ben had gotten down here right before he went nuts and attacked me?"

Minho pulled the keys out of his pocket and dangled them with a clickety-clank. "Only a few lucky toads have a set of these."

"Still . . ."

"Quit your bellyachin' and pick a couple. Make sure they're nice and sharp. Then we'll go get breakfast and pack our lunch. I wanna spend some time in the Map Room before we head out."

Thomas was pumped to hear that—he'd been curious about the squat building ever since he'd first seen a Runner go through its menacing door. He selected a short silvery dagger with a rubber grip, then one with a long black blade. His excitement waned a little. Even though he knew perfectly well what lived out there, he still didn't want to think about why he needed weapons to go into the Maze.

A half hour later, fed and packed, they stood in front of the riveted metal door of the Map Room. Thomas was itching to go inside. Dawn had burst forth in all her glory, and Gladers milled about, readying for the day. Smells of frying bacon wafted through the air—Frypan and his crew trying to keep up with dozens of starving stomachs. Minho unlocked the door, cranked the wheel-handle, spinning it until an audible click sounded from inside, then pulled. With a lurching squeal, the heavy metal slab swung open.

"After you," Minho said with a mocking bow.

Thomas went in without saying anything. A cool fear, mixed with an intense curiosity, gripped him, and he had to remind himself to breathe.

The dark room had a musty, wet smell, laced with a deep coppery scent so strong he could taste it. A distant, faded memory of sucking on pennies as a kid popped into his head.

Minho hit a switch and several rows of fluorescent lights flickered until they came on full strength, revealing the room in detail.

Thomas was surprised at its simplicity. About twenty feet across, the Map Room had concrete walls bare of any decoration. A wooden table stood in the exact center, eight chairs tucked in around it. Neatly stacked piles of paper and pencils lay about the table's surface, one for each chair. The only other items in the room were eight trunks, just like the one containing the knives in the weapons basement. Closed, they were evenly spaced, two to a wall.

"Welcome to the Map Room," Minho said. "As happy a place as you could ever visit."

Thomas was slightly disappointed—he'd been expecting something more profound. He took in a deep breath. "Too bad it smells like an abandoned copper mine."

"I kinda like the smell." Minho pulled out two chairs and sat in one of them. "Have a seat, I want you to get a couple of images in your head before we go out there."

As Thomas sat down, Minho grabbed a piece of paper and a pencil and started drawing. Thomas leaned in to get a better look and saw that Minho had drawn a big box that filled almost the entire page. Then he filled it with smaller boxes until it looked exactly like an enclosed tic-tac-toe board, three rows of three squares, all the same size. He wrote the word *GLADE* in the middle, then numbered the outside squares from one to eight, starting in the upper left corner and going clockwise. Lastly, he drew little notches here and there.

"These are the Doors," Minho said. "You know about the ones from the Glade, but there are four more out in the Maze that lead to Sections One, Three, Five, and Seven. They stay in the same spot, but the route there changes with the wall movements every night." He finished, then slid the paper over to rest in front of Thomas.

Thomas picked it up, completely fascinated that the Maze was so structured, and studied it as Minho kept talking.

"So we have the Glade, surrounded by eight Sections, each one a completely self-contained square and unsolvable in the two years since we began this freaking game. The only thing even approaching an exit is the Cliff, and that ain't a very good one unless you like falling to a horrible death." Minho tapped the Map. "The walls move all over the shuck place every evening—same time as our Doors close shut. At least, we think that's when, because we never really hear walls moving any other time."

Thomas looked up, happy to be able to offer a piece of information. "I didn't see anything move that night we got stuck out there."

"Those main corridors right outside the Doors don't ever change. It's just the ones a little deeper out."

"Oh." Thomas returned to the crude map, trying to visualize the Maze and see stone walls where Minho had penciled lines.

"We always have at least eight Runners, including the Keeper. One for each Section. It takes us a whole day to map out our area—hoping against hope there's an exit—then we come back and draw it up, a separate page for each day." Minho glanced over at one of the trunks. "That's why those things are shuck full of Maps."

Thomas had a depressing—and scary—thought. "Am I . . . replacing someone? Did somebody get killed?"

Minho shook his head. "No, we're just training you—someone'll probably want a break. Don't worry, it's been a while since a Runner was killed."

For some reason that last statement worried Thomas, though he hoped it didn't show on his face. He pointed at Section Three. "So . . . it takes you a whole day to run through these little squares?"

"Hilarious." Minho stood and stepped over to the trunk right behind them, knelt down, then lifted the lid and rested it against the wall. "Come here."

Thomas had already gotten up; he leaned over Minho's shoulder and took a look. The trunk was large enough that four stacks of Maps could fit, and all four reached the top. Each of the ones Thomas could see were very similar: a rough sketch of a square maze, filling almost the whole page. In the top right corners, *Section 8* was scribbled, followed by the name *Hank,* then the word *Day,* followed by a number. The latest one said it was day number 749.

Minho continued. "We figured out the walls were moving right at the beginning. As soon as we did, we started keeping track. We've always thought that comparing these day to day, week to week, would help us figure out a pattern. And we did—the mazes basically repeat themselves about every month. But we've yet to see an exit open up that will lead us out of the square. Never been an exit."

"It's been two years," Thomas said. "Haven't you gotten desperate enough to stay out there overnight, see if maybe something opens while the walls are moving?"

Minho looked up at him, a flash of anger in his eyes. "That's kind of insulting, dude. Seriously."

"What?" Thomas was shocked—he hadn't meant it that way.

"We've been bustin' our butts for two years, and all you can ask is why we're too sissy to stay out there all night? A few tried it in the very beginning—all of them showed up dead. You wanna spend another night out there? Like your chances of surviving again, do ya?"

Thomas's face reddened in shame. "No. Sorry." He suddenly felt like a piece of klunk. And he certainly agreed—he'd much rather come home safe and sound to the Glade every night than ensure another battle with the Grievers. He shuddered at the thought.

"Yeah, well." Minho returned his gaze to the Maps in the trunk, much to Thomas's relief. "Life in the Glade might not be sweet livin', but at least it's safe. Plenty of food, protection from the Grievers. There's no way we can ask the Runners to risk staying out there—no way. Least not yet. Not until something about these patterns gives a clue that an exit might open up, even temporarily."

"Are you close? Anything developing?"

Minho shrugged. "I don't know. It's kind of depressing, but we don't know what else to do. Can't take a chance that one day, in one spot, somewhere, an exit might appear. We can't give up. Ever."

Thomas nodded, relieved at the attitude. As bad as things were, giving up would only make them worse.

Minho pulled several sheets from the trunk, the Maps from the last few days. As he flipped through them, he explained, "We compare day to day, week to week, month to month, just like I was saying. Each Runner is in charge of the Map for his own Section. If I gotta be honest, we haven't figured out jack yet. Even more honest—we don't know what we're looking for. Really sucks, dude. Really freaking sucks."

"But we can't give up." Thomas said it in a matter-of-fact tone, as a resigned repeat of what Minho had said a moment earlier. He'd said "we" without even thinking about it, and realized he was truly part of the Glade now.

"Right on, bro. We can't give up." Minho carefully returned the papers and closed the trunk, then stood. "Well, we gotta bust it fast since we took time in here—you'll just be following me around your first few days. Ready?"

Thomas felt a wire of nervousness tighten inside him, pinching his gut. It was actually here—they were going for real now, no more talking and thinking about it. "Um . . . yeah."

"No 'ums' around here. You ready or not?"

Thomas looked at Minho, matched his suddenly hard gaze. "I'm ready."

"Then let's go runnin'."

CHAPTER 33

They went through the West Door into Section Eight and made their way down several corridors, Thomas right beside Minho as he turned right and left without seeming to think about it, running all the while. The early-morning light had a sharp sheen about it, making everything look bright and crisp—the ivy, the cracked walls, the stone blocks of the ground. Though the sun had a few hours before hitting the noon spot up above, there was plenty of light to see by. Thomas kept up with Minho as best he could, having to sprint every once in a while to catch back up.

They finally made it to a rectangular cut in a long wall to the north that looked like a doorway without a door. Minho ran straight through it without stopping. "This leads from Section Eight—the middle left square—to Section One—the top left square. Like I said, this passage is always in the same spot, but the route here might be a little different because of the walls rearranging themselves."

Thomas followed him, surprised at how heavy his breaths had already become. He hoped it was only jitters, that his breathing would steady soon.

They ran down a long corridor to the right, passing several turns to the left. When they reached the end of the passage, Minho slowed to barely more than a walk and reached behind him to pull out a notepad and pencil from a side pocket in his backpack. He jotted a note, then put them back, never fully stopping. Thomas wondered what he'd written, but Minho answered him before he could pose the question.

"I rely . . . mostly on memory," the Keeper huffed, his voice finally showing a hint of strain. "But about every fifth turn, I write something down to help me later. Mostly just related to stuff from yesterday—what's different today. Then I can use yesterday's Map to make today's. Easy-peasy, dude."

Thomas was intrigued. Minho *did* make it sound easy.

They ran for a short while before they reached an intersection. They had three possible choices, but Minho went to the right without hesitating. As he did so, he pulled one of his knives from a pocket and, without missing a beat, cut a big piece of ivy off the wall. He threw it on the ground behind him and kept running.

"Bread crumbs?" Thomas asked, the old fairy tale popping into his mind. Such odd glimpses of his past had almost stopped surprising him.

"Bread crumbs," Minho replied. "I'm Hansel, you're Gretel."

On they went, following the course of the Maze, sometimes turning right, sometimes turning left. After every turn, Minho cut and dropped a three-foot length of ivy. Thomas couldn't help being impressed—Minho didn't even need to slow down to do it.

"All right," the Keeper said, breathing heavier now. "Your turn."

"What?" Thomas hadn't really expected to do anything but run and watch on his first day.

"Cut the ivy now—you gotta get used to doing it on the run. We pick 'em up as we come back, or kick 'em to the side."

Thomas was happier than he thought he'd be at having something to do, though it took him a while to become good at it. First couple of times, he had to sprint to catch up after cutting the ivy, and once he nicked his finger. But by his tenth attempt, he could almost match Minho at the task.

On they went. After they'd run awhile—Thomas had no idea for how long or how far, but he guessed three miles—Minho slowed to a walk, then stopped altogether. "Break time." He swung off his pack and pulled out some water and an apple.

Thomas didn't have to be convinced to follow Minho's lead. He guzzled his water, relishing the wet coolness as it washed down his dry throat.

"Slow down there, fishhead," Minho yelped. "Save some for later."

Thomas stopped drinking, sucked in a big satisfied breath, then burped. He took a bite of his apple, feeling surprisingly refreshed. For some reason, his thoughts turned back to the day Minho and Alby had gone to look at the dead Griever—when everything had gone to klunk. "You never really told me what happened to Alby that day— why he was in such bad shape. Obviously the Griever woke up, but what *happened*?"

Minho had already put his backpack on. He looked ready to go. "Well, shuck thing wasn't dead. Alby poked at it with his foot like an idiot and that bad boy suddenly sprang to life, spikes flaring, its fat body rollin' all over him. Something was wrong with it, though—didn't really attack like usual. It seemed like it was mostly just trying to get out of there, and poor Alby was in the way."

"So it ran away from you guys?" From what Thomas had seen only a few nights before, he couldn't imagine it.

Minho shrugged. "Yeah, I guess—maybe it needed to get recharged or something. I don't know."

"What could've been wrong with it? Did you see an injury or anything?" Thomas didn't know what kind of answer he was searching for, but he was sure there had to be a clue or lesson to learn from what happened.

Minho thought for a minute. "No. Shuck thing just looked dead—like a wax statue. Then boom, it was back to life."

Thomas's mind was churning, trying to get somewhere, only he didn't know where or which direction to even start in. "I just wonder where it *went*. Where they always go. Don't you?" He was quiet for a second, then, "Haven't you ever thought of following them?"

"Man, you *do* have a death wish, don't you? Come on, we gotta go." And with that Minho turned and started running.

As Thomas followed, he struggled to figure out what was tickling the back of his mind. Something about that Griever being dead and then not dead, something about where it had gone once it sprang to life . . .

Frustrated, he put it aside and sprinted to catch up.

Thomas ran right behind Minho for two more hours, sprinkled with little breaks that seemed to get shorter every time. Good shape or not, Thomas was feeling the pain.

Finally, Minho stopped and pulled off his backpack once more. They sat on the ground, leaning against the soft ivy as they ate lunch, neither one of them talking much. Thomas relished every bite of his sandwich and veggies, eating as slowly as possible. He knew Minho would make them get up and go once the food disappeared, so he took his time.

"Anything different today?" Thomas asked, curious.

Minho reached down and patted his backpack, where his notes rested. "Just the usual wall movements. Nothing to get your skinny butt excited about."

Thomas took a long swig of water, looking up at the ivy-covered wall opposite them. He caught a flash of silver and red, something he'd seen more than once that day.

"What's the deal with those beetle blades?" he asked. They seemed to be everywhere. Then Thomas remembered what he'd seen in the Maze—so much had happened he hadn't had the chance to mention it. "And why do they have the word *wicked* written on their backs?"

"Never been able to catch one." Minho finished up his meal and put his lunch box away. "And we don't know what that word means— probably just something to scare us. But they have to be spies. For *them*. Only thing we can reckon."

"Who is *them*, anyway?" Thomas asked, ready for more answers. He hated the people behind the Maze. "Anybody have a clue?"

"We don't know jack about the stupid Creators." Minho's face reddened as he squeezed his hands together like he was choking someone. "Can't wait to rip their—"

But before the Keeper could finish, Thomas was on his feet and across the corridor. "What's that?" he interrupted, heading for a dull glimmer of gray he'd just noticed behind the ivy on the wall, about head high.

"Oh, yeah, that," Minho said, his voice completely indifferent.

Thomas reached in and pulled apart the curtains of ivy, then stared blankly at a square of metal riveted to the stone with words stamped across it in big capital letters. He put his hand out to run his fingers across them, as if he didn't believe his eyes.

WORLD IN CATASTROPHE:
KILLZONE EXPERIMENT DEPARTMENT

He read the words aloud, then looked back at Minho. "What's this?" It gave him a chill—it had to have something to do with the Creators.

"I don't know, shank. They're all over the place, like freaking labels for the nice pretty Maze they built. I quit bothering to look at 'em a long time ago."

Thomas turned back to stare at the sign, trying to suppress the feeling of doom that had risen inside him. "Not much here that sounds very good. Catastrophe. Killzone. *Experiment*. Real nice."

"Yeah, real nice, Greenie. Let's go."

Reluctantly, Thomas let the vines fall back into place and swung his backpack over his shoulders. And off they went, those six words burning holes in his mind.

An hour after lunch, Minho stopped at the end of a long corridor. It was straight, the walls, solid, with no hallways branching off.

"The last dead end," he said to Thomas. "Time to go back."

Thomas sucked in a deep breath, trying not to think about only being halfway done for the day. "Nothing new?"

"Just the usual changes to the way we got here—day's half over," Minho replied as he looked at his watch emotionlessly. "Gotta go back." Without waiting for a response, the Keeper turned and set off at a run in the direction from which they'd just come.

Thomas followed, frustrated that they couldn't take time to examine the walls, explore a little. He finally pulled in stride with Minho. "But—"

"Just shut it, dude. Remember what I said earlier—can't take any chances. Plus, think about it. You really think there's an exit anywhere? A secret trapdoor or something?"

"I don't know . . . maybe. Why do you ask it that way?"

Minho shook his head, spat a big wad of something nasty to his left. "There's no exit. It's just more of the same. A wall is a wall is a wall. Solid."

Thomas felt the heavy truth of it, but pushed back anyway. "How do you know?"

"Because people willing to send Grievers after us aren't gonna give us an easy way out."

This made Thomas doubt the whole point of what they were doing. "Then why even bother coming out here?"

Minho looked over at him. "Why *bother*? Because it's here—gotta be a reason. But if you think we're gonna find a nice little gate that leads to Happy Town, you're smokin' cow klunk."

Thomas looked straight ahead, feeling so hopeless he almost slowed to a stop. "This sucks."

"Smartest thing you've said yet, Greenie."

Minho blew out a big puff of air and kept running, and Thomas did the only thing he knew to do. He followed.

The rest of the day was a blur of exhaustion to Thomas. He and Minho made it back to the Glade, went to the Map Room, wrote up the day's Maze route, compared it to the previous day's. Then there were the walls closing and dinner. Chuck tried talking to him several times, but all Thomas could do was nod and shake his head, only half hearing, he was so tired.

Before twilight faded to blackness, he was already in his new favorite spot in the forest corner, curled up against the ivy, wondering if he could ever run again. Wondering how he could possibly do the same thing tomorrow. Especially when it seemed so pointless. Being a Runner had lost its glamour. After one day.

Every ounce of the noble courage he'd felt, the will to make a difference, the promise to himself to reunite Chuck with his family—it all vanished into an exhausted fog of hopeless, wretched weariness.

He was somewhere very close to sleep when a voice spoke in his head, a pretty, feminine voice that sounded as if it came from a fairy goddess trapped in his skull. The next morning, when everything started going crazy, he'd wonder if the voice had been real or part of a dream. But he heard it all the same, and remembered every word:

Tom, I just triggered the Ending.

CHAPTER 34

Thomas awoke to a weak, lifeless light. His first thought was that he must've gotten up earlier than usual, that dawn was still an hour away. But then he heard the shouts. And then he looked up, through the leafy canopy of branches.

The sky was a dull slab of gray—not the natural pale light of morning.

He jumped to his feet, put his hand on the wall to steady himself as he craned his neck to gawk toward the heavens. There was no blue, no black, no stars, no purplish fan of a creeping dawn. The sky, every last inch of it, was slate gray. Colorless and dead.

He looked down at his watch—it was a full hour past his mandatory waking time. The brilliance of the sun should've awakened him—had done so easily since he'd arrived at the Glade. But not today.

He glanced upward again, half expecting it to have changed back to normal. But it was all gray. Not cloudy, not twilight, not the early minutes of dawn. Just gray.

The sun had disappeared.

Thomas found most of the Gladers standing near the entrance to the Box, pointing at the dead sky, everyone talking at once. Based on the time, breakfast should've already been served, people should be working. But there was something about the largest object in the solar system vanishing that tended to disrupt normal schedules.

In truth, as Thomas silently watched the commotion, he didn't feel nearly as panicked or frightened as his instincts told him he ought to be. And it surprised him that so many of the others looked like lost chicks thrown from the coop. It was, in fact, ridiculous.

The sun obviously had *not* disappeared—that wasn't possible.

Though that was what it seemed like—signs of the ball of furious fire nowhere to be seen, the slanting shadows of morning absent. But he and all the Gladers were far too rational and intelligent to conclude such a thing. No, there had to be a scientifically acceptable reason for what they were witnessing. And whatever it was, to Thomas it meant one thing: the fact they could no longer see the sun probably meant they'd never been able to in the first place. A sun couldn't just disappear. Their sky had to have been—and still was—fabricated. Artificial.

In other words, the sun that had shone down on these people for two years, providing heat and life to everything, was not the sun at all. Somehow, it had been fake. Everything about this place was fake.

Thomas didn't know what that meant, didn't know how it was possible. But he knew it to be true—it was the only explanation his rational mind could accept. And it was obvious from the other Gladers' reactions that none of them had figured this out until now.

Chuck found him, and the look of fear on the boy's face pinched Thomas's heart.

"What do you think happened?" Chuck said, a pitiful tremor in his voice, his eyes glued to the sky. Thomas thought his neck must hurt something awful. "Looks like a big gray ceiling—close enough you could almost touch it."

Thomas followed Chuck's gaze and looked up. "Yeah, makes you wonder about this place." For the second time in twenty-four hours, Chuck had nailed it. The sky *did* look like a ceiling. Like the ceiling of a massive room. "Maybe something's broken. I mean, maybe it'll be back."

219

Chuck finally quit gawking and made eye contact with Thomas. "Broken? What's that supposed to mean?"

Before Thomas could answer, the faint memory of last night, before he fell asleep, came to him, Teresa's words inside his mind. She'd said, *I just triggered the Ending.* It couldn't be a coincidence, could it? A sour rot crept into his belly. Whatever the explanation, whatever that had been in the sky, the real sun or not, it was gone. And that couldn't be a good thing.

"Thomas?" Chuck asked, lightly tapping him on the upper arm.

"Yeah?" Thomas's mind felt hazy.

"What'd you mean by broken?" Chuck repeated.

Thomas felt like he needed time to think about it all. "Oh. I don't know. Must be things about this place we obviously don't understand. But you can't just make the sun disappear from space. Plus, there's still enough light to see by, as faint as it is. Where's that coming from?"

Chuck's eyes widened, as if the darkest, deepest secret of the universe had just been revealed to him. "Yeah, where *is* it coming from? What's going on, Thomas?"

Thomas reached out and squeezed the younger boy's shoulder. He felt awkward. "No clue, Chuck. Not a clue. But I'm sure Newt and Alby'll figure things out."

"Thomas!" Minho was running up to them. "Quit your leisure time with Chucky here and let's get going. We're already late."

Thomas was stunned. For some reason he'd expected the weird sky to throw all normal plans out the window.

"You're still going out there?" Chuck asked, clearly surprised as well. Thomas was glad the boy had asked the question for him.

"Of course we are, shank," Minho said. "Don't you have some sloppin' to do?" He looked from Chuck to Thomas. "If anything, gives us even more reason to get our butts out there. If the sun's really gone, won't be long before plants and animals drop dead, too. I think the desperation level just went up a notch."

The last statement struck Thomas deep down. Despite all his ideas—all the things he'd pitched to Minho—he wasn't eager to change how things had been done for the last two years. A mixture of excitement and dread swept over him when he realized what Minho was saying. "You mean we're going to stay out there overnight? Explore the walls a little more closely?"

Minho shook his head. "No, not yet. Maybe soon, though." He looked up toward the sky. "Man—what a way to wake up. Come on, let's go."

Thomas was quiet as he and Minho got their things ready and ate a lightning-fast breakfast. His thoughts were churning too much about the gray sky and what Teresa—at least, he thought it had been the girl—had told him in his mind to participate in any conversation.

What had she meant by the Ending? Thomas couldn't knock the feeling that he should tell somebody. Everybody.

But he didn't know what it meant, and he didn't want them to know he had a girl's voice in his head. They'd think he'd really gone bonkers, maybe even lock him up—and for good this time.

After a lot of deliberation, he decided to keep his mouth shut and went running with Minho for his second day of training, below a bleak and colorless sky.

They saw the Griever before they'd even made it to the door leading from Section Eight to Section One.

Minho was a few feet ahead of Thomas. He'd just rounded a corner to the right when he slammed to a stop, his feet almost skidding out from under him. He jumped back and grabbed Thomas by the shirt, pushing him against the wall.

"Shh," Minho whispered. "There's a freaking Griever up there."

Thomas widened his eyes in question, felt his heart pick up the pace, even though it had already been pumping hard and steady.

Minho simply nodded, then put his finger to his lips. He let go of Thomas's shirt and took a step back, then crept up to the corner around which he'd seen the Griever. Very slowly, he leaned forward to take a peek. Thomas wanted to scream at him to be careful.

Minho's head jerked back and he turned to face Thomas. His voice was still a whisper. "It's just sitting up there—almost like that dead one we saw."

"What do we do?" Thomas asked, as quietly as possible. He tried to ignore the panic flaring inside him. "Is it coming toward us?"

"No, idiot—I just told you it was *sitting* there."

"Well?" Thomas raised his hands to his sides in frustration. "What do we do?" Standing so close to a Griever seemed like a really bad idea.

Minho paused a few seconds, thinking before he spoke. "We have to go that way to get to our section. Let's just watch it awhile—if it comes after us, we'll run back to the Glade." He took another peek, then quickly looked over his shoulder. "Crap—it's gone! Come on!"

Minho didn't wait for a response, didn't see the look of horror Thomas had just felt widen his own eyes. Minho took off running in the direction where he'd seen the Griever. Though his instincts told him not to, Thomas followed.

He sprinted down the long corridor after Minho, turned left, then right. At every turn, they slowed so the Keeper could look around the corner first. Each time he whispered back to Thomas that he'd seen the tail end of the Griever disappearing around the next turn. This went on for ten minutes, until they came to the long hallway that ended at the Cliff, where beyond lay nothing but the lifeless sky. The Griever was charging toward that sky.

Minho stopped so abruptly Thomas almost ran him over. Then Thomas stared in shock as up ahead the Griever dug in with its spikes and spun forward right up to the Cliff's edge, then off, into the gray abyss. The creature disappeared from sight, a shadow swallowed by more shadow.

CHAPTER 35

"That settles it," Minho said.

Thomas stood next to him on the edge of the Cliff, staring at the gray nothingness beyond. There was no sign of anything, to the left, right, down, up, or ahead, for as far as he could see. Nothing but a wall of blankness.

"Settles what?" Thomas asked.

"We've seen it three times now. Something's up."

"Yeah." Thomas knew what he meant, but waited for Minho's explanation anyway.

"That dead Griever I found—it ran this way, and we never saw it come back or go deeper into the Maze. Then those suckers we tricked into jumping past us."

"Tricked?" Thomas said. "Maybe not such a trick."

Minho looked over at him, contemplative. "Hmm. Anyway, then this." He pointed out at the abyss. "Not much doubt anymore—somehow the Grievers can *leave the Maze* this way. Looks like magic, but so does the sun disappearing."

"If *they* can leave this way," Thomas added, continuing Minho's line of reasoning, "so could we." A thrill of excitement shot through him.

Minho laughed. "There's your death wish again. Wanna hang out with the Grievers, have a sandwich, maybe?"

Thomas felt his hopes drop. "Got any better ideas?"

"One thing at a time, Greenie. Let's get some rocks and test this place out. There has to be some kind of hidden exit."

Thomas helped Minho as they scrabbled around the corners and crannies of the Maze, picking up as many loose stones as possible. They got more by thumbing cracks in the wall, spilling broken chunks onto the ground. When they finally had a sizable pile, they hauled it over right next to the edge and took a seat, feet dangling over the side. Thomas looked down and saw nothing but a gray descent.

Minho pulled out his pad and pencil, placed them on the ground next to him. "All right, we gotta take good notes. And memorize it in that shuck head of yours, too. If there's some kind of optical illusion hiding an exit from this place, I don't wanna be the one who screws up when the first shank tries to jump into it."

"That shank oughtta be the Keeper of the Runners," Thomas said, trying to make a joke to hide his fear. Being this close to a place where Grievers might come out at any second was making him sweat. "You'd wanna hold on to one beauty of a rope."

Minho picked up a rock from their pile. "Yeah. Okay, let's take turns tossing them, zigzagging back and forth out there. If there's some kind of magical exit, hopefully it'll work with rocks, too—make them disappear."

Thomas took a rock and carefully threw it to their left, just in front of where the left wall of the corridor leading to the Cliff met the edge. The jagged piece of stone fell. And fell. Then disappeared into the gray emptiness.

Minho went next. He tossed his rock just a foot or so farther out than Thomas had. It also fell far below. Thomas threw another one, another foot out. Then Minho. Each rock fell to the depths. Thomas kept following Minho's orders—they continued until they'd marked a line reaching at least a dozen feet from the Cliff, then moved their target pattern a foot to the right and started coming back toward the Maze.

All the rocks fell. Another line out, another line back. All the rocks fell. They threw enough rocks to cover the entire left half of the area in front of them, covering the distance anyone—or any*thing*—could possibly jump. Thomas's discouragement grew with every toss, until it turned into a heavy mass of blah.

He couldn't help chiding himself—it'd been a stupid idea.

Then Minho's next rock disappeared.

It was the strangest, most hard-to-believe thing Thomas had ever seen.

Minho had thrown a large chunk, a piece that had fallen from one of the cracks in the wall. Thomas had watched, deeply concentrating on each and every rock. This one left Minho's hand, sailed forward, almost in the exact center of the Cliff line, started its descent to the unseen ground far below. Then it vanished, as if it had fallen through a plane of water or mist.

One second there, falling. Next second gone.

Thomas couldn't speak.

"We've thrown stuff off the Cliff before," Minho said. "How could we have ever missed that? I never saw anything disappear. Never."

Thomas coughed; his throat felt raw. "Do it again—maybe we blinked weird or something."

Minho did, throwing it at the same spot. And once again, it winked out of existence.

"Maybe you weren't looking carefully other times you threw stuff over," Thomas said. "I mean, it should be impossible—sometimes you don't look very hard for things you don't believe will or can happen."

They threw the rest of the rocks, aiming at the original spot and every inch around it. To Thomas's surprise, the spot in which the rocks disappeared proved only to be a few feet square.

"No wonder we missed it," Minho said, furiously writing down notes and dimensions, his best attempt at a diagram. "It's kind of small."

"The Grievers must barely fit through that thing." Thomas kept his eyes riveted to the area of the invisible floating square, trying to burn the distance and location in his mind, remember exactly where it was. "And when they come out, they must balance on the rim of the hole and jump over the empty space to the Cliff edge—it's not that far. If I could jump it, I'm sure it's easy for them."

Minho finished drawing, then looked up at the special spot. "How's this possible, dude? What're we looking at?"

"Like you said, it's not magic. Must be something like our sky turning gray. Some kind of optical illusion or hologram, hiding a doorway. This place is all jacked up." And, Thomas admitted to himself, kind of cool. His mind craved to know what kind of technology could be behind it all.

"Yeah, jacked up is right. Come on." Minho got up with a grunt and put on his backpack. "Better get as much of the Maze run as we can. With our new decorated sky, maybe other weird things have happened out there. We'll tell Newt and Alby about this tonight. Don't know how it helps, but at least we know now where the shuck Grievers go."

"And probably where they come from," Thomas said as he took one last look at the hidden doorway. "The Griever Hole."

"Yeah, good a name as any. Let's go."

Thomas sat and stared, waiting for Minho to make a move. Several minutes passed in silence and Thomas realized his friend must be as fascinated as he was. Finally, without saying a word, Minho turned to leave. Thomas reluctantly followed and they ran into the gray-dark Maze.

★ ★ ★

Thomas and Minho found nothing but stone walls and ivy.

Thomas did the vine cutting and all the note-taking. It was hard for him to notice any changes from the day before, but Minho pointed out without thinking about it where the walls had moved. When they reached the final dead end and it was time to head back home, Thomas felt an almost uncontrollable urge to bag everything and stay there overnight, see what happened.

Minho seemed to sense it and grabbed his shoulder. "Not yet, dude. Not yet."

And so they'd gone back.

A somber mood rested over the Glade, an easy thing to happen when all is gray. The dim light hadn't changed a bit since they'd woken up that morning, and Thomas wondered if anything would change at "sunset" either.

Minho headed straight for the Map Room as they came through the West Door.

Thomas was surprised. He thought it was the last thing they should do. "Aren't you dying to tell Newt and Alby about the Griever Hole?"

"Hey, we're still Runners," Minho said, "and we still have a job." Thomas followed him to the steel door of the big concrete block and Minho turned to give him a wan smile. "But yeah, we'll do it quick so we can talk to them."

There were already other Runners milling about the room, drawing up their Maps when they entered. No one said a word, as if all speculation on the new sky had been exhausted. The hopelessness in the room made Thomas feel as if he were walking through mud-thick water. He knew he should also be exhausted, but he was too excited to feel it—he couldn't wait to see Newt's and Alby's reactions to the news about the Cliff.

He sat down at the table and drew up the day's Map based on his memory and notes, Minho looking over his shoulder the whole time, giving pointers. "I think that hall was actually cut off here, not there," and "Watch your proportions," and "Draw straighter, you shank." He was annoying but helpful, and fifteen minutes after entering the room, Thomas examined his finished product. Pride washed through him—it was just as good as any other Map he'd seen.

"Not bad," Minho said. "For a Greenie, anyway."

Minho got up and walked over to the Section One trunk and opened it. Thomas knelt down in front of it and took out the Map from the day before and held it up side by side with the one he'd just drawn.

"What am I looking for?" he asked.

"Patterns. But looking at two days' worth isn't gonna tell you jack. You really need to study several weeks, look for patterns, anything. I know there's something there, something that'll help us. Just can't find it yet. Like I said, it sucks."

Thomas had an itch in the back of his mind, the same one he'd felt the very first time in this room. The Maze walls, moving. Patterns. All those straight lines—were they suggesting an entirely different kind of map? Pointing to something? He had such a heavy feeling that he was missing an obvious hint or clue.

Minho tapped him on the shoulder. "You can always come back and study your butt off after dinner, after we talk to Newt and Alby. Come on."

Thomas put the papers in the trunk and closed it, hating the twinge of unease he felt. It was like a prick in his side. Walls moving, straight lines, patterns . . . There had to be an answer. "Okay, let's go."

They'd just stepped outside the Map Room, the heavy door clanging shut behind them, when Newt and Alby walked up, neither one of them looking very happy. Thomas's excitement immediately turned to worry.

"Hey," Minho said. "We were just—"

"Get on with it," Alby interrupted. "Ain't got time to waste. Find anything? Anything?"

Minho actually recoiled at the harsh rebuke, but his face seemed more confused to Thomas than hurt or angry. "Nice to see you, too. Yeah, we *did* find something, actually."

Oddly, Alby almost looked disappointed. "Cuz this whole shuck place is fallin' to pieces." He shot Thomas a nasty glare as if it were all his fault.

What's wrong *with him?* Thomas thought, feeling his own anger light up. They'd been working hard all day and this was their thanks?

"What do you mean?" Minho asked. "What else happened?"

Newt answered, nodding toward the Box as he did so. "Bloody supplies didn't come today. Come every week for two years, same time, same day. But not today."

All four of them looked over at the steel doors attached to the ground. To Thomas, there seemed to be a shadow hovering over it darker than the gray air surrounding everything else.

"Oh, we're shucked for good now," Minho whispered, his reaction alerting Thomas to how grave the situation really was.

"No sun for the plants," Newt said, "no supplies from the bloody Box—yeah, I'd say we're shucked, all right."

Alby had folded his arms, still glaring at the Box as if trying to open the doors with his mind. Thomas hoped their leader didn't bring up what he'd seen in the Changing—or anything related to Thomas, for that matter. Especially now.

"Yeah, anyway," Minho continued. "We found something weird."

Thomas waited, hoping that Newt or Alby would have a positive reaction to the news, maybe even have further information to shed light on the mystery.

Newt raised his eyebrows. "What?"

Minho took a full three minutes to explain, starting with the Griever they followed and ending with the results of their rock-throwing experiment.

"Must lead to where the . . . ya know . . . Grievers *live*," he said when finished.

"The Griever Hole," Thomas added. All three of them looked at him, annoyed, as if he had no right to speak. But for the first time, being treated like the Greenie didn't bother him that much.

"Gotta bloody see that for myself," Newt said. Then murmured, "Hard to believe." Thomas couldn't have agreed more.

"I don't know what we can do," Minho said. "Maybe we could build something to block off that corridor."

"No way," Newt said. "Shuck things can climb the bloody walls, remember? Nothing *we* could build would keep them out."

But a commotion outside the Homestead shifted their attention away from the conversation. A group of Gladers stood at the front door of the house, shouting to be heard over each other. Chuck was in the group, and when he saw Thomas and the others he ran over, a look of excitement spread across his face. Thomas could only wonder what crazy thing had happened now.

"What's going on?" Newt asked.

"She's awake!" Chuck yelled. "The girl's awake!"

Thomas's insides twisted; he leaned against the concrete wall of the Map Room. The girl. The girl who spoke in his head. He wanted to run before it happened again, before she spoke to him in his mind.

But it was too late.

Tom, I don't know any of these people. Come get me! It's all fading. . . .

I'm forgetting everything but you. . . . I have to tell you things! But it's all fading. . . .

He couldn't understand how she did it, how she was inside his head.

Teresa paused, then said something that made no sense.

The Maze is a code, Tom. The Maze is a code.

CHAPTER 36

Thomas didn't want to see her. He didn't want to see anybody.

As soon as Newt set off to go and talk to the girl, Thomas silently slipped away, hoping no one would notice him in the excitement. With everyone's thoughts on the stranger waking up from her coma, it proved easy. He skirted the edge of the Glade, then, breaking into a run, he headed for his place of seclusion behind the Deadhead forest.

He crouched in the corner, nestled in the ivy, and threw his blanket over himself, head and all. Somehow, it seemed like a way to hide from Teresa's intrusion into his mind. A few minutes passed, his heart finally calming to a slow roll.

"Forgetting about you was the worst part."

At first, Thomas thought it was another message in his head; he squeezed his fists against his ears. But no, it'd been . . . different. He'd heard it with his ears. A girl's voice. Chills creeping up his spine, he slowly lowered the blanket.

Teresa stood to his right, leaning against the massive stone wall. She looked so different now, awake and alert—*standing*. Wearing a long-sleeved white shirt, blue jeans, and brown shoes, she looked—impossibly—even more striking than when he'd seen her in the coma. Black hair framed the fair skin of her face, with eyes the blue of pure flame.

"Tom, do you really not remember me?" Her voice was soft, a contrast from the crazed, hard sound he'd heard from her after she first arrived, when she'd delivered the message that *everything was going to change.*

"You mean . . . you remember *me?*" he asked, embarrassed at the squeak that escaped on the last word.

"Yes. No. Maybe." She threw her arms up in disgust. "I can't explain it."

Thomas opened his mouth, then closed it without saying anything.

"I remember *remembering,*" she muttered, sitting down with a heavy sigh; she pulled her legs up to wrap her arms around her knees. "Feelings. Emotions. Like I have all these shelves in my head, labeled for memories and faces, but they're empty. As if everything before this is just on the other side of a white curtain. Including you."

"But how do you know me?" He felt like the walls were spinning around him.

Teresa turned toward him. "I don't know. Something about before we came to the Maze. Something about us. It's mostly empty, like I said."

"You know about the Maze? Who told you? You just woke up."

"I . . . It's all very confusing right now." She held a hand out. "But I know you're my friend."

Almost in a daze, Thomas pulled the blanket completely off and leaned forward to shake her hand. "I like how you call me Tom." As soon as it came out, he was sure he couldn't have possibly said anything dumber.

Teresa rolled her eyes. "That's your *name,* isn't it?"

"Yeah, but most people call me Thomas. Well, except Newt—he calls me Tommy. Tom makes me feel . . . like I'm at home or something. Even though I don't know what home *is.*" He let out a bitter laugh. "Are we messed up or what?"

She smiled for the first time, and he almost had to look away, as if something that nice didn't belong in such a glum and gray place, as if he had no right to look at her expression.

"Yeah, we're messed up," she said. "And I'm scared."

"So am I, trust me." Which was definitely the understatement of the day.

A long moment passed, both of them looking toward the ground.

"What's . . . ," he began, not sure how to ask it. "How . . . did you talk to me inside my mind?"

Teresa shook her head. *No idea—I can just do it,* she thought to him. Then she spoke aloud again. "It's like if you tried to ride a bicycle here—if they had one. I bet you could do it without thinking. But do you remember learning to ride one?"

"No. I mean . . . I remember riding one, but not learning." He paused, feeling a wave of sadness. "Or who taught me."

"Well," she said, her eyes flickering as if she was embarrassed by his sudden gloom. "Anyway . . . it's kind of like that."

"Really clears things up."

Teresa shrugged. "You didn't tell anyone, did you? They'd think we're crazy."

"Well . . . when it first happened, I did. But I think Newt just thinks I was stressed out or something." Thomas felt fidgety, like he'd go nuts if he didn't move. He stood up, started pacing in front of her. "We need to figure things out. That weird note you had about being the last person to ever come here, your coma, the fact you can talk to me telepathically. Any ideas?"

Teresa followed him with her eyes as he walked back and forth. "Save your breath and quit asking. All I have are faint impressions—

that you and I were important, that we were *used* somehow. That we're smart. That we came here for a reason. I know I triggered the Ending, whatever that means." She groaned, her face reddening. "My memories are as useless as yours."

Thomas knelt down in front of her. "No, they're not. I mean, the fact that you knew my memory had been wiped without asking me—and this other stuff. You're way ahead of me and everybody else."

Their eyes met for a long time; it looked like her mind was spinning, trying to make sense of it all.

I just don't know, she said in his mind.

"There you go again," Thomas said aloud, though he was relieved that her trick didn't really freak him out anymore. "How do you do that?"

"I just do, and I bet you can, too."

"Well, can't say I'm too anxious to try." He sat back down and pulled his legs up, much like she had done. "You said something to me—in my head—right before you found me over here. You said 'The Maze is a code.' What did you mean?"

She shook her head slightly. "When I first woke up, it was like I'd entered an insane asylum—these strange guys hovering over my bed, the world tipping around me, memories swirling in my brain. I tried to reach out and grasp a few, and that was one of them. I can't really remember *why* I said it."

"Was there anything else?"

"Actually, yeah." She pulled up the sleeve of her left arm, exposing her bicep. Small letters were written across the skin in thin black ink.

"What's that?" he asked, leaning in for a better look.

"Read it yourself."

The letters were messy, but he could make them out when he got close enough.

Thomas's heart beat faster. "I've seen that word—*wicked*." He searched his mind for what the phrase could possibly mean. "On the little creatures that live here. The beetle blades."

"What are those?" she asked.

"Just little lizardlike machines that spy on us for the Creators—the people who sent us here."

Teresa considered that for a moment, looking off into space. Then she focused on her arm. "I can't remember why I wrote this," she said as she wet her thumb and started rubbing off the words. "But don't let me forget—it has to mean something."

The three words ran through Thomas's mind over and over. "When did you write it?"

"When I woke up. They had a pen and notepad next to the bed. In the commotion I wrote it down."

Thomas was baffled by this girl—first the connection he'd felt to her from the very beginning, then the mind-speaking, now this. "Everything about you is weird. You know that, right?"

"Judging by your little hiding spot, I'd say you're not so normal yourself. Like living in the woods, do ya?"

Thomas tried to scowl, then smiled. He felt pathetic, and embarrassed about hiding. "Well, you look familiar to me and you claim we're friends. Guess I'll trust you."

He held out his hand for another shake, and she took it, holding on for a long time. A chill swept through Thomas that was surprisingly pleasant.

"All I want is to get back home," she said, finally letting go of his hand. "Just like the rest of you."

Thomas's heart sank as he snapped back to reality and remembered how grim the world had become. "Yeah, well, things pretty much suck right about now. The sun disappeared and the sky's gone gray, they didn't send us the weekly supplies—looks like things are going to end one way or another."

But before Teresa could answer, Newt was running out of the woods. "How in the . . . ," he said as he pulled up in front of them. Alby and a few others were right behind him. Newt looked at Teresa. "How'd you get here? Med-jack said you were there one second and buggin' gone the next."

Teresa stood up, surprising Thomas with her confidence. "Guess he forgot to tell the little part about me kicking him in the groin and climbing out the window."

Thomas almost laughed as Newt turned to an older boy standing nearby, whose face had turned bright red.

"Congrats, Jeff," Newt said. "You're officially the first guy here to get your butt beat by a *girl*."

Teresa didn't stop. "Keep talking like that and you'll be next."

Newt turned back to face them, but his face showed anything but fear. He stood, silently, just staring at them. Thomas stared back, wondering what was going through the older boy's head.

Alby stepped up. "I'm sick of this." He pointed at Thomas's chest, almost tapping it. "I wanna know who you are, who this shank girl is, and how you guys know each other."

Thomas almost wilted. "Alby, I swear—"

"She came straight to you after waking up, shuck-face!"

Anger surged inside Thomas—and worry that Alby would go off like Ben had. "So what? I know her, she knows me—or at least, we used to. That doesn't mean anything! I can't *remember* anything. Neither can she."

Alby looked at Teresa. "What did you do?"

Thomas, confused by the question, glanced at Teresa to see if *she* knew what he meant. But she didn't reply.

"What did you do!" Alby screamed. "First the sky, now this."

"I triggered something," she replied in a calm voice. "Not on purpose, I swear it. The Ending. I don't know what it means."

"What's wrong, Newt?" Thomas asked, not wanting to talk to Alby directly. "What happened?"

But Alby grabbed him by the shirt. "What happened? I'll tell ya what happened, shank. Too busy makin' lovey eyes to bother lookin' around? To bother noticing what freaking *time* it is!"

Thomas looked at his watch, realizing with horror what he'd missed, knowing what Alby was about to say before he said it.

"The *walls*, you shuck. The *Doors*. They didn't close tonight."

CHAPTER 37

Thomas was speechless. Everything would be different now. No sun, no supplies, no protection from the Grievers. Teresa had been right from the beginning—everything had changed. Thomas felt as if his breath had solidified, lodged itself in his throat.

Alby pointed at the girl. "I want her locked up. Now. Billy! Jackson! Put her in the Slammer, and ignore every word that comes out of her shuck mouth."

Teresa didn't react, but Thomas did enough for the both of them. "What're you talking about? Alby, you can't—" He stopped when Alby's fiery eyes shot such a look of anger at him he felt his heart stutter. "But . . . how could you possibly blame her for the walls not closing?"

Newt stepped up, lightly placed a hand on Alby's chest and pushed him back. "How could we not, Tommy? She bloody admitted it herself."

Thomas turned to look at Teresa, paled at the sadness in her blue eyes. It felt like something had reached through his chest and squeezed his heart.

"Just be glad you ain't goin' with her, Thomas," Alby said; he gave both of them one last glare before leaving. Thomas had never wanted so badly to punch someone.

Billy and Jackson came forward and grabbed Teresa by both arms, started escorting her away.

Before they could enter the trees, though, Newt stopped them. "Stay with her. I don't care what happens, no one's gonna touch this girl. Swear your lives on it."

The two guards nodded, then walked away, Teresa in tow. It hurt Thomas even more to see how willingly she went. And he couldn't believe how sad he felt—he wanted to keep talking to her. *But I just met her,* he thought. *I don't even know her.* Yet he knew that wasn't true. He already felt a closeness that could only have come from knowing her before the memory-wiped existence of the Glade.

Come see me, she said in his mind.

He didn't know how to do it, how to talk to her like that. But he tried anyway.

I will. At least you'll be safe in there.

She didn't respond.

Teresa?

Nothing.

The next thirty minutes were an eruption of mass confusion.

Though there had been no discernible change in the light since the sun and blue sky hadn't appeared that morning, it still felt like a darkness spread over the Glade. As Newt and Alby gathered the Keepers and put them in charge of making assignments and getting their groups inside the Homestead within the hour, Thomas felt like nothing more than a spectator, not sure how he could help.

The Builders—without their leader, Gally, who was still missing— were ordered to put up barricades at each open Door; they obeyed, although Thomas knew there wasn't enough time and there weren't materials to do much good. It almost seemed to him as if the Keepers wanted people busy, wanted to delay the inevitable panic attacks. Thomas helped as the Builders gathered every loose item they could find and piled them in the gaps, nailing things together as best they could. It looked ugly and pathetic and scared him to death—no way that'd keep the Grievers out.

As Thomas worked, he caught glimpses of the other jobs going on across the Glade.

Every flashlight in the compound was gathered and distributed to as many people as possible; Newt said he planned for everyone to sleep in the Homestead that night, and that they'd kill the lights, except for emergencies. Frypan's task was to take all the nonperishable food out of the kitchen and store it in the Homestead, in case they got trapped there—Thomas could only imagine how horrible that'd be. Others were gathering supplies and tools; Thomas saw Minho carrying weapons from the basement to the main building. Alby had made it clear they could take no chances: they'd make the Homestead their fortress, and must do whatever it took to defend it.

Thomas finally snuck away from the Builders and helped Minho, carrying up boxes of knives and barbwire-wrapped clubs. Then Minho said he had a special assignment from Newt, and more or less told Thomas to get lost, refusing to answer any of his questions.

This hurt Thomas's feelings, but he left anyway, really wanting to talk to Newt about something else. He finally found him, crossing the Glade on his way to the Blood House.

"Newt!" he called out, running to catch up. "You have to listen to me."

Newt stopped so suddenly Thomas almost ran into him. The older boy turned to give Thomas such an annoyed look he thought twice about saying anything.

"Make it quick," Newt said.

Thomas almost balked, not sure how to say what he was thinking.

"You've gotta let the girl go. Teresa." He knew that she could only help, that she might still remember something valuable.

"Ah, glad to know you guys are buddies now." Newt started walking off. "Don't waste my time, Tommy."

Thomas grabbed his arm. "Listen to me! There's something about her—I think she and I were sent here to help end this whole thing."

"Yeah—end it by lettin' the bloody Grievers waltz in here and kill us? I've heard some sucky plans in my day, Greenie, but that's got 'em all beat."

Thomas groaned, wanting Newt to know how frustrated he felt. "No, I don't think that's what it means—the walls not closing."

Newt folded his arms; he looked exasperated. "Greenie, what're you yappin' about?"

Ever since Thomas had seen the words on the wall of the Maze— *world in catastrophe, killzone experiment department*—he'd been thinking about them. He knew if there was anyone who would believe him, it would be Newt. "I think . . . I think we're here as part of some weird experiment, or test, or something like that. But it's supposed to end somehow. We can't live here forever—whoever sent us here *wants* it to end. One way or another." Thomas was relieved to get it off his chest.

Newt rubbed his eyes. "And that's supposed to convince me that everything's jolly—that I should let the girl go? Because she came and everything is suddenly do-or-die?"

"No, you're missing the *point*. I don't think she has anything to do with us being here. She's just a pawn—they sent her here as our last tool or hint or whatever to help us get out." Thomas took a deep breath. "And I think they sent me, too. Just because she was the trigger for the Ending doesn't make her bad."

Newt looked toward the Slammer. "You know what, I don't buggin' care right now. She can handle one night in there—if anything, she'll be safer than us."

Thomas nodded, sensing a compromise. "Okay, we get through tonight, somehow. Tomorrow, when we have a whole day of safety, we can figure out what to do with her. Figure out what we're supposed to do."

Newt snorted. "Tommy, what's gonna make tomorrow any different? It's been two bloody years, ya know."

Thomas had an overwhelming feeling that all of these changes were a spur, a catalyst for the endgame. "Because now we *have* to solve it. We'll be forced to. We can't live that way anymore, day to day, thinking that what matters most is getting back to the Glade before the Doors close, snug and safe."

Newt thought a minute as he stood there, the bustle of the Glader preparations surrounding both of them. "Dig deeper. Stay out there while the walls move."

"Exactly," Thomas said. "That's exactly what I'm talking about. And maybe we could barricade or blow up the entrance to the Griever Hole. Buy time to analyze the Maze."

"Alby's the one who won't let the girl out," Newt said with a nod toward the Homestead. "That guy's not too high on you two shanks. But right now we just gotta slim ourselves and get to the wake-up."

Thomas nodded. "We can fight 'em off."

"Done it before, haven't you, Hercules?" Without smiling or even waiting for a response, Newt walked away, yelling at people to finish up and get inside the Homestead.

Thomas was happy with the conversation—it had gone about as well as he could've possibly hoped. He decided to hurry and talk to Teresa before it was too late. As he sprinted for the Slammer on the back side of the Homestead, he watched as Gladers started moving inside, most of them with arms full of one thing or another.

Thomas pulled up outside the small jail and caught his breath. "Teresa?" he finally asked through the barred window of the lightless cell.

Her face popped up on the other side, startling him.

He let out a small yelp before he could stop it—it took him a second to recover his wits. "You can be downright spooky, ya know?"

"That's very sweet," she said. "Thanks." In the darkness her blue eyes seemed to glow like a cat's.

"You're welcome," he answered, ignoring her sarcasm. "Listen, I've been thinking." He paused to gather his thoughts.

"More than I can say for that Alby schmuck," she muttered.

Thomas agreed, but was anxious to say what he'd come to say. "There's gotta be a way out of this place—we just have to push it, stay out in the Maze longer. And what you wrote on your arm, and what you said about a code, it all has to mean something, right?" *It has to,* he thought. He couldn't help feeling some hope.

"Yeah, I've been thinking the same thing. But first—can't you get me out of here?" Her hands appeared, gripping the bars of the window. Thomas felt the ridiculous urge to reach out and touch them.

"Well, Newt said maybe tomorrow." Thomas was just glad he'd gotten that much of a concession. "You'll have to make it through the night in there. It might actually be the safest place in the Glade."

"Thanks for asking him. Should be fun sleeping on this cold floor." She motioned behind her with a thumb. "Though I guess a Griever can't squeeze through this window, so I'll be happy, right?"

The mention of Grievers surprised him—he didn't remember talking about them to her yet. "Teresa, are you sure you've forgotten everything?"

She thought a second. "It's weird—I guess I do remember some stuff. Unless I just heard people talking while I was in the coma."

"Well, I guess it doesn't matter right now. I just wanted to see you before I went inside for the night." But he didn't want to leave; he almost wished he could get thrown in the Slammer with her. He grinned inside—he could only imagine Newt's response to *that* request.

"Tom?" Teresa said.

Thomas realized he was staring off in a daze. "Oh, sorry. Yeah?"

Her hands slipped back inside, disappeared. All he could see were her eyes, the pale glow of her white skin. "I don't know if I can do this—stay in this jail all night."

Thomas felt an incredible sadness. He wanted to steal Newt's keys and help her escape. But he knew that was a ridiculous idea. She'd just have to suffer and make do. He stared into those glowing eyes. "At least it won't get completely dark—looks like we're stuck with this twilight junk twenty-four hours a day now."

"Yeah. . . ." She looked past him at the Homestead, then focused on him again. "I'm a tough girl—I'll be okay."

Thomas felt horrible leaving her there, but he knew he had no choice. "I'll make sure they let you out first thing tomorrow, okay?"

She smiled, making him feel better. "That's a promise, right?"

"Promise." Thomas tapped his right temple. "And if you get lonely, you can talk to me with your . . . trick all you want. I'll try to answer back." He'd accepted it now, almost wanted it. He just hoped he could figure out how to talk back, so they could have a conversation.

You'll get it soon, Teresa said in his mind.

"I wish." He stood there, really not wanting to leave. At all.

"You better go," she said. "I don't want your brutal murder on my conscience."

Thomas managed his own smile at that. "All right. See you to-morrow."

And before he could change his mind, he slipped away, heading around the corner toward the front door of the Homestead, just as the last couple of Gladers were entering, Newt shooing them in like errant chickens. Thomas stepped inside as well, followed by Newt, who closed the door behind him.

Just before it latched shut, Thomas thought he heard the first eerie moan of the Grievers, coming from somewhere deep in the Maze.

The night had begun.

CHAPTER 38

Most of them slept outside in normal times, so packing all those bodies into the Homestead made for a tight fit. The Keepers had organized and distributed the Gladers throughout the rooms, along with blankets and pillows. Despite the number of people and the chaos of such a change, a disturbing silence hung over the activities, as if no one wanted to draw attention to themselves.

When everyone was settled, Thomas found himself upstairs with Newt, Alby and Minho, and they were finally able to finish their discussion from earlier in the courtyard. Alby and Newt sat on the only bed in the room while Thomas and Minho sat next to them in chairs. The only other furniture was a crooked wooden dresser and a small table, on top of which rested a lamp providing what light they had. The gray darkness seemed to press on the window from outside, with promises of bad things to come.

"Closest I've come so far," Newt was saying, "to hangin' it all up. Shuck it all and kiss a Griever goodnight. Supplies cut, bloody gray skies, walls not closing. But we can't give up, and we all know it. The buggers who sent us here either want us dead or they're givin' us a spur. This or that, we gotta work our arses off till we're dead or not dead."

Thomas nodded, but didn't say anything. He agreed completely but had no concrete ideas on what to do. If he could just make it to tomorrow, maybe he and Teresa could come up with something to help.

Thomas glanced over at Alby, who was staring at the floor,

seemingly lost in his own gloomy thoughts. His face still wore the long, weary look of depression, his eyes sunken and hollow. The Changing had been aptly named, considering what it had done to him.

"Alby?" Newt asked. "Are you gonna pitch in?"

Alby looked up, surprise crossing his face as if he hadn't known that anyone else was in the room. "Huh? Oh. Yeah. Good that. But you've seen what happens at night. Just because Greenie the freaking superboy made it doesn't mean the rest of us can."

Thomas rolled his eyes ever so slightly at Minho—so tired of Alby's attitude.

If Minho felt the same way, he did a good job of hiding it. "I'm with Thomas and Newt. We gotta quit boohooing and feeling sorry for ourselves." He rubbed his hands together and sat forward in his chair. "Tomorrow morning, first thing, you guys can assign teams to study the Maps full-time while the Runners go out. We'll pack our stuff shuck-full so we can stay out there a few days."

"What?" Alby asked, his voice finally showing some emotion. "What do you mean, *days*?"

"I mean, *days*. With open Doors and no sunset, there's no point in coming back here, anyway. Time to stay out there and see if anything opens up when the walls move. *If* they still move."

"No way," Alby said. "We have the Homestead to hide in—and if that ain't workin', the Map Room and the Slammer. We can't freaking ask people to go out there and die, Minho! Who'd volunteer for that?"

"Me," Minho said. "And Thomas."

Everyone looked at Thomas; he simply nodded. Although it scared him to death, exploring the Maze—really exploring it—was something he'd wanted to do from the first time he'd learned about it.

"I will if I have to," Newt said, surprising Thomas; though he'd never talk about it, the older boy's limp was a constant reminder that something horrible had happened to him out in the Maze. "And I'm sure all the Runners'll do it."

"With your bum leg?" Alby asked, a harsh laugh escaping his lips.

Newt frowned, looked at the ground. "Well, I don't feel good askin' Gladers to do something if I'm not bloody willing to do it myself."

Alby scooted back on the bed and propped his feet up. "Whatever. Do what you want."

"Do what I want?" Newt asked, standing up. "What's wrong with you, man? Are you tellin' me we have a choice? Should we just sit around on our butts and wait to be snuffed by the Grievers?"

Thomas wanted to stand up and cheer, sure that Alby would finally snap out of his doldrums.

But their leader didn't look in the least bit reprimanded or re-morseful. "Well, it sounds better than running *to* them."

Newt sat back down. "Alby. You gotta start talkin' reason."

As much as he hated to admit it, Thomas knew they needed Alby if they were going to accomplish anything. The Gladers looked up to him.

Alby finally took a deep breath, then looked at each of them in turn. "You guys know I'm all screwed up. Seriously, I'm . . . sorry. I shouldn't be the stupid leader anymore."

Thomas held his breath. He couldn't believe Alby had just said that.

"Oh bloody—" Newt started.

"No!" Alby shouted, his face showing humility, surrender. "That's not what I meant. Listen to me. I ain't saying we should switch or any of that klunk. I'm just saying . . . I think I need to let you guys make the decisions. I don't trust myself. So . . . yeah, I'll do whatever."

Thomas could see that both Minho and Newt were as surprised as he was.

"Uh . . . okay," Newt said slowly. As if he was unsure. "We'll make it work, I promise. You'll see."

"Yeah," Alby muttered. After a long pause, he spoke up, a hint of odd excitement in his voice. "Hey, tell you what. Put me in charge of the Maps. I'll freaking work every Glader to the bone studying those things."

"Works for me," Minho said. Thomas wanted to agree, but didn't know if it was his place.

Alby put his feet back on the floor, sat up straighter. "Ya know, it was really stupid for us to sleep in here tonight. We should've been out in the Map Room, working."

Thomas thought that was the smartest thing he'd heard Alby say in a long time.

Minho shrugged. "Probably right."

"Well . . . I'll go," Alby said with a confident nod. "Right now."

Newt shook his head. "Forget that, Alby. Already heard the bloody Grievers moaning out there. We can wait till the wake-up."

Alby leaned forward, elbows on his knees. "Hey, you shucks are the ones giving me all the pep talks. Don't start whining when I actually listen. If I'm gonna do this, I gotta do it, be the old me. I need something to dive into."

Relief flooded Thomas. He'd grown sick of all the contention.

Alby stood up. "Seriously, I need this." He moved toward the door of the room as if he really meant to leave.

"You can't be serious," Newt said. "You can't go out there now!"

"I'm going, and that's that." Alby took his ring of keys from his pocket and rattled them mockingly—Thomas couldn't believe the sudden bravery. "See you shucks in the morning."

And then he walked out.

It was strange to know that the night grew later, that darkness should've swallowed the world around them, but to see only the pale gray light outside. It made Thomas feel off-kilter, as if the urge to sleep that grew steadily with every passing minute were somehow unnatural. Time slowed to an agonizing crawl; he felt as if the next day might never come.

The other Gladers settled themselves, turning in with their pillows and blankets for the impossible task of sleeping. No one said much, the mood somber and grim. All you could hear were quiet shuffles and whispers.

Thomas tried hard to force himself to sleep, knowing it would make the time pass faster, but after two hours he'd still had no luck. He lay on the floor in one of the upper rooms, on top of a thick blanket, several other Gladers crammed in there with him, almost body to body. The bed had gone to Newt.

Chuck had ended up in another room, and for some reason Thomas pictured him huddled in a dark corner, crying, squeezing his blankets to his chest like a teddy bear. The image saddened Thomas so deeply he tried to replace it, but to no avail.

Almost every person had a flashlight by their side in case of emergency. Otherwise, Newt had ordered all lights extinguished despite the pale, deathly glow of their new sky—no sense attracting any more attention than necessary. Anything that *could* be done on such short notice to prepare for a Griever attack had been done: windows boarded up, furniture moved in front of doors, knives handed out as weapons . . .

But none of that made Thomas feel safe.

The anticipation of what might happen was overpowering, a suffocating blanket of misery and fear that began to take on a life of its own. He almost wished the suckers would just come and get it over with. The waiting was unbearable.

The distant wails of the Grievers grew closer as the night stretched on, every minute seeming to last longer than the one before it.

Another hour passed. Then another. Sleep finally came, but in miserable fits. Thomas guessed it was about two in the morning when he turned from his back to his stomach for the millionth time that night. He put his hands under his chin and stared at the foot of the bed, almost a shadow in the dim light.

Then everything changed.

A mechanized surge of machinery sounded from outside, followed by the familiar rolling clicks of a Griever on the stony ground, as if someone had scattered a handful of nails. Thomas shot to his feet, as did most of the others.

But Newt was up before anyone, waving his arms, then shushing the room by putting a finger to his lips. Favoring his bad leg, he tiptoed toward the lone window in the room, which was covered by three hastily nailed boards. Large cracks allowed for plenty of space to peek outside. Carefully, Newt leaned in to take a look, and Thomas crept over to join him.

He crouched below Newt against the lowest of the wooden boards, pressing his eye against a crack—it was terrifying being so close to the wall. But all he saw was the open Glade; he didn't have enough space to look up or down or to the side, just straight ahead. After a minute or so, he gave up and turned to sit with his back against the wall. Newt walked over and sat back down on the bed.

A few minutes passed, various Griever sounds penetrating the walls every ten to twenty seconds. The squeal of small engines followed by a grinding spin of metal. The clicking of spikes against the hard stone. Things snapping and opening and snapping. Thomas winced in fear every time he heard something.

Sounded like three or four of them were just outside. At least.

He heard the twisted animal-machines come closer, so close, waiting on the stone blocks below. All hums and metallic clatter.

Thomas's mouth dried up—he'd seen them face to face, remembered it all too well; he had to remind himself to breathe. The others in the room were still; no one made a sound. Fear seemed to hover in the air like a blizzard of black snow.

One of the Grievers sounded like it was moving toward the house. Then the clicking of its spikes against the stone suddenly turned into a deeper, hollower sound. Thomas could picture it all: the creature's metal spikes digging into the wooden sides of the Homestead, the massive creature rolling its body, climbing up toward their room, defying gravity with its strength. Thomas heard the Grievers' spikes shred the wood siding in their path as they tore out and rotated around to take hold once again. The whole building shuddered.

The crunching and groaning and snapping of the wood became the only sounds in the world to Thomas, horrifying. They grew louder, *closer*—the other boys had shuffled across the room and as far away from the window as possible. Thomas finally followed suit, Newt right beside him; everyone huddled against the far wall, staring at the window.

Just when it grew unbearable—just as Thomas realized the Griever was right outside the window—everything fell silent. Thomas could almost hear his own heart beating.

Lights flickered out there, casting odd beams through the cracks between the wooden boards. Then a thin shadow interrupted the light, moving back and forth. Thomas knew that the Griever's probes and weapons had come out, searching for a feast. He imagined beetle blades out there, helping the creatures find their way. A few seconds later the shadow stopped; the light settled to a standstill, casting three unmoving planes of brightness into the room.

The tension in the air was thick; Thomas couldn't hear anyone breathing. He thought much the same must be going on in the other rooms of the Homestead. Then he remembered Teresa in the Slammer.

He was just wishing she'd say something to him when the door from the hallway suddenly whipped open. Gasps and shouts exploded throughout the room. The Gladers had been expecting something from the window, not from behind them. Thomas turned to see who'd opened the door, expecting a frightened Chuck or maybe a reconsidering Alby. But when he saw who stood there, his skull seemed to contract, squeezing his brain in shock.

It was Gally.

CHAPTER 39

Gally's eyes raged with lunacy; his clothes were torn and filthy. He dropped to his knees and stayed there, his chest heaving with deep, sucking breaths. He looked about the room like a rabid dog searching for someone to bite. No one said a word. It was as if they all believed as Thomas did—that Gally was only a figment of their imagination.

"They'll kill you!" Gally screamed, spittle flying everywhere. "The Grievers will kill you all—one every night till it's over!"

Thomas watched, speechless, as Gally staggered to his feet and walked forward, dragging his right leg with a heavy limp. No one in the room moved a muscle as they watched, obviously too stunned to do anything. Even Newt stood mouth agape. Thomas was almost more afraid of their surprise visitor than he was of the Grievers just outside the window.

Gally stopped, standing just a few feet in front of Thomas and Newt; he pointed at Thomas with a bloody finger. "You," he said with a sneer so pronounced it went past comical to flat-out disturbing. "It's all your fault!" Without warning he swung his left hand, forming it into a fist as it came around and crashed into Thomas's ear. Crying out, Thomas crumpled to the ground, more taken by surprise than pain. He scrambled to his feet as soon as he'd hit the floor.

Newt had finally snapped out of his daze and pushed Gally away. Gally stumbled backward and crashed into the desk by the window. The lamp scooted off the side and broke into pieces on the ground. Thomas

assumed Gally would retaliate, but he straightened instead, taking everyone in with his mad gaze.

"It can't be solved," he said, his voice now quiet and distant,
spooky. "The shuck Maze'll kill all you shanks. . . . The Grievers'll kill
you . . . one every night till it's over. . . . I . . . It's better this way. . . ."
His eyes fell to the floor. "They'll only kill you one a night . . . their
stupid Variables . . ."

Thomas listened in awe, trying to suppress his fear so he could
memorize everything the crazed boy said.

Newt took a step forward. "Gally, shut your bloody hole—there's
a Griever right out the window. Just sit on your butt and be quiet—
maybe it'll go away."

Gally looked up, his eyes narrowing. "You don't get it, Newt.
You're too stupid—you've always been too stupid. There's no way
out—there's no way to win! They're gonna kill you, all of you—one
by *one*!"

Screaming the last word, Gally threw his body toward the window
and started tearing at the wooden boards like a wild animal trying to
escape a cage. Before Thomas or anyone else could react, he'd already
ripped one board free; he threw it to the ground.

"No!" Newt yelled, running forward. Thomas followed to help, in
utter disbelief at what was happening.

Gally ripped off the second board just as Newt reached him. He
swung it backward with both hands and connected with Newt's head,
sent him sprawling across the bed as a small spray of blood sprinkled the
sheets. Thomas pulled up short, readying himself for a fight.

"Gally!" Thomas yelled. "What're you *doing*!"

The boy spat on the ground, panting like a winded dog. "You shut
your shuck-face, *Thomas*. You shut up! I know who you are, but I don't
care anymore. I can only do what's right."

Thomas felt as if his feet were rooted to the ground. He was completely baffled by what Gally was saying. He watched the boy reach back and rip loose the final wooden board. The instant the discarded slab hit the floor of the room, the glass of the window exploded inward like a swarm of crystal wasps. Thomas covered his face and fell to the floor, kicking his legs out to scoot his body as far away as possible. When he bumped into the bed, he gathered himself and looked up, ready to face his world coming to an end.

A Griever's pulsating, bulbous body had squirmed halfway through the destroyed window, metallic arms with pincers snapping and clawing in all directions. Thomas was so terrified, he barely registered that everyone else in the room had fled to the hallway—all except Newt, who lay unconscious on the bed.

Frozen, Thomas watched as one of the Griever's long arms reached for the lifeless body. That was all it took to break him from his fear. He scrambled to his feet, searched the floor around him for a weapon. All he saw were knives—they couldn't help him now. Panic exploded within him, consumed him.

Then Gally was speaking again; the Griever pulled back its arm, as if it needed the thing to be able to observe and listen. But its body kept churning, trying to squeeze its way inside.

"No one ever understood!" the boy screamed over the horrible noise of the creature, crunching its way deeper into the Homestead, ripping the wall to pieces. "No one ever understood what I saw, what the Changing did to me! Don't go back to the real world, Thomas! You *don't . . . want . . .* to remember!"

Gally gave Thomas a long, haunted look, his eyes full of terror; then he turned and dove onto the writhing body of the Griever. Thomas yelled out as he watched every extended arm of the monster immediately retract and clasp onto Gally's arms and legs, making escape or rescue impossible. The boy's body sank several inches into the creature's squishy flesh, making a horrific squelching sound. Then, with surprising speed, the Griever pushed itself back outside the shattered frame of the window and began descending toward the ground below.

Thomas ran to the jagged, gaping hole, looked down just in time to see the Griever land and start scooting across the Glade, Gally's body appearing and disappearing as the thing rolled. The lights of the monster shone brightly, casting an eerie yellow glow across the stone of the open West Door, where the Griever exited into the depths of the Maze. Then, seconds later, several other monsters followed close behind their companion, whirring and clicking as if celebrating their victory.

Thomas was sickened to the verge of throwing up. He began to back away from the window, but something outside caught his eye. He quickly leaned out of the building to get a better look. A lone shape was sprinting across the courtyard of the Glade toward the exit through which Gally had just been taken.

Despite the poor light, Thomas realized who it was immediately. He screamed—yelled at him to stop—but it was too late.

Minho, running full speed, disappeared into the Maze.

CHAPTER 40

Lights blazed throughout the Homestead. Gladers ran about, everyone talking at once. A couple of boys cried in a corner. Chaos ruled.

Thomas ignored all of it.

He ran into the hallway, then leaped down the stairs three at a time. He pushed his way through a crowd in the foyer, tore out of the Homestead and toward the West Door, sprinting. He pulled up just short of the threshold of the Maze, his instincts forcing him to think twice about entering. Newt called to him from behind, delaying the decision.

"Minho followed it out there!" Thomas yelled when Newt caught up to him, a small towel pressed against the wound on his head. A patchy spot of blood had already seeped through the white material.

"I saw," Newt said, pulling the towel away to look at it; he grimaced and put it back. "Shuck it, that hurts like a mother. Minho must've finally fried his last bit of brain cells—not to mention Gally. Always knew he was crazy."

Thomas could only worry about Minho. "I'm going after him."

"Time to be a bloody hero again?"

Thomas looked at Newt sharply, hurt by the rebuke. "You think I do things to impress you shanks? Please. All I care about is getting out of here."

"Yeah, well, you're a regular toughie. But right now we've got worse problems."

"What?" Thomas knew if he wanted to catch up with Minho he had no time for this.

"Somebody—" Newt began.

"There he is!" Thomas shouted. Minho had just turned a corner up ahead and was coming straight for them. Thomas cupped his hands. "What were you doing, idiot!"

Minho waited until he made it back through the Door, then bent over, hands on his knees, and sucked in a few breaths before answering. "I just . . . wanted to . . . make sure."

"Make sure of what?" Newt asked. "Lotta good you'd be, taken with Gally."

Minho straightened and put his hands on his hips, still breathing heavily. "Slim it, boys! I just wanted to see if they went toward the Cliff. Toward the Griever Hole."

"And?" Thomas said.

"Bingo." Minho wiped sweat from his forehead.

"I just can't believe it," Newt said, almost whispering. "What a night."

Thomas's thoughts tried to drift toward the Hole and what it all meant, but he couldn't shake the thought of what Newt had been about to say before they saw Minho return. "What were you about to tell me?" he asked. "You said we had worse—"

"Yeah." Newt pointed his thumb over his shoulder. "You can still see the buggin' smoke."

Thomas looked in that direction. The heavy metal door of the Map Room was slightly ajar, a wispy trail of black smoke drifting out and into the gray sky.

"Somebody burned the Map trunks," Newt said. "Every last one of 'em."

For some reason, Thomas didn't care about the Maps that much—they seemed pointless anyway. He stood outside the window of the Slammer, having left Newt and Minho when they went to investigate the sabotage of the Map Room. Thomas had noticed them exchange an odd look before they split up, almost as if communicating some secret with their eyes. But Thomas could think of only one thing.

"Teresa?" he asked.

Her face appeared, hands rubbing her eyes. "Was anybody killed?" she asked, somewhat groggy.

"Were you *sleeping*?" Thomas asked. He was relieved to see that she appeared okay, felt himself relax.

"I was," she responded. "Until I heard something shred the Homestead to bits. What happened?"

Thomas shook his head in disbelief. "I don't know how you could've slept through the sound of all those Grievers out here."

"You try coming out of a coma sometime. See how you do." *Now answer my question,* she said inside his head.

Thomas blinked, momentarily surprised by the voice since she hadn't done it in a while. "Cut that junk out."

"Just tell me what happened."

Thomas sighed; it was such a long story, and he didn't feel like telling the whole thing. "You don't know Gally, but he's a psycho kid who ran away. He showed up, jumped on a Griever, and they all took off into the Maze. It was really weird." He still couldn't believe it had actually happened.

"Which is saying a lot," Teresa said.

"Yeah." He looked behind him, hoping to see Alby somewhere.

262

Surely he'd let Teresa out now. Gladers were scattered all over the complex, but there was no sign of their leader. He turned back to Teresa. "I just don't get it. Why would the Grievers have left after getting Gally? He said something about them killing us one a night until we were all dead—he said it at least twice."

Teresa put her hands through the bars, rested her forearms against the concrete sill. "Just one a night? Why?"

"I don't know. He also said it had to do with . . . trials. Or variables. Something like that." Thomas had the same strange urge he'd had the night before—to reach out and take one of her hands. He stopped himself, though.

"Tom, I was thinking about what you told me I said. That the Maze is a code. Being holed up in here does wonders for making the brain do what it was made for."

"What do you think it means?" Intensely interested, he tried to block out the shouts and chatter rumbling through the Glade as others found out about the Map Room being burned.

"Well, the walls move every day, right?"

"Yeah." He could tell she was really on to something.

"And Minho said they think there's a pattern, right?"

"Right." Gears were starting to shift into place inside Thomas's head as well, almost as if a prior memory was beginning to break loose.

"Well, I can't remember why I said that to you about the code. I know when I was coming out of the coma all sorts of thoughts and memories swirled through my head like crazy, almost as if I could feel someone *emptying* my mind, sucking them out. And I felt like I needed to say that thing about the code before I lost it. So there must be an important reason."

Thomas almost didn't hear her—he was thinking harder than he had in a while. "They always compare each section's Map to the one

263

from the day before, and the day before that, and the day before that, day by day, each Runner just analyzing their own Section. What if they're supposed to compare the Maps to *other* sections . . ." He trailed off, feeling like he was on the cusp of something.

Teresa seemed to ignore him, doing her own theorizing. "The first thing the word *code* makes me think of is letters. Letters in the alphabet. Maybe the Maze is trying to *spell* something."

Everything came together so quickly in Thomas's mind, he almost heard an audible click, as if the pieces all snapped into place at once. "You're right—you're right! But the Runners have been looking at it wrong this whole time. They've been analyzing it the wrong way!"

Teresa gripped the bars now, her knuckles white, her face pressed against the iron rods. "What? What're you talking about?"

Thomas grabbed the two bars outside of where she held on, moved close enough to smell her—a surprisingly pleasant scent of sweat and flowers. "Minho said the patterns repeat themselves, only they can't figure out what it means. But they've always studied them section by section, comparing one day to the next. What if each day is a separate piece of the code, and they're supposed to use all eight sections together somehow?"

"You think maybe each day is trying to reveal a word?" Teresa asked. "With the wall movements?"

Thomas nodded. "Or maybe a letter a day, I don't know. But they've always thought the movements would reveal how to escape, not spell something. They've been studying it like a map, not like a picture of something. We've gotta—" Then he stopped, remembering what he'd just been told by Newt. "Oh, no."

Teresa's eyes flared with worry. "What's wrong?"

"Oh no oh no oh no . . ." Thomas let go of the bars and stumbled back a step as the realization hit him. He turned to look at the Map

Room. The smoke had lessened, but it still wafted out the door, a dark, hazy cloud covering the entire area.

"What's wrong?" Teresa repeated. She couldn't see the Map Room from her angle.

Thomas faced her again. "I didn't think it mattered. . . ."

"What!" she demanded.

"Someone *burned* all the Maps. If there was a code, it's gone."

CHAPTER 41

"I'll be back," Thomas said, turning to go. His stomach was full of acid. "I gotta find Newt, see if any of the Maps survived."

"Wait!" Teresa yelled. "Get me out of here!"

But there was no time, and Thomas felt awful about it. "I can't— I'll be back, I promise." He turned before she could protest and set off at a sprint for the Map Room and its foggy black cloud of smoke. Needles of pain pricked his insides. If Teresa was right, and they'd been that close to figuring out some kind of clue to get out of there, only to see it literally lost in flames . . . It was so upsetting it hurt.

The first thing Thomas saw when he ran up was a group of Gladers huddled just outside the large steel door, still ajar, its outer edge blackened with soot. But as he got closer, he realized they were surrounding something on the ground, all of them looking down at it. He spotted Newt, kneeling there in the middle, leaning over a body.

Minho was standing behind him, looking distraught and dirty, and spotted Thomas first. "Where'd you go?" he asked.

"To talk to Teresa—what happened?" He waited anxiously for the next dump of bad news.

Minho's forehead creased in anger. "Our Map Room was set on fire and you ran off to talk to your shuck girlfriend? What's wrong with you?"

Thomas knew the rebuke should've stung, but his mind was too preoccupied. "I didn't think it mattered anymore—if you haven't figured out the Maps by now . . ."

Minho looked disgusted, the pale light and fog of smoke making his face seem almost sinister. "Yeah, this'd be a great freaking time to give up. What the—"

"I'm sorry—just tell me what happened." Thomas leaned over the shoulder of a skinny boy standing in front of him to get a look at the body on the ground.

It was Alby, flat on his back, a huge gash on his forehead. Blood seeped down both sides of his head, some into his eyes, crusting there. Newt was cleaning it with a wet rag, gingerly, asking questions in a whisper too low to hear. Thomas, concerned for Alby despite his recent ill-tempered ways, turned back to Minho and repeated his question.

"Winston found him out here, half dead, the Map Room blazing. Some shanks got in there and put it out, but way too late. All the trunks are burned to a freaking crisp. I suspected Alby at first, but whoever did it slammed his shuck head against the table—you can see where. It's nasty."

"Who do you think did it?" Thomas was hesitant to tell him about the possible discovery he and Teresa had made. With no Maps, the point was moot.

"Maybe Gally before he showed up in the Homestead and went psycho? Maybe the Grievers? I don't know, and I don't care. Doesn't matter."

Thomas was surprised at the sudden change of heart. "Now who's the one giving up?"

Minho's head snapped up so quickly, Thomas took a step backward. There was a flash of anger there, but it quickly melted into an odd expression of surprise or confusion. "That's not what I meant, shank."

Thomas narrowed his eyes in curiosity. "What did—"

"Just shut your hole for now." Minho put his fingers to his lips, his eyes darting around to see if anyone was looking at him. "Just shut your hole. You'll find out soon enough."

Thomas took a deep breath and thought. If he expected the other boys to be honest, he should be honest too. He decided he'd better share about the possible Maze code, Maps or no Maps. "Minho, I need to tell you and Newt something. And we need to let Teresa out—she's probably starving and we could use her help."

"That stupid girl is the last thing I'm worried about."

Thomas ignored the insult. "Just give us a few minutes—we have an idea. Maybe it'll still work if enough Runners remember their Maps."

This seemed to get Minho's full attention—but again, there was that same strange look, as if Thomas was missing something very obvious. "An idea? What?"

"Just come over to the Slammer with me. You and Newt."

Minho thought for a second. "Newt!" he called out.

"Yeah?" Newt stood up, refolding his bloody rag to find a clean spot. Thomas couldn't help noticing that every inch was drenched in red.

Minho pointed down at Alby. "Let the Med-jacks take care of him. We need to talk."

Newt gave him a questioning look, then handed the rag to the closest Glader. "Go find Clint—tell him we got worse problems than guys with buggin' splinters." When the kid ran off to do as he was told, Newt stepped away from Alby. "Talk about what?"

Minho nodded at Thomas, but didn't say anything.

"Just come with me," Thomas said. Then he turned and headed for the Slammer without waiting for a response.

"Let her out." Thomas stood by the cell door, arms folded. "Let her out, and then we'll talk. Trust me—you wanna hear it."

Newt was covered in soot and dirt, his hair matted with sweat. He certainly didn't seem to be in a very good mood. "Tommy, this is—"

"*Please*. Just open it—let her out. Please." He wouldn't give up this time.

Minho stood in front of the door with his hands on his hips. "How can we trust her?" he asked. "Soon as she woke up, the whole place fell to pieces. She even *admitted* she triggered something."

"He's got a point," Newt said.

Thomas gestured through the door at Teresa. "We can trust her. Every time I've talked to her, it's something about trying to get out of here. She was sent here just like the rest of us—it's stupid to think she's responsible for any of this."

Newt grunted. "Then what the bloody shuck did she mean by sayin' she triggered something?"

Thomas shrugged, refusing to admit that Newt had a good point. There had to be an explanation. "Who knows—her mind was doing all kinds of weird stuff when she woke up. Maybe we all went through that in the Box, talking gibberish before we came totally awake. Just let her out."

Newt and Minho exchanged a long look.

"Come on," Thomas insisted. "What's she gonna do, run around and stab every Glader to death? Come on."

Minho sighed. "Fine. Just let the stupid girl out."

"I'm not stupid!" Teresa shouted, her voice muffled by the walls. "And I can hear every word you morons are saying!"

Newt's eyes widened. "Real sweet girl you picked up, Tommy."

"Just hurry," Thomas said. "I'm sure we have a lot to do before the Grievers come back tonight—if they don't come during the day."

Newt grunted and stepped up to the Slammer, pulling his keys out as he did so. A few clinks later the door swung wide open. "Come on."

Teresa walked out of the small building, glowering at Newt as she passed him. She gave a just-as-unpleasant glance toward Minho, then stopped to stand right next to Thomas. Her arm brushed against his; tingles shot across his skin, and he felt mortally embarrassed.

"All right, talk," Minho said. "What's so important?"

Thomas looked at Teresa, wondering how to say it.

"What?" she said. "You talk—they obviously think I'm a serial killer."

"Yeah, you look so dangerous," Thomas muttered, but he turned his attention to Newt and Minho. "Okay, when Teresa was first coming out of her deep sleep, she had memories flashing through her mind. She, um"—he just barely stopped himself from saying she'd said it inside his mind—"she told me later that she remembers that the Maze is a *code*. That maybe instead of solving it to find a way out, it's trying to send us a message."

"A *code*?" Minho asked. "How's it a code?"

Thomas shook his head, wishing he could answer. "I don't know for sure—you're way more familiar with the Maps than I am. But I have a theory. That's why I was hoping you guys could remember some of them."

Minho glanced at Newt, his eyebrows raised in question. Newt nodded.

"What?" Thomas asked, fed up with them keeping information from him. "You guys keep acting like you have a secret."

Minho rubbed his eyes with both hands, took a deep breath. "We hid the Maps, Thomas."

At first it didn't compute. "Huh?"

Minho pointed at the Homestead. "We hid the freaking Maps in

270

the weapons room, put dummies in their place. Because of Alby's warning. And because of the so-called *Ending* your girlfriend triggered."

Thomas was so excited to hear this news he temporarily forgot how awful things had become. He remembered Minho acting suspicious the day before, saying he had a special assignment. Thomas looked over at Newt, who nodded.

"They're all safe and sound," Minho said. "Every last one of those suckers. So if you have a theory, get talking."

"Take me to them," Thomas said, itching to have a look.

"Okay, let's go."

CHAPTER 42

Minho switched on the light, making Thomas squint for a second until his eyes got used to it. Menacing shadows clung to the boxes of weapons scattered across the table and floor, blades and sticks and other nasty-looking devices seeming to wait there, ready to take on a life of their own and kill the first person stupid enough to come close. The dank, musty smell only added to the creepy feel of the room.

"There's a hidden storage closet back here," Minho explained, walking past some shelves into a dark corner. "Only a couple of us know about it."

Thomas heard the creak of an old wooden door, and then Minho was dragging a cardboard box across the floor; the scrape of it sounded like a knife on bone. "I put each trunk's worth in its own box, eight boxes total. They're all in there."

"Which one is this?" Thomas asked; he knelt down next to it, eager to get started.

"Just open it and see—each page is marked, remember?"

Thomas pulled on the crisscrossed lid flaps until they popped open. The Maps for Section Two lay in a messy heap. Thomas reached in and pulled out a stack.

"Okay," he said. "The Runners have always compared these day to day, looking to see if there was a pattern that would somehow help figure out a way to an exit. You even said you didn't really know *what* you were looking for, but you kept studying them anyway. Right?"

Minho nodded, arms folded. He looked as if someone were about to reveal the secret of immortal life.

"Well," Thomas continued, "what if all the wall movements had nothing to do with a map or a maze or anything like that? What if instead the pattern spelled *words*? Some kind of clue that'll help us escape."

Minho pointed at the Maps in Thomas's hand, letting out a frustrated sigh. "Dude, you have any idea how much we've studied these things? Don't you think we would've noticed if it were spelling out freaking *words*?"

"Maybe it's too hard to see with the naked eye, just comparing one day to the next. And maybe you weren't supposed to compare one day to the next, but look at it one day at a time?"

Newt laughed. "Tommy, I might not be the sharpest guy in the Glade, but sounds like you're talkin' straight out your butt to me."

While he'd been talking, Thomas's mind had been spinning even faster. The answer was within his grasp—he knew he was almost there. It was just so hard to put into words.

"Okay, okay," he said, starting over. "You've always had one Runner assigned to one section, right?"

"Right," Minho replied. He seemed genuinely interested and ready to understand.

"And that Runner makes a Map every day, and then compares it to Maps from previous days, *for that section*. What if, instead, you were supposed to compare the eight sections to *each other*, every day? Each day being a separate clue or code? Did you ever compare sections to other sections?"

Minho rubbed his chin, nodding. "Yeah, kind of. We tried to see if they made something when put together—of course we did that. We've tried everything."

Thomas pulled his legs up underneath him, studying the Maps in his lap. He could just barely see the lines of the Maze written on the second page through the page resting on top. In that instant, he knew what they had to do. He looked up at the others.

"Wax paper."

"Huh?" Minho asked. "What the—"

"Just trust me. We need wax paper and scissors. And every black marker and pencil you can find."

Frypan wasn't too happy having a whole box of his wax paper rolls taken away from him, especially with their supplies being cut off. He argued that it was one of the things he always requested, that he used it for baking. They finally had to tell him what they needed it for to convince him to give it up.

After ten minutes of hunting down pencils and markers—most had been in the Map Room and were destroyed in the fire—Thomas sat around the worktable in the weapons basement with Newt, Minho and Teresa. They hadn't found any scissors, so Thomas had grabbed the sharpest knife he could find.

"This better be good," Minho said. Warning laced his voice, but his eyes showed some interest.

Newt leaned forward, putting his elbows on the table, as if waiting for a magic trick. "Get on with it, Greenie."

"Okay." Thomas was eager to do so, but was also scared to death it might end up being nothing. He handed the knife to Minho, then pointed at the wax paper. "Start cutting rectangles, about the size of the Maps. Newt and Teresa, you can help me grab the first ten or so Maps from each section box."

"What is this, kiddie craft time?" Minho held up the knife and looked at it with disgust. "Why don't you just tell us what the klunk we're doing this for?"

"I'm done explaining," Thomas said, knowing they just had to see what he was picturing in his mind. He stood to go rummage through the storage closet. "It'll be easier to show you. If I'm wrong, I'm wrong, and we can go back to running around the Maze like mice."

Minho sighed, clearly irritated, then muttered something under his breath. Teresa had stayed quiet for a while, but she spoke up inside Thomas's head.

I think I know what you're doing. Brilliant, actually.

Thomas was startled, but he tried his best to cover it up. He knew he had to pretend he didn't have voices in his head—the others would think he was a lunatic.

Just . . . come . . . help . . . me, he tried to say back, thinking each word separately, trying to visualize the message, *send* it. But she didn't respond.

"Teresa," he said aloud. "Can you help me a second?" He nodded toward the closet.

The two of them went into the dusty little room and opened up all the boxes, grabbing a small stack of Maps from each one. Returning to the table, Thomas found that Minho had cut twenty sheets already, making a messy pile to his right as he threw each new piece on top.

Thomas sat down and grabbed a few. He held one of the papers up to the light, saw how it shone through with a milky glow. It was exactly what he needed.

He grabbed a marker. "All right, everybody trace the last ten or so days onto a piece of this stuff. Make sure you write the info on top so we can keep track of what's what. When we're done, I think we might see something."

"What—" Minho began.

"Just bloody keep cutting," Newt ordered. "I think I know where he's going with this." Thomas was relieved someone was finally getting it.

They got to work, tracing from original Maps to wax paper, one by one, trying to keep it clean and correct while hurrying as fast as possible. Thomas used the side of a stray slab of wood as a makeshift ruler, keeping his lines straight. Soon he'd completed five maps, then five more. The others kept the same pace, working feverishly.

As Thomas drew, he started to feel a tickle of panic, a sick feeling that what they were doing was a complete waste of time. But Teresa, sitting next to him, was a study in concentration, her tongue sticking out the corner of her mouth as she traced lines up and down, side to side. She seemed way more confident that they were definitely on to something.

Box by box, section by section, they continued on.

"I've had enough," Newt finally announced, breaking the quiet. "My fingers are bloody burning like a mother. See if it's working."

Thomas put his marker down, then flexed his fingers, hoping he'd been right about all this. "Okay, give me the last few days of each section—make piles along the table, in order from Section One to Section Eight. One here"—he pointed at an end—"to Eight here." He pointed at the other end.

Silently, they did as he asked, sorting through what they'd traced until eight low stacks of wax paper lined the table.

Jittery and nervous, Thomas picked up one page from each pile, making sure they were all from the same day, keeping them in order. He then laid them one on top of the other so that each drawing of the Maze matched the same day above it and below it, until he was looking at eight different sections of the Maze at once. What he saw amazed him. Almost magically, like a picture coming into focus, an image developed. Teresa let out a small gasp.

Lines crossed each other, up and down, so much so that what

Thomas held in his hands looked like a checkered grid. But certain lines in the middle—lines that happened to appear more often than any other—made a slightly darker image than the rest. It was subtle, but it was, without a doubt, there.

Sitting in the exact center of the page was the letter F.

CHAPTER 43

Thomas felt a rush of different emotions: relief that it had worked, surprise, excitement, wonder at what it could lead to.

"Man," Minho said, summing up Thomas's feelings with one word.

"Could be a coincidence," Teresa said. "Do more, quick."

Thomas did, putting together the eight pages of each day, in order from Section One to Section Eight. Each time, an obvious letter formed in the center of the crisscrossed mass of lines. After the *F* was an *L,* then an *O,* then an *A,* and a *T.* Then *C* . . . *A* . . . *T.*

"Look," Thomas said, pointing down the line of stacks they'd formed, confused, but happy that the letters were so obvious. "It spells *FLOAT* and then it spells *CAT.*"

"Float cat?" Newt asked. "Doesn't sound like a bloody rescue code to me."

"We just need to keep working," Thomas said.

Another couple of combinations made them realize that the second word was actually *CATCH. FLOAT* and *CATCH.*

"Definitely not a coincidence," Minho said.

"Definitely not," Thomas agreed. He couldn't wait to see more.

Teresa gestured toward the storage closet. "We need to go through all of them—all those boxes in there."

"Yeah," Thomas nodded. "Let's get on it."

"We can't help," Minho said.

All three of them looked at him. He returned their glares. "At least not me and Thomas here. We need to get the Runners out in the Maze."

"What?" Thomas asked. "This is way more important!"

"Maybe," Minho answered calmly, "but we can't miss a day out there. Not now."

Thomas felt a rush of disappointment. Running the Maze seemed like such a waste of time compared to figuring out the code. "Why, Minho? You said the pattern's basically been repeating itself for months—one more day won't mean a thing."

Minho slammed his hand against the table. "That's bullcrap, Thomas! Of all days, this might be the most important to get out there. Something might've changed, something might've opened up. In fact, with the freaking walls not closing anymore, I think we should try your idea—stay out there overnight and do some deeper exploring."

That piqued Thomas's interest—he *had* been wanting to do that. Conflicted, he asked, "But what about this code? What about—"

"Tommy," Newt said in a consoling voice. "Minho's right. You shanks go out and get Runnin'. I'll round up some Gladers we can trust and get workin' on this." Newt sounded more like a leader than ever before.

"Me too," Teresa agreed. "I'll stay and help Newt."

Thomas looked at her. "You sure?" He was itching to figure out the code himself, but he decided Minho and Newt were right.

She smiled and folded her arms. "If you're going to decipher a hidden code from a complex set of different mazes, I'm pretty sure you need a girl's brain running the show." Her grin turned into a smirk.

"If you say so." He folded his own arms, staring at her with a smile, suddenly not wanting to leave again.

"Good that." Minho nodded and turned to go. "Everything's fine and dandy. Come on." He started toward the door, but stopped when he realized Thomas wasn't behind him.

"Don't worry, Tommy," Newt said. "Your girlfriend will be fine."

Thomas felt a million thoughts go through his head in that moment. An itch to learn the code, embarrassment at what Newt thought of him and Teresa, the intrigue of what they might find out in the Maze—and fear.

But he pushed it all aside. Without even saying goodbye, he finally followed Minho and they went up the stairs.

Thomas helped Minho gather the Runners to give them the news and organize them for the big journey. He was surprised at how readily everyone agreed that it was time to do some more in-depth exploring of the Maze and stay out there overnight. Even though he was nervous and scared, he told Minho he could take one of the sections himself, but the Keeper refused. They had eight experienced Runners to do that. Thomas was to go with him—which made Thomas so relieved he was almost ashamed of himself.

He and Minho packed their backpacks with more supplies than usual; there was no telling how long they'd be out there. Despite his fear, Thomas couldn't help being excited as well—maybe this was the day they'd find an exit.

He and Minho were stretching their legs by the West Door when Chuck walked over to say goodbye.

"I'd go with you," the boy said in a far too jovial voice, "but I don't wanna die a gruesome death."

Thomas laughed, surprising himself. "Thanks for the words of encouragement."

"Be careful," Chuck said, his tone quickly melting into genuine concern. "I wish I could help you guys."

Thomas was touched—he bet that if it really came down to it, Chuck *would* go out there if he were asked to. "Thanks, Chuck. We'll definitely be careful."

Minho grunted. "Being careful hasn't gotten us squat. It's all or nothing now, baby."

"We better get going," Thomas said. Butterflies swarmed in his gut, and he just wanted to *move,* to quit thinking about it. After all, going out in the Maze was no worse than staying in the Glade with open Doors. Though the thought didn't make him feel much better.

"Yeah," Minho responded evenly. "Let's go."

"Well," Chuck said, looking down at his feet before returning his gaze to Thomas. "Good luck. If your girlfriend gets lonely for you, I'll give her some lovin'."

Thomas rolled his eyes. "She's not my girlfriend, shuck-face."

"Wow," Chuck said. "You're already using Alby's dirty words." He was obviously trying hard to pretend he wasn't scared of all the recent developments, but his eyes revealed the truth. "Seriously, good luck."

"Thanks, that means a lot," Minho answered with his own eye roll. "See ya, shank."

"Yeah, see ya," Chuck muttered, then turned to walk away.

Thomas felt a pang of sadness—it was possible he might never see Chuck or Teresa or any of them again. A sudden urge gripped him. "Don't forget my promise!" he yelled. "I'll get you home!"

Chuck turned and gave him a thumbs-up; his eyes glimmered with tears.

Thomas flipped up double thumbs; then he and Minho pulled on their backpacks and entered the Maze.

CHAPTER 44

Thomas and Minho didn't stop until they were halfway to the last dead end of Section Eight. They made good time—Thomas was glad for his wristwatch, with the skies being gray—because it quickly became obvious that the walls hadn't moved from the day before. Everything was exactly the same. There was no need for Mapmaking or taking notes; their only task was to get to the end and start making their way back, searching for things previously unnoticed—anything. Minho allowed a twenty-minute break and then they were back at it.

They were silent as they ran. Minho had taught Thomas that speaking only wasted energy, so he concentrated on his pace and his breaths. Regular. Even. In, out. In, out. Deeper and deeper into the Maze they went, with only their thoughts and the sounds of their feet thumping against the hard stone floor.

In the third hour, Teresa surprised him, speaking in his mind from back in the Glade.

We're making progress—found a couple more words already. But none of it makes sense yet.

Thomas's first instinct was to ignore her, to deny once again that someone had the ability to enter his mind, invade his privacy. But he *wanted* to talk to her.

Can you hear me? he asked, picturing the words in his mind, mentally throwing them out to her in some way he could never have explained. Concentrating, he said it again. *Can you hear me?*

Yes! she replied. *Really clearly the second time you said it.*

Thomas was shocked. So shocked he almost quit running. It had worked!

Wonder why we can do this, he called out with his mind. The mental effort of speaking to her was already straining—he felt a headache forming like a bulge in his brain.

Maybe we were lovers, Teresa said.

Thomas tripped and crashed to the ground. Smiling sheepishly at Minho, who'd turned to look without slowing, Thomas got back up and caught up to him. *What?* he finally asked.

He sensed a laugh from her, a watery image full of color. *This is so bizarre,* she said. *It's like you're a stranger, but I know you're not.*

Thomas felt a pleasant chill even though he was sweating. *Sorry to break it to you, but we* are *strangers. I just met you, remember?*

Don't be stupid, Tom. I think someone altered our brains, put something in there so we could do this telepathy thing. Before *we came here. Which makes me think we already knew each other.*

It was something he'd wondered about, and he thought she was probably right. Hoped it, anyway—he was really starting to like her. *Brains altered?* he asked. *How?*

I don't know—some memory I can't quite grasp. I think we did something big.

Thomas thought about how he'd always felt a connection to her, ever since she arrived in the Glade. He wanted to dig a little more and see what she said. *What are you talking about?*

Wish I knew. I'm just trying to bounce ideas off you to see if it sparks anything in your mind.

Thomas thought about what Gally, Ben and Alby had said about him—their suspicions that he was against them somehow, was someone not to trust. He thought about what *Teresa* had said to him, too, the very first time—that he and she had somehow done all of this to them.

This code has to mean something, she added. *And the thing I wrote on my arm*—WICKED is good.

Maybe it won't matter, he answered. *Maybe we'll find an exit. You never know.*

Thomas squeezed his eyes shut for a few seconds as he ran, trying to concentrate. A pocket of air seemed to float in his chest every time they spoke, a swelling that half annoyed and half thrilled him. His eyes popped back open when he realized she could maybe read his thoughts even when he wasn't trying to communicate. He waited for a response, but none came.

You still there? he asked.

Yeah, but this always gives me a headache.

Thomas was relieved to hear he wasn't the only one. *My head hurts, too.*

Okay, she said. *See you later.*

No, wait! He didn't want her to leave; she was helping the time pass. Making the running easier somehow.

Bye, Tom. I'll let you know if we figure anything out.

Teresa—what about the thing you wrote on your arm?

Several seconds passed. No reply.

Teresa?

She was gone. Thomas felt as if that bubble of air in his chest had burst, releasing toxins into his body. His stomach hurt, and the thought of running the rest of the day suddenly depressed him.

In some ways, he wanted to tell Minho about how he and Teresa could talk, to share what was happening before it made his brain explode. But he didn't dare. Throwing telepathy into the whole situation didn't seem like the grandest of ideas. Everything was weird enough already.

Thomas put his head down and drew in a long, deep breath. He would just keep his mouth shut and run.

Two breaks later, Minho finally slowed to a walk as they headed down a long corridor that ended in a wall. He stopped and took a seat against the dead end. The ivy was especially thick there; it made the world seem green and lush, hiding the hard, impenetrable stone.

Thomas joined him on the ground and they attacked their modest lunch of sandwiches and sliced fruit.

"This is it," Minho said after his second bite. "We've already run through the whole section. Surprise, surprise—no exits."

Thomas already knew this, but hearing it made his heart sink even lower. Without another word—from himself or Minho—he finished his food and readied himself to explore. To look for who-knew-what.

For the next few hours, he and Minho scoured the ground, felt along the walls, climbed up the ivy in random spots. They found nothing, and Thomas grew more and more discouraged. The only thing interesting was another one of those odd signs that read WORLD IN CATASTROPHE—KILLZONE EXPERIMENT DEPARTMENT. Minho didn't even give it a second glance.

They had another meal, searched some more. They found nothing, and Thomas was beginning to get ready to accept the inevitable—that there was nothing *to* find. When wall-closing time rolled around, he started looking for signs of Grievers, was struck by an icy hesitation at every corner. He and Minho always had knives clasped firmly in both hands. But nothing showed up until almost midnight.

Minho spotted a Griever disappearing around a corner ahead of them; and it didn't come back. Thirty minutes later, Thomas saw one do the exact same thing. An hour after that, a Griever came charging through the Maze right past them, not even pausing. Thomas almost collapsed from the sudden rush of terror.

He and Minho continued on.

"I think they're playing with us," Minho said a while later.

Thomas realized he'd given up on searching the walls and was just heading back toward the Glade in a depressed walk. From the looks of it, Minho felt the same way.

"What do you mean?" Thomas asked.

The Keeper sighed. "I think the Creators want us to know there's no way out. The walls aren't even moving anymore—it's like this has all just been some stupid game and it's time to end. And they want us to go back and tell the other Gladers. How much you wanna bet when we get back we find out a Griever took one of them just like last night? I think Gally was right—they're gonna just keep killing us."

Thomas didn't respond—felt the truth of what Minho said. Any hope he'd felt earlier when they'd set out had crashed a long time ago.

"Let's just go home," Minho said, his voice weary.

Thomas hated to admit defeat, but he nodded in agreement. The code seemed like their only hope now, and he resolved to focus on that.

He and Minho made their way silently back to the Glade. They didn't see another Griever the whole way.

CHAPTER 45

By Thomas's watch, it was midmorning when he and Minho stepped through the West Door back into the Glade. Thomas was so tired he wanted to lie down right there and take a nap. They'd been in the Maze for roughly twenty-four hours.

Surprisingly, despite the dead light and everything falling apart, the day in the Glade appeared to be proceeding business as usual—farming, gardening, cleaning. It didn't take long for some of the boys to notice them standing there. Newt was notified and he came running.

"You're the first to come back," he said as he walked up to them. "What happened?" The childlike look of hope on his face broke Thomas's heart—he obviously thought they'd found something important. "Tell me you've got good news."

Minho's eyes were dead, staring at a spot somewhere in the gray distance. "Nothing," he said. "The Maze is a big freaking joke."

Newt looked at Thomas, confused. "What's he talking about?"

"He's just discouraged," Thomas said with a weary shrug. "We didn't find anything different. The walls haven't moved, no exits, nothing. Did the Grievers come last night?"

Newt paused, darkness passing over his face. Finally, he nodded. "Yeah. They took Adam."

Thomas didn't know the name, and felt guilty for feeling nothing. *Just one person again*, he thought. *Maybe Gally was right.*

287

Newt was about to say something else when Minho freaked out, startling Thomas.

"I'm sick of this!" Minho spat in the ivy, veins popping out of his neck. "I'm sick of it! It's over! It's all over!" He took off his backpack and threw it on the ground. "There's no exit, never was, never will be. We're all shucked."

Thomas watched, his throat dry, as Minho stomped off toward the Homestead. It worried him—if Minho gave up, they were all in big trouble.

Newt didn't say a word. He left Thomas standing there, now in his own daze. Despair hung in the air like the smoke from the Map Room, thick and acrid.

The other Runners returned within the hour, and from what Thomas heard, none of them had found anything and they'd eventually given up as well. Glum faces were everywhere throughout the Glade, and most of the workers had abandoned their daily jobs.

Thomas knew that the code of the Maze was their only hope now. It had to reveal something. It had to. And after aimlessly wandering the Glade to hear the other Runners' stories, he snapped out of his funk.

Teresa? he said in his mind, closing his eyes, as if that would do the trick. *Where are you? Did you figure anything out?*

After a long pause, he almost gave up, thinking it didn't work.

Huh? Tom, did you say something?

Yeah, he said, excited he'd made contact again. *Can you hear me? Am I doing this thing right?*

Sometimes it's choppy, but it's working. Kinda freaky, huh?

Thomas thought about that—actually, he was sort of getting used to it. *It's not so bad. Are you guys still in the basement? I saw Newt but then he disappeared again.*

Still here. Newt had three or four Gladers help us trace the Maps. I think we have the code all figured out.

Thomas's heart leaped into his throat. *Serious?*

Get down here.

I'm coming. He was already moving as he said it, somehow not feeling so exhausted anymore.

Newt let him in.

"Minho still hasn't shown up," he said as they walked down the stairs to the basement. "Sometimes he turns into a buggin' hothead."

Thomas was surprised Minho was wasting time sulking, especially with the code possibilities. He pushed the thought aside as he entered the room. Several Gladers he didn't know were gathered around the table, standing; they all looked exhausted, their eyes sunken. Piles of Maps lay scattered all over the place, including the floor. It looked as if a tornado had touched down right in the middle of the room.

Teresa was leaning against a stack of shelves, reading a single sheet of paper. She glanced up when he entered, but then returned her gaze to whatever it was she held. This saddened him a little—he'd hoped she'd be happy to see him—but then he felt really stupid for even having the thought. She was obviously busy figuring out the code.

You have to see this, Teresa said to him just as Newt dismissed his helpers—they clomped up the wooden stairs, a couple of them grumbling about doing all that work for nothing.

Thomas started, for a brief moment worried that Newt could tell what was going on. *Don't talk in my head while Newt's around. I don't want him knowing about our . . . gift.*

"Come check this out," she said aloud, barely hiding the smirk that flashed across her face.

"I'll get down on my knees and kiss your bloody feet if you can figure it out," Newt said.

Thomas walked over to Teresa, eager to see what they'd come up with. She held out the paper, eyebrows raised.

"No doubt this is right," she said. "Just don't have a clue what it means."

Thomas took the paper and scanned it quickly. There were numbered circles running down the left side, one to six. Next to each one was a word written in big blocky letters.

FLOAT
CATCH
BLEED
DEATH
STIFF
PUSH

That was it. Six words.

Disappointment washed over Thomas—he'd been sure the purpose of the code would be obvious once they had it figured out. He looked up at Teresa with a sunken heart. "That's all? Are you sure they're in the right order?"

She took the paper back from him. "The Maze has been repeating those words for months—we finally quit when that became clear. Each time, after the word *PUSH,* it goes a full week without showing any letter at all, and then it starts over again with *FLOAT.* So we figured that's the first word, and that's the order."

Thomas folded his arms and leaned against the shelves next to

Teresa. Without thinking about it, he'd memorized the six words, welded them to his mind. *Float. Catch. Bleed. Death. Stiff. Push.* That didn't sound good.

"Cheerful, don't ya think?" Newt said, mirroring his thoughts exactly.

"Yeah," Thomas replied with a frustrated groan. "We need to get Minho down here—maybe he knows something we don't. If we just had more clues—" He froze, hit by a dizzy spell; he would've fallen to the floor if he hadn't had the shelves to lean on. An idea had just occurred to him. A horrible, terrible, awful idea. The worst idea in the history of horrible, terrible, awful ideas.

But instinct told him he was right. That it was something he had to do.

"Tommy?" Newt asked, stepping closer with a look of concern creasing his forehead. "What's wrong with you? Your face just went white as a ghost."

Thomas shook his head, composing himself. "Oh . . . nothing, sorry. My eyes are hurting—I think I need some sleep." He rubbed his temples for effect.

Are you okay? Teresa asked in his mind. He looked to see that she was as worried as Newt, which made him feel good.

Yeah. Seriously, I'm tired. I just need some rest.

"Well," Newt said, reaching out to squeeze Thomas's shoulder. "You spent all bloody night out in the Maze—go take a nap."

Thomas looked at Teresa, then at Newt. He wanted to share his idea, but decided against it. Instead, he just nodded and headed for the stairs.

All the same, Thomas now had a plan. As bad as it was, he had a plan. They needed more clues about the code. They needed *memories*.

So he was going to get stung by a Griever. Go through the Changing. On purpose.

CHAPTER 46

Thomas refused to talk to anyone the rest of the day.

Teresa tried several times. But he kept telling her he didn't feel good, that he just wanted to be alone and sleep in his spot behind the forest, maybe spend some time thinking. Try to discover a hidden secret within his mind that would help them know what to do.

But in truth, he was psyching himself up for what he had planned for that evening, convincing himself it was the right thing to do. The *only* thing to do. Plus, he was absolutely terrified and he didn't want the others to notice.

Eventually, when his watch showed that evening had arrived, he went to the Homestead with everyone else. He barely noticed he'd been hungry until he started eating Frypan's hastily prepared meal of biscuits and tomato soup.

And then it was time for another sleepless night.

The Builders had boarded up the gaping holes left by the monsters who'd carried off Gally and Adam. The end result looked to Thomas like an army of drunk guys had done the work, but it was solid enough. Newt and Alby, who finally felt well enough to walk around again, his head heavily bandaged, insisted on a plan for everyone to rotate where they slept each night.

Thomas ended up in the large living room on the bottom floor of the Homestead with the same people he'd slept with two nights before. Silence settled over the room quickly, though he didn't know if it was because people were actually asleep or just scared, quietly hoping against hope the Grievers didn't come again. Unlike two nights ago, Teresa was allowed to stay in the building with the rest of the Gladers. She was near him, curled up in two blankets. Somehow, he could sense that she was sleeping. Actually *sleeping*.

Thomas certainly couldn't sleep, even though he knew his body needed it desperately. He tried—he tried so hard to keep his eyes closed, force himself to relax. But he had no luck. The night dragged on, the heavy sense of anticipation like a weight on his chest.

Then, just as they'd all expected, came the mechanical, haunted sounds of the Grievers outside. The time had come.

Everyone crowded together against the wall farthest from the windows, doing their best to keep quiet. Thomas huddled in a corner next to Teresa, hugging his knees, staring at the window. The reality of the dreadful decision he'd made earlier squeezed his heart like a crushing fist. But he knew that everything might depend on it.

The tension in the room rose at a steady pace. The Gladers were quiet, not a soul moved. A distant scraping of metal against wood echoed through the house; it sounded to Thomas like a Griever was climbing on the back side of the Homestead, opposite where they were. More noises joined in a few seconds later, coming from all directions, the closest right outside their own window. The air in the room seemed to freeze into solid ice, and Thomas pressed his fists against his eyes, the anticipation of the attack killing him.

A booming explosion of ripping wood and broken glass thundered from somewhere upstairs, shaking the whole house. Thomas went numb as several screams erupted, followed by the pounding of fleeing footsteps. Loud creaks and groans announced a whole horde of Gladers running to the first floor.

"It's got Dave!" someone yelled, the voice high-pitched with terror.

No one in Thomas's room moved a muscle; he knew each of them was probably feeling guilty about their relief—that at least it wasn't them. That maybe they were safe for one more night. Two nights in a row only one boy had been taken, and people had started to believe that what Gally had said was true.

Thomas jumped as a terrible crash sounded right outside their door, accompanied by screams and the splintering of wood, like some iron-jawed monster was eating the entire stairwell. A second later came another explosion of ripping wood: the front door. The Griever had come right through the house and was now leaving.

An explosion of fear ripped through Thomas. It was now or never.

He jumped up and ran to the door of the room, yanking it open. He heard Newt yell, but he ignored him and ran down the hall, sidestepping and jumping over hundreds of splintered pieces of wood. He could see that where the front door had been there now stood a jagged hole leading out into the gray night. He headed straight for it and ran out into the Glade.

Tom! Teresa screamed inside his head. *What are you doing!*

He ignored her. He just kept running.

The Griever holding Dave—a kid Thomas had never spoken to—was rolling along on its spikes toward the West Door, churning and whirring. The other Grievers had already gathered in the courtyard and followed their companion toward the Maze. Without hesitating, knowing the others would think he was trying to commit suicide, Thomas sprinted in their direction until he found himself in the middle of the pack of creatures. Having been taken by surprise, the Grievers hesitated.

Thomas jumped on the one holding Dave, tried to jerk the kid free, hoping the creature would retaliate. Teresa's scream inside his mind was so loud it felt as if a dagger had been driven through his skull.

Three of the Grievers swarmed on him at once, their long pincers and claspers and needles flying in from all directions. Thomas flailed his arms and legs, knocking away the horrible metallic arms as he kicked at the pulsating blubber of the Grievers' bodies—he only wanted to be stung, not taken like Dave. Their relentless attack intensified, and Thomas felt pain erupt over every inch of his body—needle pricks that told him he'd succeeded. Screaming, he kicked and pushed and thrashed, throwing his body into a roll, trying to get away from them. Struggling, bursting with adrenaline, he finally found an open spot to get his feet under him and ran with all his power.

As soon as he escaped the immediate reach of the Grievers' instruments, they gave up and retreated, disappearing into the Maze. Thomas collapsed to the ground, groaning from the pain.

Newt was on him in a second, followed immediately by Chuck, Teresa, several others. Newt grabbed him by the shoulders and lifted him up, gripping him under both arms. "Get his legs!" he yelled.

Thomas felt the world swimming around him, felt delirious, nauseated. Someone, he couldn't tell who, obeyed Newt's order; he was being carried across the courtyard, through the front door of the Homestead, down the shattered hall, into a room, placed on a couch. The world continued to twist and pitch.

"What were you *doing*!" Newt yelled in his face. "How could you be so bloody stupid!"

Thomas had to speak before he faded into blackness. "No . . . Newt . . . you don't understand. . . ."

"Shut up!" Newt shouted. "Don't waste your energy!"

Thomas felt someone examining his arms and legs, ripping his clothes away from his body, checking for damage. He heard Chuck's voice, couldn't help feeling relief that his friend was okay. A Med-jack said something about him being stung dozens of times.

Teresa was by his feet, squeezing his right ankle with her hand. *Why, Tom? Why would you do that?*

Because . . . He didn't have the strength to concentrate.

Newt yelled for the Grief Serum; a minute later Thomas felt a pinprick on his arm. Warmth spread from that point throughout his body, calming him, lessening the pain. But the world still seemed to be collapsing in on itself, and he knew it would all be gone from him in just a few seconds.

The room spun, colors morphing into each other, churning faster and faster. It took all of his effort, but he said one last thing before the darkness took him for good.

"Don't worry," he whispered, hoping they could hear him. "I did it on purpose. . . ."

CHAPTER 47

Thomas had no concept of time as he went through the Changing.

It started much like his first memory of the Box—dark and cold. But this time he had no sensation of anything touching his feet or body. He floated in emptiness, stared into a void of black. He saw nothing, heard nothing, smelled nothing. It was as if someone had stolen his five senses, leaving him in a vacuum.

Time stretched on. And on. Fear turned into curiosity, which turned into boredom.

Finally, after an interminable wait, things began to change.

A distant wind picked up, unfelt but heard. Then a swirling mist of whiteness appeared far in the distance—a spinning tornado of smoke that formed into a long funnel, stretching out until he could see neither the top nor the bottom of the white whirlwind. He felt the gales then, sucking into the cyclone so that it blew past him from behind, ripping at his clothes and hair like they were shredded flags caught in a storm.

The tower of thick mist began to move toward him—or *he* was moving toward *it,* he couldn't tell—increasing its speed at an alarming rate. Where seconds before he'd been able to see the distinct form of the funnel, he now could see only a flat expanse of white.

And then it consumed him; he felt his mind taken by the mist, felt memories flood into his thoughts.

Everything else turned into pain.

CHAPTER 48

"Thomas."

The voice was distant, warbled, like an echo in a long tunnel.

"Thomas, can you hear me?"

He didn't want to answer. His mind had shut down when it could no longer take the pain; he feared it would all return if he allowed himself back into consciousness. He sensed light on the other side of his eyelids, but knew it would be unbearable to open them. He did nothing.

"Thomas, it's Chuck. Are you okay? Please don't die, dude."

Everything came crashing back into his mind. The Glade, the Grievers, the stinging needle, the Changing. *Memories.* The Maze couldn't be solved. Their only way out was something they'd never expected. Something terrifying. He was crushed with despair.

Groaning, he forced his eyes open, squinting at first. Chuck's pudgy face was there, staring with frightened eyes. But then they lit up and a smile spread across his face. Despite it all, despite the terrible crappiness of it all, Chuck smiled.

"He's awake!" the boy yelled to no one in particular. "Thomas is awake!"

The booming sound of his voice made Thomas wince; he shut his eyes again. "Chuck, do you have to scream? I don't feel so good."

"Sorry—I'm just glad you're alive. You're lucky I don't give you a big kiss."

"Please don't do that, Chuck." Thomas opened his eyes again and forced himself to sit up in the bed in which he lay, pushing his back against the wall and stretching out his legs. Soreness ate at his joints and muscles. "How long did it take?" he asked.

"Three days," Chuck answered. "We put you in the Slammer at night to keep you safe—brought you back here during the days. Thought you were dead for sure about thirty times since you started. But check you out—you look brand-new!"

Thomas could only imagine how *non*-great he looked. "Did the Grievers come?"

Chuck's jubilation visibly crashed to the ground as his eyes sank down toward the floor. "Yeah—they got Zart and a couple others. One a night. Minho and the Runners have scoured the Maze, trying to find an exit or some use for that stupid code you guys came up with. But nothing. Why do you think the Grievers are only taking one shank at a time?"

Thomas's stomach turned sour—he knew the exact answer to that question, and some others now. Enough to know that sometimes knowing sucked.

"Get Newt and Alby," he finally said in answer. "Tell them we need to have a Gathering. Soon as possible."

"Serious?"

Thomas let out a sigh. "Chuck, I just went through the Changing. Do *you* think I'm serious?"

Without a word, Chuck jumped up and ran out of the room, his calls for Newt fading the farther he went.

Thomas closed his eyes and rested his head against the wall. Then he called out to her with his mind.

Teresa.

She didn't answer at first, but then her voice popped into his thoughts as clearly as if she were sitting next to him. *That was really stupid, Tom. Really, really stupid.*

Had to do it, he answered.

I pretty much hated you the last couple days. You should've seen yourself. Your skin, your veins . . .

You hated *me?* He was thrilled she'd cared so much about him.

She paused. *That's just my way of saying I would've killed you if you'd died.*

Thomas felt a burst of warmth in his chest, reached up and actually touched it, surprised at himself. *Well . . . thanks. I guess.*

So, how much do you remember?

He paused. *Enough. What you said about the two of us and what we did to them . . .*

It was true?

We did some bad things, Teresa. He sensed frustration from her, like she had a million questions and no idea where to start.

Did you learn anything to help us get out of here? she asked, as if she didn't want to know what part she'd had in all of this. *A purpose for the code?*

Thomas paused, not really wanting to talk about it yet—not before he really gathered his thoughts. Their only chance for escape might be a death wish. *Maybe,* he finally said, *but it won't be easy. We need a Gathering. I'll ask for you to be there—I don't have the energy to say it all twice.*

Neither one of them said anything for a while, a sense of hopelessness wafting between their minds.

Teresa?

Yeah?

The Maze can't be solved.

She paused for a long time before answering. *I think we all know that now.*

Thomas hated the pain in her voice—he could feel it in his mind. *Don't worry; the Creators meant for us to escape, though. I have a plan.* He wanted to give her some hope, no matter how scarce.

Oh, really.

Yeah. It's terrible, and some of us might die. Sound promising?

Big-time. What is it?

We have to—

Before he could finish, Newt walked into the room, cutting him off.

I'll tell you later, Thomas quickly finished.

Hurry! she said, then was gone.

Newt had walked over to the bed and sat down next to him. "Tommy—you barely look sick."

Thomas nodded. "I feel a little queasy, but other than that, I'm fine. Thought it'd be a lot worse."

Newt shook his head, his face a mixture of anger and awe. "What you did was half brave and half bloody stupid. Seems like you're pretty good at that." He paused, shook his head. "I *know* why you did it. What memories came back? Anything that'll help?"

"We need to have a Gathering," Thomas said, shifting his legs to get more comfortable. Surprisingly, he didn't feel much pain, just wooziness. "Before I start forgetting some of this stuff."

"Yeah, Chuck told me—we'll do it. But why? What did you figure out?"

"It's a test, Newt—the whole thing is a test."

Newt nodded. "Like an experiment."

Thomas shook his head. "No, you don't get it. They're weeding us out, seeing if we'll give up, finding the best of us. Throwing variables at us, trying to make us quit. Testing our ability to hope and fight. Sending Teresa here and shutting everything down was only the last part, one more . . . final analysis. Now it's time for the last test. To escape."

Newt's brow crinkled in confusion. "What do you mean? You know a way out?"

"Yeah. Call the Gathering. Now."

CHAPTER 49

An hour later, Thomas sat in front of the Keepers for the Gathering, just like he had a week or two before. They hadn't let Teresa in, which ticked him off just as much as it did her. Newt and Minho trusted her now, but the others still had their doubts.

"All right, Greenie," Alby said, looking much better as he sat in the middle of the semicircle of chairs, next to Newt. The other chairs were all occupied except two—a stark reminder that Zart and Gally had been taken by the Grievers. "Forget all the beat-around-the-bush klunk. Start talking."

Thomas, still a bit queasy from the Changing, forced himself to take a second and gain his composure. He had a lot to say, but wanted to be sure it came out sounding as non-stupid as possible.

"It's a long story," he began. "We don't have time to go through it all, but I'll tell you the gist of it. When I went through the Changing, I saw flashes of images—hundreds of them—like a slide show in fast forward. A lot came back to me, but only some of it's clear enough to talk about. Other stuff has faded or is fading." He paused, gathering his thoughts one last time. "But I remember enough. The Creators are testing us. The Maze was never meant to be solved. It's all been a trial. They want the winners—or survivors—to do something important." He trailed off, already confused at what order he should tell things in.

"What?" Newt asked.

"Let me start over," Thomas said, rubbing his eyes. "Every single one of us was taken when we were really young. I don't remember how or why—just glimpses and feelings that things had changed in the world, that something really bad happened. I have no idea what. The Creators stole us, and I think they felt justified in doing it. Somehow they figured out that we have above-average intelligence, and that's why they chose us. I don't know, most of this is sketchy and doesn't matter that much anyway.

"I can't remember anything about my family or what happened to them. But after we were taken, we spent the next few years learning in special schools, living somewhat normal lives until they were finally able to finance and build the Maze. All our names are just stupid nicknames they made up—like Alby for Albert Einstein, Newt for Isaac Newton, and me—Thomas. As in Edison."

Alby looked like he'd been slapped in the face. "Our names . . . these ain't even our real names?"

Thomas shook his head. "As far as I can tell, we'll probably never know what our names were."

"What are you saying?" Frypan asked. "That we're freakin' orphans raised by scientists?"

"Yes," Thomas said, hoping his expression didn't give away just how depressed he felt. "Supposedly we're really smart and they're studying every move we make, analyzing us. Seeing who'd give up and who wouldn't. Seeing who'd survive it all. No wonder we have so many beetle blade spies running around this place. Plus, some of us have had things . . . altered in our brains."

"I believe this klunk about as much as I believe Frypan's food is good for you," Winston grumbled, looking tired and indifferent.

303

"Why would I make this up?" Thomas said, his voice rising. He'd gotten stung on *purpose* to remember these things! "Better yet, what do *you* think is the explanation? That we live on an alien planet?"

"Just keep talking," Alby said. "But I don't get why none of us remembered this stuff. I've been through the Changing, but everything I saw was . . ." He looked around quickly, like he'd just said something he shouldn't have. "I didn't learn nothin'."

"I'll tell you in a minute why I think I learned more than others," Thomas said, dreading that part of the story. "Should I keep going or not?"

"Talk," Newt said.

Thomas sucked in a big breath, as if he were about to start a race. "Okay, somehow they wiped our memories—not just our childhood, but all the stuff leading up to entering the Maze. They put us in the Box and sent us up here—a big group to start and then one a month over the last two years."

"But why?" Newt asked. "What's the bloody point?"

Thomas held up a hand for silence. "I'm getting there. Like I said, they wanted to test us, see how we'd react to what they call the Variables, and to a problem that has no solution. See if we could work together—build a community, even. Everything was provided for us, and the problem was laid out as one of the most common puzzles known to civilization—a maze. All this added up to making us think there *had* to be a solution, just encouraging us to work all the harder while at the same time magnifying our discouragement at not finding one." He paused to look around, making sure they were all listening. "What I'm saying is, there *is* no solution."

Chatter broke out, questions overlapping each other.

Thomas held his hands up again, wishing he could just zap his thoughts into everyone else's brains. "See? Your reaction proves my point. Most people would've given up by now. But I think we're different. We couldn't accept that a problem *can't* be solved—especially when it's something as simple as a maze. And we've kept fighting no matter how hopeless it's gotten."

Thomas realized his voice had steadily risen as he spoke, and he felt heat in his face. "Whatever the reason, it makes me sick! All of this—the Grievers, the walls moving, the Cliff—they're just elements of a stupid *test*. We're being used and manipulated. The Creators wanted to keep our minds working toward a solution that was never there. Same thing goes for Teresa being sent here, her being used to trigger the Ending—whatever *that* means—the place being shut down, gray skies, on and on and on. They're throwing crazy things at us to see our response, test our will. See if we'll turn on each other. In the end, they want the survivors for something important."

Frypan stood up. "And killing people? That's a nice little part of their plan?"

Thomas felt a moment of fear, worried that the Keepers might take out their anger on him for knowing so much. And it was only about to get worse. "Yes, Frypan, killing people. The only reason the Grievers are doing it one by one is so we don't all die before it ends the way it's supposed to. Survival of the fittest. Only the best of us will escape."

Frypan kicked his chair. "Well, you better start talking about this magical escape, then!"

"He will," Newt said, quietly. "Shut up and listen."

Minho, who'd been mostly silent the whole time, cleared his throat. "Something tells me I'm not gonna like what I'm about to hear."

"Probably not," Thomas said. He closed his eyes for a second and folded his arms. The next few minutes were going to be crucial. "The Creators want the best of us for whatever it is they have planned. But we have to earn it." The room fell completely silent, every eye on him. "The code."

"The code?" Frypan repeated, his voice lighting up with a trace of hope. "What about it?"

Thomas looked at him, paused for effect. "It was hidden in the wall movements of the Maze for a reason. I should know—I was there when the Creators did it."

CHAPTER 50

For a long moment, no one said anything, and all Thomas saw were blank faces. He felt the sweat beading on his forehead, slicking his hands; he was terrified to keep going.

Newt looked completely baffled and finally broke the silence. "What are you talking about?"

"Well, first there's something I have to share. About me and Teresa. There's a reason Gally accused me of so much stuff, and why everyone who's gone through the Changing recognizes me."

He expected questions—an eruption of voices—but the room was dead silent.

"Teresa and I are . . . different," he continued. "We were part of the Maze Trials from the very beginning—but against our will, I swear it."

Minho was the one to speak up now. "Thomas, what're you talking about?"

"Teresa and I were used by the Creators. If you had your full memories back, you'd probably want to kill us. But I had to tell you this myself to show you we can be trusted now. So you'll believe me when I tell you the only way we can get out of here."

Thomas quickly scanned the faces of the Keepers, wondering one last time if he should say it, if they would understand. But he knew he had to. He *had* to.

Thomas took a deep breath, then said it. "Teresa and I helped design the Maze. We helped create the whole thing."

Everyone seemed too stunned to respond. Blank faces stared back at him once again. Thomas figured they either didn't understand or didn't believe him.

"What's that supposed to mean?" Newt finally asked. "You're a bloody sixteen-year-old. How could you have created the Maze?"

Thomas couldn't help doubting it a little himself—but he knew what he'd remembered. As crazy as it was, he knew it for the truth. "We were . . . smart. And I think it might be part of the Variables. But most importantly, Teresa and I have a . . . gift that made us very valuable as they designed and built this place." He stopped, knowing it must all sound absurd.

"Speak!" Newt yelled. "Spit it out!"

"We're telepathic! We can talk to each other in our freaking heads!" Saying it out loud almost made him feel ashamed, as if he'd just admitted he was a thief.

Newt blinked in surprise; someone coughed.

"But listen to me," Thomas continued, in a hurry to defend himself. "They *forced* us to help. I don't know how or why, but they did." He paused. "Maybe it was to see if we could gain your trust despite having been a part of them. Maybe we were meant all along to be the ones to reveal how to escape. Whatever the reason, with your Maps we figured out the code and we need to use it now."

Thomas looked around, and surprisingly, astonishingly, no one seemed angry. Most of the Gladers continued to stare blankly at him or shook their heads in wonder or disbelief. And for some odd reason, Minho was smiling.

"It's true, and I'm sorry," Thomas continued. "But I can tell you this—I'm in the same boat with you now. Teresa and I were sent here just like anyone else, and we can die just as easily. But the Creators have seen enough—it's time for the final test. I guess I needed the Changing to add the final pieces of the puzzle. Anyway, I wanted you to know the truth, to know there's a chance we can do this."

Newt shook his head back and forth, staring at the ground. Then he looked up, took in the other Keepers. "The Creators—those shanks did this to us, not Tommy and Teresa. The Creators. And they'll be sorry."

"Whatever," Minho said, "who gives a klunk about all that—just get on with the escape already."

A lump formed in Thomas's throat. He was so relieved he almost couldn't speak. He'd been sure they'd put him under major heat for his confession, if not throw him off the Cliff. The rest of what he had to say almost seemed easy now. "There's a computer station in a place we've never looked before. The code will open a door for us to get out of the Maze. It also shuts down the Grievers so they can't follow us— if we can just survive long enough to get to that point."

"A place we've never *looked* before?" Alby asked. "What do you think we've been doing for two years?"

"Trust me, you've never been to this spot."

Minho stood up. "Well, where is it?"

"It's almost suicide," Thomas said, knowing he was putting off the answer. "The Grievers will come after us whenever we try to do it. All of them. The final test." He wanted to make sure they understood the stakes. The odds of everyone surviving were slim.

"So where is it?" Newt asked, leaning forward in his chair.

"Over the Cliff," Thomas answered. "We have to go through the Griever Hole."

CHAPTER 51

Alby stood up so quickly his chair fell over backward. His bloodshot eyes stood out against the white bandage on his forehead. He took two steps forward before stopping, as if he'd been about to charge and attack Thomas.

"Now you're being a shuck idiot," he said, glaring at Thomas. "Or a traitor. How can we trust a word you say if you helped design this place, put us here! We can't handle one Griever on our own ground, much less fight a whole horde of them in their little hole. What are you really up to?"

Thomas was furious. "What am I up to? Nothing! Why would I make all this up?"

Alby's arms stiffened, fists clenched. "For all we know you were sent here to get us all killed. Why should we trust you?"

Thomas stared, incredulous. "Alby, do you have a short-term memory problem? I risked my life to save you out in the Maze—you'd be dead if it wasn't for me!"

"Maybe that was a trick to gain our trust. If you're in league with the shucks who sent us here, you wouldn't have had to worry about the Grievers hurting you—maybe it was all an act."

Thomas's anger lessened slightly at that, turned into pity. Something was odd here—suspicious.

"Alby," Minho finally interjected, relieving Thomas. "That's about the dumbest theory I've ever heard. He just about got freaking torn apart three nights ago. You think that's part of the act?"

Alby nodded once, curtly. "Maybe."

"I *did it,*" Thomas said, throwing all the annoyance he could into his voice, "on the chance that I could get my memories back, help all of us get out of here. Do I need to show you the cuts and bruises all over my body?"

Alby said nothing, his face still quivering with rage. His eyes watered and veins popped out on his neck. "We can't go back!" he finally yelled, turning to look at everyone in the room. "I've seen what our lives were like—we can't go back!"

"Is *that* what this is about?" Newt asked. "Are you kidding?"

Alby turned on him, fiercely, even held up a clenched fist. But he stopped, lowered his arm, then went over and sank into his chair, put his face in his hands, and broke down. Thomas couldn't have been more surprised. The fearless leader of the Gladers was crying.

"Alby, talk to us," Newt pressed, not willing to let it drop. "What's going on?"

"I did it," Alby said through a racking sob. "I did it."

"Did what?" Newt asked. He looked as confused as Thomas felt.

Alby looked up, his eyes wet with tears. "I burned the Maps. I did it. I slammed my head on the table so you'd think it was someone else, I lied, burned it all. I did it!"

The Keepers exchanged looks, shock clear in their wide eyes and raised eyebrows. For Thomas, though, it all made sense now. Alby remembered how awful his life was before he came here and he didn't want to go back.

"Well, it's a good thing we saved those Maps," Minho said, completely straight-faced, almost mocking. "Thanks for the tip you gave us after the Changing—to protect them."

Thomas looked to see how Alby would respond to Minho's sarcastic, almost cruel, remark, but he acted as if he hadn't even heard.

Newt, instead of showing anger, asked Alby to explain. Thomas knew why Newt wasn't mad—the Maps were safe, the code figured out. It didn't matter.

"I'm telling you." Alby sounded like he was begging—near hysterical. "We can't go back to where we came from. I've seen it, remembered awful, awful things. Burned land, a disease—something called the Flare. It was horrible—way worse than we have it here."

"If we stay *here,* we'll all die!" Minho yelled. "It's worse than that?"

Alby stared at Minho a long time before answering. Thomas could only think of the words he'd just said. *The Flare.* Something about it was familiar, right on the edge of his mind. But he was certain he hadn't remembered anything about that when he'd gone through the Changing.

"Yes," Alby finally said. "It's worse. Better to die than go home."

Minho snickered and leaned back in his chair. "Man, you are one butt-load of sunshine, let me tell you. I'm with Thomas. I'm with Thomas one hundred percent. If we're gonna die, let's freakin' do it fighting."

"Inside the Maze or out of it," Thomas added, relieved that Minho was firmly on his side. He turned to Alby then, and looked at him gravely. "We still live inside the world you remembered."

Alby stood again, his face showing his defeat. "Do what you want." He sighed. "Doesn't matter. We'll die no matter what." And with that, he walked to the door and left the room.

Newt let out a deep breath and shook his head. "He's never been the same since being stung—must've been one bugger of a memory. What in the world is the Flare?"

"I don't care," Minho said. "Anything's better than dying here. We can deal with the Creators once we're out. But for now we gotta do what they planned. Go through the Griever Hole and escape. If some of us die, so be it."

Frypan snorted. "You shanks are driving me nuts. Can't get out of the Maze, and this idea of hanging with the Grievers at their bachelor pad sounds as stupid as anything I've ever heard in my life. Might as well slit our wrists."

The other Keepers burst out in argument, everyone talking over everyone else. Newt finally screamed for them to shut up.

Thomas spoke again once things settled. "I'm going through the Hole or I'll die trying to get there. Looks like Minho will, too. And I'm sure Teresa's in. If we can fight off the Grievers long enough for someone to punch in the code and shut them down, then we can go through the door *they* come through. We'll have passed the tests. Then we can face the Creators themselves."

Newt's grin had no humor in it. "And you think we can fight off Grievers? Even if we don't die, we'll probably all get stung. Every last one of them might be waiting for us when we get to the Cliff—the beetle blades are out there constantly. The Creators'll know when we make our run for it."

He'd been dreading it, but Thomas knew it was time to tell them the last part of his plan. "I don't think they'll sting us—the Changing was a Variable meant for us while we lived here. But that part will be over. Plus, we might have one thing going for us."

"Yeah?" Newt asked, rolling his eyes. "Can't wait to hear it."

"It doesn't do the Creators any good if we all die—this thing is meant to be hard, not impossible. I think we finally know for sure that the Grievers are programmed to only kill one of us each day. So somebody can sacrifice himself to save the others while we run to the Hole. I think this might be how it's supposed to happen."

313

The room went silent until the Blood House Keeper barked a loud laugh. "Excuse me?" Winston asked. "So your suggestion is that we throw some poor kid to the wolves so the rest of us can escape? *This* is your *brilliant* suggestion?"

Thomas refused to admit how bad that sounded, but an idea hit him. "Yes, Winston, I'm glad you're so good at paying attention." He ignored the glare that got him. "And it seems obvious who the poor kid should be."

"Oh, yeah?" Winston asked. "Who?"

Thomas folded his arms. "Me."

CHAPTER 52

The meeting erupted into a chorus of arguments. Newt very calmly stood up, walked over to Thomas and grabbed him by the arm; he pulled him toward the door. "You're leaving. Now."

Thomas was stunned. "Leaving? Why?"

"Think you've said enough for one meeting. We need to talk and decide what to do—*without* you here." They had reached the door and Newt gave him a gentle push outside. "Wait for me by the Box. When we're done, you and I'll talk."

He started to turn around, but Thomas reached out and grabbed him. "You gotta believe me, Newt. It's the only way out of here—we can do it, I swear. We're *meant* to."

Newt got in his face and spoke in an angry rasp of a whisper. "Yeah, I especially loved the bit where you volunteered to get yourself killed."

"I'm perfectly willing to do it." Thomas meant it, but only because of the guilt that racked him. Guilt that he'd somehow helped design the Maze. But deep down, he held on to the hope that he could fight long enough for someone to punch in the code and shut down the Grievers before they killed him. Open the door.

"Oh, really?" Newt asked, seeming irritated. "Mr. Noble himself, aren't ya?"

"I have plenty of my own reasons. In some ways it's my fault we're here in the first place." He stopped, took a breath to compose himself. "Anyway, I'm going no matter what, so you better not waste it."

Newt frowned, his eyes suddenly filled with compassion. "If you really did help design the Maze, Tommy, it's not your fault. You're a *kid*—you can't help what they forced you to do."

But it didn't matter what Newt said. What anyone said. Thomas bore the responsibility anyway—and it was growing heavier the more he thought about it. "I just . . . feel like I need to save everyone. To redeem myself."

Newt stepped back, slowly shaking his head. "You know what's funny, Tommy?"

"What?" Thomas replied, wary.

"I actually believe you. You just don't have an ounce of lying in those eyes of yours. And I can't bloody believe I'm about to say this." He paused. "But I'm going back in there to convince those shanks we should go through the Griever Hole, just like you said. Might as well fight the Grievers rather than sit around letting them pick us off one by one." He held up a finger. "But listen to me—I don't want another buggin' word about you dying and all that heroic klunk. If we're gonna do this, we'll take our chances—all of us. You hear me?"

Thomas held his hands up, overwhelmed with relief. "Loud and clear. I was just trying to make the point that it's worth the risk. If someone's going to die every night anyway, we might as well use it to our advantage."

Newt frowned. "Well, ain't that just cheery?"

Thomas turned to walk away, but Newt called out to him. "Tommy?"

"Yeah?" He stopped, but didn't look back.

"If I can convince those shanks—and that's a big *if*—the best time to go would be at night. We can hope that a lot of the Grievers might be out and about in the Maze—not in that Hole of theirs."

"Good that." Thomas agreed with him—he just hoped Newt could convince the Keepers. He turned to look at Newt and nodded.

Newt smiled, a barely-there crack in his worried grimace. "We should do it tonight, before anyone else is killed." And before Thomas could say anything, Newt disappeared back into the Gathering.

Thomas, a little shocked at the last statement, left the Homestead and walked to an old bench near the Box and took a seat, his mind a whirlwind. He kept thinking of what Alby had said about the Flare, and what it could mean. The older boy had also mentioned burned earth and a disease. Thomas didn't remember anything like that, but if it was all true, the world they were trying to get back to didn't sound so good. Still—what other choice did they have? Besides the fact that the Grievers were attacking every night, the Glade had basically shut down.

Frustrated, worried, tired of his thoughts, he called out to Teresa. *Can you hear me?*

Yeah, she replied. *Where are you?*

By the Box.

I'll come in a minute.

Thomas realized how badly he needed her company. *Good. I'll tell you the plan; I think it's on.*

What is it?

Thomas leaned back on the bench and put his right foot up on his knee, wondering how Teresa would react to what he was going to say. *We gotta go through the Griever Hole. Use that code to shut the Grievers down and open a door out of here.*

A pause. *I figured it was something like that.*

Thomas thought for a second, then added, *Unless you've got any better ideas?*

No. It's gonna be awful.

He punched his right fist against his other hand, even though he knew she couldn't see him. *We can do this.*

Doubtful.

Well, we have to try.

Another pause, this one longer. He could feel her resolve. *You're right.*

I think we're leaving tonight. Just come out here and we can talk more about it.

I'll be there in a few minutes.

Thomas's stomach tightened into a knot. The reality of what he had suggested, the plan Newt was trying to convince the Keepers to accept, was starting to hit him. He knew it was dangerous, but the idea of actually fighting the Grievers—not just running from them—was terrifying. The absolute best-case scenario was that only one of them would die—but even that couldn't be trusted. Maybe the Creators would just reprogram the creatures. And then all bets were off.

He tried not to think about it.

Sooner than Thomas expected, Teresa had found him and was sitting next to him, her body pressed against his despite plenty of room on the bench. She reached out and took his hand. He squeezed back, so hard he knew it must've hurt.

"Tell me," she said.

Thomas did, reciting every word he'd told the Keepers, hating how Teresa's eyes filled with worry—and terror. "The plan was easy to talk about," he said after he'd told her everything. "But Newt thinks we should go *tonight*. It doesn't sound so good now." It especially terrified him to think about Chuck and Teresa out there—he'd faced the Grievers down already and knew all too well what it was like. He wanted to be able to protect his friends from the horrible experience, but he knew he couldn't.

"We can do it," she said in a quiet voice.

Hearing her say that only made him worry more. "Holy crap, I'm scared."

"Holy crap, you're human. You *should* be scared."

Thomas didn't respond, and for a long time they just sat there, holding hands, no words spoken, in their minds or aloud. He felt the slightest hint of peace, as fleeting as it was, and tried to enjoy it for however long it might last.

CHAPTER 53

Thomas was almost sad when the Gathering finally ended. When Newt came out of the Homestead he knew that the time for rest was over.

The Keeper spotted them and approached at a limping run. Thomas noticed he'd let go of Teresa's hand without thinking about it. Newt finally came to a halt and crossed his arms over his chest as he looked down at them sitting on the bench. "This is bloody nuts, you know that, right?" His face was impossible to read, but there seemed to be a hint of victory in his eyes.

Thomas stood up, feeling a rush of excitement flooding his body. "So they agreed to go?"

Newt nodded. "All of them. Wasn't as hard as I thought it'd be. Those shanks've seen what happens at night with those bloody Doors open. We can't get out of the stupid Maze. Gotta try *something*." He turned and looked at the Keepers, who'd started to gather their respective work groups. "Now we just have to convince the Gladers."

Thomas knew that would be even more difficult than persuading the Keepers had been.

"You think they'll go for it?" Teresa asked, finally standing to join them.

"Not all of them," Newt said, and Thomas could see the frustration in his eyes. "Some'll stay and take their chances—guarantee it."

Thomas didn't doubt people would blanch at the thought of

making a run for it. Asking them to fight the Grievers was asking a lot. "What about Alby?"

"Who knows?" Newt responded, looking around the Glade, observing the Keepers and their groups. "I'm convinced that bugger really *is* more scared to go back home than he is of the Grievers. But I'll get him to go with us, don't worry."

Thomas wished he could bring back memories of those things that were tormenting Alby, but there was nothing. "How are you going to convince him?"

Newt laughed. "I'll make up some klunk. Tell him we'll all find a new life in another part of the world, live happily ever after."

Thomas shrugged. "Well, maybe we can. I promised Chuck I'd get him home, you know. Or at least find him a home."

"Yeah, well," Teresa murmured. "Anything's better than this place."

Thomas looked around at the arguments breaking out across the Glade, Keepers doing their best to convince people they should take a chance and battle their way through the Griever Hole. Some Gladers stomped away, but most seemed to listen and at least consider.

"So what's next?" Teresa asked.

Newt took a deep breath. "Figure out who's going, who's staying. Get ready. Food, weapons, all that. Then we go. Thomas, I'd put you in charge since it was your idea, but it's going to be hard enough to get people on our side without making the Greenie our leader—no offense. So just lay low, okay? We'll leave the code business to you and Teresa—you can handle that from the background."

Thomas was more than fine with lying low—finding that computer station and punching in the code was more than enough responsibility for him. Even with that much on his shoulders he had to fight the rising flood of panic he felt. "You sure make it sound easy," he finally said, trying his best to lighten up the situation. Or at least *sound* like he was.

Newt folded his arms again, looked at him closely. "Like you said—stay here, one shank'll die tonight. Go, one shank'll die. What's the difference?" He pointed at Thomas. "*If* you're right."

"I am." Thomas knew he was right about the Hole, the code, the door, the need to fight. But whether one person or many would die, he had no clue. However, if there was one thing his gut told him, it was not to admit to any doubt.

Newt clapped him on the back. "Good that. Let's get to work."

The next few hours were frantic.

Most of the Gladers ended up agreeing to go—even more than Thomas would've guessed. Even Alby decided to make the run. Though no one admitted it, Thomas bet most of them were banking on the theory that only one person would be killed by the Grievers, and they figured their chances of *not* being the unlucky sap were decent. Those who decided to stay in the Glade were few but adamant and loud. They mainly walked around sulking, trying to tell others how stupid they were. Eventually, they gave up and kept their distance.

As for Thomas and the rest of those committed to the escape, there was a ton of work to be done.

Backpacks were handed out and stuffed full of supplies. Frypan—Newt told Thomas that the Cook had been one of the last Keepers to agree to go—was in charge of gathering all the food and figuring out a way to distribute it evenly among the packs. Syringes of Grief Serum were included, even though Thomas didn't think the Grievers would sting them. Chuck was in charge of filling water bottles and getting them out to everyone. Teresa helped him, and Thomas asked her to sugarcoat the trip as much as she could, even if she had to flat-out lie, which was mostly the case. Chuck had tried to act brave from the time he first found out they were going for it, but his sweaty skin and dazed eyes revealed the truth.

Minho went to the Cliff with a group of Runners, taking ivy ropes and rocks to test the invisible Griever Hole one last time. They had to hope the creatures would keep to their normal schedule and not come out during daytime hours. Thomas had contemplated just jumping into the Hole right away and trying to punch in the code quickly, but he had no idea what to expect or what might be waiting for him. Newt was right—they'd better wait until night and hope that most of the Grievers were in the Maze, not inside their Hole.

When Minho returned, safe and sound, Thomas thought he seemed very optimistic that it really was an exit. Or entrance. Depending on how you looked at it.

Thomas helped Newt distribute the weapons, and even more innovative ones were created in their desperation to be prepared for the Grievers. Wooden poles were carved into spears or wrapped in barbwire; the knives were sharpened and fastened with twine to the ends of sturdy branches hacked from trees in the woods; chunks of broken glass were duct-taped to shovels. By the end of the day, the Gladers had turned into a small army. A very pathetic, ill-prepared army, Thomas thought, but an army all the same.

Once he and Teresa were done helping, they went to the secret spot in the Deadheads to strategize about the station inside the Griever Hole and how they planned to punch in the code.

"We have to be the ones to do it," Thomas said as they leaned their backs against craggy trees, the once-green leaves already starting to turn gray from the lack of artificial sunlight. "That way if we get separated, we can be in contact and still help each other."

Teresa had grabbed a stick and was peeling off the bark. "But we need backup in case something happens to us."

"Definitely. Minho and Newt know the code words—we'll tell them they have to get them punched into the computer if we . . . well, you know." Thomas didn't want to think about all the bad things that might happen.

"Not much to the plan, then." Teresa yawned, as if life were completely normal.

"Not much at all. Fight the Grievers, punch in the code, escape through the door. Then we deal with the Creators—whatever it takes."

"Six code words, who knows how many Grievers." Teresa broke the stick in half. "What do you think *WICKED* stands for, anyway?"

Thomas felt like he'd been hit in the stomach. For some reason, hearing the word at that moment, from someone else, knocked something loose in his mind and it clicked. He was stunned he hadn't made the connection sooner. "That sign I saw out in the Maze—remember? The metal one with words stamped on it?" Thomas's heart had started to race with excitement.

Teresa crinkled her forehead in confusion for a second, but then a light seemed to blink on behind her eyes. "Whoa. World In Catastrophe: Killzone Experiment Department. WICKED. *WICKED is good*—what I wrote on my arm. What does that even *mean*?"

"No idea. Which is why I'm scared to death that what we're about to do is a whole pile of stupid. Could be a bloodbath."

"Everyone knows what they're getting into." Teresa reached out and took his hand. "Nothing to lose, remember?"

Thomas remembered, but for some reason Teresa's words fell flat—they didn't have much hope in them. "Nothing to lose," he repeated.

CHAPTER 54

Just before the normal Door-closing time, Frypan prepared one last meal to carry them through the night. The mood hanging over the Gladers as they ate couldn't have been more somber or sodden with fear. Thomas found himself sitting next to Chuck, absently picking at his food.

"So . . . Thomas," the boy said through a huge bite of mashed potatoes. "Who am I nicknamed after?"

Thomas couldn't help shaking his head—here they were, about to embark on probably the most dangerous task of their lives, and Chuck was curious where he'd gotten his nickname. "I don't know, Darwin, maybe? The dude who figured out evolution."

"I bet no one's ever called him a dude before." Chuck took another big bite, and seemed to think that was the best time to talk, full mouth and all. "You know, I'm really not all that scared. I mean, last few nights, sitting in the Homestead, just waiting for a Griever to come in and steal one of us was the worst thing I've ever done. At least now we're taking it to them, *trying* something. And at least . . ."

"At least what?" Thomas asked. He didn't believe for a second that Chuck wasn't scared; it almost hurt to see him acting brave.

"Well, everyone's speculating they can only kill one of us. Maybe I sound like a shuck, but it gives me some hope. At least most of us will make it through—just leaves one poor sucker to die. Better than all of us."

It made Thomas sick to think people were hanging on to that hope of just one person dying; the more he thought about it, the less he believed it was true. The Creators knew the plan—they might reprogram the Grievers. But even false hope was better than nothing. "Maybe we can all make it. As long as everyone fights."

Chuck stopped stuffing his face for a second and looked at Thomas carefully. "You really think that, or you just trying to cheer me up?"

"We can do it." Thomas ate his last bite, took a big drink of water. He'd never felt like such a liar in his life. People were going to die. But he was going to do everything possible to make sure Chuck wasn't one of them. And Teresa. "Don't forget my promise. You can still plan on it."

Chuck frowned. "Big deal—I keep hearing the world is in klunky shape."

"Hey, maybe so, but we'll find the people who care about us— you'll see."

Chuck stood up. "Well, I don't wanna think about it," he announced. "Just get me out of the Maze, and I'll be one happy dude."

"Good that," Thomas agreed.

A commotion from the other tables caught his attention. Newt and Alby were gathering the Gladers, telling everyone it was time to go. Alby seemed mostly himself, but Thomas still worried about the guy's mental state. In Thomas's mind, Newt was in charge, but he could also be a loose cannon sometimes.

The icy fear and panic Thomas had experienced so often the last few days swept over him once again in full force. This was it. They were going. Trying not to think about it, to just act, he grabbed his backpack. Chuck did the same, and they headed for the West Door, the one leading to the Cliff.

Thomas found Minho and Teresa talking to each other near the left side of the Door, going over the hastily made plans to enter the escape code once they got into the Hole.

"You shanks ready?" Minho asked when they came up. "Thomas, this was all your idea, so it better work. If not, I'll kill ya before the Grievers can."

"Thanks," Thomas said. But he couldn't shake the twisting feeling in his gut. What if somehow he *was* wrong? What if the memories he'd had were false ones? *Planted* somehow? The thought terrified him, and he pushed it aside. There was no going back.

He looked at Teresa, who shifted from foot to foot, wringing her hands. "You okay?" he asked.

"I'm fine," she answered with a small smile, clearly not fine at all. "Just anxious to get it over with."

"Amen, sister," Minho said. He looked the calmest to Thomas, the most confident, the least scared. Thomas envied him.

When Newt finally had everyone gathered, he called for quiet, and Thomas turned to hear what he had to say. "There're forty-one of us." He pulled the backpack he was holding onto his shoulders, and hoisted a thick wooden pole with barbwire wrapped around its tip. The thing looked deadly. "Make sure you've got your weapons. Other than that, isn't a whole lot to buggin' say—you've all been told the plan. We're gonna fight our way through to the Griever Hole, and Tommy here's gonna punch in his little magic code and then we're gonna get payback on the Creators. Simple as that."

Thomas barely heard Newt, having seen Alby sulking over to the side, away from the main group of the Gladers, alone. Alby picked at the string of his bow while he stared at the ground. A quiver of arrows hung over his shoulder. Thomas felt a rising tide of worry that somehow Alby was unstable, that somehow he'd screw everything up. He decided to watch him carefully if he could.

"Shouldn't someone give a pep talk or something?" Minho asked, pulling Thomas's attention away from Alby.

"Go ahead," Newt replied.

Minho nodded and faced the crowd. "Be careful," he said dryly. "Don't die."

Thomas would have laughed if he could, but he was too scared for it to come out.

"Great. We're all bloody inspired," Newt answered, then pointed over his shoulder, toward the Maze. "You all know the plan. After two years of being treated like mice, tonight we're making a stand. Tonight we're taking the fight back to the Creators, no matter what we have to go through to get there. Tonight the Grievers better be scared."

Someone cheered, and then someone else. Soon shouts and battle calls broke out, rising in volume, filling the air like thunder. Thomas felt a trickle of courage inside him—he grasped it, clung to it, urged it to grow. Newt was right. Tonight, they'd fight. Tonight, they'd make their stand, once and for all.

Thomas was ready. He roared with the other Gladers. He knew they should probably be quiet, not bring any more attention to themselves, but he didn't care. The game was on.

Newt thrust his weapon into the air and yelled, "Hear that, Creators! We're coming!"

And with that, he turned and ran into the Maze, his limp barely noticeable. Into the gray air that seemed darker than the Glade, full of shadows and blackness. The Gladers around Thomas, still cheering, picked up their weapons and ran after him, even Alby. Thomas followed, falling into line between Teresa and Chuck, hefting a big wooden spear with a knife tied at its tip. The sudden feeling of responsibility for his friends almost overwhelmed him—made it hard to run. But he kept going, determined to win.

You can do this, he thought. *Just make it to that Hole.*

CHAPTER 55

Thomas kept a steady pace as he ran with the other Gladers along the stone pathways toward the Cliff. He'd grown used to running the Maze, but this was completely different. The sounds of shuffling feet echoed up the walls and the red lights of the beetle blades flashed more menacingly in the ivy—the Creators were certainly watching, listening. One way or another, there was going to be a fight.

Scared? Teresa asked him as they ran.

No, I love things made out of blubber and steel. Can't wait to see them. He felt no mirth or humor and wondered if there'd ever be a time again when he would.

So funny, she responded.

She was right next to him, but his eyes stayed glued up ahead. *We'll be fine. Just stay close to me and Minho.*

Ah, my Knight in Shining Armor. What, you don't think I can fend for myself?

Actually, he thought quite the opposite—Teresa seemed as tough as anybody there. *No, I'm just trying to be nice.*

The group was spread out across the full width of the corridor, running at a steady but quick pace—Thomas wondered how long the non-Runners would hold up. As if in response to the thought, Newt fell back, finally tapping Minho on the shoulder. "You lead the way now," Thomas heard him say.

Minho nodded and ran to the front, guiding the Gladers through all the turns necessary. Every step was agonizing for Thomas. What courage he'd gathered had turned to dread, and he wondered when the Grievers would finally give chase. Wondered when the fight would begin.

And so it went for him as they kept moving, those Gladers not used to running such distances gasping in huge gulps of air. But no one quit. On and on they ran, with no signs of Grievers. And as the time passed, Thomas let the slightest trickle of hope enter his system—maybe they'd make it before getting attacked. Maybe.

Finally, after the longest hour of Thomas's life, they reached the long alley that led to the last turn before the Cliff—a short corridor to the right that branched off like the stem of the letter *T*.

Thomas, his heart thumping, sweat slicking his skin, had moved up right behind Minho, Teresa at his side. Minho slowed at the corner, then stopped, holding up a hand to tell Thomas and the others to do the same. Then he turned, a look of horror on his face.

"Do you hear that?" he whispered.

Thomas shook his head, trying to squash the terror Minho's expression had given him.

Minho crept ahead and peeked around the sharp edge of stone, looking toward the Cliff. Thomas had seen him do that before, when they'd followed a Griever to this very spot. Just like that time, Minho jerked back and turned to face him.

"Oh, no," the Keeper said through a moan. "Oh, no."

Then Thomas heard it. Griever sounds. It was as if they'd been hiding, waiting, and now were coming to life. He didn't even have to look—he knew what Minho was going to say before he said it.

"There's at least a dozen of them. Maybe fifteen." He reached up and rubbed his eyes with the heels of his hands. "They're just waiting for us!"

The icy chill of fear bit Thomas harder than ever before. He looked over at Teresa, about to say something, but stopped when he saw the expression on her pale face—he'd never seen terror present itself so starkly.

Newt and Alby had moved up the line of waiting Gladers to join Thomas and the others. Apparently Minho's pronouncement had already been whispered through the ranks, because the first thing Newt said was "Well, we knew we'd have to fight." But the tremor in his voice gave him away—he was just trying to say the right thing.

Thomas felt it himself. It'd been easy to talk about—the nothing-to-lose fight, the hope that just one of them would be taken, the chance to finally escape. But now it was here, literally around the corner. Doubts that he could go through with it seeped into his mind and heart. He wondered why the Grievers were just waiting—the beetle blades had obviously let them know the Gladers were coming. Were the Creators *enjoying* this?

He had an idea. "Maybe they've already taken a kid back at the Glade. Maybe we can get past them—why else would they just be sitting—"

A loud noise from behind cut him off—he spun to see more Grievers moving down the corridor toward them, spikes flaring, metal arms groping, coming from the direction of the Glade. Thomas was just about to say something when he heard sounds from the other end of the long alley—he looked to see yet more Grievers.

The enemy was on all sides, blocking them off completely.

The Gladers surged toward Thomas, forming a tight group, forcing him to move out into the open intersection where the Cliff corridor met the long alley. He saw the pack of Grievers between them and the Cliff, spikes extended, their moist skin pulsing in and out. Waiting, watching. The other two groups of Grievers had closed in and stopped just a few dozen feet from the Gladers, also waiting, watching.

Thomas slowly turned in a circle, fought the fear as he took it all in. They were surrounded. They had no choice now—there was nowhere to go. A sharp pulsing pain throbbed behind his eyes.

The Gladers compressed into a tighter group around him, everyone facing outward, huddled together in the center of the *T* intersection. Thomas was pressed between Newt and Teresa—he could feel Newt trembling. No one said a word. The only sounds were the eerie moans and whirrs of machinery coming from the Grievers, sitting there as if enjoying the little trap they'd set for the humans. Their disgusting bodies heaved in and out with mechanical wheezes of breath.

What are they doing? Thomas called out to Teresa. *What are they waiting for?*

She didn't answer, which worried him. He reached out and squeezed her hand. The Gladers around him stood silent, clutching their meager weapons.

Thomas looked over at Newt. "Got any ideas?"

"No," he replied, his voice just the tiniest bit shaky. "I don't understand what they're bloody waitin' for."

"We shouldn't have come," Alby said. He'd been so quiet, his voice sounded odd, especially with the hollow echo the Maze walls created.

Thomas was in no mood for whining—they had to *do* something. "Well, we'd be no better off in the Homestead. Hate to say it, but if one of us dies, that's better than all of us." He really hoped the one-person-a-night thing was true now. Seeing all these Grievers close up hit home with an explosion of reality—could they really fight them all?

A long moment passed before Alby replied. "Maybe I should . . ." He trailed off and started walking forward—in the direction of the Cliff—slowly, as if in a trance. Thomas watched in detached awe—he couldn't believe his eyes.

"Alby?" Newt said. "Get back here!"

Instead of responding, Alby took off running—he headed straight for the pack of Grievers between him and the Cliff.

"Alby!" Newt screamed.

Thomas started to say something himself, but Alby had already made it to the monsters and jumped on top of one. Newt moved away from Thomas's side and toward Alby—but five or six Grievers had already burst to life and attacked the boy in a blur of metal and skin. Thomas reached out and grabbed Newt by the arms before he could go any farther, then pulled him backward.

"Let go!" Newt yelled, struggling to break loose.

"Are you nuts!" Thomas shouted. "There's nothing you can do!"

Two more Grievers broke from the pack and swarmed over Alby, piling on top of each other, snapping and cutting at the boy, as if they wanted to rub it in, show their vicious cruelty. Somehow, impossibly, Alby didn't scream. Thomas lost sight of the body as he struggled with Newt, thankful for the distraction. Newt finally gave up, collapsing backward in defeat.

Alby'd flipped once and for all, Thomas thought, fighting the urge to rid his stomach of its contents. Their leader had been so scared to go back to whatever he'd seen, he'd chosen to sacrifice himself instead. He was gone. Totally gone.

Thomas helped steady Newt on his feet; the Glader couldn't stop staring at the spot where his friend had disappeared.

"I can't believe it," Newt whispered. "I can't believe he just did that."

Thomas shook his head, unable to reply. Seeing Alby go down like that . . . a new kind of pain he'd never felt before filled his insides—an ill, disturbed pain; it felt worse than the physical kind. And he didn't even know if it had anything to do with Alby—he'd never much liked the guy. But the thought that what he'd just seen might happen to Chuck—or Teresa . . .

Minho moved closer to Thomas and Newt, squeezed Newt's shoulder. "We can't waste what he did." He turned toward Thomas. "We'll fight 'em if we have to, make a path to the Cliff for you and Teresa. Get in the Hole and do your thing—we'll keep them off until you scream for us to follow."

Thomas looked at each of the three sets of Grievers—not one had yet made a move toward the Gladers—and nodded. "Hopefully they'll go dormant for a while. We should only need a minute or so to punch in the code."

"How can you guys be so heartless?" Newt murmured, the disgust in his voice surprising Thomas.

"What do you want, Newt?" Minho said. "Should we all dress up and have a funeral?"

Newt didn't respond, still staring at the spot where the Grievers seemed to be *feeding* on Alby beneath them. Thomas couldn't help taking a peek—he saw a smear of bright red on one of the creatures' bodies. His stomach turned and he quickly looked away.

Minho continued. "Alby didn't wanna go back to his old life. He freaking *sacrificed* himself for us—and they aren't attacking, so maybe it worked. *We'd* be heartless if we wasted it."

Newt only shrugged, closed his eyes.

Minho turned and faced the huddled group of Gladers. "Listen up! Number one priority is to protect Thomas and Teresa. Get them to the Cliff and the Hole so—"

The sounds of the Grievers revving to life cut him off. Thomas looked up in horror. The creatures on both sides of their group seemed to have noticed them again. Spikes were popping in and out of blubbery skin; their bodies shuddered and pulsed. Then, in unison, the monsters moved forward, slowly, instrument-tipped appendages unfolding, pointed at Thomas and the Gladers, ready to kill. Tightening their trap formation like a noose, the Grievers steadily charged toward them.

Alby's sacrifice had failed miserably.

CHAPTER 56

Thomas grabbed Minho by the arm. "Somehow I have to get through that!" He nodded toward the rolling pack of Grievers between them and the Cliff—they looked like one big mass of rumbling, spiked blubber, glistening with flashes of lights off steel. They were even more menacing in the faded gray light.

Thomas waited for an answer as Minho and Newt exchanged a long glance. The anticipation of fighting was almost worse than the fear of it.

"They're *coming*!" Teresa yelled. "We have to do something!"

"You lead," Newt finally said to Minho, his voice barely more than a whisper. "Make a bloody path for Tommy and the girl. Do it."

Minho nodded once, a steel look of resolve hardening his features. Then he turned toward the Gladers. "We head straight for the Cliff! Fight through the middle, push the shuckin' things toward the walls. What matters most is getting Thomas and Teresa to the Griever Hole!"

Thomas looked away from him, back at the approaching monsters—they were only a few feet away. He gripped his poor excuse for a spear.

We have to stay close together, he told Teresa. *Let them do the fighting—we have to get through that Hole.* He felt like a coward, but he knew that any fighting—and any deaths—would be in vain if they didn't get that code punched, the door to the Creators opened.

I know, she replied. *Stick together.*

336

"Ready!" Minho yelled next to Thomas, raising his barbwire-wrapped club into the air with one hand, a long silver knife in the other. He pointed the knife at the horde of Grievers; a flash glinted off the blade. *"Now!"*

The Keeper ran forward without waiting for a response. Newt went after him, right on his heels, and then the rest of the Gladers followed, a tight pack of roaring boys charging ahead to a bloody battle, weapons raised. Thomas held Teresa's hand, let them all go past, felt them bump him, smelled their sweat, sensed their terror, waiting for the perfect opportunity to make his own dash.

Just as the first sounds of boys crashing into Grievers filled the air—pierced with screams and roars of machinery and wood clacking against steel—Chuck ran past Thomas, who quickly reached out and grabbed his arm.

Chuck stumbled backward, then looked up at Thomas, his eyes so full of fright Thomas felt something shatter in his heart. In that split second, he'd made a decision.

"Chuck, you're with me and Teresa." He said it forcefully, with authority, leaving no room for doubt.

Chuck looked ahead at the engaged battle. "But . . ." He trailed off, and Thomas knew the boy relished the idea though he was ashamed to admit it.

Thomas quickly tried to save his dignity. "We need your help in the Griever Hole, in case one of those things is in there waiting for us."

Chuck nodded quickly—too quickly. Again, Thomas felt the pang of sadness in his heart, felt the urge to get Chuck home safely stronger than he'd ever felt it before.

"Okay, then," Thomas said. "Hold Teresa's other hand. Let's go."

Chuck did as he was told, trying so hard to act brave. And, Thomas noted, not saying a word, perhaps for the first time in his life.

They've made an opening! Teresa shouted in Thomas's mind—it sent a quick snap of pain shooting through his skull. She pointed ahead, and Thomas saw the narrow aisle forming in the middle of the corridor, Gladers fighting wildly to push the Grievers toward the walls.

"Now!" Thomas shouted.

He sprinted ahead, pulling Teresa behind him, Teresa pulling Chuck behind her, running at full speed, spears and knives cocked for battle, forward into the bloody, scream-filled hallway of stone. Toward the Cliff.

War raged around them. Gladers fought, panic-induced adrenaline driving them on. The sounds echoing off the walls were a cacophony of terror—human screams, metal clashing against metal, motors roaring, the haunted shrieks of the Grievers, saws spinning, claws clasping, boys yelling for help. All was a blur, bloody and gray and flashes of steel; Thomas tried not to look left or right, only ahead, through the narrow gap formed by the Gladers.

Even as they ran, Thomas went through the code words again in his mind. *FLOAT, CATCH, BLEED, DEATH, STIFF, PUSH.* They just had to make it a few dozen feet more.

Something just sliced my arm! Teresa screamed. Even as she said it, Thomas felt a sharp stab in his leg. He didn't look back, didn't bother answering. The seething impossibility of their predicament was like a heavy deluge of black water flooding around him, dragging him toward surrender. He fought it, pushed himself forward.

There was the Cliff, opening out into a gray-dark sky, about twenty feet away. He surged ahead, pulling his friends.

Battles clashed on both sides of them; Thomas refused to look, refused to help. A Griever spun directly in his path; a boy, his face hidden from sight, was clutched in its claws, stabbing viciously into the thick, whalish skin, trying to escape. Thomas dodged to the left, kept running. He heard a shriek as he passed by, a throat-scorching wail that could only mean the Glader had lost the fight, met a horrific end. The scream ran on, shattering the air, overpowering the other sounds of war, until it faded in death. Thomas felt his heart tremble, hoped it wasn't someone he knew.

Just keep going! Teresa said.

"*I know!*" Thomas shouted back, this time out loud.

Someone sprinted past Thomas, bumped him. A Griever charged in from the right, blades twirling. A Glader cut it off, attacked it with two long swords, metal clacking and clanging as they fought. Thomas heard a distant voice, screaming the same words over and over, something about him. About protecting him as he ran. It was Minho, desperation and fatigue radiant in his shouts.

Thomas kept going.

One almost got Chuck! Teresa yelled, a violent echo in his head.

More Grievers came at them, more Gladers helped. Winston had picked up Alby's bow and arrow, flinging the steel-pointed shafts at anything nonhuman that moved, missing more than he hit. Boys Thomas didn't know ran alongside him, whacking at Griever instruments with their makeshift weapons, jumping on them, attacking. The sounds— clashes, clangs, screams, moaning wails, roars of engines, spinning saws, snapping blades, the screech of spikes against the floor, hair-raising pleas for help—it all grew to a crescendo, became unbearable.

Thomas screamed, but he kept running until they made it to the Cliff. He skidded to a stop, right on the edge. Teresa and Chuck bumped into him, almost sending all three of them to an endless fall. In a split second, Thomas surveyed his view of the Griever Hole. Hanging out, in the middle of thin air, were ivy vines stretching to nowhere.

Earlier, Minho and a couple of Runners had pulled out ropes of ivy and knotted them to vines still attached to the walls. They'd then tossed the loose ends over the Cliff, until they hit the Griever Hole, where now six or seven vines ran from the stone edge to an invisible rough square, hovering in the empty sky, where they disappeared into nothingness.

It was time to jump. Thomas hesitated, feeling one last moment of stark terror—hearing the horrible sounds behind him, seeing the illusion in front of him—then snapped out of it. "You first, Teresa." He wanted to go last to make sure a Griever didn't get her or Chuck.

To his surprise, she didn't hesitate. After squeezing Thomas's hand, then Chuck's shoulder, she leaped off the edge, immediately stiffening her legs, with her arms by her sides. Thomas held his breath until she slipped into the spot between the cut-off ivy ropes and disappeared. It looked as if she'd been erased from existence with one quick swipe.

"Whoa!" Chuck yelled, the slightest hint of his old self breaking through.

"*Whoa* is right," Thomas said. "You're next."

Before the boy could argue, Thomas grabbed him under his arms, squeezed Chuck's torso. "Push off with your legs and I'll give you a lift. Ready? One, two, *three!*" He grunted with effort, heaved him over toward the Hole.

Chuck screamed as he flew through the air, and he almost missed the target, but his feet went through; then his stomach and arms slammed against the sides of the invisible hole before he disappeared inside. The boy's bravery solidified something in Thomas's heart. He loved the kid. He loved him as if they had the same mom.

Thomas tightened the straps on his backpack, held his makeshift fighting spear tightly in his right fist. The sounds behind him were awful, horrible—he felt guilty for not helping. *Just do your part,* he told himself.

Steeling his nerves, he tapped his spear against the stone ground, then planted his left foot on the very edge of the Cliff and jumped, catapulting up and into the twilight air. He pulled the spear close to his torso, pointed his toes downward, stiffened his body.

Then he hit the Hole.

CHAPTER 57

A line of icy cold shot across Thomas's skin as he entered the Griever Hole, starting from his toes and continuing up his whole body, as if he'd jumped through a flat plane of freezing water. The world went even darker around him as his feet thumped to a landing on a slippery surface, then shot out from under him; he fell backward into Teresa's arms. She and Chuck helped him stand. It was a miracle Thomas hadn't stabbed someone's eye out with his spear.

The Griever Hole would've been pitch-black if not for the beam of Teresa's flashlight cutting through the darkness. As Thomas got his bearings, he realized they were standing in a ten-foot-high stone cylinder. It was damp, and covered in shiny, grimy oil, and it stretched out in front of them for dozens of yards before it faded into darkness. Thomas peered up at the Hole through which they'd come—it looked like a square window into a deep, starless space.

"The computer's over there," Teresa said, grabbing his attention.

Several feet down the tunnel, she had aimed her light at a small square of grimy glass that shone a dull green color. Beneath it, a keyboard was set into the wall, angling out enough for someone to type on it with ease if standing. There it was, ready for the code. Thomas couldn't help thinking it seemed too easy, too good to be true.

"Put the words in!" Chuck yelled, slapping Thomas on the shoulder. "Hurry!"

Thomas motioned for Teresa to do it. "Chuck and I'll keep watch, make sure a Griever doesn't come through the Hole." He just hoped the Gladers had turned their attention from making the aisle in the Maze to keeping the creatures away from the Cliff.

"Okay," Teresa said—Thomas knew she was too smart to waste time arguing about it. She stepped up to the keyboard and screen, then started typing.

Wait! Thomas called to her mind. *Are you sure you know the words?*

She turned to him and scowled. "I'm not an idiot, Tom. Yes, I'm perfectly capable of remembering—"

A loud bang from above and behind them cut her off, made Thomas jump. He spun around to see a Griever plop through the Griever Hole, appearing as if by magic from the dark square of black. The thing had retracted its spikes and arms to enter—when it landed with a squishy thump, a dozen sharp and nasty objects popped back out, looking deadlier than ever.

Thomas pushed Chuck behind him and faced the creature, holding out his spear as if that would ward it off. "Just keep typing, Teresa!" he yelled.

A skinny metallic rod burst out of the Griever's moist skin, unfolding into a long appendage with three spinning blades, which moved directly toward Thomas's face.

He gripped the end of his spear with both hands, squeezing tightly as he lowered the knife-laced point to the ground in front of him. The bladed arm moved within two feet, ready to slice his skin to bits. When it was just a foot away, Thomas tensed his muscles and swung the spear up, around, and toward the ceiling as hard as he could. It smacked the metal arm and pivoted the thing skyward, revolving in an arc until it slammed back into the body of the Griever. The monster let out an angry shriek and pulled back several feet, its spikes retracting into its body. Thomas heaved breaths in and out.

Maybe I can hold it off, he said quickly to Teresa. *Just hurry!*

I'm almost done, she replied.

The Griever's spikes appeared again; it surged ahead and another arm popped out of its skin and shot forward, this one with huge claws, snapping to grab the spear. Thomas swung, this time from above his head, throwing every bit of strength into the attack. The spear crashed into the base of the claws. With a loud clunk, and then a squishing sound, the entire arm ripped free of its socket, falling to the floor. Then, from some kind of mouth that Thomas couldn't see, the Griever let out a long, piercing shriek and pulled back again; the spikes disappeared.

"These things are beatable!" Thomas shouted.

It won't let me enter the last word! Teresa said in his mind.

Barely hearing her, not quite understanding, he yelled out a roar and charged ahead to take advantage of the Griever's moment of weakness. Swinging his spear wildly, he jumped on top of the creature's bulbous body, whacking two metal arms away from him with a loud crack. He lifted the spear above his head, braced his feet—felt them sink into the disgusting blubber—then thrust the spear down and into the monster. A slimy yellow goo exploded from the flesh, splashing over Thomas's legs as he drove the spear as far as it would sink into the thing's body. Then he released the hilt of the weapon and jumped away, running back to Chuck and Teresa.

Thomas watched in sick fascination as the Griever twitched uncontrollably, spewing the yellow oil in every direction. Spikes popped in and out of the skin; its remaining arms swung around in mass confusion, at times impaling its own body. Soon it began to slow, losing energy with every ounce of blood—or fuel—it lost.

A few seconds later, it stopped moving altogether. Thomas couldn't believe it. He absolutely couldn't believe it. He'd just defeated a

Griever, one of the monsters that had terrorized the Gladers for more than two years.

He glanced behind him at Chuck, standing there with eyes wide.

"You killed it," the boy said. He laughed, as if that one act had solved all their problems.

"Wasn't so hard," Thomas muttered, then turned to see Teresa frantically typing away at the keyboard. He knew immediately that something was wrong.

"What's the problem?" he asked, almost shouting. He ran up to look over her shoulder and saw that she kept typing the word *PUSH* over and over, but nothing appeared on the screen.

She pointed at the dirty square of glass, empty but for its greenish glow of life. "I put in all the words and one by one they appeared on the screen; then something beeped and they'd disappear. But it won't let me type in the last word. Nothing's happening!"

Cold filled Thomas's veins as Teresa's words sank in. "Well . . . why?"

"I don't know!" She tried again, then again. Nothing appeared.

"Thomas!" Chuck screamed from behind them. Thomas turned to see him pointing at the Griever Hole—another creature was making its way through. As he watched, it plopped down on top of its dead brother and another Griever started entering the Hole.

"What's taking so long!" Chuck cried frantically. "You said they'd turn off when you punched in the code!"

Both Grievers had righted themselves and extended their spikes, had started moving toward them.

"It won't let us enter the word *PUSH*," Thomas said absently, not really speaking to Chuck but trying to think of a solution . . .

I don't get it, Teresa said.

The Grievers were coming, only a few feet away. Feeling his will fade into blackness, Thomas braced his feet and held up his fists half-heartedly. It was supposed to work. The code was supposed to—

"Maybe you should just push that button," Chuck said.

Thomas was so surprised by the random statement that he turned away from the Grievers, looked at the boy. Chuck was pointing at a spot near the floor, right underneath the screen and keyboard.

Before he could move, Teresa was already down there, crouching on her knees. And consumed by curiosity, by a fleeting hope, Thomas joined her, collapsing to the ground to get a better look. He heard the Griever moan and roar behind him, felt a sharp claw grab his shirt, felt a prick of pain. But he could only stare.

A small red button was set into the wall only a few inches above the floor. Three black words were printed there, so obvious he couldn't believe he'd missed it earlier.

Kill the Maze

More pain snapped Thomas out of his stupor. The Griever had grabbed him with two instruments, had started dragging him backward. The other one had gone after Chuck and was just about to swipe at the kid with a long blade.

A button.

"Push!" Thomas screamed, louder than he'd thought possible for a human being to scream.

And Teresa did.

She pushed the button and everything went perfectly silent. Then, from somewhere down the dark tunnel, came the sound of a door sliding open.

CHAPTER 58

Almost at once the Grievers had shut down completely, their instruments sucked back through their blubbery skin, their lights turned off, their inside machines dead quiet. And that door . . .

Thomas fell to the floor after being released by his captor's claws, and despite the pain of several lacerations across his back and shoulders, elation surged through him so strongly he didn't know how to react. He gasped, then laughed, then choked on a sob before laughing again.

Chuck had scooted away from the Grievers, bumping into Teresa—she held him tightly, squeezing him in a fierce hug.

"You did it, Chuck," Teresa said. "We were so worried about the stupid code words, we didn't think to look around for something to *push*—the last word, the last piece of the puzzle."

Thomas laughed again, in disbelief that such a thing could be possible so soon after what they'd gone through. "She's right, Chuck—you saved us, man! I *told* you we needed you!" Thomas scrambled to his feet and joined the other two in a group hug, almost delirious. "Chuck's a shucking hero!"

"What about the others?" Teresa said with a nod toward the Griever Hole. Thomas felt his elation wither, and he stepped back and turned toward the Hole.

As if in answer to her question, someone fell through the black square—it was Minho, looking as if he'd been scratched or stabbed on ninety percent of his body.

"Minho!" Thomas shouted, filled with relief. "Are you okay? What about everybody else?"

Minho stumbled toward the curved wall of the tunnel, then leaned there, gulping big breaths. "We lost a ton of people. . . . It's a mess of blood up there . . . then they all just shut down." He paused, taking in a really deep breath and letting it go in a rush of air. "You did it. I can't believe it actually worked."

Newt came through then, followed by Frypan. Then Winston and others. Before long eighteen boys had joined Thomas and his friends in the tunnel, making a total of twenty-one Gladers in all. Every last one of those who'd stayed behind and fought was covered in Griever sludge and human blood, their clothes ripped to shreds.

"The rest?" Thomas asked, terrified of the answer.

"Half of us," Newt said, his voice weak. "Dead."

No one said a word then. No one said a word for a very long time.

"You know what?" Minho said, standing up a little taller. "Half might've died, but half of us shucking lived. And nobody got stung—just like Thomas thought. We've gotta get out of here."

Too many, Thomas thought. *Too many by far.* His joy dribbled away, turned into a deep mourning for the twenty people who'd lost their lives. Despite the alternative, despite knowing that if they hadn't tried to escape, *all* of them might've died, it still hurt, even though he hadn't known them very well. Such a display of death—how could it be considered a victory?

"Let's get out of here," Newt said. "Right now."

"Where do we go?" Minho asked.

Thomas pointed down the long tunnel. "I heard the door open

down that way." He tried to push away the ache of it all—the horrors of the battle they'd just won. The losses. He pushed it away, knowing they were nowhere near safe yet.

"Well—let's go," Minho answered. And the older boy turned and started walking up the tunnel without waiting for a response.

Newt nodded, ushering the other Gladers past him to follow. One by one they went until only he remained with Thomas and Teresa.

"I'll go last," Thomas said.

No one argued. Newt went, then Chuck, then Teresa, into the black tunnel. Even the flashlights seemed to get swallowed by the darkness. Thomas followed, not even bothering to look back at the dead Grievers.

After a minute or so of walking, he heard a shriek from ahead, followed by another, then another. Their cries faded, as if they were falling. . . .

Murmurs made their way down the line, and finally Teresa turned to Thomas. "Looks like it ends in a slide up there, shooting downward."

Thomas's stomach turned at the thought. It seemed like it *was* a game—for whoever had built the place, at least.

One by one he heard the Gladers' dwindling shouts and hoots up ahead. Then it was Newt's turn, then Chuck's. Teresa shone her light down on a steeply descending, slick black chute of metal.

Guess we have no choice, she said to his mind.

Guess not. Thomas had a strong feeling it wasn't a way out of their nightmare; he just hoped it didn't lead to another pack of Grievers.

Teresa slipped down the slide with an almost cheerful shriek, and Thomas followed her before he could talk himself out of it—anything was better than the Maze.

His body shot down a steep decline, slick with an oily goo that smelled awful—like burnt plastic and overused machinery. He twisted his body until he got his feet in front of him, then tried to hold his hands out to slow himself down. It was useless—the greasy stuff covered every inch of the stone; he couldn't grip anything.

The screams of the other Gladers echoed off the tunnel walls as they slid down the oily chute. Panic gripped Thomas's heart. He couldn't fight off the image that they'd been swallowed by some gigantic beast and were sliding down its long esophagus, about to land in its stomach at any second. And as if his thoughts had materialized, the smells changed—to something more like mildew and rot. He started gagging; it took all his effort not to throw up on himself.

The tunnel began to twist, turning in a rough spiral, just enough to slow them down, and Thomas's feet smacked right into Teresa, hitting her in the head; he recoiled and a feeling of complete misery sank over him. They were still falling. Time seemed to stretch out, endless.

Around and around they went down the tube. Nausea burned in his stomach—the squishing of the goo against his body, the smell, the circling motion. He was just about to turn his head to the side to throw up when Teresa let out a sharp cry—this time there was no echo. A second later, Thomas flew out of the tunnel and landed on her.

Bodies scrambled everywhere, people on top of people, groaning and squirming in confusion as they tried to push away from each other. Thomas wiggled his arms and legs to scoot away from Teresa, then crawled a few more feet to throw up, emptying his stomach.

Still shuddering from the experience, he wiped at his mouth with his hand, only to realize it was covered in slimy filth. He sat up, rubbing both hands on the ground, and he finally got a good look at where they'd arrived. As he gaped, he saw, also, that everyone else had pulled themselves together into a group, taking in the new surroundings.

Thomas had seen glimpses of it during the Changing, but didn't truly remember it until that very moment.

They were in a huge underground chamber big enough to hold nine or ten Homesteads. From top to bottom, side to side, the place was covered in all kinds of machinery and wires and ducts and computers. On one side of the room—to his right—there was a row of forty or so large white pods that looked like enormous coffins. Across from that on the other side stood large glass doors, although the lighting made it impossible to see what was on the other side.

"Look!" someone shouted, but he'd already seen it, his breath catching in his throat. Goose bumps broke out all over him, a creepy fear trickling down his spine like a wet spider.

Directly in front of them, a row of twenty or so darkly tinged windows stretched across the compound horizontally, one after the other. Behind each one, a person—some men, some women, all of them pale and thin—sat observing the Gladers, staring through the glass with squinted eyes. Thomas shuddered, terrified—they all looked like ghosts. Angry, starving, sinister apparitions of people who'd never been happy when alive, much less dead.

But Thomas knew they were not, of course, ghosts. They were the people who'd sent them all to the Glade. The people who'd taken their lives away from them.

The Creators.

CHAPTER 59

Thomas took a step backward, noticing others doing the same. A deathly silence sucked the life out of the air as every last Glader stared at the row of windows, at the row of observers. Thomas watched one of them look down to write something, another reach up and put on a pair of glasses. They all wore black coats over white shirts, a word stitched on their right breast—he couldn't quite make out what it said. None of them wore any kind of discernible facial expression—they were all sallow and gaunt, miserably sad to look upon.

They continued to stare at the Gladers; a man shook his head, a woman nodded. Another man reached up and scratched his nose—the most human thing Thomas had seen any of them do.

"Who are those people?" Chuck whispered, but his voice echoed throughout the chamber with a raspy edge.

"The Creators," Minho said; then he spat on the floor. "I'm gonna break your faces!" he screamed, so loudly Thomas almost held his hands over his ears.

"What do we do?" Thomas asked. "What are they waiting on?"

"They've probably revved the Grievers back up," Newt said. "They're probably coming right—"

A loud, slow beeping sound cut him off, like the warning alarm of a huge truck driving in reverse, but much more powerful. It came from everywhere, booming and echoing throughout the chamber.

"What now?" Chuck asked, not hiding the concern in his voice.

For some reason everyone looked at Thomas; he shrugged in answer—he'd only remembered so much, and now he was just as clueless as anyone else. And scared. He craned his neck as he scanned the place top to bottom, trying to find the source of the beeps. But nothing had changed. Then, out of the corner of his eye, he noticed the other Gladers looking in the direction of the doors. He did as well; his heart quickened when he saw that one of the doors was swinging open toward them.

The beeping stopped, and a silence as deep as outer space settled on the chamber. Thomas waited without breathing, braced himself for something horrible to come flying through the door.

Instead, two people walked into the room.

One was a woman. An actual grown-up. She seemed very ordinary, wearing black pants and a button-down white shirt with a logo on the breast—WICKED spelled in blue capital letters. Her brown hair was cut at the shoulder, and she had a thin face with dark eyes. As she walked toward the group, she neither smiled nor frowned—it was almost as if she didn't notice or care they were standing there.

I know her, Thomas thought. But it was a cloudy kind of recollection—he couldn't remember her name or what she had to do with the Maze, but she seemed familiar. And not just her looks, but the way she walked, her mannerisms—stiff, without a hint of joy. She stopped several feet in front of the Gladers and slowly looked left to right, taking them all in.

The other person, standing next to her, was a boy wearing an overly large sweatshirt, its hood pulled up over his head, concealing his face.

"Welcome back," the woman finally said. "Over two years, and so few dead. Amazing."

Thomas felt his mouth drop open—felt anger redden his face.

"*Excuse* me?" Newt asked.

Her eyes scanned the crowd again before falling on Newt. "Everything has gone according to plan, Mr. Newton. Although we expected a few more of you to give up along the way."

She glanced over at her companion, then reached out and pulled the hood off the boy. He looked up, his eyes wet with tears. Every Glader in the room sucked in a breath of surprise. Thomas felt his knees buckle.

It was Gally.

Thomas blinked, then rubbed his eyes, like something out of a cartoon. He was consumed with shock and anger.

It was *Gally*.

"What's *he* doing here!" Minho shouted.

"You're safe now," the woman responded as if she hadn't heard him. "Please, be at ease."

"At ease?" Minho barked. "Who are you, telling us to be at ease? We wanna see the police, the mayor, the president—somebody!" Thomas worried what Minho might do—then again, Thomas kind of wanted him to go punch her in the face.

She narrowed her eyes as she looked at Minho. "You have no idea what you're talking about, boy. I'd expect more maturity from someone who's passed the Maze Trials." Her condescending tone shocked Thomas.

Minho started to retort, but Newt elbowed him in the gut.

"Gally," Newt said. "What's going on?"

The dark-haired boy looked at him; his eyes flared for a moment, his head shaking slightly. But he didn't respond. *Something's off with him,* Thomas thought. Worse than before.

The woman nodded as if proud of him. "One day you'll all be

354

grateful for what we've done for you. I can only promise this, and trust your minds to accept it. If you don't, then the whole thing was a mistake. Dark times, Mr. Newton. Dark times."

She paused. "There is, of course, one final Variable." She stepped back.

Thomas focused on Gally. The boy's whole body trembled, his face pasty white, making his wet, red eyes stand out like bloody splotches on paper. His lips pressed together; the skin around them twitched, as if he were trying to speak but couldn't.

"Gally?" Thomas asked, trying to suppress the complete hatred he had for him.

Words burst from Gally's mouth. "They . . . can control me . . . I don't—" His eyes bulged, a hand went to his throat as if he were choking. "I . . . have . . . to . . ." Each word was a croaking cough. Then he stilled, his face calming, his body relaxing.

It was just like Alby in bed, back in the Glade, after he went through the Changing. The same type of thing had happened to him. What did it—

But Thomas didn't have time to finish his thought. Gally reached behind himself, pulled something long and shiny from his back pocket. The lights of the chamber flashed off the silvery surface—a wicked-looking dagger, gripped tightly in his fingers. With unexpected speed, he reared back and threw the knife at Thomas. As he did so, Thomas heard a shout to his right, sensed *movement*. Toward him.

The blade windmilled, its every turn visible to Thomas, as if the world had turned to slow motion. As if it did so for the sole purpose of allowing him to feel the terror of seeing such a thing. On the knife came, flipping over and over, straight at him. A strangled cry was forming in his throat; he urged himself to move but he couldn't.

Then, inexplicably, Chuck was there, diving in front of him. Thomas felt as if his feet had been frozen in blocks of ice; he could only stare at the scene of horror unfolding before him, completely helpless.

With a sickening, wet thunk, the dagger slammed into Chuck's chest, burying itself to the hilt. The boy screamed, fell to the floor, his body already convulsing. Blood poured from the wound, dark crimson. His legs slapped against the floor, feet kicking aimlessly with onrushing death. Red spit oozed from between his lips. Thomas felt as if the world were collapsing around him, crushing his heart.

He fell to the ground, pulled Chuck's shaking body into his arms.

"Chuck!" he screamed; his voice felt like acid ripping through his throat. *"Chuck!"*

The boy shook uncontrollably, blood everywhere, wetting Thomas's hands. Chuck's eyes had rolled up in their sockets, dull white orbs. Blood trickled out of his nose and mouth.

"Chuck . . . ," Thomas said, this time a whisper. There had to be something they could do. They could save him. They—

The boy stopped convulsing, stilled. His eyes slid back into normal position, focused on Thomas, clinging to life. "Thom . . . mas." It was one word, barely there.

"Hang on, Chuck," Thomas said. "Don't die—fight it. *Someone get help!*"

Nobody moved, and deep inside, Thomas knew why. Nothing *could* help now. It was over. Black spots swam before Thomas's eyes; the room tilted and swayed. *No,* he thought. *Not Chuck. Not Chuck. Anyone but Chuck.*

"Thomas," Chuck whispered. "Find . . . my mom." A racking cough burst from his lungs, throwing a spray of blood. "Tell her . . ."

He didn't finish. His eyes closed, his body went limp. One last breath wheezed from his mouth.

Thomas stared at him, stared at his friend's lifeless body.

Something happened within Thomas. It started deep down in his chest, a seed of rage. Of revenge. Of hate. Something dark and terrible. And then it exploded, bursting through his lungs, through his neck, through his arms and legs. Through his mind.

He let go of Chuck, stood up, trembling, turned to face their new visitors.

And then Thomas snapped. He completely and utterly *snapped*.

He rushed forward, threw himself on Gally, grasping with his fingers like claws. He found the boy's throat, squeezed, fell to the ground on top of him. He straddled the boy's torso, gripped him with his legs so he couldn't escape. Thomas started punching.

He held Gally down with his left hand, pushing down on the boy's neck, as his right fist rained punches upon Gally's face, one after another. Down and down and down, slamming his balled knuckles into the boy's cheek and nose. There was crunching, there was blood, there were horrible screams. Thomas didn't know which were louder— Gally's or his own. He beat him—*beat* him as he released every ounce of rage he'd ever owned.

And then he was being pulled away by Minho and Newt, his arms still flailing even when they only hit air. They dragged him across the floor; he fought them, squirmed, yelled to be left alone. His eyes remained on Gally, lying there, still; Thomas could feel the hatred pouring out, as if a visible line of flame connected them.

And then, just like that, it all vanished. There were only thoughts of Chuck.

He threw off Minho's and Newt's grip, ran to the limp, lifeless body of his friend. He grabbed him, pulled him back into his arms, ignoring the blood, ignoring the frozen look of death on the boy's face.

"*No!*" Thomas shouted, sadness consuming him. "*No!*"

Teresa was there, put her hand on his shoulder. He shook it away.

"I promised him!" he screamed, realizing even as he did so that his voice was laced with something wrong. Almost insanity. "I promised I'd save him, take him home! I *promised* him!"

Teresa didn't respond, only nodded, her eyes cast to the ground.

Thomas hugged Chuck to his chest, squeezed him as tightly as possible, as if that could somehow bring him back, or show thanks for saving his life, for being his friend when no one else would.

Thomas cried, wept like he'd never wept before. His great, racking sobs echoed through the chamber like the sounds of tortured pain.

CHAPTER 60

He finally pulled it all back into his heart, sucking in the painful tide of his misery. In the Glade, Chuck had become a symbol for him—a beacon that somehow they could make everything right again in the world. Sleep in beds. Get kissed goodnight. Have bacon and eggs for breakfast, go to a real school. Be happy.

But now Chuck was gone. And his limp body, to which Thomas still clung, seemed a cold talisman—that not only would those dreams of a hopeful future never come to pass, but that life had never been that way in the first place. That even in escape, dreary days lay ahead. A life of sorrow.

His returning memories were sketchy at best. But not much good floated in the muck.

Thomas reeled in the pain, locked it somewhere deep inside him. He did it for Teresa. For Newt and Minho. Whatever darkness awaited them, they'd be together, and that was all that mattered right then.

He let go of Chuck, slumped backward, trying not to look at the boy's shirt, black with blood. He wiped the tears from his cheeks, rubbed his eyes, thinking he should be embarrassed but not feeling that way. Finally, he looked up. Looked up at Teresa and her enormous blue eyes, heavy with sadness—just as much for him as for Chuck, he was sure of it.

She reached down, grabbed his hand, helped him stand. Once he was up, she didn't let go, and neither did he. He squeezed, tried to say what he felt by doing so. No one else said a word, most of them staring at Chuck's body without expression, as if they'd moved far beyond feeling. No one looked at Gally, breathing but still.

The woman from WICKED broke the silence.

"All things happen for a purpose," she said, any sign of malice now gone from her voice. "You must understand this."

Thomas looked at her, threw all his compressed hatred into the glare. But he did nothing.

Teresa placed her other hand on his arm, gripped his bicep. *What now?* she asked.

I don't know, he replied. *I can't—*

His sentence was cut short by a sudden series of shouts and commotion outside the entrance through which the woman had come. She visibly panicked, the blood draining from her face as she turned toward the door. Thomas followed her gaze.

Several men and women dressed in grimy jeans and soaking-wet coats burst through the entrance with guns raised, yelling and screaming words over each other. It was impossible to understand what they were saying. Their guns—some were rifles, other pistols—looked . . . archaic, rustic. Almost like toys abandoned in the woods for years, recently discovered by the next generation of kids ready to play war.

Thomas stared in shock as two of the newcomers tackled the WICKED woman to the floor. Then one stepped back and drew up his gun, aimed.

No way, Thomas thought. *No—*

Flashes lit the air as several shots exploded from the gun, slamming into the woman's body. She was dead, a bloody mess.

Thomas took several steps backward, almost stumbled.

A man walked up to the Gladers as the others in his group spread out around them, sweeping their guns left and right as they shot at the observation windows, shattering them. Thomas heard screams, saw blood, looked away, focused on the man who approached them. He had dark hair, his face young but full of wrinkles around the eyes, as if he'd spent each day of his life worrying about how to make it to the next.

"We don't have time to explain," the man said, his voice as strained as his face. "Just follow me and run like your life depends on it. Because it does."

With that the man made a few motions to his companions, then turned and ran out the big glass doors, his gun held rigidly before him. Gunfire and cries of agony still rattled the chamber, but Thomas did his best to ignore them and follow instructions.

"*Go!*" one of the rescuers—that was the only way Thomas could think of them—screamed from behind.

After the briefest hesitation, the Gladers followed, almost stomping each other in their rush to get out of the chamber, as far away from the Grievers and the Maze as possible. Thomas, his hand still gripping Teresa's, ran with them, bunched up in the back of the group. They had no choice but to leave Chuck's body behind.

Thomas felt no emotion—he was completely numb. He ran down a long hallway, into a dimly lit tunnel. Up a winding flight of stairs. Everything was dark, smelled like electronics. Down another hallway. Up more stairs. More hallways. Thomas wanted to ache for Chuck, get excited about their escape, rejoice that Teresa was there with him. But he'd seen too much. There was only emptiness now. A void. He kept going.

On they ran, some of the men and women leading from ahead, some yelling encouragement from behind.

They reached another set of glass doors and went through them into a massive downpour of rain, falling from a black sky. Nothing was visible but dull sparkles flashing off the pounding sheets of water.

The leader didn't stop moving until they reached a huge bus, its sides dented and scarred, most of the windows webbed with cracks. Rain sluiced down it all, making Thomas imagine a huge beast cresting out of the ocean.

"Get on!" the man screamed. "Hurry!"

They did, forming into a tight pack behind the door as they entered, one by one. It seemed to take forever, Gladers pushing and scrambling their way up the three stairs and into the seats.

Thomas was at the back, Teresa right in front of him. Thomas looked up into the sky, felt the water beat against his face—it was warm, almost hot, had a weird thickness to it. Oddly, it helped break him out of his funk, snap him to attention. Maybe it was just the ferocity of the deluge. He focused on the bus, on Teresa, on escape.

They were almost to the door when a hand suddenly slammed against his shoulder, gripping his shirt. He cried out as someone jerked him backward, ripping his hand out of Teresa's—he saw her spin around just in time to watch as he slammed into the ground, throwing up a spray of water. A bolt of pain shot down his spine as a woman's head appeared two inches above him, upside down, blocking out Teresa.

Greasy hair hung down, touching Thomas, framing a face hidden in shadow. A horrible smell filled his nostrils, like eggs and milk gone rotten. The woman pulled back enough for someone's flashlight to reveal her features—pale, wrinkly skin covered in horrible sores, oozing with pus. Sheer terror filled Thomas, froze him.

"Gonna save us all!" the hideous woman said, spit flying out of her mouth, spraying Thomas. "Gonna save us from the Flare!" She laughed, not much more than a hacking cough.

The woman yelped when one of the rescuers grabbed her with both hands and yanked her off of Thomas, who recovered his wits and scrambled to his feet. He backed into Teresa, staring as the man dragged the woman away, her legs kicking out weakly, her eyes on Thomas. She pointed at him, called out, "Don't believe a word they tell ya! Gonna save us from the Flare, ya are!"

When the man was several yards from the bus, he tossed the woman to the ground. "Stay put or I'll shoot you dead!" he yelled at her; then he turned to Thomas. "Get on the bus!"

Thomas, so terrified by the ordeal that his body shook, turned and followed Teresa up the stairs and into the aisle of the bus. Wide eyes watched him as they walked all the way to the back seat and plopped down; they huddled together. Black water washed down the windows outside. The rain drummed on the roof, heavy; thunder shook the skies above them.

What was *that?* Teresa said in his mind.

Thomas couldn't answer, just shook his head. Thoughts of Chuck flooded him again, replacing the crazy woman, deadening his heart. He just didn't care, didn't feel any relief at escaping the Maze. *Chuck . . .*

One of the rescuers, a woman, sat across from Thomas and Teresa; the leader who'd spoken to them earlier climbed onto the bus and took a seat at the wheel, cranked up the engine. The bus started rolling forward.

Just as it did, Thomas saw a flash of movement outside the window. The sore-riddled woman had gotten to her feet, was sprinting toward the front of the bus, waving her arms wildly, screaming something drowned out by the sounds of the storm. Her eyes were lit with lunacy or terror—Thomas couldn't tell which.

He leaned toward the glass of the window as she disappeared from his view up ahead.

"Wait!" Thomas shrieked, but no one heard him. Or if they did, they didn't care.

The driver gunned the engine—the bus lurched as it slammed into the woman's body. A thump almost jolted Thomas out of his seat as the front wheels ran over her, quickly followed by a second thump—the back wheels. Thomas looked at Teresa, saw the sickened look on her face that surely mirrored his own.

Without a word, the driver kept his foot on the gas and the bus plowed forward, driving off into the rain-swept night.

CHAPTER 61

The next hour or so was a blur of sights and sounds for Thomas.

The driver drove at reckless speeds, through towns and cities, the heavy rain obscuring most of the view. Lights and buildings were warped and watery, like something out of a drug-induced hallucination. At one point people outside rushed the bus, their clothes ratty, hair matted to their heads, strange sores like those Thomas had seen on the woman covering their terrified faces. They pounded on the sides of the vehicle as if they wanted to get on, wanted to escape whatever horrible lives they were living.

The bus never slowed. Teresa remained silent next to Thomas.

He finally got up enough nerve to speak to the woman sitting across the aisle.

"What's going on?" he asked, not sure how else to pose it.

The woman looked over at him. Wet, black hair hung in strings around her face. Dark eyes full of sorrow. "That's a very long story." The woman's voice came out much kinder than Thomas had expected, giving him hope that she truly was a friend—that all of their rescuers were friends. Despite the fact that they'd run over a woman in cold blood.

"Please," Teresa said. "Please tell us something."

The woman looked back and forth between Thomas and Teresa, then let out a sigh. "It'll take a while before you get your memories back, if ever—we're not scientists, we have no idea what they did to you, or how they did it."

Thomas's heart dropped at the thought of maybe having lost his memory forever, but he pressed on. "Who are they?" he asked.

"It started with the sun flares," the woman said, her gaze growing distant.

"What—" Teresa began, but Thomas shushed her.

Just let her talk, he said to her mind. *She looks like she will.*

Okay.

The woman almost seemed in a trance as she spoke, never taking her eyes off an indistinct spot in the distance. "The sun flares couldn't have been predicted. Sun flares are normal, but these were unprecedented, massive, spiking higher and higher—and once they were noticed, it was only minutes before their heat slammed into Earth. First our satellites were burned out, and thousands died instantly, millions within days, countless miles became wastelands. Then came the sickness."

She paused, took a breath. "As the ecosystem fell apart, it became impossible to control the sickness—even to keep it in South America. The jungles were gone, but the insects weren't. People call it the Flare now. It's a horrible, horrible thing. Only the richest can be treated, no one can be cured. Unless the rumors from the Andes are true."

Thomas almost broke his own advice—questions filled his mind. Horror grew in his heart. He sat and listened as the woman continued.

"As for you, all of you—you're just a few of millions orphaned. They tested thousands, chose you for the big one. The ultimate test. Everything you lived through was calculated and thought through. Catalysts to study your reactions, your brain waves, your thoughts. All in an attempt to find those capable of helping us find a way to beat the Flare."

She paused again, pulled a string of hair behind her ear. "Most of the physical effects are caused by something else. First the delusions start, then animal instincts begin to overpower the human ones. Finally it

366

consumes them, destroys their humanity. It's all in the brain. The Flare *lives* in their brains. It is an awful thing. Better to die than catch it."

The woman broke her gaze into nothingness and focused on Thomas, then looked at Teresa, then Thomas again. "We won't let them do this to children. We've sworn our lives to fighting WICKED. We can't lose our humanity, no matter the end result."

She folded her hands in her lap, looked down at them. "You'll learn more in time. We live far in the north. We're separated from the Andes by thousands of miles. They call it the Scorch—it lies between here and there. It's centered mainly around what they used to call the equator—it's just heat and dust now, filled with savages consumed by the Flare beyond help. We're trying to cross that land—to find the cure. But until then, we'll fight WICKED and stop the experiments and tests." She looked carefully at Thomas, then Teresa. "It's our hope that you'll join us."

She looked away then, gazing out her window.

Thomas looked at Teresa, raised his eyebrows in question. She simply shook her head and then laid it on his shoulder and closed her eyes.

I'm too tired to think about it, she said. *Let's just be safe for now.*

Maybe we are, he replied. *Maybe.*

He heard the soft sounds of her sleep, but he knew that sleep would be impossible for him. He felt such a raging storm of conflicting emotions, he couldn't identify any of them. Still—it was better than the dull void he'd experienced earlier. He could only sit and stare out the window into the rain and blackness, pondering words like *Flare* and *sickness* and *experiment* and *Scorch* and *WICKED.* He could only sit and hope that things might be better now than they'd been in the Maze.

But as he jiggled and swayed with the movements of the bus, felt Teresa's head thump against his shoulder every once in a while when they hit big bumps, heard her stir and fall back to sleep, heard the murmurs of other conversations from other Gladers, his thoughts kept returning to one thing.

Chuck.

Two hours later, the bus stopped.

They had pulled into a muddy parking lot that surrounded a nondescript building with several rows of windows. The woman and other rescuers shuffled the nineteen boys and one girl through the front door and up a flight of stairs, then into a huge dormitory with a series of bunk beds lined up along one of the walls. On the opposite side were some dressers and tables. Curtain-covered windows checkered each wall of the room.

Thomas took it all in with a distant and muted wonder—he was far past being surprised or overcome by anything ever again.

The place was full of color. Bright yellow paint, red blankets, green curtains. After the drab grayness of the Glade, it was as if they'd been transported to a living rainbow. Seeing it all, seeing the beds and the dressers, all made up and fresh—the sense of normalcy was almost overwhelming. Too good to be true. Minho said it best on entering their new world: "I've been shucked and gone to heaven."

Thomas found it hard to feel joy, as if he'd betray Chuck by doing so. But there was something there. Something.

Their bus-driving leader left the Gladers in the hands of a small staff—nine or ten men and women dressed in pressed black pants and white shirts, their hair immaculate, their faces and hands clean. They were smiling.

The colors. The beds. The staff. Thomas felt an impossible happiness trying to break through inside him. An enormous pit lurked in the middle of it, though. A dark depression that might never leave—memories of Chuck and his brutal murder. His sacrifice. But despite that, despite everything, despite all the woman on the bus had told them about the world they'd reentered, Thomas felt safe for the very first time since coming out of the Box.

Beds were assigned, clothes and bathroom things were passed out, dinner was served. Pizza. Real, bona fide, greasy-fingers pizza. Thomas devoured each bite, hunger trumping everything else, the mood of contentment and relief around him palpable. Most of the Gladers had remained quiet through it all, perhaps worried that speaking would make everything vanish. But there were plenty of smiles. Thomas had gotten so used to looks of despair, it was almost unsettling to see happy faces. Especially when he was having such a hard time feeling it himself.

Soon after eating, no one argued when they were told it was time for bed.

Certainly not Thomas. He felt as if he could sleep for a month.

CHAPTER 62

Thomas shared a bunk with Minho, who insisted on sleeping up top; Newt and Frypan were right next to them. The staff put Teresa up in a separate room, shuffling her away before she could even say goodbye. Thomas missed her desperately three seconds after she was gone.

As Thomas was settling into the soft mattress for the night, he was interrupted.

"Hey, Thomas," Minho said from above him.

"Yeah?" Thomas was so tired the word barely came out.

"What do you think happened to the Gladers who stayed behind?"

Thomas hadn't thought about it. His mind had been occupied with Chuck and now Teresa. "I don't know. But based on how many of us died getting here, I wouldn't like to be one of them right now. Grievers are probably swarming all over them." He couldn't believe how nonchalant his voice sounded as he said it.

"You think we're safe with these people?" Minho asked.

Thomas pondered the question for a moment. There was only one answer to hold on to. "Yeah, I think we're safe."

Minho said something else, but Thomas didn't hear. Exhaustion consuming him, his mind wandered to his short time in the Maze, his time as a Runner and how much he'd wanted it—ever since that first night in the Glade. It felt like a hundred years ago. Like a dream.

Murmurs of conversation floated through the room, but to

Thomas they seemed to come from another world. He stared at the crossed wooden boards of the bed above him, feeling the pull of sleep. But wanting to talk to Teresa, he fought it off.

How's your room? he asked in his mind. *Wish you were in here.*

Oh, yeah? she replied. *With all those stinky boys? Think not.*

Guess you're right. I think Minho's farted three times in the last minute. Thomas knew it was a lame attempt at a joke, but it was the best he could do.

He sensed her laughing, wished he could do the same. There was a long pause. *I'm really sorry about Chuck,* she finally said.

Thomas felt a sharp pang and closed his eyes as he sank deeper into the misery of the night. *He could be so annoying,* he said. He paused, thought of that night when Chuck had scared the crap out of Gally in the bathroom. *But it hurts. Feels like I lost a brother.*

I know.

I promised—

Stop, Tom.

What? He wanted Teresa to make him feel better, say something magic to make the pain go away.

Stop with the promise stuff. Half of us made it. We all would've died if we'd stayed in the Maze.

But Chuck didn't make it, Thomas said. Guilt racked him because he knew for a certainty he would trade any one of the Gladers in that room for Chuck.

He died saving you, Teresa said. *He made the choice himself. Just don't ever waste it.*

Thomas felt tears swell under his eyelids; one escaped and trickled down his right temple, into his hair. A full minute passed without any words between them. Then he said, *Teresa?*

Yeah?

Thomas was scared to share his thoughts, but did. *I wanna remember you. Remember us. Ya know, before.*

Me too.

Seems like we . . . He didn't know how to say it after all.

I know.

Wonder what tomorrow'll be like.

We'll find out in a few hours.

Yeah. Well, good night. He wanted to say more, much more. But nothing came.

Good night, she said, just as the lights went out.

Thomas rolled over, glad it was dark so no one could see the look that had settled across his face.

It wasn't a smile, exactly. Not quite a happy expression. But almost.

And for now, almost was good enough.

EPILOGUE

WICKED Memorandum, Date 232.1.27, Time 22:45
TO: My Associates
FROM: Ava Paige, Chancelor
RE: THOUGHTS ON MAZE TRIALS, Group A

By any reckoning, I think we'd all agree that the Trials were a success. Twenty survivors, all well qualified for our planned endeavor. The responses to the Variables were satisfactory and encouraging. The boy's murder and the "rescue" proved to be a valuable finale. We needed to shock their systems, see their responses. Honestly, I'm amazed that in the end, despite everything, we were able to collect such a large population of kids that just never gave up.

Oddly enough, seeing them this way, thinking all is well, has been the hardest thing for me to observe. But there's no time for regret. For the good of our people, we will move forward.

I know I have my own feelings as to who should be chosen as the leader, but I'll refrain from saying at this time so as not to influence any decisions. But to me, it's an obvious choice.

We are all well aware of what's at stake. I, for one, am encouraged. Remember what the girl wrote on her arm before losing her memory? The one thing she chose to clasp on to? *WICKED is good.*

The subjects will eventually recall and understand the purpose of the hard things we have done and plan to do to them. The mission of WICKED is to serve and preserve humanity, no matter the cost. We are, indeed, "good."

Please respond with your own reactions. The subjects will be allowed one full night's sleep before Stage 2 implementation. At this time, let's allow ourselves to feel hopeful.

Group B's trial results were also most extraordinary. I need time to process the data, but we can touch on it in the morning.

Until tomorrow, then.

END OF BOOK ONE

ACKNOWLEDGMENTS

Editor and friend Stacy Whitman, for helping me see what I could not see.

Faithful fan Jacoby Nielsen, for his feedback and constant support.

Fellow authors Brandon Sanderson, Aprilynne Pike, Julie Wright, J. Scott Savage, Sara Zarr, Emily Wing Smith, and Anne Bowen, for being there.

My agent, Michael Bourret, for making my dream a reality.

Also, sincere thanks to Lauren Abramo and everyone at Dystel & Goderich.

And Krista Marino, for an editing job that defies description. You are a genius, and your name should be on the cover with mine.

HERE IS A SPECIAL LOOK AT
THE SEQUEL TO
THE MAZE RUNNER

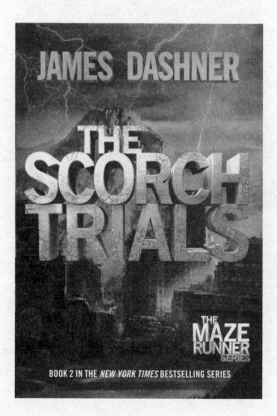

Thomas!

She screamed it. A piercing rattle in his head. He felt the first trickle of fear, but it was more like a dream. He could only sleep. And they were safe now, nothing to worry about anymore. Yeah, it had to be a dream. Teresa was fine, they were all fine. He relaxed again, let himself drown in slumber.

Other sounds snuck their way into his consciousness. Thumps. The clang of metal against metal. Something shattering. Boys shouting. More like the echo of shouts, very distant, muted. Suddenly they became more like screams. Unearthly cries of anguish. But still distant. As if he'd been wrapped in a thick cocoon of dark velvet.

Finally something pricked the comfort of sleep. This wasn't right. Teresa had called for him, told him something was wrong! He fought the deep sleep that had consumed him, clawed at the heavy weight pinning him down.

Wake up! he yelled at himself. *Wake up!*

Then something disappeared from inside him. There one instant, gone the next. He felt as if a major organ had just been ripped from his body.

It had been her. She was gone.

Teresa! he screamed out with his mind. *Teresa! Are you there?*

But there was nothing, and he no longer felt that comforting sense of her closeness. He called her name again, then again, as he continued to struggle against the dark pull of sleep.

Finally, reality swept in, washed away the darkness. Engulfed in terror, Thomas opened his eyes and shot to a sitting position on his bed, scooted out until he got his feet under him and jumped up. Looked around.

Everything had gone crazy.

The other Gladers in the room were running around, shouting. And terrible, horrible, awful sounds filled the air, like the wretched squeals of animals being tortured. There was Frypan, pointing out a window, his face pale. Newt and Minho were running to the door. Winston, hands held up to his frightened, acne-plagued face like he'd just seen a flesh-eating zombie. Others stumbling over each other to look out the different windows, but keeping their distance from the glass. Achingly, Thomas realized he didn't even know most of the names of the twenty boys who'd survived the Maze, an odd thought to have in the middle of all that chaos.

Something at the corner of his eye made him turn to look toward the wall. What he saw immediately wiped away any peace and safety he'd felt talking to Teresa in the night. Made him doubt such emotions could even exist in the same world in which he now stood.

Three feet from his bed, draped by colorful curtains, a window looked out into a bright, blinding light. The glass was broken, jagged shards leaning against crisscrossed steel bars. A man stood on the other side, gripping the bars with bloody hands. His eyes were wide and bloodshot, filled with madness. Sores and scars covered his thin, sunburnt face. He had no hair, only diseased splotches of what looked like greenish moss. A vicious slit stretched across his right cheek; Thomas could see teeth through the raw, festering wound. Pink saliva dribbled in swaying lines from the man's chin.

"I'm a Crank!" the horror of a man yelled. "I'm a bloody Crank!"

And then he started screaming two words over and over and over, spit flying with every shriek.

"Kill me! Kill me! Kill me! . . ."

A hand slammed down on Thomas's shoulder from behind; he cried out

and spun around to see Minho staring past him at the maniac screaming through the window.

"They're everywhere," Minho said. His voice had a gloom to it that
perfectly matched how Thomas felt. It seemed as if everything they'd
dared hope for the previous night had dissolved to nothing. "And there's
no sign of those shanks who rescued us," he added.

Thomas had lived in fear and terror the past few weeks, but this was
almost too much. To feel safe only to have that snatched away again.
Shocking even himself, though, he quickly set aside that small part of
him that wanted to jump back into his bed and bawl his eyes out. He
pushed away the lingering ache of remembering his mom and the stuff
about his dad and people going crazy. Thomas knew that someone had to
take charge—they needed a plan if they were going to survive this, too.

"Have any of them gotten in yet?" he asked, a strange calm washing over him. "Do all the windows have these bars?"

Minho nodded toward one of the many lining the walls of the long
rectangular room. "Yeah. It was too dark to notice them last night, especially with those stupid frilly curtains. But I'm sure glad for 'em."

Thomas looked at the Gladers around them, some running from window to window to get a look outside, others huddling in small groups.
Everyone had a look of half disbelief, half terror. "Where's Newt?"

"Right here."

Thomas turned to see the older boy, not knowing how he'd missed
him. "What's goin' on?"

"You think I have a bloody clue? Bunch of crazies want to eat us
for breakfast, by the looks of it. We need to find another room, have a
Gathering. All this noise is driving nails through my buggin' skull."

Thomas nodded absently; he agreed with the plan but hoped Newt
and Minho would take care of it. He was eager to make contact with
Teresa—he hoped her warning had just been part of a dream, a halluci-

nation from the drug of deep and exhausted slumber. And that vision of his mom . . .

His two friends moved away, calling out and waving their arms to collect Gladers. Thomas took a tremulous glance back at the shredded madman at the window, then looked away immediately, wishing he hadn't reminded his brain of the blood and torn flesh, the insane eyes, the hysterical screaming.

Kill me! Kill me! Kill me!

Thomas stumbled to the farthest wall, leaned heavily against it.

Teresa, he called out again with his mind. *Teresa. Can you hear me?*

He waited, closing his eyes to concentrate. Reaching out with invisible hands, trying to grasp some trace of her. Nothing. Not even a passing shadow or brush of feeling, much less a response.

Teresa, he said more urgently, clenching his teeth with the effort. *Where are you? What happened?*

Nothing. His heart seemed to slow until it almost stopped, and he felt like he'd swallowed a big hairy lump of cotton. Something had happened to her.

He opened his eyes to see the Gladers gathered around the green-painted door that led to the common area where they'd eaten pizza the night before. Minho was jerking on the round brass handle to no avail. Locked.

The only other door was to a shower and locker room, from which no other exits existed. There was that, and the windows. All with those metal bars. Thank goodness. Each one had raging lunatics screaming and yelling on the other side.

Even though worry ate at him like spilled acid in his veins, Thomas gave up momentarily on trying to contact Teresa and joined the other Gladers. Newt was having a go at the door, with the same useless result.

"It's locked," he muttered when he finally gave up, his arms falling weakly to his sides.

"Really, genius?" Minho said, his powerful arms folded and tensed, veins bulging all over the place. Thomas thought for a split second he could actually see the blood pumping through them. "No wonder you were named after Isaac Newton—such an amazing ability to think."

Newt wasn't in the mood. Or maybe he'd just learned long ago to ignore Minho's smart-aleck remarks. "Let's break this bloody handle off." He looked around as if he expected someone to give him a sledge-hammer.

"I wish those shuck . . . Cranks would shut up!" Minho yelled, turning to glower at the closest one, a woman who looked even more hideous than the first man Thomas had seen. A bleeding wound crossed her face, ending on the side of her head.

"Cranks?" Frypan repeated. The hairy cook had been silent until then, barely noticeable. Thomas thought he looked even more frightened than when they'd been about to battle the Grievers to escape the Maze. Maybe this was worse. When they'd settled into bed last night, everything had seemed good and safe. Yeah, maybe this *was* worse, to have that suddenly taken away.

Minho pointed at the screaming, bloody woman. "That's what they keep calling themselves. Haven't you heard it?"

"I don't care if you call 'em pussy willows," Newt snapped. "Find me something to break through this stupid door!"

"Here," a shorter boy said, carrying a slender but solid fire extinguisher he'd taken off the wall—Thomas remembered seeing it earlier. Again, he felt guilty for not even knowing this kid's name.

Newt grabbed the red cylinder, ready to pile-drive the door handle. Thomas stood as close as he could, eager to see what was on the other side of the door, though he had a very bad feeling that whatever it was, they weren't going to like it.

Newt lifted the extinguisher, then slammed it down on the round brass handle. The loud crack was accompanied by a deeper crunch, and it took only three more whacks before the entire unit of the handle crashed to the floor with a jangle of broken metal pieces. The door inched outward, cracked open just enough to show darkness on the other side.

Newt stood quietly, staring at that long, narrow gap of blackness as if he expected demons from the underworld to come flying through. Absently, he handed the extinguisher back to the boy who'd found it. "Let's go," he said. Thomas thought he heard the slightest quaver in his voice.

"Wait," Frypan called out. "We sure we wanna go out there? Maybe that door was locked for a reason."

Thomas couldn't help but agree; something felt wrong about this.

Minho stepped up to stand right next to Newt; he looked back at Frypan, then made eye contact with Thomas. "What else're we gonna do? Sit here and wait for those loonies to get in? Come on."

"Those freaks aren't breaking through the window bars anytime soon," Frypan retorted. "Let's just *think* for a second."

"Time for thinking's done," Minho said. He kicked out with his foot and the door swung completely open; if anything, it seemed to grow even darker on the other side. "Plus, you should've spoken up *before* we blasted the lock to bits, slinthead. Too late now."

"I hate when you're right," Frypan grumbled under his breath.

Thomas couldn't quit staring past the open door, into the pool of inky darkness. He felt a now-all-too-familiar clench of apprehension, knowing that something had to be wrong or the people who'd rescued them would've come for them a long time ago. But Minho and Newt were right—they had to go out there and find some answers.

"Shuck it," Minho said. "I'll go first."

Without waiting for a response he walked through the open door, his body vanishing in the gloom almost instantly. Newt gave Thomas a hesitant look, then followed. For some reason Thomas thought it should be up to him to go next, so he did.

Step by step, he left the dorm room and entered the darkness of the common area, hands reaching out in front of him.

The glow of light coming from behind didn't do much to illuminate things; he might as well have been walking with his eyes squeezed shut. And the place smelled. Horrible.

Minho yelped up ahead, then called back. "Whoa, be careful. Something . . . weird's hanging from the ceiling."

Thomas heard a slight squeak or groan, something creaking. As if Minho had bumped into a low-hanging chandelier, sending it swaying back and forth. A grunt from Newt somewhere to the right was followed by the squeal of metal dragging across the floor.

"Table," Newt announced. "Watch out for tables."

Frypan spoke up behind Thomas. "Does anyone remember where the light switches were?"

"That's where I'm heading," Newt responded. "I swear I remember seeing a set of them somewhere over here."

Thomas continued walking blindly forward. His eyes had adjusted a little; where before, everything had been a wall of blackness, now he could see traces of shadows against shadows. Yet something was off. He was still a little disoriented, but things seemed to be in places they shouldn't be. It was almost as if—

"Bluh-huh-huh," Minho groaned, a shudder of repulsion, like he'd just stepped in a pile of klunk. Another creaking sound cut through the room.

Before Thomas could ask what had happened, he bumped into something himself. Hard. Awkwardly shaped. The feel of cloth.

"Found it!" Newt shouted.

A few clicks were heard; then the room suddenly blazed with fluorescent lights, temporarily blinding Thomas. He stumbled away from the thing he'd bumped into, rubbing his eyes, ran into another stiff figure, sent it swaying away from him.

"Whoa!" Minho yelled.

Thomas squinted; his vision cleared. He forced himself to look at the scene of horror around him.

Throughout the large room, people hung from the ceiling—at least a dozen. They'd all been strung up by the neck, the ropes twisted and trenched into purple, bloated skin. The stiff bodies swung to and fro ever so slightly, pale pink tongues lolling out of their white-lipped mouths. All of them had eyes open, though glazed over with certain death. By the looks of it, they'd been that way for hours. Their clothes and some of their faces looked familiar.

Thomas dropped to his knees.

He knew these dead people.

They were the ones who'd rescued the Gladers. Just the day before.

If you love
THE MAZE RUNNER,
turn the page for a look at the first book in
James Dashner's new series, the Mortality Doctrine:

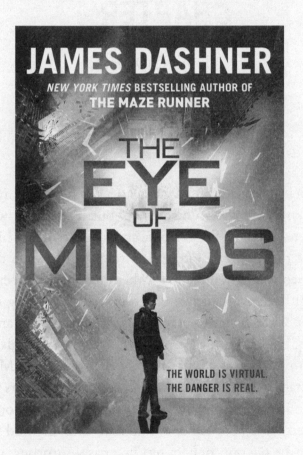

CHAPTER 1

THE COFFIN

1

Michael spoke against the wind, to a girl named Tanya.

"I know it's water down there, but it might as well be concrete. You'll be flat as a pancake the second you hit."

Not the most comforting choice of words when talking to someone who wanted to end her life, but it was certainly the truth. Tanya had just climbed over the railing of the Golden Gate Bridge, cars zooming by on the road, and was leaning back toward the open air, her twitchy hands holding on to a pole wet with mist. Even if somehow Michael could talk her out of jumping, those slippery fingers might get the job done anyway. And then it'd be lights-out. He pictured some poor sap of a fisherman thinking he'd finally caught the big one, only to reel in a nasty surprise.

"Stop joking," the trembling girl responded. "It's not a game—not anymore."

Michael was inside the VirtNet—the Sleep, to people

who went in as often as he did. He was used to seeing scared people there. A lot of them. Yet underneath the fear was usually the *knowing*. Knowing deep down that no matter what was happening in the Sleep, it wasn't real.

Not with Tanya. Tanya was different. At least, her Aura, her computer-simulated counterpart, was. Her Aura had this bat-crazy look of pure terror on her face, and it suddenly gave Michael chills—made him feel like *he* was the one hovering over that long drop to death. And Michael wasn't a big fan of death, fake or not.

"It *is* a game, and you know it," he said louder than he'd wanted to—he didn't want to startle her. But a cold wind had sprung up, and it seemed to grab his words and whisk them down to the bay. "Get back over here and let's talk. We'll both get our Experience Points, and we can go explore the city, get to know each other. Find some crazies to spy on. Maybe even hack some free food from the shops. It'll be good times. And when we're done, we'll find you a Portal, and you can Lift back home. Take a break from the game for a while."

"This has nothing to do with *Lifeblood*!" Tanya screamed at him. The wind pulled at her clothes, and her dark hair fanned out behind her like laundry on a line. "Just go away and leave me alone. I don't want your pretty-boy face to be the last thing I see."

Michael thought of *Lifeblood Deep*, the next level, the goal of all goals. Where everything was a thousand times more real, more advanced, more intense. He was three years away from earning his way inside. Maybe two. But right then he needed to talk this dopey girl out of jumping to her date with the fishes or he'd be sent back to the Suburbs for a week, making *Lifeblood Deep* that much further away.

"Okay, look . . ." He was trying to choose his words carefully, but he'd already made a pretty big mistake and knew it. Going out of character and using the game itself as a reason for her to stop what she was doing meant he'd be docked points big-time. And it was all about the points. But this girl was legitimately starting to scare him. It was that face—pale and sunken, as if she'd already died.

"Just go away!" she yelled. "You don't get it. I'm trapped here. Portals or no Portals. I'm trapped! He won't let me Lift!"

Michael wanted to scream right back at her—she was talking nonsense. A dark part of him wanted to say forget it, tell her she was a loser, let her nosedive. She was being so stubborn—it wasn't like any of it was really happening. *It's just a game.* He had to remind himself of that all the time.

But he couldn't mess this up. He needed the points. "All right. Listen." He took a step back, held his hands up like he was trying to calm a scared animal. "We just met—give it some time. I promise I won't do anything nutty. You wanna jump, I'll let you jump. But at least talk to me. Tell me why."

Tears lined her cheeks; her eyes had gone red and puffy. "Just go away. Please." Her voice had taken on the softness of defeat. "I'm not messing around here. I'm done with this—all of this!"

"Done? Okay, that's fine to be done. But you don't have

to screw it up for me, too, right?" Michael figured maybe it was okay to talk about the game after all, since she was using it as her reason to end it—to check out of the Virtual-Flesh-and-Bones Hotel and never come back. "Seriously. Walk back to the Portal with me, Lift yourself, do it the right way. You're done with the game, you're safe, I get my points. Ain't that the happiest ending you ever heard of?"

"I hate you," she spat. Literally. A spray of misty saliva. "I don't even know you and I hate you. This has nothing to do with *Lifeblood*!"

"Then tell me what it *does* have to do with." He said it kindly, trying to keep his composure. "You've got all day to jump. Just give me a few minutes. Talk to me, Tanya."

She buried her head in the crook of her right arm. "I just can't do it anymore." She whimpered and her shoulders shook, making Michael worry about her grip again. "I can't."

Some people are just weak, he thought, though he wasn't stupid enough to say it.

Lifeblood was by *far* the most popular game in the Virt-Net. Yeah, you could go off to some nasty battlefield in the Civil War or fight dragons with a magic sword, fly space-ships, explore the freaky love shacks. But that stuff got old quick. In the end, nothing was more fascinating than bare-bones, dirt-in-your-face, gritty, get-me-out-of-here real life. Nothing. And there were some, like Tanya, who obviously couldn't handle it. Michael sure could. He'd risen up its ranks almost as quickly as legendary gamer Gunner Skale.

"Come on, Tanya," he said. "How can it hurt to talk to me? And if you're going to quit, why would you want to end your last game by killing yourself so violently?"

Her head snapped up and she looked at him with eyes so hard he shivered again.

"Kaine's haunted me for the last time," she said. "He can't just trap me here and use me for an experiment—sic the KillSims on me. I'm gonna rip my Core out."

Those last words changed everything. Michael watched in horror as Tanya tightened her grip on the pole with one hand, then reached up with the other and started digging into her own flesh.